Content Area Reading:

Literacy and Learning Across the Curriculum

Content Area Reading:

Literacy and Learning Across the Curriculum

Canadian Edition

Richard T. Vacca
Kent State University

Jo Anne L. Vacca
Kent State University

Deborah L. Begoray
University of Victoria

PEARSON

Toronto

National Library of Canada Cataloguing in Publication

Vacca, Richard T.

     Content area reading : literacy and learning across the curriculum / Richard T. Vacca, Jo Anne L. Vacca, Deborah L. Begoray. – Canadian ed.

Includes bibliographical references and index.

ISBN 0-205-35795-4

     1. Content area reading. I. Vacca, Jo Anne L. II. Begoray, Deborah, 1953– III. Title.

LB1050.455.V33 2004   428.4'3   C2004-902212-1

Vice-President, Editorial Director: Michael J. Young
Executive Acquisitions Editor: Cas Shields
Signing Representation: Marc Sourisseau
Marketing Manager: Ryan St. Peters
Associate Editor: Paula Drużga
Production Editor: Charlotte Morrison-Reed
Copy Editor: Eliza Marciniak
Proofreader: Bonnie di Malta
Senior Production Coordinator: Peggy Brown
Page Layout: Phyllis Seto
Art Director: Mary Opper
Cover and Interior Design: Anthony Leung
Cover Image: Digital Vision

1 2 3 4 5   09 08 07 06 05

Printed and bound in Canada.

To our grandsons Simon, Max, and Joe
Who light up our lives
With unbridled enthusiasm
And their unquenchable desire to learn.

−Papa and Bama

For Flo,
A wise and wonderful friend
who always encouraged me to write.

−Debbie

Brief Contents

Detailed Contents

Preface to the Canadian Edition

AS CANADIAN AS POSSIBLE, UNDER THE CIRCUMSTANCES.

When Peter Gzowski was the host of CBC's *This Country in the Morning*, he ran a contest for a slogan. Listeners were to complete the phrase "As Canadian as..." The winning slogan appears above.

I was told this story by a friend, Sharon Perrin, when I was explaining to her the process of taking a well-respected but very American textbook and creating a Canadian edition. I searched for Canadian examples in the fields of history, science, literature, assessment, English as a second language... At first, the list seemed to be endless. I asked for assistance from colleagues across the country, trawled through books and websites, called Ministry of Education officials. Once I began, I quickly realized what a privilege it was to be able to do such work. I was reminded once again of the richness and diversity of life in Canada, and of the generosity of Canadian experts in a variety of content area disciplines. I endeavoured to find stories and events, ideas and inventions from every region in Canada. Readers may judge for themselves how well I succeeded.

Editing this book was not merely a matter of finding Canadian examples but also of capturing something of the Canadian philosophy of life. We hold unique perspectives on immigration, second language instruction, the contributions of Aboriginal people, multiculturalism, federal and provincial responsibilities, and responses to international events. We tend to compromise and negotiate rather than confront. Most of us uphold community values rather than individual ones. We brag less about our participation in war and more about our participation in peace. We complain about our taxes but fight to maintain our health care system. In international competitions, our students outperform our neighbours to the south consistently, across subjects and grades. We fund education generously in comparison with most other nations. We are not Americans.

Education in Canada remains in the hands of educators who believe in research and the lessons of experience rather than the political fashions of right- and left-wing politicians. Our colleagues in the United States and Great Britain are beleaguered with examinations, inspections, and government interference, which make it increasingly difficult for them to teach. Our very Canadian notion of language arts as reading and writing, listening and speaking, viewing and representing—the concept of literacy as composed of different sets of skills—is pursued in most classrooms. It is such a view of literacy that you will find reflected in this book.

In addition, the Canadian edition embraces a view of "text" as more than the traditional printed text—words on the page—to include oral texts, such as speeches and sign language; visual texts, such as charts, graphs, and art prints; and multimedia texts, such as websites and films. In my own classes with preservice teachers, such an inclusive definition of text has helped me reach a wider range of students. Music majors begin to consider how music notation can be taught as a text. Physical education students think about teacher demonstrations as a text. We discuss how each of the many sign systems has evolved to meet specific needs in the various disciplines. Ideas from the teaching of reading—broadly defined also as listening and viewing as well as comprehending printed text—can help students expand their approaches to teaching. Prereading exercises can help mathematics students "read" equations with more understanding. Prediction skills can assist geography students with "reading" graphs.

All this talk of the new literacies does not meant that this edition ignores traditional reading. In fact, it is still the dominant topic. We have a rich variety of literature in Canada, and you will find many Canadian books you know and love (and perhaps some you donít yet know) mentioned here.

Today's adolescents live in a world of visual images, but they also need to become consumers and producers of words. Canadian experts continue to research issues on how children learn to read and how they build sophisticated strategies for deep comprehension as they move through the grades. Other investigators work with struggling adolescent readers and research the reading act as complicated by gender, socioeconomic status, and culture.

In addition, students of every age must be able to critically evaluate the many texts they encounter, and consider not just speech, words, and pictures but learn to ask questions about issues of power and control. For example, whose views are not represented? Why not? Other educational jurisdictions across the globe have seen language arts narrowed to reading of printed texts, and reading itself narrowed to include only fragmented skills that can be examined in pencil and paper tests.

I believe that content area reading, or content area literacy as I prefer to call it, needs to be taught as a series of strategies to make adolescents more active, aware, and autonomous. Adolescents need to be actively involved in their learning rather than passively completing worksheets or the ubiquitous end-of-chapter questions. They need to be aware of what they know and don't know, of what strategies help them learn. Finally, they need to become more independent in their learning—able to pose their own questions, set their own goals, and work to complete them. In Canada, we can still help students to work within provincial mandates, to work in interdisciplinary teams, to involve the arts and the mass media in their learning—in short, to meet student needs in creative and original ways. Many of our international colleagues have seen this precious right eroded in recent years.

All that being said, it was also a privilege to work with Richard and Jo Anne Vacca's book. I first began to use *Content Area Reading* in 1988, when I was a sessional instructor at the University of Calgary. Dr. Chris Gordon recommended it, and I have used it ever since—at the Universities of Calgary, Winnipeg, Manitoba, and Victoria. Colleagues in secondary language arts and literacy education programs across Canada and the United States report that they still regard it as the premier textbook in the area. I have retained the order of chapters and the many features of the seventh edition of *Content Area Reading*. Many chapters, in fact, are largely unchanged from the Vaccas' original work. I owe the authors a debt of gratitude.

Supplements

Content Area Reading is supplemented by an Instructor's Manual that can be downloaded from Pearson Education Canada's protected Instructor Central website, at www.pearsoned. ca/instructor.

ACKNOWLEDGMENTS

I would like to acknowledge the help of the many people who rendered assistance and advice. These people include John Anderson, Robert Anthony, John Begoray, Catherine Caws, Eliza Churchill, Melissa Edwards, Khalid Kareem, Sylvia Pantaleo, Dan Peebles, and Tracie Smith. Thank you all.

The book you now hold in your hand is indeed as Canadian as possible under the circumstances. I hope it helps you help all your students—in universities, secondary schools, and middle schools—to teach language and literacy more effectively in all the subject areas. I look forward to your comments.

Deborah L. Begoray
Faculty of Education
University of Victoria
dbegoray@uvic.ca

part one

Teaching and Learning with Texts

chapter one

Reading Matters

*I found my freedom
through reading.*

–Lesra Martin

ORGANIZING PRINCIPLE

Lesra Martin first became famous as a member of the legal team that exonerated Rubin "Hurricane" Carter, who had been wrongly convicted of a triple murder (a story made popular in the movie *The Hurricane*). When Martin arrived in Toronto in 1979, he was befriended by a group of Canadians and offered an education. Soon his tutor discovered Martin was unable to read and write beyond a very basic level. Martin recalls, "When I was 15 and first discovered that I couldn't read or write, I became despondent. I was burdened with the thought that I was incapable of learning." But learn he did. He completed an Honours BA at the University of Toronto, obtained a law degree from Dalhousie, and became a Crown prosecutor in British Columbia. His mind and spirit, formerly wasting away in a Brooklyn ghetto, were freed by literacy.

Showing students how to use reading to learn is what content area reading is all about. Although texts are routinely assigned in content area classrooms, helping students learn how to learn with texts enters into the plans of teachers only infrequently. Teaching and learning with texts is a challenge in today's classrooms, where the range of linguistic, cultural, and academic diversity has been increasing steadily. All too often, students give up on independent learning. When students become too dependent on teachers as their primary source of information, they are rarely in a position to think and learn with text. This need not be the case. As the organizing principle of this chapter underscores: **all teachers play a critical role in helping students think and learn with text.**

Study the chapter overview. It's your map to the major ideas that you will encounter in the chapter. The overview shows the relationships that exist among the concepts you will study. Use it as an organizer. What is the chapter about? What do you already know about the content to be presented in the chapter? What do you need to learn more about?

In conjunction with the chapter overview, take a moment or two to study the *Frame of Mind* questions. This feature uses key questions to help you think about the ideas that you will read about. Our intent is to create a mental disposition for learning, a critical *frame of mind,* if you will, so that you can better interact with the ideas that we, as authors, have organized and developed in the chapter. When you finish reading, you should be able to respond fully to the "Frame of Mind" questions.

CHAPTER OVERVIEW

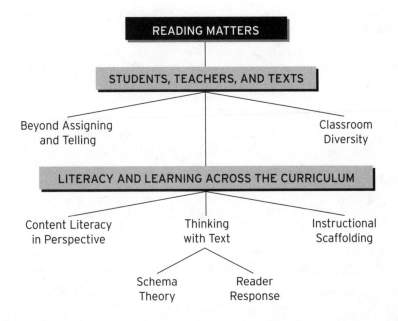

FRAME OF MIND

1. Why do "assigning and telling" stifle active learning and deny students responsibility for learning on their own?

2. In what ways are literacy and learning related?

3. What is content area literacy?

4. How are classrooms more diverse today than they were several decades ago?

5. What does it mean to think with text?

6. How do reader response and schema influence comprehending and learning?

The classroom is a crucible, a place where the special mix of *teacher, student,* and *text* come together to create wonderfully complex human interactions that stir the minds and spirits of learners. Some days, of course, are better than others. The things that you thought about doing and the classroom surprises that you didn't expect fall into place. A creative energy imbues teaching and learning.

Sometimes, however, lessons limp along. Others just bomb—so you cut them short. The four or so remaining minutes before the bell rings are a kind of self-inflicted wound. Nothing is more unnerving than waiting for the bell to ring when students don't have anything meaningful to do.

Consider a science teacher's reflection on the way things went in one of her classes. "Something was missing," she explains. "The students aren't usually as quiet and passive as they were today. Excuse the pun, but the chemistry wasn't there. Maybe the textbook assignment was too hard. Maybe I could have done something differently. Any suggestions?" This teacher, like most good teachers, cares about what she does. She wants to know how to improve her craft. She knows that when the chemistry is there, teaching is its own reward.

Good teachers bring sensitivity and a spirit of reflective inquiry to their teaching. They care about what they do and how they do it. As Eliot Eisner (1985) aptly put it:

> Teaching can be done as badly as anything else. It can be wooden, mechanical, mindless, and wholly unimaginative. But when it is sensitive, intelligent, and creative—those qualities that confer upon it the status of an art—it should, in my view, not be regarded, as it so often is by some, as an expression of unfathomable talent or luck but as an example of humans exercising the highest levels of their intelligence. (p. 77)

To be a teacher today means exercising the highest levels of intelligence in coping with difficult issues: the curriculum; content delivery; school climate; classroom control; dropout rates; accountability; children and youth at risk of failure; and ethnic, social, and cultural diversity, to name a few. There is unrelenting pressure on teachers to respond to problems of all types. What is abundantly clear is that as important as academic content is, there's more to being an artful teacher than having a rich and deep understanding of a subject.

STUDENTS, TEACHERS, AND TEXTS

A strong attraction to academic content is one of the reasons teachers are wedded to a particular discipline. Yet it is much more difficult to teach something than merely to know that something. What to teach and how to teach it are nagging problems for classroom teachers. For some, using texts to teach content contributes to the problem. For others, showing students how to learn with texts is part of the solution.

Why does reading matter? Why bring students and texts together in the classroom? Texts, after all, are but one medium for learning academic content. What is the value of learning through texts in the content areas?

Although we're not suggesting that texts are the only source for learning or that they should be, they will continue to be indispensable tools for constructing knowledge; sharing the experiences, ideas, and feelings of others; and developing new insights and perspectives. Learning how to teach with texts contributes significantly to the way you think about teaching, learning, and curriculum. Throughout this book, we invite you to examine content area teaching practices, and the assumptions underlying those practices, in the light of promising strategies for text learning and active student engagement.

All too often, academic texts are viewed as sacred canons, authoritative sources of knowledge by which the information in a field is transmitted from generation to generation of learners. The expression "learning *from* texts" has been used widely in content area reading, as if a text were indeed a canon to be mastered rather than a tool for learning and constructing meaning. The preposition *from* suggests a one-way act in which meaning flows from A (the text) to B (the reader). The shift in meaning from *from* to *with* is subtle but dramatic (Tierney & Pearson 1992). It places the act of reading to learn squarely in the context of a human transaction between two parties rather than being a transmission of information from one party to another. Learning *with* texts suggests that readers have much to contribute to the process as they interact with texts to make meaning and construct knowledge.

Although texts come with the territory, using them to help students acquire content doesn't work well for many teachers. Teaching with texts is more complex than it appears on the surface. Whether you're a novice or a veteran teacher, using texts effectively requires the willingness to explore instructional strategies and to move beyond assigning and telling.

Beyond Assigning and Telling

Your own personal history as a student, we wager, has etched into your memory an instructional blueprint that teachers in your past probably followed: *assign* a text to read (usually with questions to be answered) for homework; then, in subsequent lessons, *tell* students through question-and-answer routines what the material they read was about, explaining the ideas and information that the students encountered in print. The dominant interactional pattern between teacher and students during the class presentation of assigned material often involves calling on a student to answer a question, listening to the student's response, and then evaluating or modifying the student's response (Alvermann & Moore 1991). Such is the ebb and flow of assign-and-tell instructional routines in content area classrooms.

There is more to teaching with texts than assigning and telling. Assigning and telling are common but uninspired teaching practices that bog students down in the mire of passive learning. Assign-and-tell, more often than not, dampens active involvement in learning and denies students ownership of and responsibility for the acquisition of content. Teachers place themselves, either by design or by circumstance, in the unenviable position of being the most active participant during classroom interactions with students.

No wonder John Goodlad (1984) portrays textbook assignment, lecture, and recitation (a form of oral questioning in which teachers already know the answers to the questions they ask) as the dominant activities in the instructional repertoire of many content area teachers. Goodlad and his research associates conclude from a monumental study of schools that "the data from our observations in more than 1000 classrooms support the popular image of a teacher standing in front of a class imparting knowledge to a group of students" (p. 105). His team of researchers found that the prevalence of assign-and-tell practices increases steadily from the elementary to the senior secondary school years and that teachers often "outtalk" students by a three-to-one ratio.

Try to recall what it was like when you were in school. Well-intentioned teachers, more likely than not, assigned texts to be read as homework, only to find that for one reason or another many of the students didn't quite grasp what they were assigned to read. Some didn't read the material at all. Others read narrowly, to answer questions assigned for homework. Still others may have gotten tangled in text, stuck in the underbrush of facts and details. So class time was spent transmitting information that wasn't learned well from texts in the first place.

When teachers impart knowledge with little attention to how a learner acquires that knowledge, students soon become nonparticipants in the academic life of the classroom. Assign-and-tell practices not only result in passive reading but also influence the way students view themselves in relation to texts. The accompanying "Calvin and Hobbes" cartoon has Calvin thinking of himself as "informationally impaired."

Shifting the burden of learning from teachers' shoulders to students' is in large measure what this book is about. Yet learning with texts is all the more challenging in today's classroom, where the range of academic, cultural, and language differences has increased steadily in the past several decades. More often than not, students of diverse backgrounds are caught in a cycle of school failure that contributes to marginal achievement and a sense of helplessness and frustration with content literacy activities. Traditional approaches to instruction aren't reaching diverse learners in ways that make a difference in their academic development. Arguably, what may have worked in classrooms 10, 15, or 20 years ago isn't working well today. As a result, many teachers are in transition as they reconsider instructional beliefs and practices that neither are culturally responsive nor meet students' academic needs. They are shying away from traditional approaches in favour of strategies that reach diverse learners in ways that support literacy and learning in content area classrooms.

Students of diverse backgrounds are often placed in low-ability groups where instruction is based on a limited, watered-down version of the curriculum. The strengths they bring to learning situations typically go untapped. However, the trend away from "tracking" students by ability, the movement toward inclusive classrooms, and the increasing number of students whose first language is not English demand instruction that is strategic, with high learning expectations for all students.

Calvin and Hobbes   by Bill Watterson

Source: "Calvin and Hobbes," copyright © 1992 Bill Watterson. Reprinted with permission of Universal Press Syndicate. All rights reserved.

Classroom Diversity

Canadian teachers who began their careers in the 1970s or 1980s and who are still teaching have probably noticed significant changes in the diversity of students in their classrooms. Where school populations might have once appeared rather homogenous, it is now far more likely that teachers are working with a culturally varied population of students.

Changes to the Immigration Act in 1962 and 1967 established a point system for individuals applying for Canadian citizenship. If a person applying had training to fill certain work spaces in Canada or spoke English or French, he or she received more points toward citizenship acceptance. One consequence was that French-speaking immigrants from North Africa and the Caribbean began to appear in Canada in larger numbers. In 1969, the Royal Commission on Bilingualism and Biculturalism issued a report that paved the way to the Official Languages Act of 1971, which made both English and French the official languages of Canada. From the time of the earliest settlers, however, cultural groups speaking languages other than English or French have contributed to the Canadian society. Aboriginal peoples have inhabited Canada for thousands of years, and the number of aboriginal students in classrooms is steadily increasing. Workers from China were instrumental in the building of the transcontinental railway. Icelandic settlers helped open up Manitoba. Waves of immigrants from Europe farmed the prairies, fished in the Maritimes, and were lumberjacks in British Columbia.

More recently, Canada has become a home for immigrants from Asia, South America, and the Middle East, some admitted as refugees. In 1978, a new federal immigration act allowed "expression of concern" for individuals applying for Canadian citizenship, rather than looking only at Canada's own interests in the matter. The individual's family was also considered. This act required that all levels of government work to help immigrants adapt to Canadian society. In 1982, all Canadians were covered by the Charter of Rights and Freedoms, which was added to the Canadian Constitution. Six years later, the Canadian Multicultural Act recognized and promoted the understanding that multiculturalism reflects cultural and racial diversity in Canadian society, and ensured that all individuals received equal treatment and protection under the law (Ashworthy 2000). While the school system in Canada is under provincial jurisdiction, these rights extend to all citizens of Canada. For teachers just beginning their careers, Canada's current immigration policy will mean that schools will have more students who have faced traumatic life events.

Increasing diversity presents certain difficulties for schools and school boards across the country. For example, while most school districts oppose "tracking" of students—that is, grouping students by academic ability in separate classes—students who recently immigrated to Canada may face unintended barriers in some subjects. French immersion, an optional program in provinces other than Quebec, tends to become more homogenous as students advance. A higher proportion of students from families with lower socio-economic status than those from families with higher socio-economic status leave French immersion programs. The majority of immersion students in urban areas come from homes where at least one parent is an upper manager or professional (Lapkin 1998).

Student diversity brings challenges to teachers, but it also presents them with tremendous opportunities to enrich their students' lives by introducing them to the customs, traditions, and cultural heritage of their classmates. Developing content area literacy by having students deal with a variety of print, oral, and multimedia texts from other cultures, including novels, films, magazines, websites, music, and guest speaker presentations, will help us in our quest for more democratic, inclusive education.

Cultural and Linguistic Differences The shift in the student population in Canada can be traced to the 1960s, when people of colour, refugees, and people from developing countries began to fill Canada's classrooms. These visible minorities often faced a main-stream culture rooted in European beliefs, standards, and values, a culture that often seemed unaware of its effects on these new Canadians. Sylvia Hamilton, Canadian film-maker and writer remembers:

> In Nova Scotia high schools during the 1960s, "slave auctions" were common activities organized by student councils, sometimes as fundraisers; often just for fun. Carried on with gaiety, without interference from the school administration. Harmless. African Nova Scotian students like me were in those schools, part of the student body. We tried hard to keep our distance, not to be at school during those days. (Hamilton 2003)

In 1995, the first African Canadian woman elected to Parliament, Jean Augustine, PD, MP of Etobicoke-Lakeshore in Ontario, rose in the House to move that Parliament officially recognize February as Black History Month. The motion was carried unanimously.

African Canadian accomplishments are sometimes absent in school literature. Content area teachers might look at the work of Josiah Henson (1789–1889), who wrote his autobiography, *The Life of Josiah Henson*, in 1849. Harriet Beecher Stowe, an American writer, used this book as the basis for *Uncle Tom's Cabin* (1852). Physical education teachers may be interested in the story of boxer Sam Langford of Weymouth Falls, Nova Scotia, who was never given a chance to fight for the world title because he was considered unbeatable. Students could consider whether racial prejudice might also have been a factor.

Mathieu Da Costa (?–1607) an explorer of African descent, worked with many languages, including French and Mi'kmaq. Early Canadians often relied on interpreters to bridge linguistic gaps. Da Costa's life and work is of special interest because he represents Canadian efforts to work with differences rather than allowing them to divide us. The Department of Canadian Heritage sponsors a challenge in Da Costa's name for Canadian students interested in researching, discovering, and celebrating the contribution of aboriginal peoples and Canadians of all ethnic and racial backgrounds to the building of Canada. (For more information on this challenge, visit http://www.canadianheritage.gc.ca).

Similar stories might be told of other Canadians of non-European descent. Content area literacy offers an opportunity to redress practices that exclude part of our student population. Students can be encouraged to discover the omissions in traditional education— including those concerning minority cultures—in all subject areas. Box 1.1 provides a list of some of the multicultural resources available on the internet.

Language and Dialect Differences Cultural variation in the use of language has a strong influence on literacy learning. Even though students whose first language is not English may not have full control of English grammatical structures, pronunciation, and vocabulary, they can engage in reading and writing activities (Goodman & Goodman 1978). When students use their own culturally acceptable conversational style to talk and write about ideas they read in texts, they are likely to become more content-literate and to improve their literacy skills. Expanding literacy practices to include viewing and representing will help students continue learning through visual approaches. Accompanying

BOX 1.1	**Nothing but Net**

Multicultural Resources for Teachers and Students

Department of Cultural Heritage
www.canadianheritage.gc.ca

Literacy and Literacy Training of
Francophone Minority Groups in Canada
www.nald.ca

First Nations on SchoolNet
www.schoolnet.ca/aboriginal

The First Pugwash Conference
www.pugwash.org/about/conference.htm

Multicultural Resources
**curry.edschool.virginia.edu/go/
multicultural**

African Strategy Game
imagiware.com/mancala

Multilanguage Activities and Projects
www.kidlink.org

China the Beautiful: Chinese Art and
History
www.chinapage.org/china.html

Intercultural Email Classroom Connections
(IECC)
www.iecc.org

Judaism 101
www.jewfaq.org

Multicultural Book Reviews
**www.isomedia.com/homes/jmele/
homepage.html**

lessons with visual supports is, in fact, good practice for all students (Sadoski & Paivio 2001). Content area concepts might, for example, be represented in a chart to show the relationships between and among ideas (Early 1989).

Shouldn't students from minority backgrounds learn to use standard English? The question is a rhetorical one. As teachers, our stance toward the use of standard English is critical. Standard English, often thought of as the "news broadcast–type" English used in the conduct of business, is the language of the dominant mainstream culture in Canadian society—the "culture of power," according to Delpit (1986, 1988). Delpit explains that the rules and codes of the culture of power, including the rules and codes for language use, are acquired by students from mainstream backgrounds through interaction with their families. Students from minority backgrounds, however, whose families are outside the mainstream culture, do not acquire the same rules and codes. If these students are going to have access to opportunities in mainstream society, schools must acquaint them with the rules and codes of the culture of power. Not making standard English accessible to students from minority backgrounds puts them at a disadvantage in competing with their mainstream counterparts.

Although it is important for culturally diverse learners to receive explicit instruction in the use of standard English, *when* and *under what circumstances* become critical instructional issues. All students should understand how cultural contexts influence what they read, write, hear, say, and view. Language arts classes are probably the appropriate place to provide explicit instruction in the functional use and conventions of standard English. Although becoming proficient in standard English may be an important school goal for all students, it should not be viewed as a prerequisite for literate classroom behaviour (Au 1993). When it is viewed as a prerequisite, teachers deny students the opportunity to use their own language as a tool for learning. Increasing their command of standard English, in and of itself, will not improve students' ability to think critically, "since students' own languages can serve just as well for verbal expression and reasoning" (p. 130).

Moreover, immigrant students vary in their use of English as a second language. Some may have little or no proficiency in the use of English (*NEP:* non-English-proficient). Others may have limited English skills (*LEP:* limited-English-proficient). These students are placed in bilingual and English as a second language (ESL) programs until they are proficient enough in English to be mainstreamed into the regular curriculum.

Once mainstreamed into the regular curriculum, second-language learners often struggle with content area texts. In schools where tracking still persists as an organizational tool, a disproportionate number of second-language learners have been placed in lower-track classrooms, even though the notion that students learn best with others of similar achievement levels has not been supported by research (Allington 1983; Oakes 1985).

In mainstream classes, reading textbooks is one of the most cognitively demanding, context-reduced tasks that language-minority students will encounter (Cummins 1994). Some students may become frustrated by texts because of issues related to background knowledge. According to Kang (1994),

> Some information or concepts in textbooks may presuppose certain background knowledge that native speakers may take for granted but that may be different or lacking in some ESL students. Culture-specific background knowledge developed in students' native country, community, or home may affect their comprehension, interpretation, and development of social, cultural, historical, and even scientific concepts. Even if students possess the background knowledge presumed for a particular text, they may not be able to activate it to relate and organize new information. (p. 649)

BOX 1.2	**Nothing but Net**

ESL Resources for Teachers and Students

ESLgold
www.eslgold.com

University of Victoria's English Language Centre Study Zone
web2.uvcs.uvic.ca/elc/studyzone

WritingDen
www2.actden.com/writ_den

ESL Blues
www.collegeem.qc.ca/cemdept/anglais/trouindx.htm

Dave's ESL Café
www.pacificnet.net/~sperling/eslcafe.html

ESL Center
www.geocities.com/ResearchTriangle/Facility/4249/xindex.html

Literacy Exercises, from Digital Collections' Literacy Curriculum and Activities
collections.ic.gc.ca/literacy/le/literacy.htm

EFLweb
www.eflweb.com/sites/sites-index.htm

The vocabulary load of content area textbooks is also a problem for some second-language learners. The academic language of texts is not the language of conversational speech. If students have limited literacy skills in their own native language, they will obviously experience a great deal of frustration and failure with English texts. Moreover, if students are good readers in their native language but have minimal proficiency in English, the language barrier may inhibit them from making effective use of their literacy skills. Box 1.2 provides a list of several ESL resources available on the internet.

Achievement Differences   How students achieve or fail to achieve is often attributed to such factors as motivation, self-concept, prior knowledge of the subject, and their ability to read, to study, and to communicate effectively through oral and written language. For some low-achieving students, reading is a painful reminder of a system of schooling that has failed them. They wage a continual battle with reading as an academic activity. The failure to learn to read has contributed to these students' alienation from school. Alienated students often view teachers as uncaring and "the system" as unfair and ineffective (Wehlage & Rutter 1986). Other low-achieving students may have strategies for reading that are inappropriate for academic learning. As a result, their participation in reading-related activities is marginal. Getting through the reading task to answer homework questions is often the only reason they read at all.

Unsuccessful readers can often be found "hiding out" in classrooms. That is to say, they have developed a complex set of coping strategies to avoid reading or being held accountable for reading (Brozo 1990). These coping behaviours include avoiding eye contact with the teacher, engaging in disruptive classroom behaviour, forgetting to bring books to class, and seeking help from friends. Hiding out perpetuates a cycle of failure, ensuring that the unsuccessful reader will remain helpless in text-related learning situations. The difference between successful and unsuccessful readers usually rests in their knowledge of strategies: how to use them, when to use them, and why. Effective readers know how to approach a text and make plans for reading. They also know how to locate and summarize important points, organize, and even get out of jams when they run into trouble with difficult texts.

Learned helplessness, or a student's perception of an inability to overcome failure, is one of the chief culprits in unsuccessful reading and low achievement in content area classrooms (Vacca & Padak 1990). Unsuccessful readers often falter in reading tasks because they lack knowledge of and control over the strategies needed for effective text learning. Often they aren't sure *what* strategies are important in particular reading tasks, or *how* or *when* to use the strategies that they do possess. In addition, they have trouble recognizing *why* they read or what reading is for. Rarely do unsuccessful readers consider what their role should be as readers. Rather than take an active role in constructing meaning, they often remain passive and disengaged.

Poor self-image contributes to a sense of helplessness. Students who are at risk in text-related learning situations do not feel competent as readers and display little confidence in their ability to discover meaning in texts. They hide out, avoiding reading at all costs, because they believe that they can't learn with texts successfully. As a result, they are often ambivalent about the act of reading and fail to value what reading can do for them. For one reason or another, they have alienated themselves from the world of print. However, the more social, collaborative, and interactive teachers make reading, the less ambivalent students will be about the act of reading itself (June 1995).

Content area classrooms are filled with the potential of human activity, interaction, and collaboration. Language, and its many uses, is often the vehicle by which teachers, students, and authors communicate with one another. Human beings think *with* language. Yet it's easy to lose sight of, or take for granted, the role written language plays in teaching and learning.

LITERACY AND LEARNING ACROSS THE CURRICULUM

Imagine what classrooms would be like without talk. Try getting through a class period or an entire school day in silence. Not impossible, but difficult, isn't it?

The uses of language in content area classrooms, however, involve more than talk. Although verbal interactions between students and teachers serve learning well in various instructional contexts, other modes of language are also crucial to learning. Imagine, for example, what learning would be like without texts. Texts? Our hunch is that it's far easier for you to envision teaching and learning without texts than without talk.

Yet a *text,* by its very nature, is language. Print text may be fixed in typesetter's ink on a conventional printed page, or it may be on a computer screen in an electronic environment. Text, whether it is printed or electronic, may consist of a single word, sentence, paragraph, page, chapter, or text screen. But there are other texts as well—oral texts such as the lectures teachers deliver in classrooms, and visual texts such as photographs, diagrams, and maps. There are also multimodal texts such as websites with a mix of print text, audio, and video clips (Begoray 2002).

Teaching with texts requires its fair share of strategy. But it involves more than assigning pages to be read, lecturing, or using questions to check whether students have comprehended the assigned material. To use texts strategically, you must first be aware of the powerful bonds that link literacy and learning across the curriculum.

Content Literacy in Perspective

Content literacy is the ability to use reading and writing, listening and speaking, and viewing and representing to learn subject matter in a given discipline. To understand better what it means to be content-literate in a discipline, examine the general construct of the term *literacy* and how it is used in today's society.

Literacy is a strong cultural expectation in Canada and other technologically advanced countries. Society places a heavy premium on literate behaviour and demands that its citizens acquire literacy for personal, social, academic, and economic success. However, what does it mean to be literate?

Literacy is a term whose meaning fluctuates from one context to another. It may, for example, be used to describe how knowledgeable a person is in a particular subject. What do you know about computers and how to use them? Are you *computer-literate*? In the same vein, the term *cultural literacy* refers to what an educated person should know about the arts, literature, and other determinants of culture.

The most common use of the term *literacy* has been to denote one's ability to read and write a language. In the past century, the term has undergone variations in meaning. It has been used to depict the level of competence in reading and writing—*functional literacy*— that one needs to survive in society; one's lack of education—*illiteracy*—manifested in an inability to read and write a language; and one's lack of a reading habit—*aliteracy*—especially among those who have the ability to read and write but choose not to do so.

The more researchers inquire into literacy and what it means to be literate, the more complex and multidimensional the concept becomes. Literacy is situational. In other words, a person may be able to handle the literacy demands of a task in one situation or context but not in another. Hence *workplace literacy* refers to the situational demands placed on workers to read and write effectively (Mikulecky 1990). These demands vary from job to job. *Family literacy* is used to describe how family interactions influence the language competence of young children (Taylor 1983). Because the environments for learning literacy vary from family to family, some young children enter school more literate than others.

Suppose you were to accompany Darryl, a grade 10 student, through a typical school day. Toward the end of his first-period social studies class, where the students have been studying the events leading up to the Rebellion of 1837, the teacher calls on Darryl to read a textbook section aloud to the class describing how a group of rebels, led by William Lyon Mackenzie, attacked Toronto:

> A rebellion is an armed uprising against the government. In some cases, the leaders of the rebellion try to establish a new and independent organization in place of the existing government. For a few days in December 1837, rebellion raged in Upper Canada. Toronto, the capital city with a population of about 12 000, was under attack by between 500 and 1000 armed colonists. The rebels marched on the city to overthrow the government and bring about changes they considered important. Why would formerly law-abiding citizens take such a desperate step? And why did the rebellion fail? (Cruxton & Wilson 1997, p. 5)

Darryl reads the text quickly, completing the reading just as the bell rings. He grabs his stuff from the desk and hurries off to biology, where the class has been involved in a study of microorganisms. Five minutes into the lesson, the teacher reinforces a point she is making during her lecture by asking Darryl to read about euglenoids:

> The euglenoids, members of phylum Euglenophyta, are protists that have traits of both plants and animals. They are like plants because they contain chlorophyll and undergo photosynthesis. However, euglenoids have no cell walls. Instead of a cell wall, euglenoids have a layer of flexible, interlocking protein fibers inside the cell membrane. Euglenoids are similar to animals because they are responsive and move by using one or two flagella for locomotion. Euglenoids have a contractile vacuole that expels excess water from the cell through an opening. They reproduce asexually by mitosis. (Biggs, Emmeluth, Gentry, Hays, Lundgren, & Mollura 1991, p. 275)

Darryl navigates his way through the euglenoid passage, occasionally faltering on words like *flagella* as he reads. When asked to tell the class what the passage is about, he gropes for a word or two: "I dunno. Eugenoids [*sic*] or something." His teacher manages a smile, corrects the pronunciation of *euglenoids,* and proceeds to explain what Darryl read to the class.

Mercifully, the period ends. Darryl heads for mathematics, his favourite class. The teacher assigns students to read this passage on an alternative definition of a *function*:

> Since a function has the property that exactly one second component is related to each first component, an alternative definition of a function is the following. A *function* is a rule that associates with each element of one set exactly one element of another set.

Functions are often denoted by letters, such as *f*, *g*, and *h*. If the function defined by the rule *y* = 2*x* is called *f,* the following "arrow notation" can also be used to define the *function*:

$$f{:}x \rightarrow 2x$$

This is read "*f* is the function that associates with a number *x* the number 2*x*." (Dolciani, Graham, Swanson, & Sharron 1992, p. 84)

Darryl handles the task with more purpose and confidence than he exhibited in the reading tasks from the previous classes. Why? you might wonder.

Darryl's scenario illustrates how demanding it is to switch gears from content area to content area. What demands do the various readings place on Darryl's ability to comprehend? What demands does the task—reading aloud to the class—place on Darryl? What other factors besides the nature of the text and of the task are likely to affect his content literacy?

As you might surmise, a variety of classroom-related factors influence one's content literacy in a given discipline, some of which are the learner's prior knowledge of, attitude toward, and interest in the subject; the learner's purpose; the language and conceptual difficulty of the material; the assumptions the text creator makes about his or her audience of learners; the way the text ideas are organized; and the teacher's beliefs about and attitude toward the use of texts.

To be literate in content area classrooms, students must learn how to use reading and writing, listening and speaking, and viewing and representing to explore and construct meaning with texts, other learners, and teachers. Using literacy in the classroom to help students *think with text* doesn't require specialized training on the part of content teachers. Nor does the pursuit of content literacy diminish the teacher's role as a subject matter specialist. To help students become literate in a content area does not mean to teach them *how* to read or write, listen and speak, view and represent. Instead, reading and writing, listening and speaking, and viewing and representing are tools that students use to think and learn with text in a given subject area. A common-sense definition of reading is that it is thinking with printed symbols. Students need to know how to think with text in order to respond to, discover, organize, retrieve, and elaborate on information and ideas they encounter in content learning situations. To this end, every teacher has a role to play.

Thinking with Text

The story of Olaudah Equiano, an African slave who lived in the 1700s, illustrates what reading is all about. Equiano kept a diary that eventually was published as a book called *The Interesting Narrative of the Life of Olaudah Equiano, or Gustavus Vassa, the African, Written by Himself.* His book was first published in London in 1789 and later abridged and edited by Paul Edwards (1967). Equiano tells how he was kidnapped from his West African tribe as a child and sold into bondage to a ship's captain, how he educated himself, and how he eventually purchased his freedom. In his diary, Equiano describes the rather strange and mysterious activity that his master engaged in whenever he read books on long voyages across the seas. Although Equiano didn't know how to read, he was in awe of the relationship that his master had with books.

What was this thing that his master called reading? Equiano longed to be able to read books the way his master did. So when he was alone in his captain's cabin, he would pick up a book, open it, and begin *talking* to it. Then he would put his ears near the pages of the book in hopes that the book would *talk* back to him, but the book remained silent. Equiano felt helpless in the presence of the silent text. Reading remained a mystery to him, as it did to Lesra Martin, until he learned to read and write. Equiano may have been far more skilled in listening, speaking, viewing, and representing, but reading and writing remain important skills in our society.

Equiano was on the right track when he picked up a book and started talking to it in hopes that it would talk back to him. One way to think about reading is to liken it to a conversation between two parties. Metaphorically speaking, reading involves a conversation between the reader and the text. An author creates a text to communicate ideas to someone else. Readers engage their minds in the conversation by thinking about the text so that they can respond to, understand, and perhaps even question and challenge the author's ideas. Equiano intuitively recognized that reading is a process of communicating with text. However, he didn't know how to go about the process of thinking with text until he learned how to make books "talk" to him.

In Plato's *Theaetetus,* written more than 2000 years ago, Socrates responds to the question, "What is the thinking process?" His response was as revealing then as it is today. Socrates explains to his questioner that when the mind is thinking, it is merely talking to itself, asking questions and answering them. In more recent times, reading has been described as a *skillful* and *strategic* activity in which the reader's mind is alive with questions—*cognitive questions*, as Frank Smith (1988) calls them. Cognitive questions vary from reader to reader. Skilled readers often aren't even aware that they are raising questions while reading because reading has become an automatic process—an activity that is second nature to the skilled reader. These cognitive questions allow readers to interact with the content of the communication: What is this text about? What is the author trying to say? What is going to happen next? What does the text mean? So what? Such questions help the reader anticipate meaning, respond to the text, search for information, and infer from and elaborate on the content of the text.

When skilled readers run into trouble or have difficulty comprehending what they are reading, they often use a *strategic* approach to make sense of it. They have strategies at their command that they use to get out of trouble and to make sense of the text. Raising questions about the text *at a conscious level* is one such strategy. Teaching students to be skillful and strategic as they think and learn with text in content areas is what we explore throughout this book. Two theories related to the reading process, *reader response theory* and *schema theory*, contribute to our understanding of reading as thinking with text and underscore the active role of the reader in comprehending and learning.

Reader Response Theory Reader response theory has evolved from a literary tradition. As early as 1938, Louise Rosenblatt (1982) argued that *thought* and *feeling* are legitimate components of literary interpretation. A text, whether it is literary or informational, demands affective as well as intellectual response from its readers. Creating an active learning environment in which students respond personally and critically to what they are reading is an important instructional goal in a response-centred classroom. Often in text-learning situations, a teacher will focus on what students have learned and how much.

There is value in having what Rosenblatt calls an *efferent stance* as a reader. When readers assume an efferent stance, they focus attention on the ideas and information they encounter in a text. Reader response, however, is also likely to involve feelings, personal associations, and insights that are unique to the reader. When students assume an *aesthetic stance*, they shift attention inward to what is being created as part of the reading experience itself. An aesthetic response to text is driven by personal feelings and attitudes that are stirred by the reader's transactions with the text.

One way to encourage thinking with text is to take advantage of both efferent and aesthetic stances. This works well when students actively respond to what they are reading not only by talking but also by writing. One of the instructional strategies we explore in Chapter 8, on writing to learn, is the use of *response journals*. When students combine the use of response journals with discussion, the challenge from an instructional perspective is to create an environment in which they feel free enough to respond openly. Open response is necessary to evoke students' initial feelings and thoughts. Evoking students' initial responses to a text is crucial to further exploration of the ideas they are encountering. Open responses, however, are not final responses.

For example, a history teacher divides the class into two groups and has one group read *Keeper 'n Me* by Richard Wagamese and the other group *Underground to Canada* by Barbara Smucker. As the students read the books, they keep response journals in which they react to questions such as how the protagonists feel interacting with societies that discriminate against their race. Some students also sketch their responses. When the class meets to discuss the books, students offer ideas from their response journals to generate a comparison concerning the ways in which the Aboriginal character in *Keeper 'n Me* differs from the escaped slaves in *Underground to Canada*. From this discussion, students go on to explore the concept of "captivity" and how it changes across circumstances, societies, and historical periods.

Affect, as you can see, is a catalyst for students to respond to text. Bleich (1978) suggests that response involves both the author and the reader taking active parts in the making of meaning. Thus, the initial response of "I like this" or "I hate this" becomes the springboard for other, more complex reactions. *Why* a student likes or does not like a text becomes the genesis of discussions, drama, art, and compositions that probe the reader's intentions.

Reader response questions allow students to explore their personal responses and to take those initial reactions into more analytic realms. According to Brozo (1989), the rationale behind a reader's response to text is this: "It is through a personal connection that a text becomes meaningful and memorable" (p. 141). Following are some questions that evoke student responses to informational texts:

1. *What aspect of the text interested you the most?* (The reader identifies an idea, issue, event, character, place, or any other aspect of the content that aroused strong feelings.)

2. *What are your feelings and attitudes about this aspect of the text?* (The reader describes and explains feelings and attitudes.)

3. *What experiences have you had that help others understand why you feel the way you do?* (The reader supports feelings and attitudes with personal experiences.) (Brozo 1989, p. 142)

Student's Most Interesting Part of Text	The information about quarks was good. It was something that I didn't know before. I really thought that the names of the different types of quarks (up, down, truth, beauty, strange, and charm) were kind of weird, but these names made them easier to remember because they are so different.
Student's Feelings and Attitudes Toward Subject	The author did a good job in making all of this interesting and pretty easy to read. Quarks and their flavours and colours are kind of hard to understand when you read about them in the textbook, but I could follow this book. I think it's amazing what scientists have been able to find out about atomic particles. I especially wonder about why the universe hasn't blown up already, because the book said that it should have because of the way particles and antiparticles react. Scientists don't have the answer either. But it makes you feel a little uneasy, not knowing what holds all of this together.
Student's Personal Associations	I suppose that all of us have wondered about what keeps the universe going at some time or other. I guess what started me thinking about this was a science fiction movie I saw that showed the world exploding into outer space. A lot of people see these kinds of shows and wonder if that could really happen. Then, when you read about quarks, it makes you think.

FIGURE 1.1   **Student's Responses to Reader Response Questions for** *Atoms, Molecules, and Quarks*

Responses to these questions help readers consciously connect their own experiences to the content of the text. The questions can be used well in combination with writing and talking.

Study a student's responses to a trade book titled *Atoms, Molecules, and Quarks* (1986), by Melvin Berger, presented in Figure 1.1. Students can and do become interested in and excited about informational text when it is presented in a response-centred format.

Schema Theory Students position themselves to learn with text whenever they use prior knowledge to construct meaning for new material that they are studying. To this extent, schema reflects the experiences, conceptual understandings, attitudes, values, skills, and strategies a reader brings to a text situation. *Schema* is the technical term used by cognitive scientists to describe how people organize and store information in their heads.

Schema activation is the mechanism by which people access what they know and match it to the information in a text. In doing so, they build on the meaning they already bring to the reading situation. Indeed, *schemata* (the plural for *schema*) have been called "the building blocks of cognition" (Rumelhart 1982), because they represent elaborate networks of information that people use to make sense of new stimuli, events, and situations.

In ordinary conversation, the language by which people communicate doesn't often pose problems for comprehension. In academic content areas, however, the reader needs to be familiar with the language of a discipline, or the text will create trouble for the reader. Bransford and Stein (1984) make this clear with the passage in Box 1.3 on page 18.

BOX 1.3	**Letter to Jim**

Dear Jim,

Remember Pete, the guy in my last letter? You'll never guess what he did last week. First, he talked about the importance of mass spectrometers. He then discussed the isotopes of argon 36 and argon 38 and noted that they were of higher density than expected. He also cited the high values of neon found in the atmosphere. He has a paper that is already written, but he is aware of the need for further investigation as well.

Love,

Sandra

Source: Reprinted from J. D. Bransford & B. S. Stein (1984). *The ideal problem solver: A guide to improving thinking, learning, and creativity.* New York: W. H. Freeman and Co. Copyright © 1984 by W. H. Freeman and Company.

The passage may pose a comprehension problem if readers do not know enough about Pete or his goal. Pete, it turns out, is an astronomer, and his goal is to call into question current theories about the formation of the solar system based on data collected from a NASA spaceship's voyage to Venus. Does this information help you better comprehend the letter? Maybe. Bransford and Stein (1984) point out, "Most people feel that [information about Pete's goal] helps comprehension to some extent. However, unless they are knowledgeable about astronomy, they are unable to make many inferences about the letter" (p. 54). For example, what is the relationship, if any, between the high density of the isotopes of argon and theories of the formation of the solar system? To answer the question requires that readers make an inferential leap by using what they know to fill in gaps in the information presented in the letter.

Schemata influence comprehending and learning. When a match occurs between students' prior knowledge and text material, schema functions in at least three ways.

First, schema provides a framework for learning that allows readers to *seek and select* information that is relevant to their purposes for reading. In the process of searching and selecting, readers are more likely to *make inferences* about the text. You make inferences when you *anticipate* content and *make predictions* about upcoming material or, as we just suggested, you *fill in gaps* in the material during reading.

Second, schema helps readers *organize* text information. The process by which you organize and integrate new information into old facilitates the ability to *retain and remember* what you read. A poorly organized text is difficult for readers to comprehend. We illustrate this point in more detail when we discuss the influences of text structure on comprehension and retention in later chapters.

Third, schema helps readers *elaborate* information. When you elaborate what you have read, you engage in a cognitive process that involves deeper levels of insight, judgment, and evaluation. You are inclined to ask, "So what?" as you engage in conversation with an author.

BOX 1.4	**Prereading Activity for "Ordeal by Cheque"**

Here are the essential bits of information contained in the first few cheques of the story:

Entry date:	Paid to:	Amount:	Signed by:
8/30/03	A baby shop	$ 148.00	Lawrence Exeter
9/2/03	A hospital	100.00	Lawrence Exeter
10/3/03	A physician	475.00	Lawrence Exeter Sr.
12/19/03	A toy company	83.20	Lawrence Exeter Sr.
10/6/09	A private school for boys	1250.00	Lawrence Exeter Sr.
4/18/10	A bicycle company	52.50	Lawrence Exeter Sr.
8/26/15	A military academy	2150.00	Lawrence Exeter Sr.
9/3/21	A Cadillac dealer	3885.00	Lawrence Exeter Sr.
9/7/21	An auto repair shop	228.76	Lawrence Exeter Sr.

What is the story about? Who are the main characters and what do you know about them? What do you think will happen in the remainder of the story?

A Reader Response, Schema-Based Demonstration   To illustrate thinking with text in action, we will use a workshop activity. In workshops for content teachers, we occasionally read the short story "Ordeal by Cheque" by Wuther Crue (first published in *Vanity Fair* magazine in 1932). The story is extraordinary in that it is told entirely through the bank cheques of the Exeter family over a 28-year span. The workshop participants interact in small groups, and each group is assigned the task of constructing the meaning of the story. At first glance, the groups don't know what to make of their task. "You must be kidding!" is a typical response. At this point, we engage the groups in a prereading activity to activate prior knowledge, declare the purposes for reading, and arouse interest in the story. We assign them the activity in Box 1.4, which depicts in chart form the essential bits of information contained on the first nine cheques of the story. Group members collaborate as they respond to the task of answering the three questions that accompany the chart: What is the story about? Who are the main characters and what do you know about them? What do you predict will happen in the remainder of the story? We invite you to analyze the information in the chart. Are you able to construct what has taken place so far in the story? What inferences did you make about the characters? Here are some typical responses to these questions:

"A baby boy was born. He's named after his father."

"The Exeters must be 'fat cats.' The old man's loaded."

"He spends $83 for toys in 1903! He probably bought out the toy store."

"Lawrence Jr. must be a spoiled brat!"

"Yeah, how can any kid born with a silver spoon in his mouth not turn out spoiled?"

'Let's not jump to conclusions. Why is he spoiled?"

"Look, the family sent him to a military academy after he screwed up at the private school."

"No, no. It was fashionable in those days to send your child first to a private school until he was old enough for military school. The rich sent their children to exclusive schools—it's as simple as that."

"Maybe so, but the kid is still a spoiled brat. His father buys him a Cadillac, probably for graduation from the academy, and four days later, it's in the body shop for repair."

"The father indulges his son. I wonder what will happen to Junior when he has to make it on his own?"

This demonstration illustrates that readers not only read the lines to determine what an author says but also read between the lines to infer meaning and beyond the lines to elaborate the message. Now read "Ordeal by Cheque" in its entirety on pages 21–24. As you read, you will undoubtedly find yourself responding, raising questions, predicting, searching for relationships among the pieces of information contained in each cheque, inferring, judging, and elaborating.

■■■ Read *Ordeal by Cheque* on pages 21-24 ■■■

The statements made about Lawrence Exeter and his son are the result of schema activation. We often ask workshop participants to examine the basis for their initial responses about the father and the son in the story. Some speak with authority, citing knowledge and beliefs about how the rich live. Others express their inferences about the Exeters as hunches that need to be pursued as more information is revealed in the story.

The activity also activates the workshop participants' prior knowledge of stories. Some use their *story schema* to establish a setting and identify a problem around which the remainder of the story will revolve. Based on the information from the chart in Box 1.4 on page 19, what appears to be the problem in the story? And how do you predict it will be resolved?

The 15 or so minutes that it takes to complete the *prereading activity* is time well spent. Not only do participants have a framework in which to construct meaning for the story, but their expectations have also been raised about the content of the cheques they have yet to read. The predictions they make for the remainder of the story, though general, often suggest that they have surmised the author's intent.

The insights into thinking with text presented here are developed in succeeding chapters within the framework of instructional strategies related to content area reading. What these insights tell the classroom teacher is this: readers must "work" with print in an effort to explore and construct meaning. Reading is first and foremost a conversation, a give-and-take exchange, between the reader and the text. However, the burden of learning is always on the reader. There are times when a text may be too difficult for students to handle on their own. In situations where text is difficult, teachers are in an ideal position to guide students' reading through various forms of instructional activity. Scaffolding learning with texts, then, is a primary responsibility of the teacher—one that we also explore throughout this book.

Ordeal by Cheque

LOS ANGELES, CALIF. *Apr. 18th* 19 *10* No.____
HOLLYWOOD STATE BANK 90-984
6801 SANTA MONICA BOULEVARD
PAY TO THE ORDER OF *City Bicycle Co.* $ *52.50*
Fifty two ———————— *50/* DOLLARS
Lawrence Exeter Sr.

LOS ANGELES, CALIF. *Aug 30th* 19 *03* No.____
HOLLYWOOD STATE BANK 90-984
6801 SANTA MONICA BOULEVARD
PAY TO THE ORDER OF *Goosie Gander Baby Shoppe* $ *148.50*
One hundred & forty eight ——— *50/* DOLLARS
Lawrence Exeter

LOS ANGELES, CALIF. *Aug 26th* 19 *15* No.____
HOLLYWOOD STATE BANK 90-984
6801 SANTA MONICA BOULEVARD
PAY TO THE ORDER OF *Columbia Military Acad.* $ *2,150.00*
Twenty-one hundred & fifty ——— *XX* DOLLARS
Lawrence Exeter Sr.

LOS ANGELES, CALIF. *Sept 2nd* 19 *03* No.____
HOLLYWOOD STATE BANK 90-984
6801 SANTA MONICA BOULEVARD
PAY TO THE ORDER OF *Hollywood Hospital* $ *100.00*
One hundred ———————— *XX* DOLLARS
Lawrence Exeter

LOS ANGELES, CALIF. *Sept 3rd* 19 *21* No.____
HOLLYWOOD STATE BANK 90-984
6801 SANTA MONICA BOULEVARD
PAY TO THE ORDER OF *Hollywood Cadillac Co.* $ *3,885.00*
Thirty eight hundred & eighty five *XX* DOLLARS
Lawrence Exeter Sr.

LOS ANGELES, CALIF. *Oct 3rd* 19 *03* No.____
HOLLYWOOD STATE BANK 90-984
6801 SANTA MONICA BOULEVARD
PAY TO THE ORDER OF *Dr. David M. McCoy* $ *475.00*
Four hundred & seventy five ——— *XX* DOLLARS
Lawrence Exeter Sr.

LOS ANGELES, CALIF. *Sept. 7th* 19 *21* No.____
HOLLYWOOD STATE BANK 90-984
6801 SANTA MONICA BOULEVARD
PAY TO THE ORDER OF *Wilshire Auto Repair Service* $ *288.76*
Two hundred & eighty-eight ——— *76/* DOLLARS
Lawrence Exeter Sr.

LOS ANGELES, CALIF. *Dec 19th* 19 *03* No.____
HOLLYWOOD STATE BANK 90-984
6801 SANTA MONICA BOULEVARD
PAY TO THE ORDER OF *California Toyland Co.* $ *83.20*
Eighty Three ———————— *20/* DOLLARS
Lawrence Exeter, Sr.

LOS ANGELES, CALIF. *Oct. 15th* 19 *21* No.____
HOLLYWOOD STATE BANK 90-984
6801 SANTA MONICA BOULEVARD
PAY TO THE ORDER OF *Stanford University* $ *339.00*
Three hundred & thirty-nine ——— *XX* DOLLARS
Lawrence Exeter Sr.

LOS ANGELES, CALIF. *Oct. 6th* 19 *09* No.____
HOLLYWOOD STATE BANK 90-984
6801 SANTA MONICA BOULEVARD
PAY TO THE ORDER OF *Palisades School for Boys* $ *1,250.00*
Twelve hundred & fifty ——— *XX* DOLLARS
Lawrence Exeter, Sr.

LOS ANGELES, CALIF. *June 1st* 19 *23* No.____
HOLLYWOOD STATE BANK 90-984
6801 SANTA MONICA BOULEVARD
PAY TO THE ORDER OF *Miss Daisy Windsor* $ *25,000.00*
Twenty-five thousand ———————— *XX* DOLLARS
Lawrence Exeter Sr.

LOS ANGELES, CALIF. June 9th 19 23 No. _____
HOLLYWOOD STATE BANK 90-984
6801 SANTA MONICA BOULEVARD
PAY TO THE ORDER OF French Line, Ile de France $585.00
Five hundred & eighty-five ——— XX DOLLARS
Lawrence Exeter Sr.

LOS ANGELES, CALIF. Nov. 18th 19 26 No. _____
HOLLYWOOD STATE BANK 90-984
6801 SANTA MONICA BOULEVARD
PAY TO THE ORDER OF Beverly Diamond & Gift Shoppe $678.45
Six hundred & seventy-eight ——— 45/ DOLLARS
Lawrence Exeter Sr.

LOS ANGELES, CALIF. Aug. 23rd 19 23 No. _____
HOLLYWOOD STATE BANK 90-984
6801 SANTA MONICA BOULEVARD
PAY TO THE ORDER OF Banque de France $5,000.00
Five thousand ——— XX DOLLARS
Lawrence Exeter Sr.

LOS ANGELES, CALIF. Nov. 16th 19 26 No. _____
HOLLYWOOD STATE BANK 90-984
6801 SANTA MONICA BOULEVARD
PAY TO THE ORDER OF Hawaii Steamship Co. $560.00
Five hundred & sixty ——— XX DOLLARS
Lawrence Exeter Sr.

LOS ANGELES, CALIF. Feb. 13th 19 26 No. _____
HOLLYWOOD STATE BANK 90-984
6801 SANTA MONICA BOULEVARD
PAY TO THE ORDER OF University Club Florists $76.50
Seventy-six ——— 50/ DOLLARS
Lawrence Exeter Sr.

LOS ANGELES, CALIF. Nov. 21st 19 26 No. _____
HOLLYWOOD STATE BANK 90-984
6801 SANTA MONICA BOULEVARD
PAY TO THE ORDER OF Lawrence Exeter, Junior $200,000
Two hundred thousand ——— XX DOLLARS
Lawrence Exeter Sr.

LOS ANGELES, CALIF. June 22nd 19 26 No. _____
HOLLYWOOD STATE BANK 90-984
6801 SANTA MONICA BOULEVARD
PAY TO THE ORDER OF University Club Florists $312.75
Three hundred & twelve ——— 75/ DOLLARS
Lawrence Exeter Sr.

LOS ANGELES, CALIF. Nov. 22 rd 19 26 No. _____
HOLLYWOOD STATE BANK 90-984
6801 SANTA MONICA BOULEVARD
PAY TO THE ORDER OF Ambassador Hotel $2,250.00
Twenty-two hundred & fifty ——— XX DOLLARS
Lawrence Exeter Sr.

LOS ANGELES, CALIF. Aug 11th 19 26 No. _____
HOLLYWOOD STATE BANK 90-984
6801 SANTA MONICA BOULEVARD
PAY TO THE ORDER OF Riviera Heights Land Co. $56,000.00
Fifty-six Thousand ——— XX DOLLARS
Lawrence Exeter Sr.

LOS ANGELES, CALIF. Dec. 1st 19 26 No. _____
HOLLYWOOD STATE BANK 90-984
6801 SANTA MONICA BOULEVARD
PAY TO THE ORDER OF University Club Florists $183.50
One hundred & eighty-three ——— 50/ DOLLARS
Lawrence Exeter Sr.

LOS ANGELES, CALIF. Oct. 30th 19 26 No. _____
HOLLYWOOD STATE BANK 90-984
6801 SANTA MONICA BOULEVARD
PAY TO THE ORDER OF Renaissance Interior Decorators $22,000.00
Twenty-two thousand ——— XX DOLLARS
Lawrence Exeter Sr.

LOS ANGELES, CALIF. Feb. 18 19 27 No. _____
HOLLYWOOD STATE BANK 90-984
6801 SANTA MONICA BOULEVARD
PAY TO THE ORDER OF Cocoanut Grove Sweet Shoppe $27.00
Twenty seven ——— DOLLARS
Lawrence Exeter Jr.

LOS ANGELES, CALIF. July 16 19 27 No. ____
HOLLYWOOD STATE BANK 90-984
6801 SANTA MONICA BOULEVARD
PAY TO THE ORDER OF Parisian Gown Shoppe $25.00
Nine hundred twenty five ———— DOLLARS
Lawrence Exeter, Jr.

LOS ANGELES, CALIF. Aug. 30 19 29 No. ____
HOLLYWOOD STATE BANK 90-984
6801 SANTA MONICA BOULEVARD
PAY TO THE ORDER OF Tony Spagoni $126.00
One hundred twenty six ———— DOLLARS
Lawrence Exeter, Jr.

LOS ANGELES, CALIF. Dec. 1 19 27 No. ____
HOLLYWOOD STATE BANK 90-984
6801 SANTA MONICA BOULEVARD
PAY TO THE ORDER OF Anita Lingerie Salon $750.00
Seven hundred, fifty ———— DOLLARS
Lawrence Exeter, Jr.

LOS ANGELES, CALIF. May 25 19 30 No. ____
HOLLYWOOD STATE BANK 90-984
6801 SANTA MONICA BOULEVARD
PAY TO THE ORDER OF University Club Florists $87.00
Eighty seven ———— DOLLARS
Lawrence Exeter, Jr.

LOS ANGELES, CALIF. April 1 19 28 No. ____
HOLLYWOOD STATE BANK 90-984
6801 SANTA MONICA BOULEVARD
PAY TO THE ORDER OF Parisian Gown Shoppe $1,150.00
Eleven hundred fifty ———— DOLLARS
Lawrence Exeter, Jr.

LOS ANGELES, CALIF. May 28 19 30 No. ____
HOLLYWOOD STATE BANK 90-984
6801 SANTA MONICA BOULEVARD
PAY TO THE ORDER OF Broadway Diamond Co. $575.00
Five hundred, seventy five ———— DOLLARS
Lawrence Exeter, Jr.

LOS ANGELES, CALIF. Nov. 1 19 28 No. ____
HOLLYWOOD STATE BANK 90-984
6801 SANTA MONICA BOULEVARD
PAY TO THE ORDER OF Moderne Sportte Shoppe   562.00
Five hundred, sixty two ———— DOLLARS
Lawrence Exeter, Jr.

LOS ANGELES, CALIF. Nov. 13 19 30 No. ____
HOLLYWOOD STATE BANK 90-984
6801 SANTA MONICA BOULEVARD
PAY TO THE ORDER OF Miss Flossie Wentworth $50,000.00
Fifty thousand ———— DOLLARS
Lawrence Exeter, Jr.

LOS ANGELES, CALIF. July 1 19 29 No. ____
HOLLYWOOD STATE BANK 90-984
6801 SANTA MONICA BOULEVARD
PAY TO THE ORDER OF The Bootery $145.25
One hundred, forty five 25/100 DOLLARS
Lawrence Exeter, Jr.

LOS ANGELES, CALIF. Nov. 14 19 30 No. ____
HOLLYWOOD STATE BANK 90-984
6801 SANTA MONICA BOULEVARD
PAY TO THE ORDER OF Wall & Smith, attys. at Law $525.00
Five hundred twenty five ———— DOLLARS
Lawrence Exeter, Jr.

LOS ANGELES, CALIF. Aug 23 19 29 No. ____
HOLLYWOOD STATE BANK 90-984
6801 SANTA MONICA BOULEVARD
PAY TO THE ORDER OF Tony Spagoni $126.00
One hundred twenty six ———— DOLLARS
Lawrence Exeter, Jr.

LOS ANGELES, CALIF. Nov. 15 19 30 No. ____
HOLLYWOOD STATE BANK 90-984
6801 SANTA MONICA BOULEVARD
PAY TO THE ORDER OF Mrs. Lawrence Exeter, Jr. $5000.00
Five thousand ———— DOLLARS
Lawrence Exeter, Jr.

INSTRUCTIONAL SCAFFOLDING

When texts serve as tools for learning in content area classrooms, teachers have a significant role to play. That role can be thought of in a metaphorical way as "instructional scaffolding." One of the benchmarks of content-literate students, as we suggested earlier, is that they know how to learn with texts independently. Yet many students in today's diverse classrooms have trouble handling the conceptual demands inherent in reading material when left to their own devices to learn with text. A gap often exists between the ideas and relationships they are studying and their prior knowledge, interests, attitudes, cultural background, language proficiency, or reading ability. In a nutshell, instructional scaffolding allows teachers to support readers' efforts to make sense of texts while showing them how to use strategies that will, over time, lead to independent learning.

Used in construction, scaffolds serve as supports, lifting up workers so that they can achieve something that otherwise would not have been possible. In teaching and learning contexts, scaffolding means helping learners do what they cannot do at first (Bruner 1986). Instructional scaffolds support text learners by helping them achieve literacy tasks that would otherwise have been out of reach. Applebee (1991) explains that instructional scaffolding provides the necessary support that students need as they attempt new tasks; at the same time, teachers model or lead the students through effective strategies for completing these tasks. Providing the "necessary support" often means understanding the diversity that exists among the students in your class, planning active learning environments, and supporting students' efforts to learn through the use of instructional strategies and authentic texts beyond the textbook—all of which are explored more closely in the chapters that follow.

LOOKING BACK, LOOKING FORWARD

In this chapter, we invited you to begin an examination of content literacy practices, and the assumptions underlying those practices, for text learning and active student involvement. Teachers play a critical role in helping students realize a potentially powerful use of language: learning with text. Learning with text is an active process. Yet assigning and telling are still common teaching practices and often have the unfortunate consequence of dampening students' active involvement in learning.

In addition, changes in the racial and ethnic composition of our student population have been dramatic. Not only are classrooms more linguistically and culturally diverse than they were two or three decades ago but they have also changed academically. The linguistic, cultural, and achievement differences of students contribute to the complexities of classroom diversity. Students of diverse backgrounds (who may be distinguished by their ethnicity, social class, language, or achievement level) often struggle in classrooms. They exhibit a learned helplessness characterized by a lack of control over reading strategies, a poor self-image, and an ambivalent attitude toward reading. As a result, diverse learners tend to avoid reading or being held accountable for reading in school. They challenge teachers to look for and experiment with instructional strategies that will actively involve them in the life of the classroom.

To shift the burden of learning from teacher to student requires an understanding of the importance of the relationships that exist between a more broadly conceived definition of literacy (reading, writing, listening, speaking, viewing, and representing) and learning across the curriculum. As a result, we explored the role that literacy plays in the acquisition of content knowledge. Learning and thinking with a variety of texts is what content area literacy is all about. Instead of teaching students how to read or write, we use reading and writing and other literacy skills as tools to construct knowledge—to discover, to clarify, and to make meaning—in a given discipline.

Content literacy, then, underscores the situational demands placed on students to use reading and writing, listening and speaking, and viewing and representing to learn subject matter. Content teachers are in an ideal position to show students how to use the literacy strategies that are actually needed to construct content knowledge.

Perhaps the single most important resource in learning with texts is reader's prior knowledge. Therefore, we explored some of the influences and processes underlying reading to learn in content classrooms. In particular, we emphasized the roles that reader response and schema play in thinking with text.

Instructional scaffolding is a concept used throughout this book. Instructional scaffolding supports text learners in achieving literacy tasks that would otherwise be out of reach.

In the next chapter, we shift our focus to texts. If teachers are going to meet the academic, linguistic, and cultural needs of students, they need to reconsider the role that textbooks play in classroom learning. How do teachers move beyond the use of textbooks by integrating a variety of trade books and electronic texts into the curriculum? We argue that trade books and electronic texts should be used interchangeably with textbooks to give students an intense and extensive involvement with subject matter.

 # MINDS-ON

1. Review the passages read by Darryl in Canadian history, biology, and mathematics classes. In small groups, create lists of the varying situational demands that each text selection places on Darryl's ability to read. Discuss possible factors besides the nature of the text and of the task that are likely to affect his content literacy. How are Darryl's attitude and willingness to be an active learner affected by these factors? What might the teachers of these various classes have done to create a more student-centred learning experience?

2. Focus on the elements of a student-centred curriculum. Obviously, the teacher's beliefs and instructional approach play a large role in permitting students to become actively involved in an ongoing lesson, but what visible signs of student involvement would exist in the physical environment of the classroom? Just by looking, would it be possible to detect a classroom where student-centred lessons are the norm? If so, what physical evidence would be present, and what would that evidence indicate to you, the observer?

3. Picture a classroom in your content area of 25 students from diverse backgrounds— different social classes, different ethnicity, and varying achievement levels. Describe some classroom strategies you might use to respond to individual differences while maintaining high standards of content literacy and learning.

4. In the next 10 years, the representation of visible minorities in Canada is expected to continue to rise so that, by the year 2016, children from visible minorities will constitute approximately 25 percent of the population (Kelly 1995; Esses & Gardner 1996). How do you believe this change will influence learning strategies in the classroom?

5. Imagine that during lunch, several teaching colleagues comment that since many students in their courses "can't read," these teachers rarely use books. They argue that students learn content just as well through audiovisual aids and discussions.

   Divide a small group of six class members into two smaller groups of three: one representing the teachers who believe books are unnecessary and one representing those who believe books are essential. For 10 minutes, role-play a lunchtime debate on the pros and cons of using all literacy skills—reading, writing, listening, speaking, viewing, and representing—in content areas. What might be the result if we use only reading? If we use only visual materials? After the time has elapsed, discuss the arguments used by the role players. Which did you find valid, and with which did you disagree?

6. Your supervisor observes a lesson in which you use a large block of time for students to read. Afterward, the supervisor says that you should assign reading as homework, rather than "wasting" valuable class time. She adds that if you continue with lessons like this, your students will be lucky to finish one or two books over the entire year. Consequently, you request a meeting with the supervisor. What arguments might you bring to this meeting to help convince her of the validity of your approach?

 ## HANDS-ON

1. With a small group, examine the following well-known passage and attempt to supply the missing words. Note that all missing words, regardless of length, are indicated by blanks in the passage.

   We have gathered from coast to coast to _____ , from one ocean to another, united in our grief, to say _____ .

   But this is not the end. He left _____ in '84. But he came back for Meech. He came back for _____ . He came back to remind us of who we are and what we're all capable of. But he won't be coming back anymore. It's all up to us, all of us, now.

   The woods are _____ , dark and deep. He has kept his _____ and earned his sleep.

   Je t'aime _____ .

   After you have filled in the blanks, discuss the processes by which decisions on possible responses were made and any problems encountered. How did prior knowledge of the passage's topic assist your reading process? (After you have completed this experiment, review Justin Trudeau's speech at the end of the "Hands-On" section in Chapter 4.)

   In what ways was your experience similar to that of a student who attempts to decipher a content passage but who has little background knowledge of its content?

2. Bring the following materials to class: a large paper bag, five paper plates, four buttons, three cardboard tubes, scraps of material, six pipe cleaners, three sheets of construction paper, scissors, tape, and a stapler. Your instructor will silently give each group a written directive to create a replica of a living creature (cat, dog, rhinoceros, aardvark, etc.) with *no* verbal communication permitted.

After your group has constructed its creature, list the communication difficulties, and discuss how each was overcome. Finally, have a spokesperson from each group share these difficulties with the rest of the class.

3. Rewrite Lewis Carroll's poem "Jabberwocky" using "real" words.

Jabberwocky

'Twas brillig, and the slithy toves
Did gyre and gimble in the wabe;
All mimsy were the borogoves,
And the mome raths outgrabe.

"Beware the Jabberwock, my son!
The jaws that bite, the claws that catch!
Beware the Jubjub bird and shun
The frumious Bandersnatch!"

He took his vorpal sword in hand:
Long time the manxome foe he sought—
So rested he by the Tumtum tree,
And stood awhile in thought.

And, as in uffish thought he stood,
The Jabberwock, with eyes of flame,
Came whiffling through the tulgey wood,
And burbled as it came!

One, two! One, two! And through and through
The vorpal blade went snicker-snack!
He left it dead, and with its head
He went galumphing back.

Compare your efforts with those of other members of your small group, and discuss the following questions:

a. Why are there differences in the translations?
b. Does your translation change the intended meaning of the poem?
c. Do the differences affect your enjoyment of the poem?
d. What personal experiences and prior knowledge that you brought to your reading of the poem may have influenced your translation?

SUGGESTED READINGS

Allington, R. L., Boxer, N. J., & Broikou, K. H. (1987). Jeremy, remedial reading and subject matter classes. *Journal of Reading, 30,* 643–645.

Anderson, R. C. (1994). Role of the reader's schema in comprehension, learning, and memory. In R. Ruddell, M. Ruddell, & H. Singer (Eds.), *Theoretical models and processes of reading* (4th ed.) (pp. 469–482). Newark, DE: International Reading Association.

Ashworthy, M. (2000). *Effective teachers, effective schools.* Toronto: Pippin Publishing Corporation.

Au, K. H. (1993). *Literacy instruction in multicultural settings.* Orlando, FL: Harcourt Brace.

Banks, J. A. (1994). *An introduction to multicultural education.* Boston, MA: Allyn & Bacon.

Begoray, D. (2002). Not just reading any more: Literacy, community and the pre-service teacher. *English Quarterly, 34*(3&4), 34–45.

Brooks, J., & Brooks, M. (1993). *The case for constructivist classrooms.* Alexandria, VA: Association for Curriculum and Supervision Development.

Delpit, L. (1995). *Other people's children: Conflict in the classroom.* New York: The New Press.

Delpit, L. D. (1988). The silenced dialogue: Power and pedagogy in educating other people's children. *Harvard Educational Review, 58,* 280–298.

Esses, V. M., & Gardner, R. C. (1996). Multiculturalism in Canada: Context and current status. Retrieved November 16, 2003, from http://www.cpa.ca/cbjsnew/1996/ful_edito.html.

Garrett-Petts, W. F., & Lawrence, D. (1996). *Integrating visual and verbal literacies.* Winnipeg: Inkshed Publications.

Ghosh, R. (1996). *Redefining multicultural education.* Toronto: Harcourt Brace Canada.

Goodlad, J. (1984). *A place called school.* New York: McGraw-Hill.

Graves, M., & Graves, B. (1994). *Scaffolding reading experiences: Designs for student success.* Norwood, MA: Christopher-Gordon.

Hiebert, E. H. (Ed.). (1991). *Literacy for a diverse society: Perspectives, practices, policies.* New York: Teachers College Press.

Johnston, P., & Winograd, P. (1990). Passive failure in reading. *Journal of Reading Behavior, 17,* 279–301.

Kang, H-W, & Golden, A. (1994). Vocabulary learning and instruction in a second or foreign language. *International Journal of Applied Linguistics, 4*(1), 57–77.

Kovacs, E. (1994). *Writing across cultures: A handbook on writing poetry & lyrical prose.* Portland, OR: Blue Heron Publishing.

Lapkin, S. (1998). *French second language education in Canada: Empirical studies.* Toronto: University of Toronto Press.

Marshall, N. (1996). The students: Who are they and how do I reach them? In D. Lapp, J. Flood, & N. Farnan (Eds.), *Content area reading and learning: Instructional strategies* (pp. 27–38). Boston, MA: Allyn & Bacon.

McAloon, N. M. (1994). Content area reading: It's not my Job! *Journal of Reading, 37,* 332–334.

Met, M. (1994). Teaching content through a second language. In F. Genesee (Ed.), *Educating second language children* (pp. 159–182). Cambridge, England: Cambridge University Press.

Moje, E. B. (1996). "I teach students, not subjects": Teacher-student relationships as contexts for secondary literacy. *Reading Research Quarterly, 31,* 172–195.

Moore, D. W. (1996). Contexts for literacy in secondary schools. In D. J. Leu, C. K. Kinzer, & K. A. Hinchman (Eds.), *Literacies for the twenty-first century: Research and practice* (pp. 15–46). Chicago: National Reading Conference.

Peregoy, S. F., & Boyle, O. F. W. (1997). *Reading, writing, & learning in ESL: A resource book for K–12 teachers* (2nd ed.). New York: Longman.

Piper, T. (2001). *And then there were two: Children and second-language learning.* Toronto: Pippin.

Sadoski, M., & Paivio, A. (2001). *Imagery and text: A dual coding theory of reading and writing.* Mahwah, NJ: Erlbaum.

Schumm, J. S., Vaughn, S., & Saumell, L. (1992). What do teachers do when the textbook is tough: Students speak out. *Journal of Reading Behavior, 24,* 481–503.

Ward, A., & Bouvier, R. (2001). *Resting lightly on Mother Earth: The Aboriginal experience in urban educational settings.* Calgary: Detselig Enterprises.

chapter two

Learning with Textbooks, Trade Books, and Electronic Texts

> *The internet is rapidly becoming a part of everyday life, and, used properly, it opens the door to a huge range of knowledge which has no national boundaries.*
>
> –Queen Elizabeth II

ORGANIZING PRINCIPLE

Books are familiar fixtures in classrooms. They are as much a part of the physical makeup of most classrooms as desks, tables, chairs, chalkboards, and bulletin boards. Although highly visible in a well-furnished classroom, books are much more than decoration. They are made to be read for a variety of purposes, not the least of which is to learn. One type of book, the textbook, has been scrutinized by educational critics who contend that textbooks have been "dumbed down" and rendered useless. Shallow and superficially written textbooks may as well be made for decoration rather than learning. In this chapter, we explore the value of textbooks but also recognize their limitations as resources for learning. Whereas 10 or 15 years ago textbooks were used almost exclusively in content learning situations, this isn't necessarily the case in today's rapidly changing classrooms. The speed at which the world of the classroom is mutating requires teachers to rethink business as usual. Technological changes, brought on by the digital forces of the computer, are transforming the way we communicate and disseminate information. Electronic texts, constructed and displayed on a computer screen, are not fixed entities cast in typesetter's print. Highly interactive and engaging electronic texts, especially those that are available over the internet, as Queen Elizabeth notes, have become an integral part of life. These texts have both benefits and shortcomings.

Coupled with unprecedented opportunities for literacy learning in electronic environments is another relatively recent phenomenon that is bringing about a radical departure from traditional text experiences in the classroom. A healthy resurgence of print media has resulted in a veritable mother lode of fiction and nonfiction trade books for children and adolescents about every topic imaginable. Trade books, as distinguished from textbooks, are published for distribution to the general public through booksellers. Trade books are informative as well as entertaining. They have a built-in appeal for people of all ages. Trade books have the potential to provide students with intense involvement in a subject and the power to develop in-depth understanding in ways not imagined a few years ago.

CHAPTER OVERVIEW

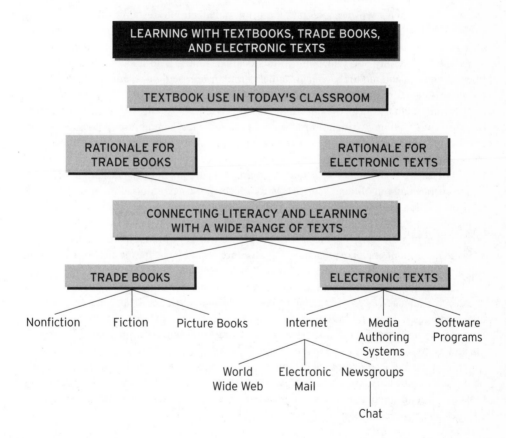

FRAME OF MIND

1. What are some problems associated with textbook use?
2. Why use trade books to learn subject matter?
3. Why use electronic texts?
4. What kinds of trade books can teachers use in their classrooms?
5. What kinds of electronic texts can be integrated into the curriculum?
6. What are some concerns about using the internet as a classroom resource?
7. How do the roles of teachers change when they make trade books and electronic texts an integral part of subject matter learning?

As teachers, how will we integrate the print and electronic resources that are quickly working their way into the curriculum? How will our roles and interactions with students change as the nature and kinds of text change in our classrooms? Should textbooks be abandoned? Certainly not. Our point in this chapter, rather, is to underscore the value of integrating print and multimedia environments into the curriculum: **trade books and electronic texts extend and enrich the curriculum.**

Learning with text begs the question, "What is a text?" Usually, the word *text* refers to the words of something written or printed; a single sentence, a paragraph, a passage of several paragraphs, a chapter, or a book can rightly be called texts, but texts are more than words written or in print. Texts represent sets of potential meanings. Louise Rosenblatt (1983) defines a text "as merely scratches, marks on parchment or paper until some reader makes meaning out of them" (p. 13). More recently, the definition of the term has shifted. Lori Neilsen (1998) defines texts as all constructions that form "sets of meaning and signifying practices" (p. 4). A text can occur in print format, such as a biography of Terry Fox, or in another format, such as a film by Atom Egoyan or even a lab demonstration by a secondary school chemistry teacher. For Rosenblatt and Neilsen, the text is a blueprint for meaning.

Texts need readers, viewers, listeners. Kit Pearson, author of popular fiction books for adolescents such as *The Sky is Falling* (1989), talks about how her ideas come from a variety of sources: "my own childhood and adolescence ... from history ... from stories I've heard from family and friends and from being incurably curious. I'm always staring at people and eavesdropping on their conversations."

In this chapter, we explore three types of texts that need readers—textbooks, trade books, and electronic texts. Each of these texts has the potential to make unique contributions to learning in content areas. Each can serve as a blueprint for meaning as students connect literacy and learning across the curriculum.

TEXTBOOK USE IN TODAY'S CLASSROOMS

A familiar ritual occurs in classrooms practically everywhere at the beginning of each school year. The ritual, of course, is the "distribution of textbooks" captured brilliantly in the accompanying Funky Winkerbean cartoon.

Textbooks are more the rule than the exception in most classrooms. Les Moore, the teacher in the cartoon, mouths the words that many teachers have either spoken aloud or

Source: Reprinted with special permission of King Features Syndicate.

thought about as part of the "distribution of textbooks" ritual. Textbooks, after all, are expensive. School districts, depending on their size, invest hundreds of thousands of dollars on a textbook adoption. Textbooks are purchased to last several years or more before the next adoption period. Mr. Moore expects his course textbooks to be returned at the end of the year in the same condition as the beginning of the year: "Although," he says somewhat wryly, "some signs of use would be nice!"

The cartoon hits home. Textbooks remain unread by too many students, even though teachers attempt to use textbooks with the best of intentions. Often we have heard teachers note with regret that students "just don't read assigned textbook material anymore." Yet it's not that the majority of students can't read. Most choose not to, primarily because they have never been shown how to think and learn with textbooks.

Textbooks are not without their problems. The quality of textbooks has come under criticism, but so has the manner in which teachers use them to drive instruction. A predominant practice in content area teaching involves the use of one type of text—*the* textbook, often at the exclusion of other types of texts. In conventional classrooms, reading assignments come almost exclusively from textbooks, the students' primary source of information. Because of their comprehensive and encyclopedic nature, most textbooks do not treat subject matter with the breadth and depth necessary to fully develop ideas and concepts. The very nature of textbooks often restricts their use in content area classrooms.

When grade 11 and 12 students in physics classes were queried about the use of their textbook, one student in the course said flatly, "I don't mess with the textbook. It's confusing." Another responded, "I should be telling you that the text is the best way to learn information. I would tell you that [for] all of my other classes. I learn by reading, and I read a lot. [But] I just can't understand this textbook. It's way above my head." These revealing comments came from interviews that were part of a study on the use of texts in science classes (Hynd, Guzzetti, & Lay 1994). The researchers, who interviewed a mix of students in science classes, were struck by the similarities in the students' comments, despite assumed differences in their ability, motivation, and background. Various student comments revealed insightful perspectives, including the belief that textbooks assume too much student knowledge, textbooks need fuller explanations and more relevant examples, and textbooks should be better organized.

Textbooks provide extensive, not intensive, treatment of subject matter. No wonder students voice concern about textbooks assuming that the students know too much. Textbook authors cast a wide net in an effort to be comprehensive. As a result, they often make erroneous assumptions about what students already know in relation to the content under

development. Rather than building a rich context and background for understanding difficult concepts, textbooks often err on the side of providing the minimum essentials necessary for understanding before moving on to another subject. This process of distilling content to its minimal essentials is undoubtedly associated with the second perspective voiced
by students: textbooks often do not supply full explanations.

A case in point is the Addison Wesley Longman textbook *History of the Canadian
Peoples*, which tells Canada's story in two volumes. Each volume is more than 500 pages
in length. The design of the two volumes, like many of the content area textbooks developed in the 1990s, is attractive and includes many eye-catching and instructionally helpful
features throughout each chapter: black-and-white photos, an array of visual aids (timelines, maps, tables, graphs, and cartoons). All of these design features serve several purposes: to support students' reading, to make learning more visual and appealing, and to
break up written text into manageable chunks of writing.

The authors of *History of the Canadian Peoples* write in an appealing manner to capture students' interest and hold their attention. Take, for example, a passage from a subsection of text describing women's suffrage:

> Western Canada produced the one individual most identified with the suffrage cause: Nellie L.
> McClung. Born in Grey Country, Ontario, she migrated to Manitoba as a young girl, married a
> druggist, raised five children, and had a successful career as a fiction writer. Her sense of
> humour and clever repartee enabled her to survive the many taunts that came her way. In 1914,
> she packed Winnipeg's Walker theatre for a performance of "How the Vote was Won." To thun-
> dering applause, she played the role of premier of a Women's Parliament, and punctured the pre-
> tensions of Conservative premier Sir Rodmond Roblin ... (Finkel & Conrad 1998, p. 150)

Much to the authors' credit, the passage they write highlights the Canadian flair for
political satire (continued in more recent years by women such as Mary Walsh of CBC's
This Hour Has 22 Minutes). Yet despite the importance of women's suffrage as a historical event and its profound political and social implications, the authors limit their coverage to six paragraphs as part of a comprehensive chapter on community responses to the
Age of Industry. Six paragraphs! Even though coverage is cursory at best, the authors
accomplish their purpose for the chapter: to chronicle events and people and to describe
the social results of major industrial changes in Canada from 1867 to 1921. The coverage
of the drive toward women's right to vote in *History of the Canadian Peoples*, we contend,
illustrates the major problem with textbooks in general. They aren't designed to provide in-
depth coverage. A textbook conveys a body of knowledge and is, by its very nature, comprehensive and encyclopedic. No wonder textbooks are often described as being "a mile
wide and an inch deep." Problems arise, however, when the textbook *becomes* the curriculum. In these instances, curriculum decisions often revolve around content coverage.

Time constraints in a textbook-driven curriculum are real. Teachers feel enormous
pressure to cover *x* amount of content in *x* amount of time before students move on to the
next chapter or unit of study. Return to the women's vote example. If pressed for time to
cover changes in Canadian life from 1867 to 1921 in three or four weeks, a Canadian social
studies teacher's concern is likely to be "How can I cover over 50 years of history in the
time allotted?" rather than "How do I involve students intellectually and emotionally in the
people, places, events, issues, ideas, and consequences associated with the Age of
Industry?" Teachers who operate under time constraints often view textbooks as efficient
informational resources that support what students are studying in a particular subject at a

particular time. Textbook-driven instruction relies on lecturing and other means of information-giving when content coverage is the primary purpose. The downside, from a content literacy perspective, is this: when reading merely chronicles events, students dismiss the power of text to inform and to transform their lives.

Increasing numbers of teachers are using a variety of print and nonprint media as resources for learning across the curriculum. Trade books and electronic texts are authentic alternatives to textbooks. So are magazines, newspapers, films, and any number of other print and nonprint learning tools. Unlike textbooks, which publishers distribute almost exclusively for use in schools, trade books, technology, and primary documents are preferred learning resources *outside* of school (Palmer & Stewart 1997). Trade books and electronic texts are more likely to be intrinsically motivating than textbooks. Students who absolutely refuse to read anything in schoolbooks may read a book of choice, visit a website, or interact with multimedia on a CD-ROM. Surfing the net or curling up in a chair with a good book attracts students to the genuine uses of texts—to inform, to entertain, to solve problems, to explore—and helps them make meaningful connections to reading, writing, and discussion.

RATIONALE FOR TRADE BOOKS

Trade books, rich in narrative and informational content, allow learners to interact with people, places, and ideas. Learning with trade books involves exposure to many different genres, all of which are potential sources of information for the active learner. A nonfiction or fiction trade book has the potential to be a magnifying glass that enlarges and enhances the reader's personal interaction with a subject. When teachers use textbooks and trade books in tandem, they help learners think critically about content. Diane Swanson (1994) has researched and written more than 20 nature books, such as *Safari Beneath the Sea* (1994) and *Buffalo Sunrise* (1996), and she emphasizes the importance of having a critical, inquiring mind. Reader involvement in a story, the potential to examine a topic in depth or explore a wide range of topics through multiple texts all contribute to extending students' reading experiences.

McGowan & Guzzetti (1991) identify four compelling reasons to use trade books across the curriculum:

- *Variety.* A wide range of books should be available and consistent with student ability and interest levels.
- *Interest.* Informative, entertaining, and engaging formats and writing styles keep readers interested.
- *Relevance.* Connections can be made to students' life experiences and prior knowledge.
- *Comprehensibility.* The books should focus on the development of concepts and relationships among concepts.

Variety

In instructional situations where teachers plan on using trade books to explore and examine a theme or topic, variety becomes an important consideration. There are numerous trade books for teachers and students to choose from dealing with important themes and topics in all content areas. Because of the wide range of books available to students, it is possible, with some advance planning and preparation, to guide students into books that will close the gap between students' reading levels and the levels of difficulty of the books. Reviews and recommendations of trade books often include appropriate age and reading levels, guidelines that may help teachers help students make good choices.

Also, exposing learners to a variety of trade books, especially nonfiction, gives them much needed practice reading informational texts (Cullinan 1993). Students need extended practice reading nonfiction texts to become proficient in the genre. The reality is that many students do not know how to read to learn with informational texts because their school experiences have been limited to textbook-only reading. For some students, the only historical, mathematics, or science materials they will ever read in a lifetime are in textbooks!

Interest and Relevance

Trade book writers are conscious not only of providing information but of entertaining readers as well—and that makes all the difference between a book and a textbook chapter on the same topic. The combination of storytelling and informing is an ancient concept that can be traced to the beginnings of the oral tradition when storytellers were the newscasters, entertainers, and teachers who kept society intact and growing. The ancient storyteller knew that "if lore can be encoded into stories, it can be made more memorable than by any other technique" (Egan 1989, p. 282). A student can learn the dates and the names of important battles for a test covering World War II, but it takes reading books such as Aranka Siegal's *Upon the Head of the Goat: A Childhood in Hungary, 1939–1944* (1983) to begin to understand the real stories of that time period.

Certain trade books relate to students' personal needs and interests because they are written from the viewpoint of children and adolescents. Editors categorize trade books as children's or young adults' by criteria such as the type of book (e.g., picture book, concept book, or novel), the age of the protagonist(s), and the perceived interest level of the story. Trade book selection for different age groups is often arbitrary and based on subjective criteria. But one thing is sure: people of all ages tend to be attracted to books that speak to them in some kind of personal way.

The primary motivation for including trade books in any classroom should be to capture students' attention and thus engage them in learning. Teachers in the sciences are finding that students learn better when they are actively engaged in the topic through trade books and actual experiences with scientific and mathematical concepts (Daisey 1994b).

At the beginning of a science lesson, an excerpt from a book read aloud to the class or a picture book can serve as an enjoyable preview of the lesson's contents. Trade books thus play a supporting role by introducing a part of or a perspective on the lesson that may entice students to want to know more. The verbal imagery of a text and the visual stimuli of picture books appeal to all age groups and help activate schemata that are crucial to further learning. For example, an excellent introduction to a study of the building instincts of animals and birds would be Kitchen's *And So They Build* (1993). Students might look at the detailed drawings before starting the unit and predict how each type of shelter is constructed. They might speculate on comparisons of the animals' and birds' building strategies to those of people. In addition, the teacher might read several of the examples in the book to the class and conduct a discussion of how they will be used in the forthcoming unit.

In science classes, popular books, or portions of them, may also be used in a preview to stimulate prediction and thinking about a topic. For example, the preface to Watson's *Double Helix* (1968) tells how scientists actually work. If students are familiar with the traditional scientific method, an initial reading of this book's introductory pages will inspire speculations about how the method can go awry. When the concept of objectivity (or the lack of it) in all human endeavours is discussed, students will gain valuable insight into both the *science* and the *art* of discovery and problem solving (Daisey 1996).

When students are given opportunities to interact with high-quality trade books, a number of things happen. Perhaps the most important is that they have a better chance of becoming lifelong learners. Textbooks alone cannot motivate students to continue their learning, particularly in the case of reluctant or academically diverse readers, who are often frustrated and defeated by textbooks in the first place. Trying to comprehend unfamiliar, difficult material in textbooks hinders some readers to the point that they quit trying altogether. Students need to be able to read trade books that capture their imagination and that appeal to their affective and cognitive needs.

Comprehensibility

Trade books help readers make sense and develop concepts in ways that are not possible with textbooks. Historical trade books, for example, help readers acquire a *framework for remembering and understanding* historical content. The same holds for content in science and in other subject areas. As Dole and Johnson (1981) indicate, popular science books—fact or fiction—provide background knowledge for science concepts covered in class and help students relate these concepts to their everyday lives.

Stories go beyond facts to get to the heart of a matter. They consider the human side of things by focusing on people and how they react to an infinite number of ideas and experiences in this world. Stories personalize ideas for readers by allowing them to experience a situation vicariously—that is, to share the thoughts of another person. People of all ages encounter aspects of human dilemmas in trade books that are not usually covered by a textbook. Readers who are invited to participate in a tale of a chimney sweep in the nineteenth century are likely to find themselves experiencing the information, instead of merely memorizing it for a test.

This is not to say that textbooks are useless. Students need diversity in the material they read so that they can compare information and make informed judgments. Though textbooks give students a broad base of information, such books cannot convey what lies below the surface. When topics are given only minimal exposure, a great deal of information is left out—information that is crucial to real learning. Levstik (1990), for example, describes young learners who were willing to delve into historical novels and other literature to find answers to questions they raised after reading their textbooks. These students expressed their interest in historical topics in terms of "needing to know" about a topic and of wanting to learn "the truth" or "what really happened." The logical source of answers to their questions and concerns was a good book.

Trade books in the content area classroom provide a variety of perspectives from which students can examine a topic. By comparing expository and narrative texts on a subject, students learn to read more critically. In other words, *reading strengthens the reading process.* Reading about a topic can dramatically improve the comprehension of related reading on the same topic. Crafton (1983) found that this was indeed the case when secondary school students read two different texts on the same subject. Not only did comprehension of the second text improve, but the students also read more actively. Reading experiences allow readers to construct background knowledge that they can use to comprehend other kinds of related texts.

Trade books are available to serve the needs of every student in every academic discipline. Box 2.1 on pages 40 and 41 provides a list of references to help teachers in selecting good books for their classrooms.

TRADE BOOKS IN THE CLASSROOM

When students have opportunities to learn with trade books, they are in a position to explore and interact with many kinds of texts, both fiction and nonfiction.

Learning with Nonfiction Books

Informational books have blossomed in recent years to attain the level of art. It is evident in recent historical writing, for example, that really good historical writers do not invent the past; instead, they give it artistic shape to connect with the reader (Meltzer 1988). No longer is nonfiction strictly objective in tone and literal in content; it often contains ele-

TABLE 2.1 Qualifications for Choosing High-Quality Nonfiction Books		
Genre	**Essential Qualities**	**Organization and Scope**
Informational books	Gives information and facts; relates facts to concepts; stimulates curiosity; "starter," not "stopper"	From simplest to most complex; from known to unknown; from familiar to unfamiliar; from early to later developments; chronological; slight narrative for younger reader
Biography	Gives accurate, verifiable facts and authentic picture of period; subject worthy of attention	Assumes no omniscience; shows individual, not stereotype; does not ignore negative qualities of subject; focuses not only on events but also on nature of person

Source: From Rebecca J. Luken's, *A Critical Handbook of Children's Literature* (5th ed.).
Copyright © 1995 by Allyn & Bacon. Reprinted by permission.

ments of fiction that flesh out the details and provide a component of entertainment in what Donelson and Nilsen (1997) call "the new journalism." This is the kind of meaty material that students can sink their teeth into and become involved in while learning something about the content area, too.

The range of nonfiction books is enormous, spanning all types of topics and book designs. There are biographies and autobiographies about all sorts of people, including rock stars (*Bryan Adams: The Inside Story*, 1992), writers (*Margaret Atwood: A Biography*, 1998; *Remembering Leacock: An Oral History*, 1983), scientists (*Frederick Banting: Discoverer of Insulin*, 1991), and classical music composers (*Mozart Tonight*, 1991). There are books about careers, about drugs and alcohol (*On the Mend*, 1991), about AIDS (*Fighting Back*, 1991) and other health issues, and about manners. There are even collections of essays written with young readers in mind, such as *Busted Lives: Dialogues with Kids in Jail* (1982), by Ann Zane Shanks, which offers first-person perspectives of prison life.

Perhaps the greatest difficulty teachers face when selecting nonfiction books for the classroom is deciding which to choose from the large number available. An important thing to keep in mind is that variety is truly the spice of life where reading and learning are concerned. No one book will satisfy all readers. The point of using nonfiction trade books in the classroom is to expose students to more than one point of view and in a form that is at once informational and readable. Although a great number of nonfiction books sound like textbooks packaged in pretty covers, teachers can choose high-quality books that adhere to the qualifications suggested in Table 2.1.

Style	Tone	Illustration
Imagery, figurative language, all devices; comparisons extremely useful; flawed if style is monotonous, repetitious, fragmented	Wonder, not mystery; respect; objectivity; occasional humour; fostering scientific attitude of inquiry; flawed by condescension, anthropomorphism, oversimplication, and when facts from opinions	Diagrams and drawings often clearer than photographs
Storytelling permissible for youngest reader; too much destroys credibility	Interest; enthusiasm; objectivity; didacticism and preaching to be avoided	Authentic

BOX 2.3	**Nothing but Net**

The Alan Review (Assembly on Literature for Adolescents, National Council of Teachers of English). Published three times a year; articles and "Clip and File" reviews. Urbana, IL: National Council of Teachers of English.

Appraisal: Children's Science Books for Young People. Published quarterly by Children's Science Book Review Committee. Reviews written by children's librarians and subject specialists.

Association for Library Service to Children. (2002). *The Newbery & Caldecott Awards: A guide to the medal and honor books.* Chicago: American Library Association. Available at http://www.ala.org. Provides short annotations for the winners and runners-up of ALA-sponsored awards.

Beers, G. K., Cart, M., & Lesesne, T. S. (Eds.). (2001). *Books for you: A booklist for senior high students* (14th ed.). Urbana, IL: National Council of Teachers of English. Available at http://www.ncte.org. Provides annotations for both fiction and nonfiction written for students, organized into 50 categories.

Book Links: Connecting Books, Libraries, and Classrooms. Published six times a year by the American Library Association to help teachers integrate literature into the curriculum. Includes bibliographies in different genres and subjects, as well as suggestions for innovative use in the classroom.

Booklist. Published twice a month by the American Library Association. Reviews of children's trade books and nonprint materials (video, audio, and computer software). Approximate grade levels are given; separate listing for nonfiction books.

Books for the Teen Age. Published annually by the Office of Young Adult Services, New York Public Library. Recommendations from young adult librarians in the various branches of the New York Public Library.

Bulletin of the Center for Children's Books. Published monthly by the University of Chicago Press; detailed reviews and possible curriculum uses are noted.

Canadian Book Review Annual. Available at http://www.interlog.com/~cbra. A yearly volume with summaries and evaluative comments on fiction, nonfiction, poetry, and plays.

The Canadian Children's Book Centre. (1999). *The storymakers: Illustrating children's books.* Markham, ON: Pembroke Publishers. A series of biographies and book lists of Canadian illustrators.

The Canadian Children's Book Centre. (2000). *The storymakers: Writing children's books.* Markham, ON: Pembroke Publishers. A series of biographies and book lists of Canadian authors.

Canadian Children's Literature Service. Available at http://www.nlc-bnc.ca/childrenliterature/index-e.html. The National Library of Canada maintains this website with reviews on books in both English and French.

Canadian Review of Materials (CM). Available at http://www.umanitoba.ca/cm/. An online serial with annotations and reviews of books, videos, and other resources for all ages.

Friedberg, J. B. (1992). *Portraying persons with disabilities: An annotated bibliography of nonfiction for children and teenagers* (2nd ed.). New Providence, NJ: Bowker. Provides comprehensive listings of nonfiction dealing with physical, mental, and emotional disabilities.

Gillespie, J. T. (1991). *Best books for junior high readers.* New Providence, NJ: Bowker. Lists more than 6000 books for young adolescents; fiction is listed by genre, nonfiction by subject.

Hoebener, M., Homa, L.L., & Screck, A. L. (Eds.). *Elementary school library collection: A guide to books and other media, phases 1, 2, 3* (22nd ed.). Williamsport, PA: Bordart Books. Reviews of books and other media in all subject areas for elementary and middle school students. Books rated by interest level and reading level.

The Horn Book Magazine. Published six times a year by Horn Book, Inc.; articles by noted children's authors, illustrators, and critics on aspects of children's literature, including its use in the classroom. Nonfiction books are reviewed in a separate section.

International Reading Association. "Children's Choices," a list of exemplary, "reader-friendly" children's literature, is published every October in *The Reading Teacher.*

Jones, R., & Stott, J. (2000). *Canadian children's books: a critical guide to authors and illustrators.* Don Mills, ON: Oxford University Press. Discusses information about the lives and work of many Canadian authors and illustrators.

McClure, A. A. (Ed.). (2002). *Adventuring with books: A booklist for pre-K–grade 6* (13th ed.). Urbana, IL: National Council of Teachers of English. Summaries of nearly 1800 books published between 1988 and 2001, arranged by genre and topics within content areas.

Montenegro, V. J., O'Connell, S. M., & Wolff, K. (Eds.). (1987). *AAA's science book list, 1978–1986.* Available at http://www.aaas.org. Reviews science and mathematics books for middle and secondary school students. Books reviewed by experts.

Montenegro, V. J., O'Connell, S. M., & Wolff, K. (Eds.). (1989). *The best science books and materials for children.* Washington, DC: American Association for the Advancement of Science. Reviews more than 800 science and mathematics books, graded K–9. Books reviewed by experts.

Notable children's trade books in the field of social studies. National Council for the Social Studies. Published yearly in the spring issue of *Social Education*; annotates notable fiction and nonfiction books, primarily for children in grades K–8.

Outstanding Science Trade Books for Children. National Science Teachers Association. Published each year in the spring issue of *Science and Children*; contains information consistent with current scientific knowledge; is pleasing in format; illustrated; and is nonsexist, nonracist, and nonviolent.

Quill & Quire. Information available at http://www.quillandquire.com. This Canadian monthly about the book industry in Canada features reviews of new books for young readers in every issue.

Resource links: Connecting classrooms, libraries & Canadian learning resources. Published five times a year for the Council for Canadian Learning Resources. Includes learning resources for all ages in print and electronic formats.

Rudman, M. K. (1995). *Children's literature* (3rd ed.). New York: Longman. Includes extensive annotated bibliographies of books that promote children's understanding of sensitive issues (e.g., divorce, death, siblings, heritage).

School Library Journal. Published by R. R. Bowker; articles on all aspects of children's literature, including its use in content areas; reviews by school and public librarians.

Walker, E. (Ed.). (1988). *Book bait: Detailed notes on adult books popular with young people* (4th ed.). Chicago: American Library Association. Extensive annotations of 100 books, including plot summaries and discussions of appeal for adolescents.

The Young Adult Canadian Book Award. Available at http://www.cla.ca/awards. A chronological listing of the winners, which is very useful for recommending books to middle school students and for guiding purchases for classroom and school libraries.

Learning with Fiction Books

Fiction entices readers to interact with texts from a number of perspectives that are impossible to achieve in nonfiction alone. Fantasy and traditional works (e.g., folktales and myths) and historical and realistic fiction, for example, help readers step outside their everyday world for a while to consider a subject from a different point of view. By doing so, readers learn something about what it means to be a human being on this planet of ours.

Ray Bradbury (1989), an acclaimed contemporary author, likens the ability to fantasize to the ability to survive. Although fantasy seems an unlikely addition to the required reading list in a content area classroom, consider the possibilities for a moment. Robert C. O'Brien's *Z for Zachariah* (1975) and Louise Lawrence's *Children of the Dust* (1985) contemplate the aftermath of a nuclear holocaust and the fate of the people who are left alive. Can students really know enough about nuclear issues without considering the crises described in these books? Probably not. The facts concerning the effects of nuclear war are too large and too disconnected from our present reality to understand. Only by focusing on the possible experiences of a small group of people can readers begin to understand the ramifications of such an event.

Monica Hughes's science fictions books such as *The Keeper of the Isis Light* (1980) discuss the role of free will and have much to offer readers about social conditions of modern life that need to be examined and changed. *The Ghost Dance Caper* (1986), for example, questions attitudes of mainstream culture toward First Nations peoples. We can see ourselves more objectively when we consider our lives from the distance of these stories.

Perhaps even more unlikely in a middle or secondary school curriculum would be the inclusion of traditional or folk literature because of its associations with younger children; however, the protagonists of most folktales are adolescents who have much to say to today's young adults. Robin McKinley's *Beauty* (1978) and Robert Nye's *Beowulf* (1968) continue to teach readers that strength of character is the crucial ingredient in changing the world. The human dimension of slavery is powerfully told in *Underground to Canada* (1978) by Barbara Smucker. Novels such as *Obasan* (1981) and *A Child in Prison Camp* (1971) reveal life in Japanese internment camps during World War II. A host of folktale collections from around the world is also readily available to add insight to the study of history, social studies, and geography. Folk literature is the "cement" or "mirror" of society (Sutherland & Arbuthnot 1986, p. 163) and thus gives readers an insider's view of a culture's beliefs and attitudes that is not found in the study of population density and manufacturing trends.

Poetry and drama also provide fascinating insight into a myriad of topics. Marilyn Dumont's *A Really Good Brown Girl* (1996) and Scofield's *Native Canadiana: Songs from the Urban Rez* (1996) will lead students into discussions on Aboriginal issues. And although the reading of drama takes a special kind of skill, it is possible to handle it well. For example, students can read Athol Fugard's *"Master Harold"... and the Boys* (1984) to comprehend more fully and actively the racial tensions of South Africa under apartheid and Ian Ross' *fareWel* (1997) to understand realities of modern aboriginal life. For teachers who are uncomfortable with group plays, Murray's *Modern Monologues for Young People* (1982) provides a forum for single-character sketches that cover a broad range of concepts.

Even cartoons have their place in the classroom, particularly when they are as well written as Art Spiegelman's *Maus: A Survivor's Tale* (1986). In this graphic novel, the story of the Holocaust is vividly told with the Nazis depicted as cats and the Jewish people as mice. Rather than detracting from the seriousness of the subject, the cartoon format lends force to the plight of the Nazis' victims.

The variety of fiction books runs the gamut of problem realism, animal realism, sports stories, mysteries, adventure stories, historical fiction, regional realism, and romance books. Although many books in each of these categories have formulized plots, stereotypical characters, and overly sentimental themes, a large body of high-quality literature is also available. Many worthy works are found on the annual *Young Adults' Choices List*, established by research sponsored by the International Reading Association. In some provinces, students vote for their favourite Canadian books. The results of these competitions, such as Ontario Red Maple Award and Young Reader's Choice Awards can be found on Canadian Children's Book Centre website (http://www.bookcentre.ca). These lists reflect the diversity of children's and young adults' literature, including titles dealing with social and political issues, such as drunk driving, women's rights, death, and war.

The host of realistic fiction books available can do much to enhance and clarify the content curriculum. An author's ability to bring lifelike characters into sharp focus against a setting that smacks of real places results in compelling reading.

Learning with Picture Books

Some of the most interesting but often overlooked books that can be used at all grade levels are picture books. William Kaplan's *One More Border* (1998), concerning one Eastern European family's journey three quarters of the way around the world to Canada, for example, offers a wealth of information that can be gleaned both from the print text (both narrative and expository) and from the variety of illustrations: historical and modern photographs, maps, and paintings. This is a book for all ages, as are David Macaulay's scholarly picture books. The practical question becomes: what role do picture books play in middle and secondary school classrooms?

Picture books aren't only for children anymore. Advanced technology and high-quality artistry have led to the production of unique and aesthetically pleasing books that appeal to all age groups. These books cover a wide range of subject matter and can be used to enhance any content area. Not only do the books invite students to mull over the illustrations, but they also teach lessons through the integration of pictures and text. Neal and Moore (1991) offer the following principles of using picture books with adolescents:

1. Themes of many picture books have universal value and appeal for all age levels.
2. Some of the best picture books may have been missed when students were younger or may have been published since that time.
3. Many issues demand a maturity level that young children do not possess.
4. The short format of these books facilitates incorporating picture books into lessons.
5. Our visually oriented society has conditioned students to employ pictures as comprehension aids. (pp. 290–291)

Readers construct meaning with a picture book in much the same way that they do with other types of texts; the readers' purposes for reading, prior knowledge, attitudes, and conceptual abilities determine in large part what and how the readers comprehend. As a result, the author's intent and the readers' purpose interact to form an interpretation. Picture books

BOX 2.2	**Picture Books for Adolescents**

Aliki. (1986). *A Medieval Feast.* New York: HarperCollins.

Anno, M. (1970). *Topsy-Turvies: Pictures to Stretch the Imagination.* New York: Weatherhill.

Anno, M. (1982). *Anno's Counting House.* New York: Philomel.

Anno, M. (1989). *Anno's Math Games II.* New York: Philomel.

Baker, J. (1991). *Window.* New York: Greenwillow.

Bang, M. (1991). *Picture This: Perception and Composition.* New York: Bullfinch Press.

Bunting, E. (1994). *Smoky Night.* Orlando, FL: Harcourt Brace.

Chekhov, A. (1991). *Kashtanka.* Trans. R. Pevear. Ill. B. Moser. New York: Putnam.

Edwards, M. (1982). *Alef-Bet: A Hebrew Alphabet Book.* New York: Lothrop, Lee & Shepard.

Feelings, M. (1971). *Moja Means One: Swahili Counting Book.* Ill. T. Feelings. New York: Dial.

George, J. C. (1995). *Everglades.* New York: HarperCollins.

Goodall, J. (1979). *The Story of an English Village.* New York: Atheneum.

Goodall, J. (1987). *The Story of a Main Street.* New York: Macmillan.

Goodall, J. (1990). *The Story of the Seashore.* New York: Macmillan.

Granfield, L. (1995). *In Flanders Fields: The Story of the Poem by John McCrae.* Ill. J. Wilson. Toronto: Lester Publishing.

Grifalconi, A. (1993). *Kinda Blue.* New York: Little, Brown.

Innocenti, R. (1991). *Rose Blanche.* New York: Stewart, Tiboria Chang.

Kaplan, W. (1998). *One More Border.* Toronto: Groundwood Books.

Lewis, J. P. (1992). *The Moonbow of Mr. B. Bones.* Ill. D. Zimmer. New York: Knopf.

Lobel, A. (1981). *On Market Street.* New York: Greenwillow.

Lowe, S. (1990). *Walden.* New York: Philomel.

Macauley, D. (1973). *Cathedral.* Boston: Houghton Mifflin.

Macauley, D. (1978). *Castle.* Boston: Houghton Mifflin.

produce a variety of meanings because the illustrations enhance the story, clarify and define concepts, and set a tone for the words. Box 2.2 lists some excellent examples of this genre.

There are several types of picture books to consider:

- *Wordless books.* The illustrations completely carry the story; no text is involved. Example: *Vagabul Escapes* (1983) by J. Marol.

- *Picture books with minimal text.* The illustrations continue to carry the story, but a few words are used to enhance the pictures. Example: *Bored—Nothing to Do!* (1978) by Peter Spier.

- *Picture storybooks.* More print is involved; pictures and text are interdependent. Example: *The Moonbow of Mr. B. Bones* (1992) by J. Patrick Lewis, illustrated by Dirk Zimmer.

- *Books with illustrations.* These books have more words than pictures, but the illustrations remain important to the text. Example: *Kashtanka* (1991) by Anton Chekhov, illustrated by Barry Moser.

Macauley, D. (1982). *Pyramid.* Boston: Houghton Mifflin.

Macauley, D. (1988). *The Way Things Work.* Boston: Houghton Mifflin.

Markle, S. (1995). *Outside and Inside Snakes.* New York: Macmillan.

Markle, S. (1995). *Pioneering Ocean Depths.* New York: Atheneum.

Marol, J. (1983). *Vagabul Escapes.* Mankato, MN: Creative Education.

Maruki, T. (1982). *Hiroshima No Pika.* New York: Lothrop, Lee & Shepard.

Maruki, T. (1985). *The Relatives Came.* Ill. S. Gammell. New York: Bradbury.

McGugan, J. (1994). *Josepha: A Prairie Boy's Story.* Ill. M. Kimber. Red Deer: Red Deer College Press.

McKee, D. (1978). *Tusk Tusk.* London, England: Random House.

O'huigin, S. (1985). *Atmosfear.* Windsor, ON: Black Moss Press.

Polacco, P. (1994). *Pink and Say.* New York: Scholastic.

Schwartz, D. M. (1985). *How Much Is a Million?* New York: Scholastic.

Schwartz, D. M. (1989). *If You Made a Million.* New York: Lothrop, Lee & Shepard.

Service, R. (1986). (Illus. Ted Harrison). *The Cremation of Sam McGee.* Toronto: Greenwillow Books.

Seuss, Dr. (1984). *The Butter Battle Book.* New York: Random House.

Simon, R. (1990). *Oceans.* New York: Morrow Junior Books.

Sis, P. (1996). *Starry Messenger: Galileo Galilei.* Toronto: Douglas & McIntyre.

Spier, P. (1978). *Bored—Nothing to Do!* New York: Doubleday.

Taylor, J. (2002). *Full Moon Rising.* Toronto: Tundra Books.

Trottier, M. (2000). *Storm at Batoche.* Ill. J. Mantha. Toronto: Stoddart.

Van Allsburg, C. (1987). *The Z Was Zapped.* Boston: Houghton Mifflin.

Van Allsburg, C. (1990). *Just a Dream.* Boston: Houghton Mifflin.

Van De Griek, S. (2002). *The Art Room.* Toronto: Groundwood Books.

Volkmer, J. A. (1990). *Song of the Chirimia: A Guatemalan Folktale.* Minneapolis: Carolrhoda.

Wisniewski, D. (1996). *Golem.* New York: Clarion.

A number of picture books lend themselves to use in science and mathematics classes. Several of Mitsumasa Anno's books can be used only with older students who have a firm grasp of mathematical concepts. *Anno's Counting House* (1982), *Anno's Math Games II* (1989), and *Topsy-Turvies: Pictures to Stretch the Imagination* (1970) inspire critical analysis of the notion of sets and logical possibilities presented in the detailed illustrations. *Moja Means One: Swahili Counting Book* (1971), by Muriel and Tom Feelings, is an excellent introduction to African traditions and to learning to count in Swahili. And Macaulay's *Pyramid* (1982) is a historically accurate look at the mathematical genius of the ancient Egyptians.

Environmental issues can be explored in books such as *Atmosfear* (1985) by Sean O'huigin, a story about the possible effects of pollution, Lowe's *Walden* (1990), Van Allsburg's *Just a Dream* (1990), and Baker's wordless *Window* (1991). Each of these books provides a thought-provoking story concerning human beings and their relationship to the earth. *The Story of the Seashore* (1990), by Goodall, and *Oceans* (1990), by Simon, offer fascinating scientific information about the sea. Goodall's book is a wordless historical overview, whereas Simon's book is an exquisite collection of photographs and colour drawings combined with informative and poetic text.

For history classes, Macauley's *Castle* (1978) and *Cathedral* (1973) are rich in detail, in both the text and the illustrations. Both books focus on the medieval world and they nicely complement Aliki's *Medieval Feast* (1986) and Goodall's *Story of a Main Street* (1987) and *Story of an English Village* (1979). Aliki's book follows the preparations of a wealthy landowner's dinner for the king, and Goodall's books give wordless historical overviews from medieval times to the present. All of these books offer a profusion of information that is impossible to find in history textbooks.

Many picture books focus on the events surrounding the World Wars. *In Flanders Fields: The Story of the Poem by John McCrae* (1995) by Linda Granfield offers an illustrated look at perhaps the most famous Canadian poem about war and remembrance, while Maruki's *Hiroshima No Pika* (1982) is a controversial book about a family's experiences when the atomic bombs were dropped on Japan in 1945. Innocenti's *Rose Blanche* (1991) offers a look at a young girl's discovery of a Nazi concentration camp near her home and her attempts to comfort the inmates there until she is killed by a Nazi soldier. In *The Butter Battle Book* (1984), Dr. Seuss explores the illogical nature of war and poses the question, Which country will "push the button" first? These picture books and countless others can be integrated into your curricular area. They can be used with older students as interesting schema builders, anticipatory sets to begin lessons, motivators for learning, read-alouds, and springboards into discussion and writing.

RATIONALE FOR ELECTRONIC TEXTS

The potential for technology to make a difference in students' literacy and learning was evident in the early 1980s when computers began to play an increasingly more important role in classrooms. However, computer-related technologies several decades ago were primitive compared to the powerful technologies that are available today. The internet as a technology for communication and information retrieval had little or no impact on classroom learning until recently (Mike 1996). In the 1980s, the computer's potential for classroom learning revolved mainly around its uses as a tool for word processing and as a teaching machine for computer-assisted instruction (CAI).

CAI entails the use of instructional software programs to help students learn. CAI programs in the 1980s included the use of drills, tutorials, games, and simulations. Some computer programs, mainly simulations such as *Fort Walsh*, were engaging and interactive, but many weren't. Drill and tutorial software, for example, often provided students with dull, uninviting "electronic worksheets" to practise skills and reinforce concepts.

Times have changed, however, with the development of powerful technologies that make learning with electronic texts highly engaging and interactive. CD-ROM disks and now DVD, for example, permit much larger storage capacity for text, graphics, and sound and offer tremendous retrieval capabilities not possible with floppy disks. Moreover, online learning opportunities on the internet allow students to communicate with others throughout the world and to access significant and relevant content in ways not imagined just a few years ago. However, the internet is also problematic for students, as some sites have content inappropriate for school use and the web has become haven for marketing schemes of all kinds.

Today computer-related technologies create complex electronic learning environments. Reading and writing with computers allow students to access and retrieve information, construct their own texts, and interact with others. Computers are now the preferred tool for processing visual images and are rapidly becoming the preferred tool for processing video as well. Reinking (1995) argues that computers are changing the way we communicate and disseminate information, how we approach reading and writing, and how we think about people becoming literate. Although electronic texts often enhance learning, Reinking contends that reading and writing with computers have the power to transform the way we teach and learn.

Some of the reasons for the use of electronic texts across the curriculum parallel those associated with trade books: variety, interest, relevance, and comprehensibility. Highly engaging and interactive computer software programs—many of which provide multimedia learning environments—and the internet make it possible for students to have access to thousands of interesting and relevant information resources. Not only is there wide access to information, but electronic texts on a relevant topic of study can help students read extensively and think critically about content central to the curriculum. In addition, text that students construct electronically can help them examine ideas, organize and report research findings, and communicate with others. *Word processing*, *graphics applications*, and *digital video editing*, for example, allow students to develop content and multimedia presentations relevant to curriculum objectives. Moreover, *email* allows students to engage in learning conversations with others within the same community or throughout the world.

We suggest a rationale for integrating electronic texts into the curriculum based on the following concepts as they apply to technology-based learning:

- *Interactivity*. Students are capable of manipulating texts (that is, all digital media), and text is responsive to student's interests, purposes, and needs.
- *Communication*. Telecommunication networks enhance electronic text interaction with others throughout the world.
- *Information search and retrieval*. A wide range of information resources and search capabilities enhance student research and information gathering.
- *Multimedia environments*. Images, sound, and text are highly engaging and extend students' understanding.
- *Socially mediated learning*. Students collaboratively construct meaning as part of literacy learning.

Interactivity

Throughout this book, we use the word *interaction* to refer to the reader's active role in learning with text. Recall from Chapter 1 that active readers engage in meaning-making whenever they interact with texts. Reinking (1995), however, points to the imprecision of the term *interaction* as it applies to printed texts. He correctly notes that the interaction between reader and printed text has a metaphorical, not literal, meaning. Reinking's point is well taken: "Printed texts are fixed, inert entities that stand aloof from the influence and needs of a particular reader" (p. 22). Yet this is not the case with electronic texts. An interactive literacy event in an electronic environment is one in which a text is responsive to the actions of the reader. Some electronic texts (but not others, such as CD-ROMs) differ from printed texts in that they have the capability to be modified and manipulated by readers according to their individual needs, interests, and purposes for reading.

Communication and Information Search and Retrieval

What better way is there to establish authentic communication than through reading and writing with computers? Digital technologies make it possible for students to participate in communication exchanges, searches for information, and retrieval of information from a multitude of resources throughout the world. One such technology, the internet, offers users "a natural blend of communication and information retrieval functions incorporated within a framework that literally encompasses the world" (Mike 1996, p. 4). The internet— also called *cyberspace*, the *information superhighway*, the *infobahn*, or simply the *net* in popular culture—consists of a worldwide collection of computers able to communicate with each other with little or no central control. Through computers, the internet connects people and resources. All you need to access this vast collection of computer networks is a computer, appropriate communication software, a modem, and an account with an internet service provider.

One of the most compelling rationales for using the internet and CD-ROM software programs is that they create multimedia environments for learning.

Multimedia Environments

Sound, graphics, photographs, video, and other nonprint media constitute electronic texts. They offer a learning environment far beyond the limitations of printed texts. If students want to find out about space exploration, for example, they can access a site on the World Wide Web. They can then choose to click on the term *space shuttle* for a definition and a computer-generated model of the space shuttle, click on the highlighted word *history* for a brief overview and history of the space program, digress to an audio recording and video clip of Neil Armstrong as he sets foot on the moon, or engage in a live interview with a NASA scientist or astronaut (http://www.nasa.gov). Students can also visit the website for the Canadian Space Agency (http://www.space.gc.ca) and look at the many webcasts available on topics such as space robotics or hear interviews with Marc Garneau and Chris Hadfield.

The concept of hypermedia is crucial to understanding the interactions between reader and text in a multimedia environment. Its structure is much less linear than that of the printed text (for example, a newspaper article). If you were reading a document in a hypermedia environment, you could scroll through it on a screen in a linear fashion, much as you would read a printed text paragraph by paragraph, but the hypermedia format also offers a "web" of text that allows you to link to other related documents and resources on demand. When sound, graphics, photographs, video, and other nonprint media are incorporated, the electronic environment is called *hypermedia*.

Socially Mediated Learning

Electronic texts create a medium for social interactions—whether we have students use the internet to communicate or assign them to learning teams as they share a computer to access information on a CD-ROM or the web. Literacy learning with computers is social and collaborative. Students learn with electronic texts by sharing their discoveries with others. Leu (1996) underscores this type of literacy learning: "Multimedia environments, because they are powerful and complex, often require us to communicate with others in order to make meaning from them. Thus, learning is frequently constructed through social interactions in these contexts, perhaps even more naturally and frequently than in traditional print environments" (p. 163). What are the implications of socially mediated learning events in the classroom? As teachers, we need to support and encourage social interactions in electronic environments and have our students take the lead in making discoveries and sharing knowledge with other students and with us.

ELECTRONIC TEXTS IN THE CLASSROOM: CONNECTING LITERACY AND LEARNING

There are unlimited possibilities for learning with electronic texts. Access to the internet means, quite literally, that students have at their fingertips a virtual library of electronic texts for subject matter learning. People use reading and writing almost entirely to interact with information or with other people on the internet. With the internet, it is possible, as suggested by Williams (1995), to engage in a variety of communication and information search and retrieval activities. Through the internet you can send and receive email. You can participate in discussion groups and newsgroups. You can access text documents, video, images, and sound from around the world. You can also communicate with others in real time through chat, voice, and even video.

Let's examine several of the opportunities that students have for learning with electronic texts.

Learning with Hypermedia

Hypermedia enriches and extends any literacy learning event in the content areas. With hypermedia, highlighted and linked texts (consisting of both words and images), called *hyperlinks* (or simply *links*), enable you to move between documents in a nonlinear manner. This process is possible because in hypermedia there are many "branches" or pathways that readers may choose to follow in many different orders, depending on their interests and purposes. If your students were to make a cyberspace visit to the home page of one of best science museums for young people, Ontario Science Centre's SciZone (www. ontariosciencecentre.ca/scizone), they would be able to participate in a variety of interactive exhibits simply by selecting the links in which they were interested. Suppose that students clicked on the link "Marshlands." In a second or two, they would be transported to the marsh site. The students could then decide to link to the banner marked "Secrets of the Marsh" to participate in a game that teaches about food webs by having students actually build one based on plant and animal life in the marsh.

Through the use of hyperlinks, students can move to other related text or nonprint media simply by clicking on a highlighted word or icon in the document. As a result, they can "jump around" or digress to explore related branches of text at their own pace, navigating in whatever direction they choose. Jumping around in a hypertext gives a sense of freedom with the text that is unattainable with printed text. The possibility for multiple digressions, according to Reinking (1997), is the defining attribute of hypertext. As he puts

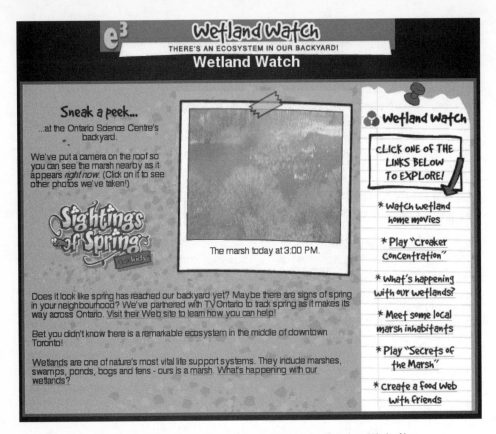

FIGURE 2.1   Wetland Watch at the Ontario Science Centre Website

Source: © 2004 Ontario Science Centre, http://www.ontariosciencecentre.ca/scizone/e3/wetland/default.asp

it, "Trying to write a hypertext means being free to digress and to assume that readers will willingly share in that same freedom. Digression can be positive and enjoyable in a hypertext because there is no compulsion to stick closely to only one main idea" (p. 629).

From an instructional perspective, the branching options offered in hypertext and hypermedia serve two important functions: to scaffold students' learning experiences and to enhance and extend thinking. For readers who may struggle with text or with difficult concepts, the resources available on demand in a hypermedia environment include pronunciations of keywords and terms, definitions and explanations, audio versions of the text, video recordings, digital movies, photographs, graphics, interactive exercises, and student-centred projects. These links have the potential to arouse curiosity, stimulate interest, and reinforce and extend students' thinking about a subject.

Keep in mind, however, a cautionary note about hypermedia learning environments. Computer software programs and the internet are technologies that lend themselves to *extensive* explorations of information resources. A key instructional concern is to avoid the more superficial experiences with technology that are fun but do not necessarily support students' literacy learning or critical thinking about content central to the curriculum (Leu 1996). Because multimedia environments are highly engaging and seductive, student discoveries, in Leu's words, "spread like wildfire" in the classroom. Whenever you plan a lesson or unit that involves students in multimedia learning environments, you run the risk of having them ignore substantive content in favour of superficial discoveries. As a result, students might navigate multimedia environments to explore topics extensively at only a superficial level of understanding without reading and thinking deeply about a specific or single topic. How teachers scaffold intensive literacy experiences and in-depth explorations of electronic and printed texts remains a key instructional issue that we explore throughout this book.

Online Learning

Harry Noden (1995), a middle school teacher in Hudson, Ohio, describes an electronic conversation that he had with a teacher, Ken Blystone, from Texas. Blystone explained that he was having difficulty securing funding for internet connections in his school district because some school administrators considered the internet a high-tech frill rather than a substantive tool for literacy and learning. According to Noden, Blystone "approached his principal early one morning before school and asked him how much it would be worth investing to get students so excited about reading and writing that they would stand in line for the opportunity." The principal chuckled at the notion until Blystone "invited him to walk to the library. There, a half an hour before school had started, gathered around the one computer connected to the internet, stood a large group of students ... standing in line waiting for the opportunity to read and write" (p. 26).

World Wide Web

The internet has been described by some as providing the "textbooks of tomorrow." And then some! The World Wide Web of the internet is fertile ground for learning with electronic texts on every subject imaginable. Access to the web on the internet means access to a hypermedia system. The web represents the universe of servers (computers) that allows text, graphics, sound, and images to be mixed together. The internet existed long before the web. Initially it was used for exchanging mail and for participating in discussion groups. What we now know as the World Wide Web started as a way for scientists to exchange technical documents. The web can now be used to exchange a rich variety of media content. Although initially only a part of the internet, the web has grown to represent the vast majority of internet traffic, to the point where many people no longer distinguish between the internet and the web. This interchangeable usage of the two terms is the approach taken here.

Alvarez (1996) describes a project called Explorers of the Universe for secondary school students in grades 9 through 12 enrolled in an astronomy class. In this class, the web became an important tool for gathering information and communicating ideas. Students worked in teams of two and three to conduct research using library resources as well as resources on the web. The internet was also used as a medium to publish students' research reports, broaden their knowledge base in specific areas, and make inquiries to other students and astronomers in the field.

Alvarez notes that the web serves a function similar to the library except that access to information resources is nearly instantaneous and students are able to contact authors of web documents directly to clarify issues or gather additional information. The teachers involved in Explorers of the Universe used textbooks in tandem with internet connections.

They found that the textbook became a resource as opposed to a singular source of science information. Preliminary findings of the project show that students related new information to their existing world knowledge, analyzed their sources more carefully, and attempted to identify new sources of information (Alvarez 1996).

To use the web effectively, students will need to develop expertise at navigating through this hypertext world. For students not experienced with browsing or surfing the web, try scaffolding activities, such as guided tours and scavenger hunts, to familiarize beginners with how to navigate. Also, use bookmarks that take students directly to locations that you want them to visit on the web. One of the most useful resource books for literacy and learning, *Teaching with the Internet: Lessons from the Classroom* (Leu & Leu 2000), provides many suggestions for developing navigation skills and numerous website locations for content area study.

Box 2.3 on pages 54 and 55 lists some frequently visited websites by content area. A visit to several of these sites will give you insight into the possibilities for subject matter learning that await students. Information resources and websites can easily be integrated into units of study in your content area.

Email, Newsgroups, and Chat

On the internet, students (and teachers) can send and receive messages anywhere in the world via email. Email messages are sent electronically from one computer to another through the use of special software. Email communication can generate important learning connections for students by making "reading and writing across the planet" a reality (Noden & Vacca 1994). Imagine the possibilities: on Monday, two students from Yakeala, Finland, talk to your students about minority groups in their country—the Roma and the Lapps. On Tuesday, students discuss the environmental problems of the Amazon jungle with students in Lima, Peru. On Wednesday, a wheelchair-bound student from Palatka, Florida, drops in to give his one- to five-star reviews of the latest video games. On Thursday, teenage refugees from Bosnia tell how most of their relatives "just disappeared" and how the young people managed to escape. On Friday, a student from Keene, New Hampshire, shares a visit from a survivor of the Holocaust.

These are only some of the email learning events that occurred in Harry Noden's grade 8 class in the course of a week (Noden Vacca 1994). To allow this to happen, Noden first made email connections with other teachers through the use of *electronic bulletin boards*, sites where students and teachers can post ideas for exchanges and internet projects. Leu and Leu (2000) recommend the following sites as "jumping-off points" for internet projects:

Kidlink
www.kidlink.org/english/general/sub.html

Email-based projects aimed at students aged 10 to 15 are featured.

The GLOBE Program
www.globe.gov

This site highlights environmental science projects that connect students and scientists around the world.

In one internet project, preservice teachers from Walsh University in Ohio engaged in email exchanges with grade 4 students from a local elementary school (McKeon 2000).

The collaborative project revolved around "booktalks" and literature discussions. Each preservice teacher was paired with a student. Throughout the semester, the email partners discussed the books they were reading. These electronic conversations provided natural opportunities for the partners to engage in authentic talk about books and for the preservice teachers to blend instructional strategies into the discussion. For example, in one correspondence just prior to reading the book *A Taste of Blackberries* (Smith 1973), a preservice teacher invites his partner to make predictions about the book:

> Just to let you know before you start reading, the book is very sad and it involves people dying. I would like you to brainstorm a little bit about the name of the book and give me some guesses of what you think the story may be about. Then we will take your guesses, and after we read the book, we can find out how close you were with some of your guesses. I am really looking forward to hearing from you.

Not only was the email project successful in making important learning connections during the literature discussions, but also in the course of a semester, the email partners got to know each other socially as they shared information and asked questions about college life, hobbies, interests, and family life.

In addition to individual messages, a person can send messages to and receive messages from groups of people by subscribing to a *mailing list* or *listserv*. These groups, often called *discussion groups*, allow students and teachers to ask questions, share information, and locate resources. In Noden's class, students received a collection of memoirs compiled by students at Hiroshima Jogakuin High School. The memoirs, written by survivors of the atomic bomb, stimulated a great deal of discussion among students, prompting them to investigate additional information sources in the library and on the web.

Leu and Leu (2000) suggest several of the most popular mailing lists for discussion groups, including this one:

Liszt Select

www.liszt.com

This comprehensive site contains more than 50 000 lists. You can either do a search for lists in your interest area or click the Liszt Select box for a much smaller annotated list of sites.

Learning with Media Authoring Systems

Reading and writing on the internet play an important role in learning. But merely using computer-related technologies in your classrooms doesn't guarantee more effective or meaningful learning. As one teacher put it,

> Students must be good communicators. In my classroom, students whose writing skills are lacking will not spend nearly as much time on the computer as those with more competency. Does this make some students strive to be more competent so they can use the computers? Yes indeed, and that brings up a positive aspect of computers; they provide incentive and encouragement for improvement. (Jasper 1995, p. 17)

Not only do computers provide incentive for improvement, but they can also be an important tool for developing students' writing abilities.

Computers as word processors allow writers to create a text and change it in any way desired. Word processing software programs have the potential to make students more active in brainstorming, outlining, exploring and organizing ideas, revising, and editing a text.

BOX 2.3	**Nothing but Net**

Selected Websites Across the Curriculum

The websites that we have selected illustrate some of the possibilities for locating information resources on the internet in various content areas. Because links change, search with keywords and look for new links. Home pages usually stay the same. (For additional websites in each content area, see Appendix A.)

THE ARTS

Canada's Digital Collections
collections.ic.gc.ca

The Canadian Encylopedia
www.thecanadianencyclopedia.com

National Gallery of Canada
national.gallery.ca

Glenbow Museum
www.glenbow.org

The Provincial Museum of Alberta Virtual Exhibits
www.pma.edmonton.ab.ca

McMichael Canadian Art Collection
www.mcmichael.com

Music
cln.org/subjects/music_inst.html

Asian Arts
www.asianart.com

ENGLISH LANGUAGE ARTS

The Children's Literature Web Guide
www.acs.ucalgary.ca/~dkbrown

The English Server
eserver.org

Links to Language Arts Educator Websites
www.waterloo.k12.wi.us/whs/infocenter/edlang.htm

Canadian Language Arts Education Resources
www.aldershot.ednet.ns.ca/curricullum/CanadianResources/canadiansubjects/languagearts.html

University of Toronto English Library
www.library.utoronto.ca/utel/

Early Canadiana Online
www.canadiana.org

CBC
www.cbc.ca

National Public Radio
www.npr.org

Discovery Channel Canada
exn.ca

PBS
www.pbs.org

Computer-Assisted Language Learning (CALL)
www.ohiou.edu/opie/index.html

FOREIGN LANGUAGE

Teaching French (and other languages)
aix1.uottawa.ca/~weinberg/french.html

ACELF
www.acelf.ca

Educaserve
www.educaserve.com/premiere.ph

Elementary Spanish Curriculum
www.veen.com/veen/leslie/Curriculum/

Japanese-Language Education
**www.japanfoundationcanada.org/JFlang/
JFlang.html**

Aboriginal Languages
language.firstnationschools.ca

HEALTH: IDEAS FOR HEALTH LESSONS

Ideas for Developmentally Appropriate
Physical Education
www.pecentral.org

British Columbia Ministry of Children and
Family Development
www.gov.bc.ca/mcf

Health Canada Online
www.hc-sc.gc.ca

MATHEMATICS

MathEd: Mathematics Education 21st
Century Problem Solving
**www2.hawaii.edu/suremath/
home1.html**

MathMagic
mathforum.org/mathmagic

SCIENCE

The Royal Ontario Museum
www.rom.on.ca

Ontario Science Centre's SciZone
www.ontariosciencecentre.ca/scizone

Environmental Education
www.eelink.net

The Official Website of NASA
www.nasa.gov

Canadian Space Agency
www.space.gc.ca

SOCIAL STUDIES

Canadian History Portal
www.canadianhistory.ca

Canada History
www.canadahistory.com

CBC Archives
archives.cbc.ca

Canadian Heritage
www.pch.gc.ca

Alexander Graham Bell
**collections.ic.gc.ca/heirloom_series/
volume4/210-215.htm**

Russian History
**www.friends-partners.org/oldfriends/mes/
russia/history.html**

Interactive Egyptian History Site
**www.iwebquest.com/egypt/
ancientegypt.htm**

A Massive History Database Online
www.thehistorynet.com

The Story of John McCrae
**www.museum.guelph.on.ca/
mccraejohn.htm**

VOCATIONAL EDUCATION

Career Management and Job Search
english.monster.ca

Statistics Canada
www.statcan.ca

Youth Employment Information
jeunesse.gc.ca

Academic-related writing is one of the most cognitive as well as physically demanding tasks required of students in school. Computers can make writing easier by taking away some of the sheer physical demands of putting ideas on paper with a pen or pencil. This is not to say that communicating with paper and pen is less effective than with a computer. A computer, however, frees students from the laborious physical tasks associated with drafting, editing, and revising a text so that they can expend more cognitive energy on the communication itself. One of the best reasons people use computers to write and communicate with others is that it takes a complex activity like writing and expedites the process. Suid and Lincoln (1989), somewhat "tongue in cheek," draw this analogy: "You can cook terrific meals on a wood-burning stove. But if you're like most people, you prefer a modern range. It's easier. It's faster. And it lets you do more" (p. 318). One of the things that a computer lets you do in a classroom is generate a finished and attractive text that others can read.

Student-generated texts and reports shouldn't be for the teacher's eyes only. They should be read by other students and can become "minibooks" for classroom learning. *Desktop publishing* programs, which combine text and graphics in varied arrangements, can help students produce attractive reports as part of thematic and topical units of study. Students can also design multimedia projects using hypermedia programs such as HyperStudio, Linkway, or HyperCard. Hypermedia programs encourage active engagement with information and extend the composing process through the interaction of various media. These programs are called *authoring systems* and are often used in research projects designed by students as part of a thematic or topical unit of study.

Lapp and Flood (1995), for example, describe a middle-grade classroom where they observed small groups of students using HyperStudio to design geology-related science projects. The students used the authoring software to help them organize their multimedia reports on a unit dealing with the causes and effects of tornadoes. One group of students located a National Geographic Society *laser disk* containing some footage of an actual tornado and used the authoring software program to incorporate the footage into their presentation. A *laser disk* is a computer peripheral on which large amounts of video and audio are stored. A student in another group found some photographs taken by his aunt of a tornado and the destruction it left in its wake. The student used a *scanner* to incorporate the photos into the multimedia presentation. A *scanner* is another peripheral used to convert pictures, texts, graphs, or charts into an image that can then be used in a computer presentation.

Even simple authoring software packages like PowerPoint and web authoring software packages like FrontPage and Dreamweaver allow students to develop multimedia projects and presentations that wed visual images, sound, graphics, and text. The premise underlying authoring systems is not as complicated as it may appear if you are a novice with the use of hypermedia technologies. Authoring software programs facilitate multimedia compositions and encourage students to communicate what they are learning through the construction of computer "**cards**" and "**buttons**." The student (or small group of students) creates the multimedia presentation by filling in computer cards with information (referred to as textual "fields") and with pictures, drawings, graphics, photographs, video, music, and voice messages. Buttons are then created to link the network of completed cards.

Students not familiar with authoring systems need to learn how to use hypermedia tools and peripherals to scan in photographs, create pictures and graphics, and record video and sounds. They will also need instructional support in planning, researching, and designing projects and in learning how to use authoring software effectively.

Learning with Software Programs

The proliferation of educational software programs can make it difficult for teachers to choose appropriate CAI programs for classroom use. Most of the major publishers of printed textbooks have entered the educational software market. Pearson, for example, has developed highly interactive multimedia CD-ROM software in most of the content areas. One Pearson program, Multimedia Math, appropriate for use in the middle grades, allows students to interact with and experience mathematics concepts through engagement in "math investigations" and "hot pages" using a rich, three-dimensional, multisensory environment. Another of its software programs, Chemedia, designed for use in secondary school chemistry courses, combines videodisks with simulation software to engage students in visual explorations of interesting phenomena otherwise not available in the classroom.

In addition to software development by major publishing houses, hundreds of smaller companies, specializing exclusively in technology-related programs, have mushroomed in the past decade, inundating the educational landscape with innovative software in all content areas for all age levels. Because of the prolific development of educational software, most of the major content area educational associations and societies offer program reviews in their professional journals.

Making decisions about educational software is no easy task. Rose and Fernlund (1997), speaking directly to social studies teachers, suggest asking a set of reflective questions related to CAI and multimedia use that is applicable to all content teachers who are interested in using educational software to enhance instruction. To guide the evaluation of computer-based instructional products, consider the questions posed in Box 2.4 on pages 58 and 59.

Learning with Electronic Books

Innovations in educational software have led to the development of the *electronic book*. Anderson-Inman and Horney (1997) use stringent criteria to distinguish electronic books from other forms of educational software:

- Electronic books must have electronic text presented to the reader visually.
- They must use the metaphors of a book by adapting some of the conventions associated with books, such as a table of contents, pages, and a bookmark, so that readers will feel that they are reading a book.
- They must have an organizing theme of an existing book or a central focus if they are not based on an equivalent printed book.
- They must be primarily text-centred. When media enhancements other than text are available in the software, they are incorporated primarily to support the text presentation.

Many electronic books—some available on CD-ROM, others via online subscription or in other formats—make excellent reference resources. *Encarta* offers readers thousands

BOX 2.4	**Evaluating Computer-Based Educational Software: Questions to Consider**

HARDWARE-RELATED QUESTIONS TO CONSIDER

1. What are the instructional tasks and levels of complexity? Do I have the necessary technology?

2. Do my computers have enough memory to run the desired software application?

3. What type of technical delivery system will be used: single computer(s) or computers attached to a local area network (LAN), a wide area network (WAN), and/or the internet?

4. Is the speed of the network sufficient to accomplish the instructional task in an efficient and timely manner?

SOFTWARE-RELATED QUESTIONS TO CONSIDER

1. How does this computer program help achieve my objectives for this unit of study? Can I modify the program to fit my plans better?

2. Does my computer system have the right hardware to run this program (required memory, printers, speech synthesizer, other peripherals)?

Source: From "Using Technology for Powerful Social Studies Learning," by S. A. Rose and P. M. Fernlund. *Social Education,* March 1997. Copyright © National Council for the Social Studies. Reprinted with permission.

of articles and easy-to-use features that make searching and retrieving information uncomplicated. Many electronic books are informational and focus on in-depth studies of subjects. *In the Company of Whales* (Discovery Communications), intended for use in middle and secondary schools, provides students with well-organized informative text, pictures, action footage, and sound. The electronic text shows how whales are studied and introduces students to some of the people who study them. Still other electronic books are for recreational reading. Highly interactive storybooks such as *Afternoon* (Eastgate Systems) and Walt Disney's *Animated Storybooks* are suitable for younger as well as older readers. In studies of interactive electronic books, researchers find that children generally respond positively to stories presented through electronic media over printed versions (Matthew 1996) and that reading from electronic books increases comprehension when students read longer and more difficult narratives (Greenlee-Moore & Smith 1996).

LOOKING BACK, LOOKING FORWARD

Trade books and electronic texts in content area classrooms extend and enrich information across the curriculum. Often textbooks are not equipped to treat subject matter with the depth and breadth necessary to develop ideas and concepts fully and engage in critical inquiry. Alternatives to the textbook have the potential to capture students' interest in people, places, events, and ideas and help them develop their imagination.

3. Is the program easy for students to use? What preparation do students need? What preparation do I need?

4. Does the publisher offer technical assistance, free or inexpensive updates, network licences?

5. Does the program offer multiple options for delivery? For example, can the program be used over the internet or linked to sites on the World Wide Web?

MULTIMEDIA-USE QUESTIONS TO CONSIDER

1. Do I have the necessary technology to use this multimedia package, includ-ing sufficient computer memory, a videodisk player/CD-ROM drive if needed, a large screen monitor or pro-jection device for large class viewing?

2. What is the perspective of this com-mercial package? How does this viewpoint differ from other resources that I plan to have students use?

3. Is this product to be used by teachers or students? Do I want to use the entire package or select particular parts?

4. In what ways will this use of technol-ogy enhance my students' learning? How can I assess the impact on learn-ing?

Whereas textbooks compress information, trade books and electronic texts provide students with intensive and extensive involvement in a subject. Trade books and electronic texts offer students a variety of interesting, relevant, and comprehensible text experiences. With trade books, students are likely to develop an interest in and an emotional commitment to the subject. Trade books are schema builders. Reading books helps students generate background knowledge and provides them with vicarious experiences. Many kinds of trade books, both nonfiction and fiction, can be used in tandem with textbooks.

Electronic texts are highly engaging and interactive. Hypermedia makes it possible to interact with text in ways not imaginable a short while ago. Text learning opportunities in electronic environments are interactive, enhance communication, engage students in multimedia, create opportunities for inquiry through information searches and retrieval, and support socially mediated learning. Reading and writing with computers has changed the way we think about literacy and learning. Whether students are navigating the internet or interacting with innovative educational software, an array of electronic text learning experiences awaits them.

In the next chapter, we explore another dimension of the changing world of classrooms as we shift our attention to authentic forms of assessment in the content area classroom. Concern about assessment is one of the major issues in education in Canada today. What role do standardized and large-scale, criterion-referenced assessments play in the lives of classroom teachers? How do naturalistic forms of assessment inform instructional decisions? How can teachers use portfolios and make decisions about the texts they use? The key to assessment in content areas, as we contend in the next chapter, is to make it as authentic as possible. Let's find out how and why this is the case.

MINDS-ON

1. Read this statement: "One way of thinking about a textbook is that it takes a subject and distils it to its minimal essentials. In doing so, a textbook runs the risk of taking world-shaking events, monumental discoveries, profound insights, intriguing and far-away places, colourful and influential people, and life's mysteries and processes and compresses them into a series of matter-of-fact statements." Can you think of a book you have read that opened new perspectives on a topic of which you had previously had only textbook knowledge? What do you believe is the ideal balance between the use of textbooks and the use of fiction books, nonfiction books, and picture books in a content classroom?

2. To what extent do you believe students should participate in the selection of documents from websites for use in a content course? Would you answer this question differently for students of various ages?

3. How often have you been assigned readings outside the content textbook at any level of schooling? What types of materials did you read? What later use did the teacher make of those readings? How often have you used electronic texts as part of subject matter learning? In your estimation, did the teacher use the outside reading assignment to its full potential? If not, in what additional ways might the readings have been explored?

4. Why do many students seem to dislike doing research in a library but are enthusiastic about surfing the net for information resources?

HANDS-ON

1. Select two texts that you would use together in the classroom. There are a variety of possibilities: a news clipping of a current event and the video coverage of that same event; a nonfiction work and a fictionalized account (novel, drama, poem, or dialogue) of the same event; the treatments of an event in an electronic text and in a textbook on the same topic. Analyze the two texts by making a comparison. How are they alike? How are they different? Come to class prepared to share your analysis.

2. Select a recent news event and conduct a search for information resources on the web. Select several resources and compare them for treatment, reliability, and accuracy. What does it mean to develop a healthy skepticism when interacting with texts on the web?

3. Select two picture books that you might coordinate with a particular unit you now teach or with a unit you have planned or observed. Explain why you chose these particular books and how you will use them with your students. Describe the activities that will follow the initial use or reading of the book.

SUGGESTED READINGS

Bamford, R. A., & Kristo, J. V. (Eds.). (1998). *Making facts come alive: Choosing quality nonfiction literature, K–8.* Norwood, MA: Christopher-Gordon.

Bamford, R. A., & Kristo, J. V. (2000). *Checking out nonfiction K–8: Good choices for best learning.* Norwood, MA: Christopher-Gordon.

Bohning, G., & Radencich, M. (1989). Informational action books: A curriculum resource for science and social studies. *Journal of Reading, 32,* 434–439.

Booksearch: Recommended historical fiction. (1989). *English Journal, 79,* 84–86.

Borasi, R., Sheedy, J. R., & Siegel, M. (1990). The power of stories in learning mathematics. *Language Arts, 67,* 174–189.

Carnes, E. J. (1988). Teaching content area reading through nonfiction book writing. *Journal of Reading, 31,* 354–360.

Doige, L. A. C. (1999). Beyond cultural differences and similarities: Student teachers encounter aboriginal children's literature. *Canadian Journal of Education, 24*(4), 383–397.

Donelson, K. L., & Nilsen, A. P. (1997). *Literature for today's young adults* (5th ed.). New York: Longman.

Egoff, S., & Saltman, J. (1990). *The new republic of childhood: A critical guide to Canadian children's literature in English.* Toronto: Oxford University Press.

Hancock, J. (Ed.). (1999). *Teaching literacy using information technology.* Newark, DE: International Reading Association.

Jacobsen, M., Clifford, P., & Friesen, S. (2002). Preparing teachers for technology integration: Creating a culture of inquiry in the context of use and teacher educators. *Contemporary Issues in Technology and Teacher Education, 2*(3). Retrieved February 5, 2004, from http://www.cite-journal.org/vol2/iss3/currentpractice/article2.cfm.

Jones, R., & Stott, J. (2000). *Canadian children's books: A critical guide to authors and illustrators.* Toronto: Oxford University Press.

Leu, D. J., Jr., & Leu, D. D. (2000). *Teaching with the internet: Lessons from the classroom* (3rd ed.). Norwood, MA: Christopher-Gordon.

Neal, J. C., & Moore, K. (1991). *The Very Hungry Caterpillar* meets *Beowulf* in secondary classrooms. *Journal of Reading, 35,* 290–296.

Pantaleo, S. (2002). A canon of literature in Canadian elementary schools? *English Quarterly, 34* (1,2), 19–26.

Tiedt, I. M. (2000). *Teaching with picture books in the middle school.* Newark, DE: International Reading Association.

Wepner, S. B., Valmont, W. J., & Thurlow, R. (Eds.). (2000). *Linking literacy and technology: A guide for K–8 classrooms.* Newark, DE: International Reading Association.

chapter three

Making Authentic Assessments

One never steps into the same river twice.

–Ancient Chinese proverb

ORGANIZING PRINCIPLE

Making authentic assessments in content area classrooms means that students and teachers are actively engaged in an ongoing process of evaluation and self-evaluation. Instead of measuring learning by a score on a standardized test, the learning process is combined with assessment of authentic tasks. Such an assessment involves students doing reading and writing tasks that look like real-life tasks, with students primarily in control of the task (Farr and Tone 1998, pp. 18–19). Directly connected to teaching and the improvement of practice, this kind of assessment is growing in popularity. It helps students and teachers make sense of how and what is taught and learned at any given time; thus, it captures the very nature of content area instruction. As the Chinese proverb suggests, things do not remain the same—especially students in the learning process.

Teachers who believe that assessment and instruction are mutually supportive processes understand that they must become actively involved in developing and scoring assessments, communicating with students about work for portfolios, and helping students reflect on their own performance and solve problems. These teachers want to depend on authentic measures to make decisions about instruction appropriate for each student. To understand assessment, you need to differentiate between two major, yet contrasting, approaches: a formal, high-stakes approach and an informal, authentic approach.

As depicted in the chapter overview, these major views of assessment form the base from which alternative practices, such as the use of portfolios, have emerged. Tests, observations, anecdotal records, checklists, interviews, inventories, writing folders, and conferences with students are some of the methods and techniques that make authentic assessments possible. Authentic assessments help us understand student performance and provide a basis for making instructional decisions; they help create a framework for both students and teachers to judge the difficulty of subject matter materials and reflect on learning and teaching.

Assessing for instruction should, first and foremost, provide the opportunity to gather and interpret useful information about students: their prior knowledge; their attitudes toward reading, writing, listening, speaking, viewing, representing, and subject matter; and their ability to use reading and writing, listening and speaking, and viewing and representing to learn with texts. Through portfolio assessment—a process of collecting authentic evidence of student work over time—both students and teachers gather information to better reflect on, understand, and communicate those factors that affect literacy and learning and characterize an individual's performance. The organizing principle of this chapter holds that assessment should be authentic and responsive to teacher decision making: **instructional assessment is a continuous process of gathering multiple sources of relevant information for instructional purposes.**

CHAPTER OVERVIEW

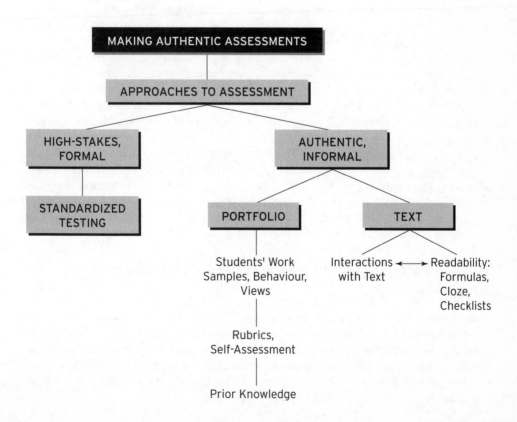

FRAME OF MIND

1. How does assessment aid in setting instructional goals?

2. How does a formal, high-stakes approach differ from an informal, authentic approach?

3. What are the advantages of ongoing assessment that occurs in the natural context of the classroom?

4. What are portfolios, and what process do content teachers follow to implement them in the classroom?

5. Why do teachers have some concerns about using portfolio assessment?

6. How can teachers assess students' background knowledge?

7. How does the teacher assess students' interactions with text?

8. When and how might teachers use professional judgment in analyzing the difficulty of textbooks?

9. What are predictive measures of readability, and how do they differ from performance measures?

You are in a good position to identify and emphasize the strengths that your students bring to learning situations whenever you engage in an ongoing process of assessment. This is why efforts at assessment should centre on the classroom context, where the focus of assessment is not only on students but also on texts and on teacher–student–text interaction. In this sense, *diagnostic teaching* is one of the most worthwhile activities in which content area teachers participate. Nevertheless, the prospect of diagnosing is often formidable because it evokes images of expertise and specialization beyond your domain.

This need not be the case. What, then, do you need to know about students and texts to plan classroom activities better? As you go about the tasks of planning and decision making, several areas of assessment are essential. First, you will want to assess students' prior knowledge in relation to thematic units and specific text lessons. Second, you will want to assess student knowledge and use of strategies to learn with texts. Third, you should consider assessing the texts you use. Each of these areas of assessment is integral to understanding some of the dynamics of the context operating in your classroom. If your purpose is to improve your understanding of that context, an informal, authentic approach to assessment is likely to be more useful than a formal, high-stakes one.

HIGH-STAKES AND AUTHENTIC APPROACHES TO ASSESSMENT

Teachers sometimes know intuitively that what they do in class is working. More often, however, information for making decisions is best obtained through careful observation of students. Their strengths and weaknesses as they interact with one another and with texts can be assessed as they participate in small groups, contribute to class discussions, respond to questions, and complete written assignments. This approach to assessment is informal and authentic; it is student centred and classroom based.

The two major views of assessment, high-stakes and authentic, are like different sides of the same coin. They represent the almost opposite perspectives of policy makers on one side, and teachers on the other. The policy makers are responding to the public and its demands for assurances that students will leave school well prepared to enter either the workforce or post-secondary education. Teachers and other educators are calling for better, more authentic assessment practices that will improve instruction and result in learning. As Tierney (1998) put it, one focuses on "something you *do to* students," and the other focuses on "something you *do with* them or help them *do for themselves*" (p. 378).

Authentic methods often include some combination of observations, interviews, anecdotal records, and student-selected performances and products. The information gained from an authentic assessment can be organized into a rich description or portrait of your content area classroom or into student *portfolios*. Concerns that emerge, whether about individual students or about the delivery of instructional strategies, are likely to make sense because they come directly from the classroom context and often result from teacher–student or student–student interaction.

Consider how an authentic approach differs from a more formal, high-stakes one. In Table 3.1 on page 66, the two approaches are compared in several categories. Certainly there are many grey areas in assessment, where the formal and informal overlap. In this table, however, differences between the two approaches are emphasized. Traditional, formal assessments are product oriented. They are more tangible and can be obtained at predetermined points in time. Authentic assessments are informal and process oriented. The process is ongoing, providing as much information about the student as learner as the product. Together, they permit a more balanced approach through a combination of traditional, formal and authentic, informal practices. The end result is an understanding of *why* particular results are obtained in formal assessment, which informs the *how* of the teacher decision-making process.

The Role of High-Stakes Testing

An assessment based on standardized test information is different from an assessment that evolves from authentic methods. A standardized reading test is more formal, is administered at a predetermined date, and uses test methods that are considered objective. Along with test results, schools receive reports of their students' strengths and weaknesses in subskill areas. In Canada, education is a provincial responsibility. Each province has a ministry of education. Secondary school testing in Canada is largely confined to grade 12 examinations, although Ontario has introduced grade 10 examinations as well. These secondary school exit tests are curriculum based and are not generally used to determine pass/fail, though some count for a percentage of a student's grade 12 final mark.

The Council of Ministries of Education also does sampling studies in the form of the School Achievement Indicators Program (SAIP) in three cycles, one each for reading/writing, mathematics, and science. Ontario now has a testing group called the Education Quality and Accountability Office (EQAO), with more emphasis on using test results for accountability purposes and publishing both board and school results for the general public.

International large-scale assessment efforts to test students worldwide often appear in newspaper headlines, citing how well or how poorly Canadian students performed in comparison to students in other countries in a given subject. In 1999, international comparative results in mathematics and science achievement were made available for grade 8 stu-

TABLE 3.1	Comparisons of Two Approaches to Assessment	
	High-Stakes, Formal	Authentic, Informal
Orientation	Formal; developed by expert committees and test publishers	Informal; developed by teachers and students
Administration	Testing one-time performance; paper-and-pencil, multiple-choice; given to groups at one seating	Continuously evolving and intermittent throughout an instructional unit; small group, one on one
Methods	Objective; standardized reading achievement tests designed to measure levels of current attainment; province-wide proficiency testing of content knowledge	Classroom tests, checklists, observations, interviews, etc., designed to evaluate understanding of course content; real-life reading and writing tasks
Uses	Compare performance of one group with that of students in other schools or classrooms; estimate range of reading ability in a class; select appropriate materials for reading; identify students who need further diagnosis; align curriculum; allocate classroom time	Make qualitative judgments about students' strengths and instructional needs in reading and learning content subjects; select appropriate materials; adjust instruction when necessary; self-assess strengths and weaknesses
Feedback format	Reports, printouts of subtest scores; summaries of high and low areas of performance; percentiles, norms, stanines	Notes, profiles, portfolios, discussions, recommendations that evolve throughout instructional units; expansive (relate to interests, strategies, purpose for learning and reading)

dents around the world in the International Association for the Evaluation of Educational Achievement's Third International Mathematics and Science Study (TIMSS). We learned that Singapore was the top-performing country in mathematics, Korea was the top-performing country in science, and Japan, Canada, and Australia also performed well. Another international assessment, the Organization of Economic Co-operation and Development's Programme of International Student Assessment (OECD-PISA), which also tests reading, mathematics, and science, found that in the year 2000, Finland, Korea, and Canada scored first, second, and third respectively in reading.

Often, standardized tests are not intended to be used to make decisions about individual students. Test publishers have developed them with a prescribed content, directions to adhere to, and a scoring arrangement to maintain a standardized analysis of the responses given. Above all, standardized tests measure performance on a test. Hence, you need to proceed with caution: make doubly sure to understand what performance on a particular reading test means before using test results to judge the ability of a reader. A student who is a good reader of social studies texts may be a poor reader of mathematics or science texts.

There are several drawbacks to the use of high-stakes testing. Because of the serious consequences associated with the test scores, preparation for high-stakes tests often results in a narrowing of the curriculum and a loss of instructional time. Rather than focusing on actual gains in reading achievement and the understanding of concepts being taught, teachers tend to teach to the test in an effort to ensure higher test scores.

What Teachers Need to Know About Standardized Tests

Standardized reading tests are formal, usually machine-scorable instruments in which scores for the tested group are compared with standards established by an original, normative population. The purpose of a standardized reading test is to show where students rank in relation to other students based on a single performance.

To make sense of test information and to determine how relevant or useful it may be, you need to be thoroughly familiar with the language, purposes, and legitimate uses of standardized tests. For example, as a test user, it is your responsibility to know about the norming and standardization of any reading test used by your school district. Consult a test manual for an explanation of what the test is about, the rationale behind its development, and a clear description of what the test purports to measure. Not only should test instructions for administering and scoring be clearly spelled out, but also information related to norms, reliability, and validity should be easily defined and made available.

Norms represent average scores of a sampling of students selected for testing according to factors such as age, sex, ethnicity, grade, or socioeconomic status. Once a test maker determines norm scores, those scores become the basis for comparing the test performance of individuals or groups to the performance of those who were included in the norming sample. *Representativeness*, therefore, is a key concept in understanding student scores. It's crucial to make sure that the norming sample used in devising the reading test resembles the characteristics of the students you teach.

Norms are extrapolated from raw scores. A *raw score* is the number of items a student answers correctly on a test. Raw scores are converted to other kinds of scores so that comparisons can be made among individuals or groups of students. Three such conversions—percentile scores, stanine scores, and grade-equivalent scores—are often represented by test makers as they report scores.

Percentile scores describe the relative standing of a student at a particular grade level. For example, the percentile score of 85 of a student in grade 5 means that his or her score is equal to or higher than the scores of 85 percent of comparable grade 5 students.

Stanine scores are raw scores that have been transformed to a common standard to permit comparison. In this respect, stanines represent one of several types of standard scores. Because standard scores have the same mean and standard deviation, they permit the direct comparison of student performance across tests and subtests. The term *stanine* refers to a *standard nine*-point scale, in which the distribution of scores on a test is divided into nine parts. Each stanine indicates a single digit ranging from 1 to 9 in numerical value. Thus a stanine of 5 is at the midpoint of the scale and represents average performance. Stanines 6, 7, 8, and 9 indicate increasingly better performance; stanines 4, 3, 2, and 1 represent decreasing performance. As teachers, we can use stanines effectively to view a student's approximate place above or below the average in the norming group.

Grade-equivalent scores provide information about reading-test performance as it relates to students at various grade levels. A grade-equivalent score is a questionable abstraction. It suggests that growth in reading progresses throughout a school year at a constant rate; for example, a student with a grade-equivalent score of 7.4 is supposedly performing at a level that is average for students who have completed four months of the seventh grade. At best, this is a silly and spurious interpretation: "Based on what is known about human development generally and language growth specifically, such an assumption [underlying grade-equivalent scores] makes little sense when applied to a human process as complex as learning to read" (Vacca, Vacca, & Gove 2000, p. 530).

Reliability refers to the consistency or stability of a student's test scores. A teacher must raise the question, "Can similar test results be achieved under different conditions?" Suppose your students were to take a reading test on Monday, their first day back from vacation, and then take an equivalent form of the same test on Thursday. Would their scores be about the same? If so, the test may indeed be reliable.

Validity, by contrast, tells the teacher whether the test is measuring what it purports to measure. Validity, without question, is one of the most important characteristics of a test. If the test purports to measure reading comprehension, what is the test maker's concept of reading comprehension? Answers to this question provide insight into the *construct validity* of a test. Other aspects of validity include *content validity* (Does the test reflect the domain or content area being examined?) and *predictive validity* (Does the test predict future performance?).

Standardized test results are probably more useful at the school or board level rather than the classroom level. A school, for example, may wish to compare itself in reading performance against a provincial or national norm. Or local board-wide norms may be compared with national norms. In general, information from standardized tests may help screen for students who have major difficulties in reading, compare general reading-achievement levels or different classes or grades of students, assess group reading achievement, and assess the reading growth of groups of students (Allington & Strange 1980).

However, you need useful information about students' reading-related behaviour and background knowledge. You would be guilty of misusing standardized test results if you were to extrapolate about students' background knowledge or ability to comprehend course materials on the basis of standardized reading-test performance. Alternatives to high-stakes, formal assessments are found in an informal, authentic approach to assessment. One of the most useful tools for inquiry into the classroom is observation.

Teachers as Observers

In a high-stakes approach to assessment, the *test* is the major tool; in an authentic approach, the *teacher* is the major tool. Who is better equipped to observe students, to provide feedback, and to serve as a key informant about the meaning of classroom events? You epitomize the process of assessing students in an ongoing, natural way because you are in a position to observe and collect information continuously (Valencia 1990). Consequently, you become an observer of the relevant interactive and independent behaviour of students as they learn in the content area classroom.

Observation is one unobtrusive measure that ranges from the occasional noticing of unusual student behaviour to frequent anecdotal jottings to regular and detailed written field notes. Besides the obvious opportunity to observe students' oral and silent reading, there are other advantages to observation. Observing students' appearance, posture, mannerisms, enthusiasm, or apathy may reveal information about self-image. However, unless you make a systematic effort to tune in to student performance, you may lose valuable insights. You have to be a good listener to and watcher of students. Observation should be a natural outgrowth of teaching; it increases teaching efficiency and effectiveness. Instructional decisions based on accurate observations help you zero in on what and how to teach in relation to reading tasks.

However, before this can happen, you must view yourself as a participant observer and as an active researcher and problem solver. You need to systematically collect information about and samples of students' work in relation to instructional goals, with an eye to what you think best represents students' capabilities (Resnick & Resnick 1991).

Today's teachers are expected to meet the special needs of all students. Consequently, the challenges of teaching diverse learners in the classroom may cause nonspecialist teachers to feel frustrated and unprepared. Understanding and accepting differences in students can, however, lead to effective instructional adaptations. Here's how Kim Browne, a grade 7 teacher of language arts, used observational assessment to help deal with her "inclusion section":

> One of the most frequent questions I'm asked at parent meetings and IEP [individual educational plan] meetings is, "How does my child interact with his or her peers?" I planned to collect data on each student by using a simple observation checklist when the students are participating in their literary circles after reading *Take Me Out to the Ball Game*. I keep an index card file on each student by the class period; my focus is on peer relationships, noting any overt behaviour that may be indicative of boredom or confusion, as well as cooperative interactions. Additional observations can be added to a large label stuck to the back of the card.

In addition to the basic format for time sample or interval data, Kim included two other sections. One was *other information*, where she noted any support the student may be receiving in or out of school and whether the student was on an IEP plan; in this section, she asked a specific question about the student. Under *tentative conclusions*, she made comments about what she just observed and what to focus on in the next observation. Figure 3.1 on page 70 illustrates Kim's recent observation of Neil, a student with special needs in her late-morning section.

To record systematic observations, to note significant teaching–learning events, or simply to make note of classroom happenings, you need to keep a notebook or index cards on hand. Information collected purposefully constitutes *field notes*. They aid in classifying information, inferring patterns of behaviour, and making predictions about the effectiveness of innovative instructional procedures. As they accumulate, field notes may serve as anecdotal records that provide documentary evidence of students' interactions over periods of time.

Teachers and others who use informal, authentic tools to collect information almost always use more than one means of collecting data, a practice known as *triangulation*. This helps ensure that the information is valid and that what is learned from one source is corroborated by what is learned from another source. A grade 5 science teacher recounted how he combined the taking of field notes with active listening and discussion to assess his students' current achievement and future needs in the subject:

Date: Sept. 13, 2004   Time: Start: 11:15   Stop: 11:25

School: Hadley   Grade: 7

Subject: Lang. Arts   Period: 5

Other information: Neil is on an IEP that indicates A.D.D. with mild Tourette. Does Neil contribute to literary circle? Does he exhibit overt signs of Tourette or frustration?

Time interval used: 3 min

Time: 11:15   Behaviour: Neil willingly joins in a small group. He asked a question, then began to listen.

Time: 11:18   Behaviour: Shrugs shoulders often. Makes a frown. Contributes orally to group.

Time: 11:21   Behaviour: Put head down on desk. Pointed to text, laughing at what someone said.

Conclusions if possible: It is possible that Neil didn't fully understand what he read in Take Me Out to the Ball Game last night. Shoulder shrugging & head down may indicate confusion. He seemed to enjoy being part of literary circle.

FIGURE 3.1   A Time Sample Observation

I briefly document on individual cards how students behave during experiments conducted individually, within a group, during reading assignments, during phases of a project, and during formal assessments. Knowing which students or what size group tends to enhance or distract a student's ability to stay on task helps me organize a more effective instructional environment. When students meet to discuss their projects and the steps they followed, I listen carefully for strategies they used or neglected. I sometimes get insights into what a particular student offered this group; I get ideas for topics for future science lessons and projects or mini-lessons on time management, breaking up a topic into "chunks," and so on.

In addition to providing valid information, informal assessment strategies are useful to teachers during parent–teacher conferences for discussing a student's strengths and weaknesses. They also help build an ongoing record of progress that may be motivating for students to reflect on and useful for their other teachers in planning lessons in different subjects. And finally, the assessments themselves may provide meaningful portfolio entries from both a teacher's and a student's perspective, serving "as the essential link among curriculum, teaching, and learning" (Wilcox 1997, p. 223).

Many students want to establish a personal rapport with their teachers. They may talk of myriad subjects, seemingly unrelated to the unit. It is often during this informal chatter, however, that you find out about the students' backgrounds, problems, and interests. This type of conversation, in which you assume the role of active listener, can provide suggestions about topics for future lessons and materials and help the student's voice emerge.

Discussion, both casual and directed, is also an integral part of assessment. You need to make yourself available, both before and after class, for discussion about general topics, lessons, and assignments. For an assessment of reading comprehension, nothing replaces one-on-one discussion of the material, whether before, during, or after the actual reading. Finally, you may even encourage students to verbalize their positive and negative feelings about the class itself as well as about topics, reading, and content area activities.

A note of caution: it's important to realize that "no matter how careful we are, we will be biased in many of our judgments" (MacGinitie 1993, p. 559). Yet teachers who observe with any sort of regularity soon discover that they are able to acquire enough information to process "in a meaningful and useful manner" (Fetterman 1989, p. 88). They can then make reliable decisions about instruction with observation and other techniques in portfolio assessment.

PORTFOLIO ASSESSMENT

One of the most exciting and potentially energizing developments in assessment is the emergence of portfolios. *Portfolio assessment*—the use of global, alternative, balanced practices in gathering information about students—is a powerful concept that has immediate appeal and potential for accomplishing the following purposes:

- Providing and organizing information about the nature of students' work and achievements
- Involving students themselves in reflecting on their capabilities and making decisions about their work
- Using the holistic nature of instruction as a base from which to consider attitudes, strategies, and responses
- Assisting in the planning of appropriate instruction to follow
- Showcasing work mutually selected by students and teacher
- Revealing diverse and special needs of students as well as talents
- Displaying multiple student-produced artifacts collected over time
- Integrating assessment into the daily instruction as a natural, vital part of teaching and learning
- Expanding both the quantity and the quality of evidence by means of a variety of indicators

Portfolios are vehicles for ongoing assessment. They are composed of purposeful collections that examine achievement, effort, improvement, and, most important, processes (selecting, comparing, sharing, self-evaluation, and goal setting), according to Tierney, Carter, and Desai (1991). As such, they lend themselves beautifully to instruction in content areas ranging from mathematics and science to English, history, and health education.

Significant pieces that go into student portfolios are *collaboratively* chosen by teachers and students. Selections represent processes and activities more than products. A distinct value underlying the use of portfolios is a commitment to students' evaluation of their own understanding and personal development.

Contrasting portfolios with traditional assessment procedures, Walker (1991) submits that instead of a contrived task representing knowledge of a subject, portfolios are an "authentic" assessment that measures the process of the construction of meaning. The *students* make choices about what to include; these choices in turn encourage self-reflection on their own development, their own evaluation of their learning, and personal goal setting. Advantages of portfolios are more easily visualized when compared with traditional assessment practices as displayed in Table 3.2, adapted from Tierney, Carter, and Desai (1991, p. 44).

Adapting Portfolios to Content Area Classes

You can, by making some individual adjustments, adapt portfolios to meet your needs. Techniques such as interviewing, observing, and using checklists and inventories provide good sources of information about students in the classroom. The use of portfolios is in many ways a more practical method of organizing this type of information. Linek (1991) suggests that many kinds of data be collected for a thorough documentation of attitudes, behaviours, achievements, improvement, thinking, and reflective self-evaluation. For example, students may begin a mathematics course with poor attitudes and may constantly challenge the validity of the content by saying things such as, "What are we learning this for anyway? It's got nothing to do with me and my life." If you provide opportunities for functional application in realistic situations, comments may change over time to, "Boy, I never realized how important this was going to be for getting a job in real life!"

TABLE 3.2	Portfolios Versus Testing: Different Processes and Outcomes
Portfolio	**Testing**
Represents the range of learning activities in which students are engaged	Assesses students across a limited range of assignments that may not match what students do
Engages students in assessing their progress or accomplishments and establishing ongoing learning goals	Mechanically scored or scored by teachers who have little input
Measures each student's achievement while allowing for individual differences between students	Assesses all students on the same dimensions
Represents a collaborative approach to assessment	Assessment process is not collaborative
Has a goal of student self-assessment	Student assessment is not a goal
Addresses improvement, effort, and achievement	Addresses achievement only
Links assessment and teaching to learning	Separates learning, testing, and teaching

Source: From *Portfolio Assessment in the Reading-Writing Classroom* by Tierney, Carter, and Desai. Copyright © 1991 Christopher Gordon Publishers, Inc. Reprinted by permission of Christopher-Gordon Publishers, Inc.

Much more than a folder for housing daily work, a record file, or a grab bag, a portfolio is a comprehensive profile of each student's progress and growth. In mathematics class, whether it's arithmetic, algebra, or trigonometry, teachers would decide with students what types of samples of student-produced work should be included. According to Stenmark (1991), a mathematics portfolio might include samples of student-produced written descriptions of the results of practical or mathematical investigations, pictures and dictated reports by younger students, extended analyses of problem situations and investigations, reflections on problem-solving processes (see Figure 3.2), and statistical studies and graphic presentations. Still other "likely candidates for inclusion in a mathematics portfolio are: coordinate graphs of arithmetic, algebra, and geometry; responses to open-ended

Name: _Jeff Brandon_   Course: _Mathematics_

Grade: _9_   Date: _2-14-05_

Problem:

Little Caesar's Pizza commercial states that a person can purchase 2 pizzas with at most 5 toppings on each pizza for $22.00. The little kid in the commercial states that there are 1 048 576 possibilities. Little Caesar's offers a choice of 12 toppings. Do you agree or disagree with the little kid? Explain.

Reflection:

For the piece on problem solving I selected the Little Caesars problem. I know I got the problem wrong, but I really liked the way I went about solving the problem. I believe my problem-solving technique is pretty accurate, but I missed one minor detail, which made the answer incorrect. I spent a lot of time preparing the portfolio, and this is one portfolio where I am very proud of my problem-solving skills.

I solved this by using a smaller problem then applying it to the real problem. I first attacked this problem by writing out all of the possibilities for a smaller problem. Then I checked to see whether using combinations would work, because I knew that I couldn't count out all of the possibilities for the real problem. Then I checked and revised it. I believe that I put forth a lot of time and energy into this portfolio.

FIGURE 3.2   **A Problem-Solving Reflection for Mathematics**

Source: A Problem-Solving Reflection for Mathematics, developed by Laura Anfany and Carol Caroff, Solon High School, Solon, OH.

questions or homework problems; group reports and photographs of student projects; copies of awards or prizes; video, audio, and computer-generated examples of student work" (p. 63). In addition to these suggestions, a mathematics portfolio might also, in one sense, be considered a mathematical biography because it may contain important information about a student's attitude toward mathematics.

Implementing Portfolios in the Classroom   Before you implement the portfolio assessment process, certain logical steps must be taken and certain decisions need to be made:

1. *Discuss with your students the notion of portfolios as an interactive vehicle for assessment.* Explain the concept and show some examples of items that might be considered good candidates for the portfolio. Provide some examples from other fields, such as art and business, where portfolios have historically recorded performance and provided updates.

2. *Specify your assessment model.* What is the purpose of the portfolio? Who is the audience for the portfolio? How much will students be involved? Purposes, for example, may be to showcase students' best work; to document or describe an aspect of their work over time (to show growth); to evaluate by making judgments by using either certain standards agreed on in advance or the relative growth and development of each individual; or to document the process that goes into the development of a single product, such as a unit of work on the Cold War or the Middle East or nutrition.

3. *Decide what types of requirements will be used, approximately how many items, and what format will be appropriate for the portfolio.* Furthermore, will students be designing their own portfolios? Might they include videos or computer disks? Or will they have a uniform look? Plan an explanation of portfolios for your colleagues and the principal; also decide on the date when this process will begin.

4. *Consider which contributions are appropriate for your content area.* The main techniques for assessing students' behaviour, background knowledge, attitudes, interests, and perceptions are writing samples, video records, conference notes, tests and quizzes, standardized tests, pupil performance objectives, self-evaluations, peer evaluations, daily work samples, a collection of written work, personal progress sheets (see Figure 3.3), vocabulary-matching exercises, structured overviews, semantic maps, your own questions, freewriting, and group projects, along with checklists, inventories, and interviews.

Cherrie Jackman, a grade 5 teacher, wanted to experiment with portfolios as an assessment tool for writing and science.

To begin this procedure in my class, I followed certain steps:

■ First, I explained the concept of portfolios and discussed why they are important. We thought of how local businesses use portfolios, and how certain types of professions (architecture, art, journalism) depend on them.

■ Next, I explained the purposes of our portfolio: to describe a portion of students' work over the quarter, showing how it has improved; to reflect on and evaluate their own work in writing and science; and to compile a body of work that can travel with them from year to year.

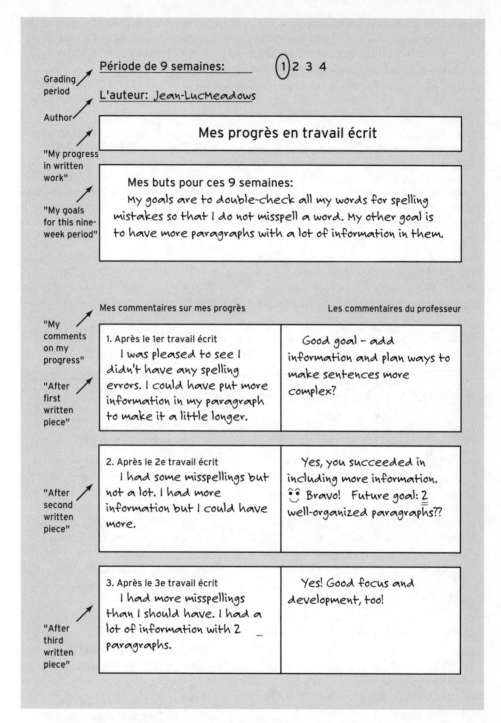

Grading period

Author

"My progress in written work"

"My goals for this nine-week period"

"My comments on my progress"

"After first written piece"

"After second written piece"

"After third written piece"

Période de 9 semaines: _____ (1) 2 3 4

L'auteur: Jean-LucMeadows

Mes progrès en travail écrit

Mes buts pour ces 9 semaines:
My goals are to double-check all my words for spelling mistakes so that I do not misspell a word. My other goal is to have more paragraphs with a lot of information in them.

Mes commentaires sur mes progrès | Les commentaires du professeur

1. Après le 1er travail écrit
I was pleased to see I didn't have any spelling errors. I could have put more information in my paragraph to make it a little longer.

Good goal – add information and plan ways to make sentences more complex?

2. Après le 2e travail écrit
I had some misspellings but not a lot. I had more information but I could have more.

Yes, you succeeded in including more information. Bravo! Future goal: 2 well-organized paragraphs??

3. Après le 3e travail écrit
I had more misspellings than I should have. I had a lot of information with 2 paragraphs.

Yes! Good focus and development, too!

FIGURE 3.3   **A Personal Progress Sheet for French**

Source: A Personal Progress Sheet for French, developed by Davara Potel, Solon High School, Solon, OH.

- Then we discussed the requirements for our portfolio: to select one or two pieces of work from science and writing that each student feels is representative of the best that he or she has done for the quarter; to add one piece for each subject area each quarter; and at the end of the school year, to evaluate students' overall progress.

- I gave examples of the kinds of contributions that would be appropriate: writing samples, self-evaluations (reflections) on a particular project, semantic maps, group projects, peer evaluations—all are acceptable pieces of work to place into the portfolio.

- Finally, we discussed the ongoing process of conferencing that will occur in our classroom. I will meet with students on an individual basis to discuss work in progress and assist in deciding which pieces might be placed in the portfolio. Time in class will be scheduled during the week for students to write reflections, ask for peer evaluations, or hold discussions with teachers about the portfolios. Although the actual work may be done at another time (writing, science), the assessment of the work could be done during this regularly scheduled time.

Grading Period: Quarter   1   ②   3   4

Author: Tawana Holiday

My Progress in the Writing Process

My Goals for This Quarter:

1) Write interesting essays.

2) Use the writing process (prewriting first draft, revising, editing).

3) Relax and have fun!

	My comments on my progress	My teacher's comments
1st essay attempt *plus I didn't have much fun.*	It was hard to get started, but once I picked my topic it went better. I went through the four steps of the writing process, and revising was hardest.	Nice job! Don't be so hard on yourself, Tawana. Your recycling topic is very interesting. Remember part of your goal is to have fun!
2nd essay	I tried to relax and have fun. It was a little easier this time. I had a short writer's block, but it passed. I like this essay better than the first one.	Don't be discouraged—writer's block happens to the best writers. I enjoyed your essay on your father; well-done description.
3rd essay	I went back and revised my first essay again. It's much better now. I like the writing process.	I'm glad you've learned the importance of relaxation in writing. Your revised 1st essay is terrific (and well developed). I'm happy that you didn't give up.

FIGURE 3.4   **A Personal Progress Sheet for Writing**

Portfolios are a process! I really want students to understand that their portfolios are a work in progress. I want them to feel comfortable selecting a piece, critiquing others' work, and asking questions. I want them to feel ownership for their own work!

Two examples of Cherrie's students' contributions are a personal progress sheet on writing goals (see Figure 3.4) and a personal reflection on an experiment done in science (see Figure 3.5).

Sometimes teachers simply want to implement portfolios in one subject. Here's how Lynn Fagerholm had her students construct portfolios as ongoing assessment and direction for their language arts activities over an entire school year. By using chronological ordering as her organizer, each procedure or product was easy to identify as an outcome measure or evidence being collected for later use.

1. *Attitude assessment.* During the first week of school, students will complete a reading assessment.

Name *Karen Manto*
Course *Science*

Grade *5*
Date *Oct. 15, 2004*

Experiment:

They're All Wet.—Determine what effect soaking seeds has on the time it takes them to sprout. In a group of four, develop an experiment using the scientific procedure. Evaluate your group from a scientific and cooperative point of view.

Reflection:

I selected the experiment "They're All Wet" as my best work in science for a number of reasons.

① My group worked very well together. Everyone was assigned a job (reader, recorder, speaker, organizer), and everyone got to talk.

② We wrote a sound hypothesis and design for our experiment because we took our time and we thought about the process.

③ We kept very good records of our observations, and then everyone participated in telling about them.

④ Even though our experiment did not prove our hypothesis, I learned many things from this experiment (see above).

Next time maybe my results will support my hypothesis, but I did learn the proper way to conduct an experiment.

FIGURE 3.5 **A Personal Reflection for Science**

2. *Tape of oral reading.* During the first week, students will also read a selection from their science or social studies textbook aloud into a tape recorder to demonstrate reading fluency.

3. *Written paragraph.* Students will compose a paragraph describing characteristics of a good reader and how well they fit that description. (This paragraph will demonstrate knowledge of reading ability and the student's ability to express ideas in written form.)

4. *Reading log.* Students will maintain a running record of all books read during the year.

5. *Genre explorations.* Students will explore the various genres and create presentations for each. These presentations should include

   ■ Book selected by student.

   ■ Complete story map.

   ■ Sticky notes discussion forum: Student places sticky notes with comments on relationships, personal reflections, or questions throughout the book. These are used during literature conferences held with the teacher periodically as the book is read. Teacher records the conference on a dated discussion form, noting the types of comments and questions raised by the student and the quality of the discussion.

   ■ Project: Students may elect to present in a variety of ways (script, drama, cartoon, advertisement, book talk, poster, letter).

   ■ Evaluation and goals: After the presentation, students write an evaluation of the process, the presentation, and goals for the future.

6. *Quarter presentation selection.* At the end of each nine-week period, students will evaluate the contents of their portfolio and select the best presentation from that quarter. Students will write a brief paragraph explaining what sets the piece of work apart from the rest. At the end of the year, the portfolio will contain four student-selected genre explorations, along with other pieces of writing that the student considers superior or significant and wishes to include.

7. *Attitude assessment.* During the last few weeks of school, students will again take the reading attitude assessment and compare the results with those from the first week of school.

8. *End-of-year assessment.* At the end of the last grading period, students will review the entire contents of their portfolios and compose a carefully written paper discussing progress made.

9. *Tape of oral reading.* Students will read a selection from the same social studies or science book used at the beginning of the year. They will compare the two recordings, listening for differences and improvements.

10. *Written paragraph.* Students will compose a written paragraph describing what a good reader is and how well they now fit that description. Afterward, they will compare this paragraph with the one written early in the year, noting differences and improvements.

Concerns of Teachers Teachers everywhere, from preschool through adult levels, have been engaged in the implementation of portfolio assessment as they participate in efforts to balance traditional and alternative assessment practices. For the most part, they are doing so without much, if any, formal training in alternative assessment techniques.

In a study of mathematics teachers in the United States, Cooney, Bell, Fisher-Cauble, and Sanchez (1996) interviewed and observed teachers who were attempting to implement some of the new assessment standards developed by the National Council of Teachers of Mathematics. Five major issues were of concern to teachers:

1. *Loss of predictability* creates some risk for teachers who are more comfortable in a well-organized and predictable classroom in which there is a correct answer to every question. Also, teachers expressed concerns about being observed by administrators who won't realize what you're doing and might "mark you down because your class is kind of loud" (p. 486).

2. *Content coverage and performance on high-stakes tests* are of great concern to teachers of secondary school mathematics courses who need to prepare students to "take the next course" and do well on grade 12 tests. Middle school teachers, for example, are more likely to use journal writing and portfolios.

3. Students need to be trained by their teachers in *expectations for responding to open-ended questions*. Students used to being graded by the "right" answer will benefit from developing and using scoring rubrics (categories of performance response).

4. *Increased demands on time* suggest that it's a good idea to "start small and go from there" (p. 486). Until teachers actually go through the process from the beginning of the year to the end, they don't have a realistic idea of the amount of time it will take to incorporate portfolios into their classrooms.

5. *Communicating with parents* is essential, especially in terms of helping them interpret their child's grades and understand their child's assignments. Once they have a sense of what the teacher is trying to accomplish, parents can provide considerable support.

Assessing Students' Behaviour and Views

Informal assessment techniques such as checklists, interviews, and content area reading inventories (discussed later in this chapter) are different from natural, open-ended observation. They often consist of categories or questions that have already been determined; they impose an *a priori* classification scheme on the observation process. A checklist is designed to reveal categories of information the teacher has preselected. When constructing a checklist, you should know beforehand which reading and study tasks or attitudes you plan to observe. Individual items on the checklist then serve to guide your observations selectively.

The selectivity that a checklist offers is both its strength and its weakness as an observational tool. Checklists are obviously efficient because they guide your observations and allow you to zero in on certain kinds of behaviour, but a checklist can also restrict observation by limiting the breadth of information recorded, excluding potentially valuable raw data. Figure 3.6 on page 80 presents sample checklist items that may be adapted to specific instructional objectives in various content areas.

In addition to checklists, observations, and inventories, interviews should be considered part of the portfolio assessment repertoire. There are several advantages of using interviews, "be they *formal,* with a preplanned set of questions, or *informal*, such as a conversation about a book" (Valencia, McGinley, & Pearson 1990, p. 14). First, students and

Reading and Study Behaviour	Minh	Pat	Frank	Karthika	Jerry	Doug	Mike	Gina
Comprehension								
1. Follows the author's message	A	B	B	A	D	C	F	C
2. Evaluates the relevancy of facts								
3. Questions the accuracy of statements								
4. Critical of an author's bias								
5. Comprehends what the author means								
6. Follows text organization								
7. Can solve problems through reading								
8. Develops purposes for reading								
9. Makes predictions and takes risks								
10. Applies information to come up with new ideas								
Vocabulary								
1. Has a good grasp of technical terms in the subject under study								
2. Works out the meaning of an unknown word through context or structural analysis								
3. Knows how to use a dictionary effectively								
4. Sees relationships among key terms								
5. Becomes interested in the derivation of technical terms								
Study Habits								
1. Concentrates while reading								
2. Understands better by reading orally than silently								
3. Has a well-defined purpose in mind when studying								
4. Knows how to take notes during lecture and discussion								
5. Can organize material through outlining								
6. Skims to find the answer to a specific question								
7. Reads everything slowly and carefully								
8. Makes use of book parts								
9. Understands charts, maps, tables in the text								
10. Summarizes information								

Grading Key: A = always (excellent)
B = usually (good)
C = sometimes (average)
D = seldom (poor)
E = never (unacceptable)

FIGURE 3.6 **Sample Checklist Items for Observing Reading and Study Behaviour**

teachers interact in collaborative settings. Second, an open-ended question format is conducive to the sharing of students' own views. Third, it reveals to what extent students are in touch with their internal disposition toward reading subject matter material.

In general, there are several *types of interviews*: structured, semistructured, informal, and retrospective. As described by Fetterman (1989, pp. 48–50), these types blend and overlap in actual practice.

1. *Formally structured and semistructured.* Verbal approximations of a questionnaire; allow for comparison of responses put in the context of common group characteristics; useful in securing baseline data about students' background experiences.

2. *Informal.* More like conversations; useful in discovering what students think and how one student's perceptions compare with another's; help identify shared values; useful in establishing and maintaining a healthy rapport.

3. *Retrospective.* Can be structured, semistructured, or informal; used to reconstruct the past, asking students to recall personal historical information; may highlight their values and reveal information about their worldviews.

One technique developed to interview students about the comprehension process is the Reading Comprehension Interview (RCI) (Wixson, Bosky, Yochum, & Alvermann 1984). Designed for grades 3 through 8, it takes about 30 minutes per student to administer in its entirety. The RCI explores students' perceptions of (1) the purpose of reading in different instructional contexts and content areas, (2) reading task requirements, and (3) strategies the student uses in different contexts.

The RCI's main uses are to help identify patterns of responses (in the whole group and individuals) that then serve as guides to instruction and to analyzing an individual's flexibility in different reading activities.

Several questions on the RCI are particularly appropriate for content area reading. Although the RCI was developed for grades 3 through 8, secondary school teachers can make good diagnostic use of some of the questions.

Rather than conduct an interview of each student individually, we suggest the following adaptation: have each student keep a learning log. In these logs, students write to themselves about what they are learning. For example, they can choose to focus on problems they are having with a particular reading assignment or activity. A variation on this general purpose would be to ask students to respond to some of the more pertinent questions on the RCI—perhaps one or two at any one time over several weeks.

In relation to a particular content area textbook, examine the kinds of questions students can write about from the RCI:[1]*

1. What is the most important reason for reading this kind of material? Why does your teacher want you to read this book?

2. Who's the best reader you know in (*content area*)? What does he/she do that makes him/her such a good reader?

3. How good are *you* at reading this kind of material? How do you know?

4. What do you have to do to get a good grade in (*content area*) in your class?

5. If the teacher told you to remember the information in this story/chapter, what would be the best way to do this? Have you ever tried (*name a strategy, e.g., outlining*)?

---

[1] From K. Wixson, A. Boskey, M. Yochum, and D. Alvermann, "An Interview for Assessing Students' Perceptions of Classroom Reading Tasks." *The Reading Teacher*, January 1984. Reprinted with permission of K. Wixson and the International Reading Association.

6. If your teacher told you to find the answers to the questions in this book, what would be the best way to do this? Why? Have you ever tried (*name a strategy, e.g., previewing*)?

7. What is the hardest part about answering questions like the ones in this book? Does that make you do anything differently?

Having students respond to these questions in writing does not deny the importance of interviewing individuals. However, it does save an enormous amount of time while providing a teacher with a record of students' perceptions of important reading tasks related to comprehension.

Another way to get at some of the same perceptions that students have about reading activities is through a questionnaire. Hahn (1984) developed a 10-item questionnaire based on modifications of a research instrument used by Paris and Meyers (1981). On the questionnaire, five items—2, 3, 4, 6, and 10—represent *positive reading strategies* (procedures students should use to comprehend effectively), and five items—1, 5, 7, 8, and 9—depict *negative reading strategies* (procedures that are ineffective and should be avoided); see Box 3.1.

Students who rate positive strategies as not very helpful can easily be identified when the questionnaire is scored. These students may benefit from some explicit instruction in the strategies. Also, a good point of discussion would be why the negative strategies are not helpful for effective *studying*.

Rubrics and Self-Assessments

Students need to play a role in the assessment of their own literacy products and processes. Teachers who want to help students get more involved in assessment invite them to participate in setting goals and to share how they think and feel. What are the students' perceptions of their achievements? McCullen (1998) described how she begins this process with middle-grade students:

> I usually start by envisioning the possible outcomes of each assignment. Then the students and I develop a standard of excellence for each facet of the process and convert the outcomes into a rubric. Thus, before the students begin their research, they know the goals of the assignment and the scope of the evaluation. (p. 7)

Rubrics are categories that range from very simple and direct to comprehensive and detailed. Some are designed to help individual students self-assess; often they are designed to be used by small groups or by an individual student and teacher. In Figure 3.7 on page 84, a basic rubric serves the dual purpose of involving each student in evaluating the group's work on their Internet Inquiry Project and in self-evaluating.

A more detailed rubric, shown in Figure 3.8 on page 85, was developed in a grade 7 life science class by the teacher and her students for a unit exploring the five senses. The teacher gave the students copies of the rubric in advance so they could monitor themselves. Using a scale of 0 to 3, students were graded individually and as part of a group by their teacher and by themselves. This rubric may be time-consuming to develop. Rubrics containing less detail and those developed in partnership with students may take less time to construct. They surely help involve students in assessing their own learning in an authentic, meaningful way that keeps the focus on *why* and *how* we do *what* we do.

BOX 3.1	**Questionnaire on Reading Strategies**

Does it help you understand a text selection (or a story) if you ...

1. Think about something else while you are reading?

    _____ always _____ almost always _____ almost never _____ never

2. Write it down in your own words?

    _____ always _____ almost always _____ almost never _____ never

3. Underline important parts of the selection?

    _____ always _____ almost always _____ almost never _____ never

4. Ask yourself questions about the ideas in the selection?

    _____ always _____ almost always _____ almost never _____ never

5. Write down every single word in the selection?

    _____ always _____ almost always _____ almost never _____ never

6. Check through the selection to see if you remember all of it?

    _____ always _____ almost always _____ almost never _____ never

7. Skip the parts you don't understand in the selection?

    _____ always _____ almost always _____ almost never _____ never

8. Read the selection as fast as you can?

    _____ always _____ almost always _____ almost never _____ never

9. Say every word over and over?

    _____ always _____ almost always _____ almost never _____ never

10. Ask questions about parts of the selection that you don't understand?

    _____ always _____ almost always _____ almost never _____ never

Source: Amos Hahn, "Assessing and Extending Comprehension: Monitoring Strategies in the Classroom," *Reading Horizons, 24*, 1984, pp. 225–230. Used by permission of Western Michigan University, College of Education.

Assessing Students' Prior Knowledge

As we mentioned in Chapter 1, one of the reasons for the recent increase in attention given to prior knowledge is the popularization of a schema-theoretic view of reading. Understanding the role of a schema in reading comprehension provides insights into why students may fail to comprehend text material. Pearson and Spiro (1982) argue that "schema inadequacies" are responsible for a great many roadblocks to reading comprehension.

Fifth-Grade Internet Inquiry Project

Name: _____

Directions: Evaluate your group's performance in each of the following categories. Be honest. Please also make comments about parts of this project you found successful and parts you found unsuccessful.

Content	Points Possible	Points Earned	Comments
Selection of topic	5		
Evidence of planning	15		
Bibliography of print resources (minimum of 3 per person)	15		
Time on task while doing research in the library computer lab	5		
Websites (minimum of 5): usefulness, appropriateness	20		
Website summaries	30		
Evidence of cooperation	10		
Total	100		

FIGURE 3.7   Rubric for Self-Evaluation

Three kinds of schema-related problems can interfere with understanding. The first deals with *schema availability*. Students may lack the relevant background knowledge and information needed to comprehend a text assignment. A teacher might ask, "Does my student have the schema necessary to make sense of a particular text selection?"

A second schema inadequacy is *schema selection*. Students who have sufficient background knowledge may fail to bring it to bear as they read. For example, students may be unaware that what they already know about the topic is of importance in the reading process. How a teacher evaluates and activates an available schema is essential to effective reading instruction in content areas.

A third type of schema inadequacy involves *schema maintenance*. Students may not be aware or skilled enough to recognize when shifts in a schema occur during reading. They may not know how or when to adapt and change schemata as a particular reading situation demands. In other words, how does a teacher help students maintain reader–text interac-

	Group Evaluation	Individual Evaluation
3	■ Worked well together every day ■ Thoroughly completed the lab activity ■ Developed a well-organized, very neatly presented handout that combined all group members' work, including at least one visual aid ■ Worked independently on most days	■ Used at least four sources, including one Website and one traditional source; correctly listed the sources ■ Thoroughly answered the assigned question ■ Came up with and answered thoroughly two related questions ■ Participated in an experiment and engaged in a thoughtful reflection around that experiment ■ Cooperated with and helped group members every day
2	■ Worked well together most days ■ Completed the lab activity with some effort ■ Developed a well-organized, fairly neatly presented handout that combined all group members' work; may or may not have included a visual aid ■ Worked independently on some days	■ Used at least three sources, including one Website and one traditional source; listed the sources ■ Thoroughly answered the assigned question ■ Came up with and tried to answer two related questions ■ Participated in an experiment and engaged in a thoughtful reflection around that experiment ■ Cooperated with and helped group members most days
1	■ May or may not have worked well together ■ Completed the lab activity ■ Developed a handout that combined all group members' work; did not include a visual aid ■ Did not work independently	■ Used at least two sources; listed the sources ■ Answered the assigned question ■ Came up with and tried to answer one related question ■ Participated in an experiment and engaged in a reflection around that experiment ■ Cooperated with and helped group members some days
0	■ Did not work well together ■ Did not complete the lab activity ■ Did not develop a handout that combined all group members' work ■ Did not work independently	■ Used fewer than two sources ■ Did not answer the assigned question ■ Did not come up with any related questions ■ May have participated in an experiment but did not reflect on that experiment ■ May or may not have cooperated

Grading Scale

■ 70% of your grade is based on your individual score
■ 30% of your grade is based on the group score

Final Score	Letter Grade
2.5–3.0	A
2.0–2.4	B
1.4–1.9	C
0.6–1.3	D
Below 0.6	F

FIGURE 3.8   Scoring Rubric for Sense Inquiry Project

tions during reading? The question implies that readers may have a schema available for a text selection and that it has been activated for reading. But somewhere during reading, the reading process breaks down. Students may get lost in a welter of details or bogged down in the conceptual complexity of the selection. Or they may be unable to interact with the text because of the way it is written: the author's language may be too complex, convoluted, or stylized. As a result, readers process only bits and pieces of the text and fail to grasp the author's broad message or intent.

Determining whether students possess, select, or maintain schemata helps the teacher make decisions about content area reading instruction. For example, one critical decision involves how much prereading preparation students will need for a text assignment. Another might be to decide how much background building and skill direction will be necessary. Seeking information to help make decisions such as these requires that teachers adapt and use the informal, naturalistic procedures that we have already outlined.

One assessment strategy might be to informally test the students' knowledge of the material to be learned. The teacher should construct a background knowledge inventory according to the content objectives—the major ideas and concepts—to be covered in a unit of study. The inventory or pretest can be a checklist, a short-answer quiz, or a set of open-ended essay questions. Many teachers combine short-answer questions with open-ended ones.

The pretest should not be graded; it should be discussed with the class. In fact, use the pretest to introduce students to the major concepts that will be developed in the unit. Explain why you chose to ask certain questions. Share your content objectives with the class. Students will get a sense of what they already know as a result of the discussion, but the discussion should also underscore *what students need to know* about the new material to be studied.

New and experienced teachers alike need to find out what their students already know about the subject matter to be taught. While Susan Courtney was doing her field experiences for her mathematics courses before student teaching, she worked with small groups of children twice a week, teaching the material requested by their teacher. Susan developed a "get to know you" activity that dovetailed with her hands-on style of assessment and instruction with manipulatives. Her goal was to ascertain the student's

> comfort level with the subject matter and their background knowledge on an individual basis. I then based lessons on the information I gathered from this assessment. The checklist helped me meet the children on their instructional level—where they were, instead of where I had expected them to be.

The assessment checklist in Figure 3.9 is one Susan used with her students studying geometry and fractions.

Alternatives to background knowledge pretesting include assessment procedures that are instructionally based. For example, the prereading plan (PreP) developed by Langer (1981) may be used to estimate background knowledge that students bring to text assignments. It is presented in Chapter 6 as a prereading activity. PreP provides the teacher with practical evaluative information about the extent to which students' language and concepts coincide with the text and promote comprehension.

ASSESSING TEXT DIFFICULTY

Evaluating texts and assessing students' interactions with texts are crucial tasks for content area teachers and students—and they call for sound judgment and decision making. One

Geometry

Using pattern blocks:

_____ Can identify triangles   _____ Can identify squares

_____ Can identify rhombuses   _____ Can identify trapezoids

_____ Can identify hexagons   _____ Can identify parallelograms

Using Geoboards

Can construct shapes that contain:

_____ right angles   _____ parallel lines

_____ a quadrilateral   _____ congruent sides

_____ perpendicular lines

_____ Can give the properties of a square

_____ Can identify lines of symmetry

Fractions

_____ Knows equivalent fractional parts must be equal

_____ Can give other names for "1"

_____ Can give other names for "1/2" (generate an equivalent fraction)

_____ Can give another name for "5/4" (rename fractions greater than 1)

_____ Can add fractions with like denominators

_____ Can subtract fractions with like denominators

_____ Can add fractions with unlike but related denominators

_____ Can compare fractions with unlike but related denominators

FIGURE 3.9   Checklist for Mathematics

of the best reasons we know for making decisions about the quality of texts is that the assessment process puts you and students in touch with their textbooks. To judge well, you must approach text assessment in much the same manner as you make decisions about other aspects of content area instruction. Any assessment suffers to the extent that it relies on a single source or perspective on information rather than on multiple sources or perspectives. Therefore, it makes sense to consider evidence in the student's portfolio along with several other perspectives.

One perspective or source of information to consider is publisher-provided descriptions of the design, format, and organizational structure of the textbook along with grade-level readability designations. Another perspective is your acquired knowledge of and interactions with the students in the class. A third perspective or source of information is your own sense of what makes the textbook a useful tool. A fourth source is the student perspective, so that instructional decisions are not made from an isolated teacher perception of the student perspective. To complement professional judgment, several procedures can provide you with useful information: readability formulas, cloze procedure, readability checklists, and a content area framework for student analysis of reading assignments. The first order of business, then, if content area reading strategies are to involve students in taking control of their own learning, is to find out how students are interacting with the text.

Assessing Students' Interactions with the Text

Teacher-made tests provide another important indicator of how students interact with text materials in content areas. A teacher-made *content area reading inventory* (CARI) is an alternative to the standardized reading test. The CARI is informal. As opposed to the standard of success on a norm-referenced test, which is a comparison of the performance of the tested group with that of the original normative population, success on the CARI test is measured by performance on the task itself. The CARI measures performance on reading materials actually used in a course. The results of the CARI can give a teacher some good insights into *how* students read course material.

Administering a CARI involves several general steps. First, explain to your students the purpose of the test. Mention that it will be used for evaluation only, to help you plan instruction, and that grades will not be assigned. Second, briefly introduce the selected portion of the text to be read and give students an idea direction to guide silent reading. Third, if you want to find out how the class uses the textbook, consider an open-book evaluation, but if you want to determine students' ability to retain information, have them answer test questions without referring to the selection. Finally, discuss the results of the evaluation individually in conferences or collectively with the entire class.

A CARI can be administered piecemeal over several class sessions so that large chunks of instructional time will not be sacrificed. The bane of many content area instructors is spending an inordinate amount of time away from actual teaching.

A CARI elicits the information you need to adjust instruction and meet student needs. It should focus on students' ability to comprehend text and to read at an appropriate rate of comprehension. Some authorities suggest that teachers also evaluate additional competency areas, such as study skills—skimming, scanning, outlining, taking notes, and so forth. We believe, however, that the best use of reading inventories in content areas is on a much smaller scale. A CARI should seek information related to basic reading tasks. For this reason, we recommend that outlining, note taking, and other useful study techniques be assessed through observation and analysis of student work samples.

Levels of Comprehension Teachers estimate their students' ability to comprehend text material at different levels of comprehension by using inventories like those in Figure 3.10 for science and Figure 3.11 on page 90 for history. These teachers wanted to assess how their students responded at *literal* (getting the facts), *inferential* (making some interpreta-

General directions: Read the assigned pages. Then look up at the board and note the time it took you to complete the selection. Record this time in the space provided on the response sheet. Close your book and answer the first question. You may then open your textbook to answer the remaining questions.

STUDENT RESPONSE FORM

Reading time: _____ min _____ s.

I.   *Directions:* Close your book and answer the following question: In your words, what was this selection about? Use as much space as you need on the back of this page to complete your answer.

II.   A.   *Directions:* Open your book and answer the following questions.

   1.   An insect has six legs and a three-part body.
        a. True
        b. False
        c. Can't tell
   2.   Insects go through changes called *metamorphosis*.
        a. True
        b. False
        c. Can't tell
   3.   Most insects are harmful.
        a. True
        b. False
        c. Can't tell
   4.   Bees help flowers by moving pollen from flower to flower.
        a. True
        b. False
        c. Can't tell

   B.   *Directions:* Answers to these questions are not directly stated by the author. You must "read between the lines" to answer them.

   1.   How is a baby cecropia moth different from a full-grown moth?
        _____

   2.   Why does a caterpillar molt?

        _____

        _____

   3.   What are the four stages of a complete metamorphosis?

        _____

   C.   *Directions:* Answers to these questions are not directly stated by the author. You must "read beyond the lines" to answer them.

   1.   Why do you suppose the caterpillar spins a long thread of silk around itself?
        _____

   2.   During which season would the full-grown cecropia moth leave the cocoon? Why?
        _____

   3.   Why do you think the moth leaves in that season rather than in another?
        _____

FIGURE 3.10 **Sample Comprehension Inventory in Science**

General directions: Read the assigned pages in your textbook, *Challenge of the West*. Then look up at the board and note the time it took you to complete the selection. Record this time in the space provided on the response sheet. Close your book and answer the first question. You may then open your textbook to answer the remaining questions.

STUDENT RESPONSE FORM

*Reading time:*_____ min _____ s.

I. *Directions:* Close your book and answer the following question: in your own words, what was this section about? Use as much space as you need on the back of this page to complete you answer.

II. *Directions*: Open your book and answer the following questions.

   1. In 1774, a Spanish ship anchored off Vancouver Island.
     a. True
     b. False

   2. Captain George Vancouver was the first European explorer to land in what is now British Columbia.
     a. True
     b. False

   3. Simon Fraser was a member of the Hudson's Bay Company.
     a. True
     b. False

   4. The Oregon Treaty set Canada's border at the 49th parallel.
     a. True
     b. False

III. *Directions:* Answers to these questions are not directly stated by the author. You must "read between the lines" to answer them.

   1. Give an example of how the aboriginal peoples helped early European explorers in British Columbia.

   2. How did Simon Fraser feel about his trip down the Fraser River?

   3. What is one main difference between the explorations of Cook and Thompson?

IV. *Directions:* Answers to these questions are not directly stated by the author. You must "read beyond the lines" to answer them.

   1. If the Chinese had not paid high prices for sea otter pelts, what difference might this lack of interest have made to the early exploration of British Columbia?

   2. Why do you think Britain and the United States argued over the ownership of the area west of the Rocky Mountains? How might Canada's history be different if the United States had been successful in establishing its claim to British Columbia?

   3. Which of the early European explorers of British Columbia would you call the most important? Why?

FIGURE 3.11 **Sample Comprehension Inventory in Canadian History**

tions), and *applied* (going beyond the material) levels of comprehension. At this time you can also determine a measure of reading rate in relation to comprehension.

You can construct a comprehension inventory using these steps:

1. *Select an appropriate reading selection from the second 50 pages of the book.* The selection need not include the entire unit or story but should be complete within itself in overall content. In most cases, two or three pages will provide a sufficient sample.

2. *Count the total number of words in the excerpt.*

3. *Read the excerpt, and formulate 10 to 12 comprehension questions.* The first part of the test should ask an open-ended question such as, "What was the passage about?" Then develop three or more questions at each level of comprehension.

4. *Prepare a student response sheet.*

5. *Answer the questions.* Include specific page references for discussion purposes after the testing is completed.

While students read the material and take the test, the teacher observes, noting work habits and student behaviour, especially of students who appear frustrated by the test. The science and history teachers of Figures 3.10 and 3.11 allowed students to check their own work as the class discussed each question. Other teachers prefer to evaluate individual students' responses to questions first and then to discuss them with students either individually or during the next class session.

Rates of Comprehension To get an estimate of students' rates of comprehension, follow these steps:

1. *Have students note the time it takes to read the selection.* This can be accomplished efficiently by recording the time in five-second intervals by using a "stopwatch" that is drawn on the board.

2. *As students complete the reading, they look up at the board to check the stopwatch.* The number within the circle represents the minutes that have elapsed. The numbers along the perimeter of the circle represent the number of seconds.

3. *Later, students or the teacher can figure out the students' rate of reading in words per minute.*

   Example:
   Words in selection: 1500
   Reading time: 4 min 30 s
   Convert seconds to a decimal fraction. Then divide time into words.

   $$\frac{1500}{4.5} = 333 \text{ words per minute}$$

4. *Determine the percentage of correct or reasonable answers on the comprehension test.* Always evaluate and discuss students' rate of reading in terms of their comprehension performance.

In summary, information you glean from a CARI will help you organize specific lessons and activities. You can decide on the background preparation needed, the length of reading assignments, and the reading activities when you apply your best judgment to the information you have learned from the assessment.

Readability

There are many readability formulas that classroom teachers can use to estimate textbook difficulty. Most popular formulas today are quick and easy to calculate. They typically involve a measure of sentence length and word difficulty to determine a grade-level score for text materials. This score supposedly indicates the reading achievement level that students need to comprehend the material. Because of their ease, readability formulas are used to make judgments about materials. These judgments are global and are not intended to be precise indicators of text difficulty.

A readability formula can best be described as a "rubber ruler" because the scores that it yields are estimates of text difficulty, not absolute levels. These estimates are often determined along a single dimension of an author's writing style: sentence complexity (as measured by length) and vocabulary difficulty (also measured by length). These two variables are used to predict text difficulty. But even though they have been shown to be persistent correlates of readability, they only indirectly assess sentence complexity and vocabulary difficulty. Are long sentences always more difficult to comprehend than short ones? Are long words necessarily harder to understand than short ones? When a readability formula is used to rewrite materials by breaking long sentences into short ones, the inferential burden of the reader actually increases (Pearson 1974–1975).

And while we're examining inferential burden, keep in mind that a readability formula doesn't account for the experience and knowledge that readers bring to content material. Hittleman (1973) characterizes readability as a moment in time. He maintains that readability estimates should include the reader's emotional, cognitive, and linguistic background. A person's human makeup interacts at the moment with the topic, the proposed purposes of reading, and the semantic and syntactic structures in the material. Formulas are not designed to tap the variables operating in the reader. Our purpose, interest, motivation, and emotional state as well as the environment that we're in during reading contribute to our ability to comprehend text.

The danger, according to Nelson (1978), is not in the use of readability formulas: "The danger is in promoting the faulty assumptions that matching the readability score of materials to the reading achievement scores of students will automatically yield comprehension" (p. 622). She makes these suggestions to content area teachers:

1. Learn to use a simple readability formula as an aid in evaluating text.

2. Whenever possible, provide materials containing the essential facts, concepts, and values of the subject at varying levels of readability within the reading range of your students.

3. Don't assume that matching readability level of material to reading achievement level of students results in automatic comprehension. Remember there are many factors that affect reading difficulty besides those measured by readability formulas.

4. Don't assume that rewriting text materials according to readability criteria results in automatic reading ease. Leave rewriting of text material to the linguists, researchers, and editors who have time to analyze and validate their manipulations.

5. Recognize that using a readability formula is no substitute for instruction. Assigning is not teaching. Subject area textbooks are not designed for independent reading. To enhance

reading comprehension in your subject area, provide instruction which prepares students for the assignment, guides them in their reading, and reinforces new ideas through rereading and discussion. (pp. 624–625)

Within the spirit of these suggestions, let's examine a popular readability formula and an alternative, the cloze procedure.

The Fry Graph The readability graph developed by Edward Fry (1977) is a quick and simple readability formula. The graph was designed to identify the grade-level score for materials from grade 1 through post-secondary education. Two variables are used to predict the difficulty of the reading material: sentence length and word length. Sentence length is determined by the total number of sentences in a sample passage. Word length is determined by the total number of syllables in the passage. Fry recommended that three 100-word samples from the reading be used to calculate readability. The grade-level scores for each of the passages can then be averaged to determine overall readability. According to Fry, the readability graph predicts the difficulty of the material within one grade level. See Figure 3.12 on page 94 for the graph and expanded directions for the Fry formula.

Cloze Procedure The cloze procedure does not use a formula to estimate the difficulty of reading material. Originated by Wilson Taylor in 1953, a cloze test determines how well students can read a particular text or reading selection as a result of their interaction with the material. Simply defined, then, the *cloze procedure* is a method by which you systematically delete words from a text passage and then evaluate students' ability to accurately supply the words that were deleted. An encounter with a cloze passage should reveal the interplay between the prior knowledge that students bring to the reading task and their language competence. Knowing the extent of this interplay will be helpful in selecting materials and planning instructional procedures. Box 3.2 on page 95 presents part of a cloze test passage developed for an art history class. Here is how to construct, administer, score, and interpret a cloze test.

1. *Construction*
   a. Select a reading passage of approximately 275 words from material that students have not yet read but that you plan to assign.
   b. Leave the first sentence intact. Starting with the second sentence, select at random one of the first five words. Delete every fifth word thereafter, until you have a total of 50 words for deletion. Retain the remaining sentence of the last deleted word. Type one more sentence intact. For children below grade 4, deletion of every tenth word is often more appropriate.
   c. Leave an underlined blank of 15 spaces for each deleted word as you type the passage.

2. *Administration*
   a. Inform students that they are not to use their textbooks or to work together in completing the cloze passage.
   b. Explain the task that students are to perform. Show how the cloze procedure works by providing several examples on the board.
   c. Allow students the time they need to complete the cloze passage.

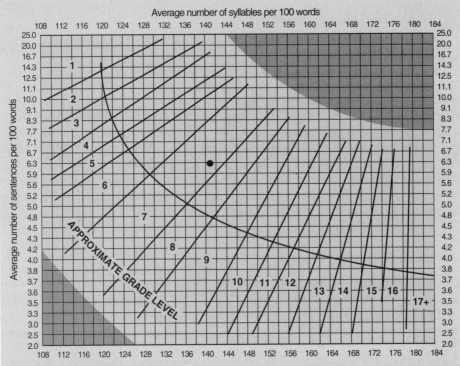

Average number of syllables per 100 words

EXPANDED DIRECTIONS FOR WORKING READABILITY GRAPH

1. Randomly select three (3) sample passages and count out exactly 100 words each, beginning with the beginning of a sentence. Do count proper nouns, initializations, and numerals.
2. Count the number of sentences in the 100 words, estimating length of the fraction of the last sentence to the nearest one-tenth.
3. Count the total number of syllables in the 100-word passage. If you don't have a hand counter available, an easy way is simply to put a mark above every syllable over one in each word; then, when you get to the end of the passage, count the number of marks and add 100. Small calculators can also be used as counters by pushing numeral 1, then pushing the + sign for each word or syllable.
4. Enter graph with *average* sentence length and *average* number of syllables; plot dot where the two lines intersect. Area where dot is plotted will give you the approximate grade level.
5. If a great deal of variability is found in syllable count or sentence count, putting more samples into the average is desirable.
6. A word is defined as a group of symbols with a space on either side; thus *1945* is one word.
7. A syllable is defined as a phonetic syllable. Generally, there are as many syllables as vowel sounds. For example, *stopped* is one syllable and *wanted* is two syllables. When counting syllables for numerals and initializations, count one syllable for each symbol. For example, *1945* is four syllables.

FIGURE 3.12 **Fry Readability Graph**

Source: From Edward Fry, *Elementary Reading Instruction.* Copyright © 1977 by McGraw-Hill. Reprinted by permission of The McGraw-Hill Companies.

BOX 3.2	**Sample Portion of a Cloze Test**

If the symbol of Rome is the Colosseum, then Paris's symbol is without doubt the Eiffel Tower. Both are monuments unique (1) planning and construction, both (2) admiration by their extraordinary (3), and bear witness (4) our inborn will to (5) something capable of demonstrating (6) measure of our genius. (7) tower was erected on (8) occasion of the World (9) in 1889. These were the (10) of the Industrial Revolution, (11) progress and of scientific (12). The attempt was made (13) adapt every art to (14) new direction which life (15) taken and to make (16) human activity correspond to (17) new sensibility created by (18) changing times.

ANSWERS

1. in	5. build	9. fair	13. to	17. the
2. stir	6. the	10. years	14. every	18. rapidly
3. dimensions	7. the	11. of	15. had	
4. to	8. the	12. conquests	16. every	

3. *Scoring*
   a. Count as correct every *exact* word students apply. *Do not* count synonyms even though they may appear to be satisfactory. Counting synonyms will not change the scores appreciably, but it will cause unnecessary hassles and haggling with students. Accepting synonyms also affects the reliability of the performance criteria, because they were established on exact word replacements.
   b. Multiply the total number of exact word replacements by 2 to determine the student's cloze percentage score.
   c. Record the cloze scores on a sheet of paper for each class. For each class, you now have one to three instructional groups that can form the basis for differentiated assignments (see Figure 3.13 on page 96).

4. *Interpretation*
   a. A score of 60 percent or higher indicates that the passage can be read competently by students. They may be able to read the material on their own without guidance.
   b. A score of 40 to 60 percent indicates that the passage can be read with some competency by students. The material will challenge students if they are given some form of reading guidance.
   c. A score below 40 percent indicates that the passage will probably be too difficult for students. They will need either a great deal of reading guidance to benefit from the material or more suitable material.

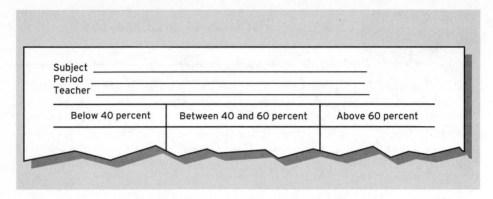

FIGURE 3.13 Headings for a Cloze Performance Chart

The cloze procedure is an alternative to a readability formula because it gives an indication of how students will actually perform with course materials. Unfortunately, the nature of the test itself will probably be foreign to students. They will be staring at a sea of blank spaces in running text, and having to provide words may seem a formidable task. Don't expect a valid score the first time you administer the test. It's important to discuss the purpose of the cloze test and to give students ample practice with and exposure to it.

Readability Checklist

Despite the many factors to be considered in text evaluation, *teachers ultimately want texts that students will understand, be able to use, and want to use*. To help guide your assessment and keep it manageable, a checklist that focuses on *understandability*, *useability*, and *interestability* is useful. One such checklist is shown in Box 3.3, an adaptation of the Irwin and Davis (1980) Readability Checklist.

The domain of *understandability* provides information about how likely a given group of students is to comprehend adequately. It helps the teacher assess relationships between the students' own schemata and conceptual knowledge and the text information. When teachers judge textbooks for possible difficulties, it is imperative to decide whether the author has taken into consideration the knowledge students will bring to the text. The match between what the reader knows and the text will have a strong influence on the understandability of the material.

Armbruster and Anderson (1981) indicate that one way to judge the author's assumptions about students' background knowledge and experiences is to decide if enough relevant ideas are presented in a text to satisfy the author's purpose. Often, authors use headings to suggest their purposes for text passages. Convert the headings to questions. If the passage content answers the questions, the authors have achieved their purposes and the passage is *considerate*. If an author hasn't provided enough information to make a passage meaningful, the passage is *inconsiderate*.

The second major domain is *useability*. Is the text coherent, unified, and structured enough to be useable? Divided into two subsections on the Readability Checklist, this sec-

BOX 3.3	**General Textbook Readability Checklist**

In the blank before each item, indicate ✔ for "yes," + for "to some extent," or x for "no" or "does not apply."

UNDERSTANDABILITY

_____ 1. Are the assumptions about students' vocabulary knowledge appropriate?

_____ 2. Are the assumptions about students' prior knowledge of this content area appropriate?

_____ 3. Are the assumptions about students' general experiential background appropriate?

_____ 4. Does the teacher's manual provide the teacher with ways to develop and review the students' conceptual and experiential background?

_____ 5. Are new concepts explicitly linked to the students' prior knowledge or to their experiential background?

_____ 6. Does the text introduce abstract concepts by accompanying them with many concrete examples?

_____ 7. Does the text introduce new concepts one at a time, with a sufficient number of examples for each one?

_____ 8. Are definitions understandable and at a lower level of abstraction than the concept being defined?

_____ 9. Does the text avoid irrelevant details?

_____ 10. Does the text explicitly state important complex relationships (e.g., causality and conditionality) rather than always expecting the reader to infer them from the context?

_____ 11. Does the teacher's manual provide lists of accessible resources containing alternative readings for the very poor or very advanced readers?

_____ 12. Is the readability level appropriate (according to a readability formula)?

USABILITY

External Organizational Aids

_____ 1. Does the table of contents provide a clear overview of the contents of the textbook?

_____ 2. Do the chapter headings clearly define the content of the chapter?

(continued)

BOX 3.3 | **(Cont.)**

USABILITY (CONT.)

_____ 3. Do the chapter subheadings clearly break out the important concepts in the chapter?

_____ 4. Do the topic headings provide assistance in breaking the chapter into relevant parts?

_____ 5. Does the glossary contain all the technical terms in the textbook?

_____ 6. Are the graphs and charts clear and supportive of the textual material?

_____ 7. Are the illustrations well done and appropriate to the level of the students?

_____ 8. Is the print size appropriate to the level of student readers?

_____ 9. Are the lines of print an appropriate length for the level of the students who will use the textbook?

_____ 10. Is a teacher's manual available and adequate for guidance to the teachers?

_____ 11. Are the important terms in italic or boldface type for easy identification by readers?

_____ 12. Are the end-of-chapter questions on literal, interpretive, and applied levels of comprehension?

Internal Organizational Aids

_____ 1. Are the concepts spaced appropriately, rather than being too many in too short a space or too few words?

_____ 2. Is an adequate context provided to allow students to determine the meanings of technical terms?

_____ 3. Are the sentence lengths appropriate to the level of students who will be using the textbook?

_____ 4. Is the author's style (word length, sentence length, sentence complexity, paragraph length, numbers of examples) appropriate to the level of students who will be using the textbook?

_____ 5. Does the author use a predominant structure or pattern of organization (compare–contrast, cause–effect, time order, problem–solution) within the writing to assist students in interpreting the textbook?

INTERESTABILITY

_____ 1. Does the teacher's manual provide introductory activities that will capture students' interests?

_____ 2. Are the chapter titles and subheadings concrete, meaningful, or interesting?

_____ 3. Is the writing style of the text appealing to the students?

_____ 4. Are the activities motivating? Will they make the student want to pursue the topic further?

_____ 5. Does the book clearly show how what is being learned might be used by the learner in the future?

_____ 6. Are the cover, format, print size, and visuals appealing to the students?

_____ 7. Does the text provide positive and motivating models for both sexes as well as for other ethnic and socio-economic groups?

_____ 8. Does the text help students generate interest as they relate experiences and develop visual and sensory images?

SUMMARY RATING

Circle one choice for each item.

The text rates highest in understandability / usability / interest.

The text rates lowest in understandability / usability / interest.

My teaching can best supplement understandability / usability / interest.

I would still need assistance with understandability / usability / interest.

STATEMENT OF STRENGTHS:

STATEMENT OF WEAKNESSES:

tion provides information about the presentation and organization of content. It will help the teacher assess pertinent factors that will contribute to the day-to-day use of the text in teaching and the students' use in learning. These items help pinpoint for a teacher exactly what needs supplementing or what may take additional preparation time or class time to compensate.

Essentially, a teacher's response to these items is another way of deciding if a text is considerate or inconsiderate. A considerate text not only fits the reader's prior knowledge but also helps "the reader to gather appropriate information with minimal cognitive effort"; an inconsiderate text "requires the reader to put forth extra effort" to compensate for poorly organized material (Armbruster & Anderson 1981, p. 3).

The third domain, *interestability*, is intended to ascertain whether features of the text will appeal to a given group of students. Illustrations and photos may have instant appeal; students can relate to drawings and photographs depicting persons similar to themselves. The more relevant the textbook, the more interesting it may be to students.

Experiment with the Readability Checklist by trying it out on a textbook in your content area. Once you've completed the checklist, sum up your ratings at the end. Does the text rate high in understandability, usability, or interestability? Is a low rating in an area you can supplement well through your instruction, or is it in an area in which you could use more help? Also, summarize the strengths and weaknesses of the textbook. If you noted two areas in which you'd still need assistance, this text is less likely than another to meet your needs. Finally, decide how you can take advantage of the textbook's strengths and compensate for its weaknesses.

LOOKING BACK, LOOKING FORWARD

Making authentic assessments is a continuous process in which teachers and students collect and analyze information about classroom interactions and texts and themselves. Multiple methods of gathering relevant data are taken from two distinct approaches to assessment: a formal, high-stakes one and an informal, authentic one. To develop goals and objectives for teaching, you need (1) to assess students' prior knowledge in relation to instructional units and text assignments, (2) to assess student knowledge and use of reading strategies to learn from texts, and (3) to assess materials.

An informal, authentic approach is a precursor to portfolio assessment. Through the use of portfolios, a more balanced approach to collecting and organizing many kinds of information can inform decision making. Careful observation of students' strengths and weaknesses as the students interact with one another and with content-specific material sheds light on the *why* as well as the *what* in teaching and learning.

In this chapter, the key terms, major purposes, and legitimate uses of standardized tests were presented. Contrasts were drawn between portfolios and testing. As teachers engage learners in a process of portfolio assessment, they make adaptations appropriate for their subject matter and consider issues that have been raised about using portfolios. Suggestions for assessing students' background knowledge included interviews, pretesting, and instructionally based strategies. Interpreting interviews, surveys, scales, and observations and developing rubrics help in assessing and self-assessing students' behaviours and views. For insights into how students interact with text material and a measure of performance on the reading materials used in a course, teacher-made content area reading inventories were suggested.

Assessing the difficulty of text material requires both professional judgment and quantitative analysis. Text assessment takes into account various factors within the reader and the text, the exercise of professional judgment being as useful as calculating a readability formula. Teachers, therefore, must be concerned about the quality of the content, format, organization, and appeal of the material. We supplied three types of procedures for assessing text difficulty: readability formulas, the cloze procedure, and readability checklists.

MINDS-ON

1. You are about to teach your first class of the school year in a school where grade 12 test scores have been extremely low during the past few years. Although a textbook has been chosen for your class, you have a wide range of auxiliary reading materials and teaching materials to choose from. Keep in mind, however, that the superintendent is interested in improving test scores. Develop a complete plan of assessment, and give the rationale for your choices.

2. For keeping records, most portfolios of student work include a cover page, one that reflects the teacher's philosophy of assessment. With the members of your group, select a content area and design a cover page that reflects your vision of authentic assessment.

3. Imagine that you are a new teacher, reviewing the required textbook you will be using in the fall. Initially, you find the book fascinating and you are certain it will excite many of your students. Yet after analyzing the work, you discover that its readability appears to be above the reading level of most of your students. How might you use this textbook effectively?

4. Readability formulas are predictive measures. How do predictive measures differ from performance measures in helping you determine how difficult reading materials will be for your students?

HANDS-ON

1. In small groups, evaluate a standardized reading test used at the secondary level. If possible, perform this evaluation by examining a copy of the technical manual that accompanies each standardized test. Consider questions such as, "What is the declared validity of the test? Its reliability? Its norming population? Its passage content? Its passage length? What conclusions can you draw from your evaluation? Will this test meet the needs of your students?"

2. Develop an observation checklist for the assessment of reading and study behaviour in your content area. Compare your checklist with those developed by others in the class for similar content areas. What conclusions might you draw?

3. Each member of your group should locate one sample of printed text material on the same topic from these sources: an elementary content area textbook, a secondary content area textbook, a newspaper, and a popular magazine. Determine the readability of a sample passage from each by using two different readability formulas. Compare your

findings by using two additional readability formulas. What conclusions can you draw from the comparison?

4. Two members of your group should be designated as observers. The other members should collaboratively attempt to solve the following mathematics problem:

    Calculate the surface area of a cylinder that is 30 cm long and 13 cm in diameter.

    Note any observations that you believe might be useful in assessing the group's performance. What types of useful information do observations like these provide?

SUGGESTED READINGS

Anderson, J. O. (1999). Modeling the development of student assessment. *Alberta Journal of Educational Research, 45*(3), 278–287.

Anthony, R. J., Johnson, T. D., Mickelson, N. I., & Preece, A. (1991). *Evaluating literacy: A perspective for change.* Toronto: Irwin Publishing.

Barrentine, S. J. (1999). *Reading assessment: Principles and practices for elementary teachers.* Newark, DE: International Reading Association.

Farr, R., & Tone, B. (1998). *Assessment portfolio and performance* (2nd ed.). Orlando, FL: Harcourt Brace.

Fry, E. (1989). Reading formulas—maligned but valid. *Journal of Reading, 32,* 292–297.

International Reading Association. (1999). *High-stakes assessments in reading: A position paper of the International Reading Association.* Newark, DE: International Reading Association.

International Reading Association and National Council of Teachers of English. (1994). *Standards for the assessment of reading and writing.* Newark, DE: International Reading Association.

Jongsma, E., & Farr, R. (1993). A themed issue on literacy assessment. *Journal of Reading, 36,* 516–600.

Kibby, M. (1993). What reading teachers should know about reading proficiency in the U.S. *Journal of Reading, 37,* 28–41.

Moje, E., Brozo, W., & Haas, J. (1994). Portfolios in a high school classroom: Challenges to change. *Reading Research and Instruction, 33,* 275–292.

Nagy, P. (2000). The three roles of assessment: Gatekeeping, accountability, and instructional diagnosis. *Canadian Journal of Education, 25*(4), 262–279.

Ohanian, S. (1999). *One size fits few: The folly of educational standards.* Portsmouth, NH: Heinemann.

Organisation for Economic Co-operation and Development. Programme for International Student Assessment (PISA). http://www.pisa.oecd.org.

Rhodes, L. (Ed.). (1993). *Literacy assessment: A handbook of instruments.* Portsmouth, NH: Heinemann.

The School Achievement Indicators Program (SAIP). http://www.cmec.ca/saip.

Tierney, R. J. (1998). Literacy assessment reform: Shifting beliefs, principled possibilities, and emerging practices. *The Reading Teacher, 51,* 374–390.

Tierney, R. J., Carter, M. A., & Desai, L. E. (1991). *Portfolio assessment in the reading–writing classroom.* Norwood, MA: Christopher-Gordon.

Trends in International Mathematics and Science Study. http://nces.ed.gov/timss.

Vacca, J. L., Vacca, R. T., & Gove, M. K. (2000). *Reading and learning to read* (4th ed.). New York: Longman.

Valencia, S., Hiebert, E., & Afflerbach, P. (Eds.). (1993). *Authentic assessment: Practices possibilities.* Newark, DE: International Reading Association.

Valencia, S., McGinley, W., & Pearson, P. D. (1990). Assessing reading and writing. In G. Duffy (Ed.), *Reading in the middle school* (pp. 124–153). Newark, DE: International Reading Association.

Wiggins, G. (1993). Assessment to improve performance, not just monitor: Assessment reform in the social sciences. *Social Science Record, 30,* 5–12.

Wilson, R. J. (1996). *Assessing students in classrooms and schools.* Scarborough, ON: Allyn Bacon.

Wolf, K., & Siu-Runyan, Y. (1996). Portfolio purposes and possibilities. *Journal of Adolescent and Adult Literacy, 40,* 30–37.

chapter four

Bringing Students and Texts Together

The use of these interrelated language processes [speaking, listening, reading, viewing, writing, and other ways of representing] is fundamental to the development of language abilities, cultural understandings, and critical and creative thinking.

–Atlantic Canada English Language Arts Curriculum

ORGANIZING PRINCIPLE

Students are changing. Classrooms are changing. Theories of what it means to teach and learn are changing. Even notions of what constitutes a text are changing. For many of today's students, a text quite legitimately may be a favourite television show, movie, or video game (Neilsen 1998). Various types of media, as well as computers, are quickly redefining what counts as literacy. Yet, the rapid growth of the trade book industry for children and adolescents suggests that books are not dead or obsolete among our student population. All forms of texts need readers. Bringing students and texts together may very well be one of the most important functions of teachers in content area learning situations.

Bringing students and texts together, however, is not without its risks or its rewards. Without risks, teaching often lacks adventure and innovation. Adventuresome teachers have enough confidence in themselves to experiment with instructional practices, even if they are uncertain of the outcomes. They are willing to go out on a creative limb and then reflect on what they do and why. If there is such a thing as glory in teaching, it often accompanies the teacher who dares to depart from the norm.

Showing students how to use literacy to learn is worth doing—and worth doing well. The time it takes to plan literacy experiences will get you the results you want:

active and purposeful learning of text materials. Planning gives you a blueprint for making decisions. The blueprint may be for a text assignment or for multiple reading experiences involving a variety of printed and electronic texts. The organizing principle underscores the importance of active text learning in content area classrooms: **bringing students and texts together involves instructional plans and practices that result in active student engagement and collaboration.**

How teachers plan lessons and units of study is the cornerstone of content literacy and learning. As you prepare to read this chapter, ask yourself why *the classroom context*—the physical, psychological, and social environments that evolve from the interactions among teachers, students, and texts—is at the top of the chapter overview.

CHAPTER OVERVIEW

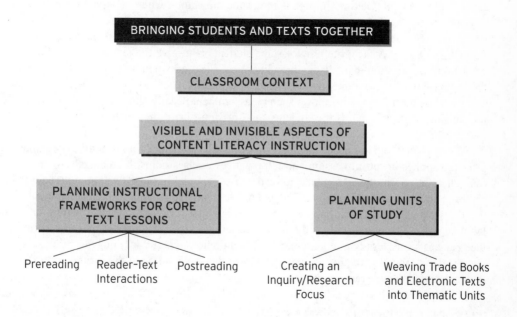

FRAME OF MIND

1. How can content area teachers plan instruction so that students will become actively engaged in reading and writing, listening and speaking, and viewing and representing? Why do students need structure?

2. What is involved in designing an instructional framework for a core text lesson?

3. How does planning a thematic unit help the teacher coordinate instructional activities and texts?

4. How do teachers create an inquiry/research focus for thematic units?

Good teachers know their subject matter. A colleague's professional competence is often judged by how well informed and up-to-date she or he is in a particular field. Good teachers also know that an intimate knowledge of a subject isn't in itself a sure ticket to success in the classroom. Another aspect of professional competence lies in getting content across to students.

Getting content across is always a challenging task. The challenge is more pronounced than ever when texts become tools for learning. Bringing learners and texts together isn't easy, but it isn't impossible either.

Assign-and-tell practices are deeply rooted in the culture of schools. A teacher shouting a reading assignment to students as they hustle out the door at the end of the period is probably a more common sight than we would like to admit. Under these conditions, the reading assignment is often purposeless. Why read it? The answer students give too frequently is, "Because it was assigned." The only real purpose for such reading is to get through the material. Getting through is the prime motivation when the assignment lacks any consideration of where students are going and how they will get there.

Answering questions at the end of the selection is an important part of the getting-through syndrome. A favourite ploy of some students is to give the teacher a three-liner: an answer to a question that fills up three lines on a sheet of paper. Regardless of whether the response is thoughtful or fully developed, three lines suffice.

The class discussion that follows such an assignment usually slips quickly away from the students to the teacher. If the students can't or won't learn the material through reading, they'll get it through lecture or other means.

Mark Twain wrote in *Life on the Mississippi*, "I'll learn him or I'll kill him!" The same principle applies in spirit to assign-and-tell practices in classrooms. If students learn anything, they learn that they don't have to read course material because there are alternative routes to acquiring the information. The end result is passive reading or no reading at all.

Texts should be an important part of the *classroom context* in which teaching and learning occur. The interactions and transactions among teachers, students, and texts form the very basis for classroom communication, comprehension, and learning. To bring students and texts together requires an appreciation and understanding of the various contexts in which teaching and learning occur.

THE CLASSROOM CONTEXT

What happens in a particular class on a particular day depends on the interactions that occur between the teacher, the students, and the material being studied. The classroom context, generally speaking, includes all the factors that influence what happens during teaching and learning. These factors operate on different levels.

More Than Simply a Room: The Physical Context

On one level, for example, the *physical context* influences what happens in the classroom. Space may restrict participation, depending on how a teacher interprets the situation. You see, the decision is still the teacher's to make. A mathematics teacher explained why she permitted small-group work in one class but not in another: "Several overly rambunctious students and not enough room to spread them apart." Some teachers use their surroundings to promote learning. Bulletin boards reflect themes or topics being studied; a display area prominently exhibits students' written work for others to read. Of course, some teachers remain oblivious of the physical environment that they and their students inhabit together. A room, after all, is just a room. Yet the physical environment of the classroom affects the nature and types of interactions that will occur. Straight rows of desks, for example, are conducive to classroom lectures and turn-taking routines in which students, one by one, recite answers to a teacher's questions.

A room isn't simply a room for teachers who seek to make the physical environment compatible with interactive learning. Interactive learning invites thinking, reading, writing, listening, speaking, viewing, representing, and sharing. Such classrooms are arranged for individuals rather than for the class as a whole; they welcome students as active participants rather than pigeonhole them as passive recipients (Noden & Vacca 1994). Various physical arrangements encourage interactive learning, such as the one illustrated in Figure 4.1 on page 108, but they depend on the size of the room and the furniture that is available.

With the design in Figure 4.1, a class can be organized for individual, group, or whole-class activities. Students are initially assigned seats at a combination of small and large tables. However, when the students work individually or in groups, they are free to abandon the assigned seating. The board (and/or screen for overhead transparencies or for the display from a data projector attached to a computer) occupies a central position in the room to accommodate whole-class study.

First and foremost, interactions are social and because they are social, interactions involve language use. The physical context, then, is necessarily tied to another dimension of the classroom: its social context.

Working Together: The Social Context

The *social context* for learning has a tremendous effect on what happens in the classroom. The social environment depends on what the teacher and students do together. Classroom learning is as much collaborative as it is individual. It often involves on-the-spot decision making: Who gets to do what? With whom? When? Where? Because most learning situations in the classroom are face-to-face encounters, they necessarily entail language. Most instructional routines, therefore, build on a series of conversational acts between teacher and students and between students and students. These acts are governed by rules (Wilkinson & Silliman 2000). Students quickly learn the rules and interact with the teacher or with other students accordingly.

In content area classrooms, communication between teacher and students, students and other students, and students and texts always occurs within a *language context*—that is, the *pragmatic*, or practical, situation in which reading, writing, talking, and listening take place.

A mathematics teacher assigns a chapter section on the topic "angles," as well as several problems to be solved using information from the text. The context includes the students' purpose, the reading task, the set of relationships established over time between the mathematics teacher and the students, the relationship of the students to the textbook, and all the conditions surrounding the learning situation. The context affects the way students interact with the text and the quality of that interaction. The students' purpose, for example, will influence how they read the material. The task—reading to solve problems—also affects how students approach the text and tackle the assignment.

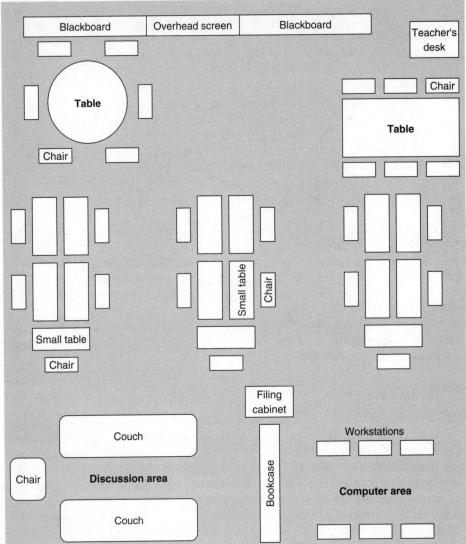

FIGURE 4.1   A Physical Arrangement Conducive to Social Interaction in the Classroom

Active Minds, Engaged Readers: The Psychological Context

The physical and social factors that influence the classroom context contribute heavily to the psychological and intellectual climate of content area classrooms. A healthy psychological context, as we have suggested in earlier chapters, is one that promotes student engagement. Engaged students are knowledgeable, strategic, motivated, and socially interactive. Engaged readers/viewers/listeners are architects of their own learning. They use prior knowledge and a variety of strategies to construct meaning with texts. Furthermore, they are internally motivated to succeed in learning tasks that involve literacy and choose to read and write as a way of knowing and enjoying (Guthrie & Wigfield 2000).

Creating the physical, social, and psychological environments for content literacy is no easy matter. Yet the classroom context is a source of study for teachers who search for meaning in what they do. How you influence the use of learning strategies—both explicitly and implicitly—depends on understanding the differences between the *visible* and *invisible* aspects of content literacy instruction.

VISIBLE AND INVISIBLE ASPECTS OF CONTENT LITERACY INSTRUCTION

Content literacy has the potential to play an important role in the school lives of children and adolescents. A credible knowledge base, grounded in theory and research on the relationships between reading and learning, supports the visible and invisible dimensions of content area reading instruction (Vacca 2001). The *visible aspects* of content literacy emphasize the explicit development of literacy strategies that enable students to think and learn with text. There is a convincing body of research that supports the role of strategic learning in students' literacy development (Pressley 2000). Content literacy instruction in the development and use of learning strategies is visible in the sense that teachers engage in explicit procedures to develop students' metacognition of strategies and the self-regulated use of these strategies to comprehend and learn with texts.

There are strong traditions in the reading field that underscore the importance of visible instruction in the development and use of reading strategies. Often, reading and language arts teachers have been charged with the responsibility of teaching reading strategies explicitly inside or outside of content area learning situations. Yet content area teachers also have a responsibility to show students, especially those who struggle with their texts, how to develop and use reading strategies to better understand and learn subject matter. In Chapter 11, we explore in more detail the role of visible, explicit instruction in the development and use of strategies for readers who struggle with text.

As crucial as explicit instruction may be to children and adolescents' literacy development, another equally important dimension of content literacy is its *invisible aspects* across the curriculum. Just as the metaphysical concept of "soul" is invisible to the physical concept of "body," the use of learning strategies should be an invisible dynamic underlying subject matter learning. When the invisible aspects of content literacy are operating in the classroom, the teacher is able to integrate reading, writing, listening, speaking, viewing, and representing, as well as subject matter learning, in seamless fashion, putting language and literacy to use to scaffold students' learning. To a casual observer of a text-related lesson, the invisible dimensions of content literacy would be difficult to categorize as a "reading lesson." What the observer might conclude, however, is that the teacher used a variety of instructional strategies that engaged students actively in learning the content under study.

Teachers make content literacy invisible through the design of well-planned text lessons and units of study. Someone in the world of business once said that 90 percent of your results come from activities that consume 10 percent of your time. When this saying is applied to education, the time teachers take to plan and organize active learning environments is time well spent. Planning appropriate frameworks for instruction may include the design of *core text lessons* and *thematic units* revolving around student-centred inquiry and self-selection from an array of text possibilities. A *core text lesson* implies that all of the students in class are reading the same text. These lessons usually evolve from textbook assignments or from a whole-class reading of a trade book, frequently referred to as a *core book study*. A *thematic unit*, by contrast, suggests a departure from an exclusive focus on a core text. Units are designed around central themes or concepts and free students to pursue questions that intrigue or puzzle them in relation to the theme or topic under study. Because inquiry is at the heart of a thematic unit, students will read, view, and listen to a wide range of texts related to the thematic explorations they are pursuing.

Lessons and units provide a blueprint for action. Whether the focus is on a core text or a thematic exploration, having a plan in advance of actual practice is simply good common sense. The organization of the lesson or unit is a thread that runs through content area instruction. A game plan is essential because students respond well to structure. When learning text material, they need to sense where they are going and how they will get there. Classroom experiences without rhyme or reason lack the direction and stability that students need to grow as learners.

Lessons should be general enough to include all students and flexible enough to allow the teacher to react intuitively and spontaneously when a particular plan is put into actual practice. In other words, lessons shouldn't restrict decisions about the instruction that is in progress; instead, they should encourage flexibility and change.

Some teachers, no doubt, will argue that a lesson plan is an educational artifact and that it's too restrictive for today's learners. Yet we're convinced that "to say that lesson planning is not appropriate is to say that thinking in advance of acting is inappropriate" (Mallan & Hersh 1972, p. 41). A good lesson plan provides a framework for making decisions—nothing more, nothing less.

Teachers tend to do their planning by focusing on activities they will do with students rather than proceeding from a list of objectives to instructional activities. The preparation of core text lessons should focus on what will be happening in the classroom—for example, what the teacher will be doing and what the students will be doing. The value of imagining should not be underestimated as a planning tool. Teachers think about instruction by envisioning in their minds how classroom activities are likely to unfold for a particular group of students in a particular instructional context. This thinking through of a lesson is like playing an imaginary videotape of the lesson in which the teacher plans the questions to be asked, the sequence of instructional activity, and the adjustments to be made should something not work.

Planning an Instructional Framework for Core Text Lessons

There's no one way to plan an effective core text lesson. The instructional framework (IF) offers the content area teacher a fairly representative approach to lesson organization (Herber 1978). Regardless of which type of plan is used, certain provisions must be made for any text-centred lesson to be effective. If we consider "reading" to mean, in general, any interaction with a text that might include viewing and listening, what the teacher does *before reading*, *during reading*, and *after reading* is crucial to active and purposeful reading.

The IF can help teachers envision a single lesson involving reading. A lesson doesn't necessarily take place in a single class session; several class meetings may be needed to achieve the objectives of the lesson. Nor do all the components of an IF necessarily receive the same emphasis in any given reading assignment; the difficulty of the material, students' familiarity with the topic, and your judgment all play a part when you decide on the sequence of activities you will organize. What the IF tells you is that readers need varying degrees of guidance. As we show throughout this book, there are prereading, reading, and postreading activities that support students' efforts to make meaning and construct knowledge through integrated language use. The components of an IF can be examined in Figure 4.2.

Prereading An IF that includes activity and discussion before reading reduces the uncertainty that students bring to an assignment. Prereading activities get students ready to read, to approach text material critically, and to seek answers to questions they have raised about the material. During the prereading phase of instruction, a teacher often places emphasis on one or more of the following: (1) motivating readers, (2) building and activating prior knowledge, (3) introducing key vocabulary and concepts, and (4) developing metacognitive awareness of the task demands of the assignment and the strategies necessary for effective learning.

A key factor related to motivation is activating students' interest in the text. However, considering how to motivate students, we must first raise a fundamental question: why should students be interested in this lesson? A teacher may even wish to consider whether he or she is interested in the material! If teachers are going to be models of enthusiasm for students, then the first step is to find something in the material about which they can get really excited. Enthusiasm—it is almost too obvious to suggest—is contagious.

Building and activating prior knowledge for a lesson and presenting key vocabulary and concepts are also essential to prereading preparation. In making decisions related to prior knowledge, it's important to review previous lessons in light of present material. What does yesterday's lesson have to do with today's? Will students make the connection to previously studied material? Sometimes several minutes of review before forging into

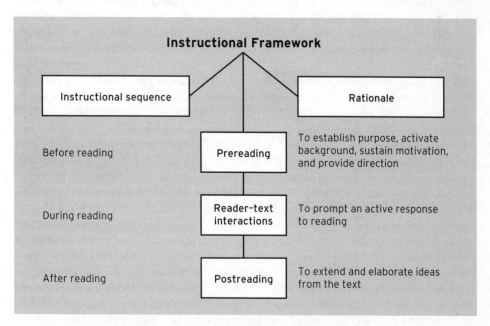

FIGURE 4.2   The Instructional Framework (IF) in Content Areas

uncharted realms of learning can make all the difference in linking new information to old. Furthermore, when deciding which vocabulary terms to single out for prereading instruction, we emphasize three questions that should be considered: What keywords will students need to understand? Are all the terms equally important? Which new words carry heavy concept loads? If students are dealing with a visual text, such as a map, they need to be introduced to the use of details such as, perhaps, the use of contour lines. If the text is oral or multimodal, students might need to understand the use of emphasis to communicate meaning.

Prereading may also include discussions that develop an awareness of the learning task at hand and of the strategies needed to handle the task effectively. These are metacognitive discussions. Providing direction is another way of saying that students will develop task knowledge and self-knowledge about their own learning strategies. Helping students analyze the reading task ahead of them and modelling a learning strategy that students will need during reading are two metacognitive activities that quickly come to mind. Here are some general questions to ask in planning for a metacognitive discussion: What are the most important ideas in the lesson? What strategies will students need to learn these ideas? Are the students *aware* of these strategies?

An IF also includes provisions for guiding the search for meaning during reading. In other words, students need to be shown how to think with texts as they read.

Reader–Text Interactions Teachers easily recognize the important parts of a text assignment. Most students don't. Instead, they tend to read (if indeed they read at all) every passage in every chapter in the same monotonous way. Each word, each sentence, each paragraph is treated with equal reverence. Visual material may be ignored altogether or regarded by many students with a sense of relief—a picture means that there are fewer words on the page! No wonder a gap often exists between the text material and the student.

The gap between text and student is especially wide in content areas where readers must interact with highly specialized and technical language. Musical notation is one example; another is mathematical notation. Mathematics texts are tersely written in a highly condensed system of language (Curry 1989). Students must perceive and decode mathematical symbols, construct meanings for specialized and technical vocabulary and concepts, analyze and interpret relationships, and apply interpretations to the solution of problems.

Study how two mathematics teachers adapt the lesson structure of the IF to scaffolding reader–text interactions. The first teaches classes in a middle school. The students are studying probability, and the objective of the teacher's IF is to ensure that the class will be able to determine the probability of a simple event. As part of prereading, the students explore the questions: Why do some sporting events, such as football, use the flipping of a coin to begin a game? Is the coin flip a fair way to decide which team will kick off? The questions tap into the students' prior knowledge and their conceptions (some naive, some sophisticated) of probability.

As part of the lesson, the teacher asks the students to use their mathematics journals to write definitions of several terms associated with probability: *odds*, *chances*, *outcomes*, *events*, and *sample space*. The students' definitions are discussed as the teacher builds on what the students know to arrive at a set of class definitions of the terms. He then pairs the students in "study buddy" teams and asks them to use what they already know about probability to read the assigned section from the textbook. The "study buddies" read the text section and complete the "selective reading guide" illustrated in Box 4.1.

BOX 4.1	**Using a Selective Reading Guide in Mathematics to Scaffold Reader-Text Interactions**

Before reading, think about the ways in which we have defined *probability* in class discussion. Now compare our definitions with the one in the book. Develop in your own words a definition of *probability* based on what you know and what you have read.

Probability: _____

Now read and define other key terms in this section.

Outcomes: _____

Events: _____

Sample space: _____

Example 1. Read the example and answer the following:

What is the probability of rolling a 5? _____

How do you know? _____

Example 2. Read this example slowly, and when you finish:

Define odds in favour: _____

Example 3. Put on your thinking caps to answer the following:

What are the odds? _____

What is the difference between finding the probability and finding the odds? _____

You're on your own!

Complete the assigned problems with your study buddy.

Together, the study buddies discuss the assigned material as they work through the guide. Selective reading guides are one way of scaffolding reader–text interactions by providing a "road map" to the important concepts in the material. These guides are discussed more fully in Chapter 10.

The second teacher, a secondary school mathematics teacher, also adapts the structure of the IF to guide students' interactions with the text and to help them make important connections between reading and mathematics. When she first started teaching, she noticed with some dismay that students almost never read the text. Nor did they talk about mathematics with one another. Therefore, she makes a conscious effort to incorporate literacy and cooperative learning principles whenever instructional situations warrant them.

One such situation occurred when her students were studying the concepts of ratio, proportion, and percentage. The focus of the lesson was a section that dealt with the development of scale drawings as an application of proportion. She initiated the lesson by having students take five minutes to write "admit slips." *Admit slips* are students' "tickets of admission" to the lesson. The teacher can use them in a variety of ways to find out what students are feeling and thinking as they begin the class period. A more detailed discussion of admit slips occurs in Chapter 8 within the larger context of using writing as a tool for learning subject matter.

The teacher triggered admit-slip writing with the prompt: "If you had a younger brother or sister in grade 6, how would you describe a scale drawing in words that he or she would understand?" Using half-sheets of paper distributed by the teacher, the students wrote freely for several minutes until instructed to "wind down" and complete the thoughts on which they were working. The teacher collected the admit slips and shared a few of the students' descriptions with the class. The discussion that followed revolved around the students' conceptions of scale drawings and what it means to be "in proportion."

The teacher then formed five-member cooperative groups to guide students' interactions with the text section on scale drawings. Each team was assigned to draw a scale model of the recreation room in its "dream house." First, the teams had to decide what facilities would be included in the recreation room. Once they developed the list of facilities, the team members read the text section and discussed how to develop a scale that would fit all of the facilities into the space provided for each team at the chalkboard. The lesson concluded with the teams' describing their scale drawings. The teacher then asked the students to regroup and develop a list of the important ideas related to scale models.

Postreading   Guidance during reading bridges the gap between students and text so that students learn how to distinguish important from less important ideas, to perceive relationships, and to respond actively to meaning.

Ideas encountered before and during reading may need clarification and elaboration after reading. Postreading activities create a structure that refines emerging concepts. For example, a social studies teacher who was nearing completion of a unit on Southeast Asia asked her students to reflect on their reading by using the activity in Box 4.2. The writing prompt in part II of the postreading activity is based on a reading–writing strategy called RAFT, which is described in Chapter 8. The writing and follow-up discussion refined and extended the students' thinking about the ideas under study. The questions, "Who is best qualified?" and "Who is the specialist in the field?" prompted students to sort out what they had learned. The teacher provided just enough structure by listing topics from various facets of Southeast Asian culture to focus students' thinking and help them make distinctions.

Activities such as the one in Box 4.2 reinforce and extend ideas. Writing/representing activities, study guides, and other postreading elements are springboards to thinking and form the basis for discussing and articulating the ideas developed through reading.

Some Examples of Core Text Lessons

Middle School Science Class   A group of middle school students were assigned a text selection on how bees communicate. The text told the story of Karl von Frisch, an entomologist who had studied bees for years, and focused on his experimental observations

BOX 4.2	**Postreading Activity for a Southeast Asia Lesson**

I. *Directions:* A rice farmer, a Buddhist monk, a government official, and a geographer all feel competent to speak on any of the following topics. Who is really best qualified? Who is the specialist in each field? On the blank line preceding each topic, place the letter of the correct specialist.

A. Rice farmer
B. Buddhist monk
C. Government official
D. Geographer

    _____   1. The forested regions of Thailand

    _____   2. The life of Siddhartha Gautama

    _____   3. The amount of rice exported each year

    _____   4. The monsoon rains in Southeast Asia

    _____   5. Harvesting rice

    _____   6. The causes of suffering

    _____   7. The art of meditation

    _____   8. The Me Nam River Basin

    _____   9. The amount of rice produced per hectare

    _____ 10. The pagodas in Thailand

    _____ 11. The number of Buddhists living in Bangkok

    _____ 12. The virtues of a simple life

    _____ 13. The rice festival in Bangkok

    _____ 14. The Temple of the Emerald Buddha

    _____ 15. The attainment of nirvana

II. *Directions:* Pretend you are the rice farmer, the Buddhist monk, the government official, or the geographer. Write a "guest editorial" for the local newspaper revealing your professional attitude toward and opinion about the approaching monsoon season.

leading to the discovery of bees' communication behaviour. The teacher's objectives were to (1) involve students in an active reading and discussion of the text assignment and (2) have them experience some of the steps scientists go through when performing laboratory or field experiments.

Here's how she planned her instructional activities:

I. Prereading

   A. Before introducing the text, determine what students now know about bees.

1. Who has observed bees close up?
2. What do you notice about bees that seems unique to them?
3. When you see a bee, is it usually by itself or in a group?
4. Why do you think bees swarm?

B. Connect students' responses to these questions to the text assignment. Introduce the story and its premise.

C. Form small groups of four students each, and direct each group to participate in the following situation:

Karl von Frisch worked with bees for many years. He was puzzled by something he had observed again and again. When he set up a table on which he placed little dishes of scented honey, he attracted bees. Usually, he had to wait hours or days for a bee to discover the feeding place. But as soon as one bee discovered it, many more came to it in a short time. Evidently, the first bee was able to communicate the news of food to the other bees in its hive.

Pretend that you are a scientist helping von Frisch discover how bees communicate. How do they tell each other where food is located? List 10 things you could do to find out the answers to this question.

D. Have the students share their group's top five ideas with the class, and write them on the chalkboard.

II. Reader–Text Interactions

A. Assign the selection to be read in class.

B. During reading, direct students to note the similarities and differences between their ideas on the board and von Frisch's experimental procedures.

III. Postreading (Day 2)

A. Discuss the previous day's reading activity. How many of the students' ideas were similar to von Frisch's procedures? How many were different?

B. Extend students' understanding of the inquiry process that scientists, such as von Frisch, follow. Divide the class into groups of four students to work on the following exercise:

All scientists follow a pattern of research to find answers to the questions they have about different subjects. For example, von Frisch wanted to know about how bees communicated. He (1) formed a question, (2) formulated an experiment to answer the question, (3) observed his subjects in the experiment, and (4) answered the question based on his observations.

Now it's your turn! Tomorrow we are going on a field trip to the park to experiment with ants and food. Your first job as a scientist is to devise a question and an experiment to fit your question. After we return, you will write your observations and the answer to your question. You will be keeping notes on your experiment while we are in the park.

Question: _____

Experiment: _____

Observations/Sketches: _____

Answer: _____

C. Conduct the experiment the next day at the park. Each group will be given a small amount of food to place near an existing anthill. The students will make visual/verbal notes and take them back to the classroom. Each group's discoveries will be discussed in class.

Secondary School French Class By way of contrast, study how a secondary school French teacher taught Guy de Maupassant's short story "L'Infirme" to an advanced class of language students. The story is about two men riding in a train. Henri Bonclair is sitting alone in a train car when another passenger, Revalière, enters the car. This fellow traveller is handicapped, having lost his leg during the war. Bonclair wonders about the type of life he must lead. As he looks at the handicapped man, Bonclair senses that he met him a few years earlier. He asks the man if he is not the person he met. Revalière is that man. Now Bonclair remembers that Revalière was to be married. He wonders if he got married before or after losing the leg or at all. Bonclair inquires. No, Revalière has not married, refusing to ask the girl to put up with a deformed man. However, he is on his way to see her, her husband, and her children. They are all very good friends. The French teacher formulated five objectives for the lesson:

1. To teach vocabulary dealing with the concept of "infirmity"
2. To foster students' ability to make inferences about the reading material from their own knowledge
3. To foster students' ability to predict what will happen in the story in light of the background they bring to the story
4. To foster students' ability to evaluate their predictions once they have read the story
5. To use the story as a basis for writing a dialogue in French

Two of the activities, the *graphic organizer* and the *inferential strategy*, used in the French teacher's plan are explained in depth in Part 2 of this book. The steps in the plan are outlined here:

I. Prereading
   A. Begin the lesson by placing the title of the story on the board: "L'Infirme." Ask students to look at the title and compare it to a similar English word (or words). Determine very generally what the story is probably about. (A handicapped person.)
   B. On the overhead, introduce keywords used in the story by displaying a *graphic organizer*:

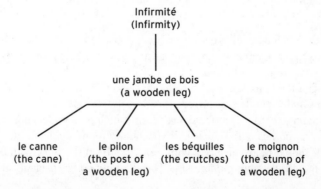

Infirmité
(Infirmity)

une jambe de bois
(a wooden leg)

le canne   le pilon   les béquilles   le moignon
(the cane)   (the post of   (the crutches)   (the stump of
                 a wooden leg)   a wooden leg)

C. Use the *inferential strategy.* Ask and discuss with the class the following three sets of questions. Have the students write down their responses.

1. *Vous avez peut-être vu quelqu'un qui est très estropiè à cause de la perte d'une jambe ou d'un bras. Qu'est-ce qui traverse votre esprit? De quoi est-ce que vous vous demandez?*
    (You may have seen someone who is very crippled because of the loss of a leg or an arm. When you see such a person, what crosses your mind? What do you wonder about?)

2. *Dans l'histoire, Bonclair voit ce jeune infirme qui a perdu la jambe. Qu'est-ce que vous pensez traverse son esprit?*
    (In the story, Bonclair sees this crippled young man who has lost his leg. What do you think crosses his mind?)

3. *Quand vous voyez quelqu'un qui a l'air vaguement familier, qu'est-ce que vous voulez faire? Qu'est-ce que vous faites? Quels sont souvent les rèsultats?*
    (When you see someone who looks vaguely familiar, what do you want to do? What do you do? What are often the results?)

4. *Dans cette histoire, Bonclair se souvient vaguement qu'il a fait la connaissance de cet infirme. Prèdites ce qu'il fera et prèdites les rèsultats.*
    (In this story, Bonclair remembers vaguely having met this cripple. Predict what he does and the results.)

5. *Imaginez que vous êtes fiancè(e) à un jeune homme ou à une jeune femme. Puis vous avez un accident qui vous rend estropiè(e). Qu'est-ce que vous feriez? Voudriez-vous se marier? Pourriez-vous compter sur l'autre de vous aimer encore?*
    (Imagine that you are engaged to a young man or woman. Then you have an accident that leaves you crippled. What would you do? Would you still want to marry? Could you still expect the other to love you?)

6. *Dans notre histoire, Revalière a eu un accident juste avant son marriage. Prèdites ce qu'il fera et ce qu'il comptera de la jeune fille. Prèdites les rèsultats.*
    (In our story, Revalière has had an accident just before his marriage. Predict what he did and what he expected of the young woman. Predict the results.)

II. Reader–Text Interactions

A. Assign the reading, instructing the students to keep in mind their prior knowledge and predictions.

B. Ask them to note possible changes in their predictions.

III. Postreading

A. After the reading, conduct a follow-up discussion with the class. Relate their predictions to what actually happened, noting how our background knowledge and experience of the world lead us to think along certain lines.

B. Through the discussion, note the changes and refinements in the students' predictions and when they occurred.

C. *Vocabulary exercise.* Distribute a sheet on which is reproduced a *vocabulary-context reinforcement exercise.* All vocabulary items studied in the prereading section should be listed, along with sentences from the story with blanks to be filled in with the appropriate word. There should be fewer blanks than word choices. Allow 7 or 8 minutes for this exercise; then ask the students to read the complete sentence (in clear French).

D. Have the class form groups of four with at least one male and one female in each group. Establish the following situation:

Une jeune fille vient d'être estropièe dans un accident de natation. Son fiancè lui a tèlèphonè. Il veut lui parler. Qu'est-ce qu'il veut lui dire? On frappe à la porte. C'est lui.

(A young lady was recently crippled in a swimming accident. Her fiancè has called her. He wants to talk to her. What does he want to talk about? There is a knock at the door. It is he.)

1. Think together, drawing on your past knowledge or experience of situations like this. Write a 15- to 20-line group dialogue in French between the girl and her fiancè. What might he have to tell her? How might she react?
2. Select a boy and a girl to present the group's dialogue to the class.

Middle School Music Class In an ambitious core text lesson, a grade 6 music teacher, Donna Mitchell, combines literacy-related practices within the context of studying the components of an opera and engaging students in the understanding and appreciation of Richard Wagner's opera *The Flying Dutchman*. As part of the prereading component of the lesson, students worked in teams to complete a *cloze activity sheet* (see Box 4.3 on page 120) in the form of a playbill. (We described the cloze procedure as an assessment tool in the previous chapter.) Cloze as an instructional activity is described in Chapter 5.

The playbill serves to activate students' prior knowledge about opera. Students fill in the playbill with the words and names provided at the bottom of the playbill activity sheet in Box 4.3. When the student teams complete the activity, they share their answers with the class. Mrs. Mitchell then reads to the class a brief biographical sketch of Richard Wagner. She directs the student teams to check their playbills after listening to some of the events and highlights in Wagner's life to determine if the biographical sketch cleared up any of the teams' questions related to the cloze activity. Students then brainstorm what *The Flying Dutchman* is about.

As part of the reader–text interactions phase of the lesson, Mrs. Mitchell dims the lights in the classroom and invites students to close their eyes as they listen to the overture to *The Flying Dutchman*. In this context, the term *overture* is redefined by the class. After establishing the mood of the opera, students rethink their ideas about what the story is about. During the next several class sessions, Mrs. Mitchell reads the story, stopping each day at a turning point of the story to pique students' curiosity. She ends each read-aloud with an enthusiastic, "To be continued!" and then engages students in a discussion of the story that has occurred thus far. Toward the end of each discussion, she elicits predictions about what the students think will happen next. Throughout this process, excerpts of the music are played at appropriate places in the lessons.

At the conclusion of the story, students enter the postreading phase of the lesson. Mrs. Mitchell follows procedures associated with the discussion web strategy (see Chapter 7). The discussion web is a collaborative strategy that requires students to explore multiple perspectives around a key question. First, the students work in "think-pair-share" dyads to respond to the question, "Did Senta need to throw herself off the cliff into the sea?" from yes/no perspectives. They then form groups of four to share their perspectives in a larger forum and to reach a conclusion, which the groups share with the class.

BOX 4.3	Cloze Playbill for the Opera, *The Flying Dutchman*

The Flying Dutchman

An _____ by _____

_____ in _____ with _____

subtitles on overhead screen

_____–Taken from a Norwegian legend

_____–The shores of Norway

_____–Maestro George Szell

Chorus–_____

_____–Constructed and designed by Marc Chagall

_____–Designed by Mademoiselle Choé

• •

_____–The Cleveland Orchestra

_____–Aboard the ship

Dutchman–Sung by _____

Daland–Sung by _____

_____–On Shore

Senta–Sung by _____

German	Act II	Setting	Spoken	Sung
Costumes	Choreographer	Conductor	Libretto	Scenery
Opera	Richard Wagner	Overture	Tenor	Baritone
English	Townspeople	Soprano	Sailors	Act I

Source: Donna Kowallek Mitchell © 2000. Reprinted with permission.

These text lessons all have the same underlying structure. Each plan provides a set of experiences designed to move students from preparation to interaction with the text to extension and elaboration of the concepts in the material under study. The lessons show how teachers translate knowledge about content area reading into plans for active learning.

How teachers imagine instructional activities in core text lessons vary by grade level and the sophistication of the students. The same is true of developing plans for a thematic unit. In the next section, we go beyond planning core text lessons to decisions related to thematic learning involving multiple literacy experiences.

Planning Thematic Units

Thematic units organize instruction around objectives, activities, print and nonprint resources, and inquiry experiences. A thematic unit may be designed for a single discipline or may be interdisciplinary, integrating two or more content areas. In secondary schools, where content area teachers are teamed in learning "communities" or "families," opportunities abound to develop interdisciplinary thematic units. Interdisciplinary units require coordination and cooperation by all of the content area teachers teamed within a learning community. Team planning helps students make connections not otherwise possible among many knowledge domains. Canso High School in Canso, Nova Scotia, for example, has developed a thematic unit around the topic of offshore energy. Students are able to take an interdisciplinary look at this topic through the perspectives of physics, chemistry, and history.

The thematic unit is a planning tool that includes (1) a title reflecting the theme or topic of the unit, (2) the major concepts to be learned, (3) the texts and information sources to be studied by students, (4) the unit's instructional activities, and (5) provisions for assessing what students have learned from the unit.

Content analysis is a major part of teacher preparation in the development of a unit of study. Content analysis results in the *what* of learning—the major concepts and understandings that students should learn from reading the unit materials. Through content analysis, the major concepts become the objectives for the unit. It doesn't matter whether these content objectives are stated in behavioural terms. What really matters is that you know which concepts students will interact with and develop. Therefore, it's important to decide on a manageable number of the most important understandings to be gained from the unit. This means setting priorities; it's impossible to cover every aspect of the material that students will read or to which they will be exposed.

A thematic unit on spatial relationships for a secondary school art class provides an example of how a teacher planned content objectives, activities, and materials. First, she listed the major concepts to be taught in the unit:

1. Humans are aware of the space about them as functional, decorative, and communicative.

2. Space organized intuitively produces an aesthetic result, but a reasoned organization of space also leads to a pleasing outcome if design is considered.

3. Occupied space and unoccupied space each has positive and negative effects on mood and depth perception.

4. The illusion of depth can be created on a two-dimensional surface.

5. The direction and balance of lines or forms create feelings of tension, force, and equilibrium in the space that contains them.

6. Seldom in nature is the order of objects so perfect as to involve no focal point or force or tension.

Then she developed the activities and identified the texts to be used in the unit (see Figure 4.3 on page 122). As you study the figure, keep in mind that some of the text-related activities suggested will be explored later in this book.

Text-Related Activities	Texts
1. Graphic organizer	Graham Collier, <u>Form, Space, and Vision</u>
2. Vocabulary and concept bulletin board	
3. Prereading	Chapter 3, Collier
4. Prereading	Chapters 6 and 7
5. Art journal	Chapters 6 and 7
6. K–W–L	Chapter 11
7. Vocabulary exercise	Chapter 3
8. Vocabulary exercise	Chapters 6 and 7
9. Vocabulary exercise	Chapter 11
10. Student's choice (list of projects for research study)	H. Botten, Do <u>You See What I See?</u>
	H. Helfman, <u>Creating Things That Move</u>
	D. McAgy, <u>Going for a Walk with a Line</u>
	L. Kampmann, <u>Creating with Space and Construction</u>
	G. LeFevre, <u>Junk Sculpture</u>
	J. Lynch, <u>Mobile Design</u>
11. Hands-On	
Ink dabs	
Straw painting	
Dry seed arrangement	
Cardboard sculpture	
Positive-negative cutouts	
Perspective drawing	<u>Calder's Universe</u>
Large-scale class sculpture	
Mobiles	
Space frames	Displays of artist's works with questionnaires
12. Filmstrip	to be filled out about them
13. Field trip to studio of a sculptor	
14. Field trip to museum	
15. Learning corner	

FIGURE 4.3 **Activities and Texts**

The actual framework of thematic units will vary. For example, you might organize a unit entirely on a sequence of lessons from assignments in a single textbook. This type of organization is highly structured and is even restrictive, in the sense that it often precludes the use of various kinds of other literature rich in content and substance. However, a thematic unit can be planned so that the teacher will (1) use a single textbook to begin the unit and then branch out into multiple-text study and differentiated activities, (2) organize the unit entirely on individual or group inquiry and research, or (3) combine single-text instruction with multiple-text activities and inquiry.

Branching out provides the latitude to move from a core text lesson to independent learning activities. The move from single- to multiple-information sources exposes students to a wide range of texts that may be better suited to their needs and interests (see Figure 4.4).

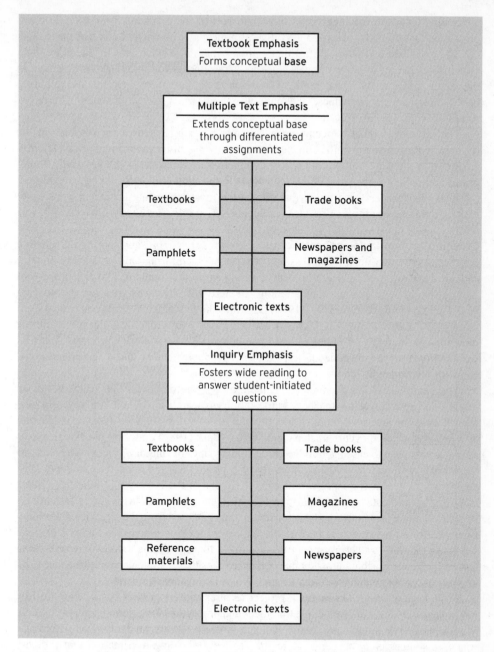

FIGURE 4.4 "Branching Out" in a Thematic Unit: Using a Wide Range of Texts

Although a thematic unit may include multiple-text opportunities, the textbook is not necessarily excluded from the unit. Thematic unit planning simply provides more options to coordinate a variety of information sources. In single-discipline units, prereading, reading, and postreading activities become an integral part of unit teaching.

Listing texts and resources is an important part of the preparation for a single-discipline unit. One reason a unit is so attractive as a means of organization is that the teacher can go beyond the textbook—or, for that matter, bypass it. A wide array of literature, both imaginative and informational, gives students opportunities for an intense involvement in the theme under study. Trade books, electronic texts, pamphlets, periodicals, reference books, newspapers, magazines, and audiovisual materials are all potential alternative routes to acquiring information.

The internet is quickly becoming a valuable planning resource for teachers in the development of thematic units. You can access many useful ideas for integrating electronic texts into thematic units of study. By conducting a search using the keywords, "integrated technology + thematic units," you will find a number of websites to be explored. For example, teachers have found that one of the most interesting Canadian websites to visit on the internet for planning ideas is SchoolNet, at http://www.schoolnet.ca.

Creating an Inquiry/Research Focus Gathering, organizing, and sharing information are crucial to both academic success and success in our information-rich society. Inquiry should, therefore, play a major role in learning important content, and the process of inquiry should be woven into thematic units of study. *The Western Canadian Protocol for Collaboration in Basic Education* (1998) describes the fundamental skills and strategies of inquiry as follows: "Students learn to activate prior knowledge, ask questions, define directions for inquiry, and gather and evaluate information for specific purposes. They also learn to manage time, meet deadlines, explore personal questions, and discover additional areas for investigation."

The centrepiece of a thematic unit, therefore, is the emphasis that teachers put on inquiry and research. How teachers guide inquiry/research projects is the key to a successful unit. The process of inquiry, like the process of writing that we describe in Chapter 9, works best when it occurs in steps and stages. Clark (1987) draws on his experience as a former journalist to ease his middle-grade students into the inquiry process. The students use human resources from the community to conduct their inquiries. The students must decide whom they will interview and what the focus of the inquiry will be. They collect data for their projects through interviews. Clark then encourages his budding researchers to write about their inquiries using information they gathered from the interviews. He identifies the following stages as part of the inquiry process in which his students engage: searching for ideas, gathering and sifting, finding a focus, building momentum, rethinking and revising, and reaching an audience. Clark realizes that if students are to be successful, he must encourage inquiry through learner choice and teacher guidance.

Each stage of an inquiry/research project requires careful support by a teacher. In Box 4.4 on pages 126 and 127, we outline the stages and procedures for guiding inquiry/ research.

When teachers simply assign and evaluate research reports, students often paraphrase whatever sources come to hand rather than actively pursuing information that they are eager to share with others. Genuine inquiry is always a messy endeavour characterized by false starts, unexpected discoveries, changes in direction, and continual decision making. Too much guidance can be as dangerous as too little.

In an in-depth study of two middle school research projects, Rycik (1994) found that teachers may lose their focus on genuine inquiry as they establish procedures for guiding all students to complete a project successfully. The teachers in the study were very concerned with providing sufficient guidance, so they broke their projects down into a series of discrete steps (such as making note cards) that could be taught, completed, and evaluated separately. As the projects moved forward, the teachers gradually came to believe that mastering the procedure for each step was the primary outcome of the project, even more important than learning content information.

Rycik (1994) concluded that inquiry should not be confined to one big research paper because teachers cannot introduce and monitor the wide range of searching, reading, thinking, and writing skills that students need to complete such projects. Good researchers, like good writers, must learn their craft through frequent practice in a variety of contexts. This means that students should research from a variety of sources and express their findings for a variety of audiences in a variety of forms. Some recommendations for integrating research into the classroom routine include the following:

- Make identifying questions and problems as important in your classroom as finding answers.
- Provide frequent opportunities to compare, contrast, and synthesize information from multiple sources.
- Present findings of research in a variety of products and formats, including charts, graphs, and visual or performing arts.
- Discuss possible sources for information presented in the class or for answering questions posed by the teacher or students (e.g., personal interviews, diaries, experiments).

The research process opens the way to reading many different kinds of materials. Developing inquiry-centred projects helps students understand and synthesize what they're learning.

The teacher must carefully plan inquiry-centred projects, giving just the right amount of direction to allow students to explore and discover ideas on their own. The research process isn't a do-your-own-thing proposition, for budding researchers need structure. Many a project has been wrecked on the shoals of nondirection. The trick is to strike a balance between teacher guidance and student self-reliance. A research project must have just enough structure to give students (1) a problem focus, (2) physical and intellectual freedom, (3) an environment in which they can obtain data, and (4) feedback situations in which to report the results of their research.

Weaving Trade Books and Electronic Texts into Thematic Units The literature-based movement in elementary schools serves as a prototype for the use of trade books in middle and secondary school classrooms. In addition, technology makes it possible to access and explore information sources through CD-ROM programs, electronic books, and the internet. Although textbooks may be used to provide an information base, the foundation for individual and group inquiry into a theme or topic is built on students' use of multiple information resources, both printed and electronic. Trade books and electronic texts are geared to students' interests and inquiry needs.

Say that in a middle-grade classroom, students are engaged in a thematic unit on the environment. What might you observe over several weeks? For starters, the teacher may conduct several whole-class lessons at the beginning of the unit using the textbook to develop a conceptual framework for individual and group investigation. As the weeks progress, however, whole-class activity is less prevalent. Instead, small groups work on research projects or in discussion teams using Monica Hughes's *The Other Place* (1999)

BOX 4.4	**Procedures for Guiding Inquiry/ Research Projects**

I. Raise questions, identify interests, organize information.

  A. Discuss interest areas related to the unit of study.

  B. Engage in goal setting.
  1. Arouse curiosities.
  2. Create awareness of present levels of knowledge.

  C. Pose questions relating to each area and/or subarea.
  1. "What do you want to find out?"
  2. "What do you want to know about?"
  3. Record the questions or topics.
  4. "What do you already know about?"

  D. Organize information; have students make predictions about likely answers to gaps in knowledge.
  1. Accept all predictions as possible answers.
  2. Encourage thoughtful speculations in a nonthreatening way.

II. Select materials.

  A. Use visual materials.
  1. Trade books and encyclopedias
  2. Magazines, catalogues, directories
  3. Newspapers and comics
  4. Indexes, atlases, almanacs, dictionaries, readers' guides, computer catalogues
  5. Films, filmstrips, slides
  6. Videotapes, television programs
  7. Electronic texts: CD-ROMs, website documents, videodisks

  B. Use nonvisual materials.
  1. Audiotapes
  2. Records
  3. Radio programs
  4. Field trips

  C. Use human resources.
  1. Interviews
  2. Letters
  3. On-site visits
  4. Discussion groups
  5. Email
  6. Listservs
  7. Chat rooms

  D. Encourage self-selection of materials.
  1. "What can I understand?"
  2. "What gives me the best answers?"

III. Guide the information search.

    A. Encourage active research.

        1. Reading

        2. Writing

        3. Listening

        4. Speaking

        5. Viewing

        6. Representing

    B. Facilitate with questions.

        1. "How are you doing?"

        2. "Can I help you?"

        3. "Do you have all the materials you need?"

        4. "Can I help you with ideas you don't understand?"

    C. Have students keep records.

        1. Learning log that includes plans, procedures, sketches, notes, and rough drafts

        2. Records of sources with complete citations

        3. Record of conferences with the teacher

IV. Consider different forms of writing.

    A. Initiate a discussion of sharing techniques.

    B. Encourage a variety of writing and representing forms.

        1. Essay or paper

        2. Lecture to a specific audience

        3. Case study

        4. Story: adventure, science fiction, other genre

        5. Dialogue, conversation, interview

        6. Dramatization/demonstration

        7. Commentary or editorial

        8. Thumbnail sketch

        9. Illustration/diagram/chart

      10. Website

V. Guide the composing process.

    A. Help students organize information.

    B. Guide first-draft writing/representing.

    C. Encourage responding, revising, and redrafting.

    D. "Publish" finished products through individual/group presentations.

and *Keeper of the Isis Light* (2000) and Lydia Bailey's (1999) *Animals at Risk.* Individual students are also working on inquiries with books such as Wayne Grady's *The Quiet Limit of the World* (1997) and Ric Careless's *To Save the Wild Earth* (1997), and films such as the National Film Board's *Red Run* (2001).

In addition, the students are conducting research online, tapping into the rich information resources of the World Wide Web. Several students investigate the websites of Canadian Wildlife Federation, Canadian Wildlife Service, and Bird Studies Canada. Toward the end of the unit, the class completes culminating activities, which may involve panel discussions, report writing, and oral/visual presentations in which individuals or groups share knowledge gleaned from the various activities and texts. In this class, what you would observe is that everyone has something to contribute.

Brozo and Tomlinson (1986) define several steps that facilitate the uses of trade books in thematic units. We have expanded their plan to include electronic texts.

1. *Identify salient concepts that become the content objectives for the unit.*

   a. What are the driving human forces behind the events?
   b. What patterns of behaviour need to be studied?
   c. What phenomena have affected or may affect ordinary people in the future?

2. *Identify appropriate trade books, websites, and software that will help in the teaching of these concepts.*

3. *Teach the unit.*

   a. Use the textbook, trade books, and electronic texts interchangeably.
   b. Use strategies such as read-aloud in which a trade book or electronic text becomes a schema builder before students read the textbook.
   c. Use trade books and electronic texts to elaborate and extend content and concepts related to the unit.

4. *Follow up.*

   a. Engage students in strategies and activities that involve collaboration, inquiry, and various forms of expression and meaning construction.
   b. Evaluate students' learning by observing how they interpret and personalize new knowledge.

Here are two examples of thematic units at the middle and secondary school levels. The first integrates trade books and internet sites; the second combines textbook study with trade books.

GRADE 8 LIFE SCIENCE: DIVERSITY OF WILDLIFE—BIRDS. A life science teacher in a middle school uses a textbook and literature interchangeably for a unit on birds within a study on the diversity of wildlife. In his classes, students have already mastered the concept of warm-blooded animals. Birds are the first group of warm-blooded animals that the students study. Because the students have varying degrees of prior knowledge about birds, the unit is focused on a wide variety of species and the economic and aesthetic value of birds.

The students engage first in a study of the relationship between birds and reptiles. Then they explore the characteristics of birds as a class of animals and the many and varied adaptations birds have made to their environment, including adaptations for flight and migration. The students also examine the importance of birds as indicators of the health of the environment. The final phase of the unit centres on the economic and aesthetic value of birds. Figure 4.5 displays the relationships among the key concepts that students will master as a result of their studies.

The teacher weaves trade books and internet investigations into the unit. Students engage in a variety of activities. For example, the teacher supplements textbook study with outside readings. He also requires the use of a science notebook in which students set aside a section to respond to the texts they are reading as part of the unit. The centrepiece of the unit, however, is a group investigation of birds. The students participate in groups to investigate several of the main concepts of the unit. Each group member investigates a different concept and then reports his or her findings to the group. As preparation for the report, students temporarily meet in expert groups (all of the students in an expert group are responsible for teaching the same concept to their teammates) to share and discuss what they are investigating. Box 4.5 on pages 130 and 131 contains a list of information resources available to the students during their investigations.

The teacher also uses different types of texts as part of direct instruction in the teaching of specific concepts. This approach often results in an opportunity to combine reading, writing, and representing experiences. For example, the teacher will read to the class poems about birds such as Randall Jarrell's "Bird of Night," Robert Francis's "Seagulls," and Ogden Nash's "Up from the Egg: The Confessions of a Nuthatch Avoider" and excerpts from novels such as Ted Harrison's *The Blue Raven* and Farley Mowat's *Owls in the Family*. After each reading, the students write and sketch in their notebooks for three minutes on how the poem made them feel. They then share their responses with others in the class. Next, the students are asked to write for another three minutes on a memory they may have associated with the poem that influenced their initial response. As another part of their response to the poem, the students choose one word that they believe summarizes the poem and write about the reasons for their choice. As a follow-up activity, the students write haiku and illustrate their poems using birds as the basic theme.

GRADE 10 CANADIAN HISTORY: RIEL REBELLIONS. A Canadian history teacher designed this unit to explain the interrelatedness of the events of the Riel rebellions and their effects on later Canadian history.

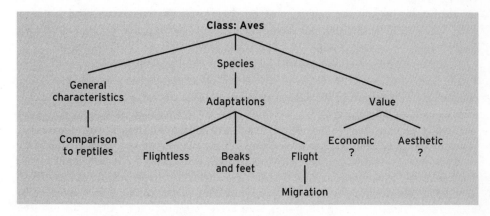

FIGURE 4.5 **Graphic Organizer for a Unit on Birds**

BOX 4.5	**Information Resources for a Unit on Diversity of Wildlife: Birds**

TEXTBOOK

Roberts, D. (1991). *Science Directions 8.* Edmonton, AB: Arnold Publishing.

NONFICTION

Alsop, F. J. (2002). *Birds of Canada.* Toronto: Dorling Kindersley.

Bull, J., & Ferrand, J., Jr. (1977). *The Audubon Society Field Guide to North American Birds.* New York: Knopf.

Canning, R., & Cannings, S. (2002). *The BC Roadside Naturalist.* Vancouver: Greystone Publishing.

Dawe, N. (2000). *The Hummingbird Book and Feeders.* Toronto: Somerville House.

Federation of Ontario Naturalists. (1997). *A Nature Guide to Ontario.* Toronto: University of Toronto Press.

Jonker, P., & Rowe, J. (2001). *The Sand Dunes of Lake Athabasca.* Saskatoon: University Extension Press.

Kavanagh, J. (1993). *Nature BC: An Illustrated Guide to Common Plants and Animals.* Vancouver: Lone Pine Publishing.

Robbins, C. S., Bruun, B., & Zim, H. (1966). *A Guide to Field Identification: Birds of North America.* New York: Golden Press.

Schutz, W. E. (1970). *How to Attract, House, and Feed Birds.* New York: Collier.

Stokes, D., & Stokes, L. (1987). *The Bird Feeder Book.* New York: Little, Brown.

Suzuki, D., & Vanderlinden, K. (2001). *Eco-fun: Great Projects, Experiments and Games for a Greener Earth.* Vancouver: Greystone Publishing.

Thurston, H. (1990). *Tidal Life: A Natural History of the Bay of Fundy.* Halifax: Nimbus Publishing.

Whitfield, P. (1988). *The Macmillan Illustrated Encyclopedia of Birds.* New York: Collier.

In planning the unit, the teacher constructed a list of the major concepts and then identified literature for group and individual investigation. The literature for the unit included the annotated bibliography in Box 4.6 on pages 132 and 133.

The teacher wove literature into the unit in two ways. She had students first self-select a fiction or nonfiction book related to the Riel rebellions and then set up an ongoing journal. She explained to the students:

> You will keep a journal of the book that you are reading. The journal will help you record your feelings, reactions, and personal insights about the book. Decide how many pages you will read at a time. After reading each section of the book, make an entry in your journal. What moved you the most in the section? How did the section make you feel? Why do you think you felt that way? What did you learn from the reading? Be sure to include details or quotations from the book so that someone who hasn't read it would understand why you were moved by the reading.

INTERNET RESOURCES

Bird Studies Canada
www.bsc-eoc.org

Canadian Nature Federation
www.cnf.ca

Canadian Wildlife Federation
www.cwf-fcf.org

Canadian Wildlife Service
www.cws-scf.ec.gc.ca

Cornell Lab of Ornithology
www.birds.cornell.edu

The Great Backyard Bird Count Program
www.birdsource.org/gbbc

National Audubon Society
www.audubon.org

Peterson Online (Houghton Mifflin)
www.petersononline.com

Smithsonian Migratory Bird Center
natzoo.si.edu/smbc/

Wild Birds Unlimited FeederCam
www.wbu.com/feedercam_home.htm

The teacher, Wei-Lin, and the students decided on three due dates, each covering about one-third of the book, for turning in the journal. In class, Wei-Lin periodically put the students in "book-talk" groups to discuss their reactions to what they were reading.

In addition to keeping the journal, the students engaged in literature study through an inquiry-centred project (see Box 4.7 on page 134). The inquiry allowed the class members to work in pairs to investigate a historical figure from the Riel rebellions. The inquiry resulted in a written interview that each pair of students role-played for the class.

Instructional activities within a unit may be initiated through flexible grouping patterns. Whole-class, small-group, and individual learning are all important vehicles for classroom interaction.

BOX 4.6	**Annotated Bibliography for a Unit on the Riel Rebellions**

CORE TEXT

Cruxton, J., & Wilson, W. (1997). *Challenge of the West: A Canadian Retrospective from 1815–1914.* Toronto: Oxford University Press.

A survey of main events and important people in the settlement of Western Canada. Features information and skill development sections, full-colour visual aids. Suitable for secondary school readers.

FICTION

Bayle, B. (2000). *Battle Cry at Batoche.* Vancouver: Beach Holme Publishing.

Fifteen-year-old twins, a boy and a girl, become involved with Gabriel and his wife, Madelaine Dumont, and the battle of Batoche. Suitable for middle school readers.

Lavallee, R. (trans. P. Claxton). (1994). *Tchipayuk or the Way of the Wolf.* Vancouver: Talonbooks.

A coming-of-age book that follows the life of a Métis boy and the fate of the Métis people in the late 1800s. Focuses on the Riel rebellions as primarily a land dispute. Detailed listing of sources. Suitable for secondary school readers.

Richards, D. (1993). *Soldier Boys.* Saskatoon: Thistledown Press.

The story of two boys, one on each side in the Battle of Fish Creek. Dramatic, rollicking style and accurate historical detail. Suitable for middle school readers.

Richards, D. (1999). *The Lady at Batoche.* Saskatoon: Thistledown Press.

The adventures of the Winnipeg Rifles during the last battle before the rebellion is over. Focuses on Gabriel Dumont and the Dakota and Cree allies of the Métis cause. Lively action and accurate historical detail. Suitable for middle school readers.

Silver, A. (1990). *Lord of the Plains.* New York: Ballantine.

A novel concentrating on the life of Gabriel and Madelaine Dumont from their meeting to Madelaine's death and Gabriel's later life as a performer in Buffalo Bill's Wild West Show. Strong afterword by the author on the use of history in writing fiction. Suitable for secondary school readers.

Trottier, M., & Mantha, J. (2000). *Storm at Batoche.* Toronto: Stoddart Kids.

A picture book that includes a fictional encounter between a young boy lost in a storm and Louis Riel. Illustrations of exceptional quality are suitable for all readers. Includes a recipe for flatbread and a brief historical overview of Riel's life. Suitable for middle school readers.

NONFICTION

Beale, B., & Macleod, R.(1984). *Prairie Fire: The 1885 North-West Rebellion.* Edmonton: Hurtig Publishers.

A comprehensive history of the rebellion in a readable style. Balanced point of view on controversies. Historical black-and-white photos, maps, and diagrams. Suitable for secondary school students and teachers looking for a source of information on the battles, maps, and key figures. Detailed index.

Brown, Chester. (2003). *Louis Riel: A Comic-Strip Biography.* Montreal: Drawn and Quarterly.

While this book is not as helpful for gaining knowledge about Riel's life as some other sources, many readers will be drawn by the graphic content. Also useful as an example of an alternative way to present history and to provoke critical discussion around the appropriateness of such representations.

Brown, W. (2001). *Steele's Scouts: Samuel Benfield Steele and the North-West Rebellion.* Surrey, BC: Heritage House.

A lively history of a key figure in the North West Mounted Police and the rebellion told in detail by a writer who is a fan of Steele's and also a promoter of Canadian history. The book contains many visuals, including maps and photographs. Brown encourages readers to seek out the original locations of key events for themselves. Good bibliography for those seeking further information. Suitable for secondary school readers.

Bumsted, J. (1996). *The Red River Rebellion.* Winnipeg: Watson and Dwyer Publishing.

Bumsted is one of Canada's best regarded academics in the study of Canadian and Manitoba history. This book looks at the rebellion in Manitoba's Red River colony when the government of Canada annexed the area. Told from the perspective of the participants. Suitable for secondary school readers.

Bumsted, J. (2001). *Louis Riel v. Canada: The Making of a Rebel.* Winnipeg: Great Plains Publications.

A scholarly and highly readable account of the law surrounding Riel and the rebellions. Suitable for secondary school readers.

Doyle, D. (2000). *From the Gallows: The Lost Testimony of Louis Riel.* Summerland, BC: Ethnic Enterprises.

Large font. Creative nonfiction account of Riel's last days using his own words. Invites readers to join in the debate around the charge of high treason. Suitable for middle school readers.

Dumont, G. (1993). *Gabriel Dumont Speaks.* Trans. M. Barnholden. Vancouver: Talonbooks.

A first-person account of the Riel rebellions by Dumont as dictated in 1903. Contains versions of battle history are different from conventional accounts. Suitable for middle school readers.

Neering, R. (1977). *Louis Riel.* Don Mills, ON: Fitzhenry & Whiteside.

A short (60-page) historical overview of the main events of Riel's life. Suitable for older middle school readers and others looking for an introduction.

Siggins, M. (1994). *Riel: A Life of Revolution.* Toronto: HarperCollins.

A biography of Louis Riel featuring accounts of key events (the Northwest Rebellion, the Red River Rebellion, the trial in Regina) but also less well-known elements of his story, such as Riel's poetry and the women who were most influential in his life. Suitable for older secondary school readers.

Stonechild, B., & Waiser, B. (1997). *Loyal till Death: Indians and the North-West Rebellion.* Calgary: Fifth House Publishers.

A rare look at the involvement of aboriginal people in the Riel rebellions, written using oral history from elders as well as more conventional texts. Contains numerous visuals including photographs and maps. Suitable for secondary school readers.

Strong-Boag, V., & Fellman, A. (1986). *Rethinking Canada: The Promise of women's history.* Copp Clark Pitman.

Contains chapter by Sylvia van Kirk on the role of First Nation's women in early Canadian fur trade. Advanced reading.

BOX 4.7	Inquiry Project for a Unit on the Riel Rebellions

Directions: Congratulations! You have been chosen to anchor the new series *PastTense.* This show features the same type of in-depth interview as CBC news documentaries, except you have a time machine. You can go back in time and interview someone from the Riel rebellions. Here are the rules:

1. Work in pairs. Both of you will do research and write the interview. Decide who will be the interviewer and who will be the interviewee. Decide on a historical interview date.

2. Your interviewee may be an actual historical figure (for example, Gabriel Dumont), or you may create a fictional eyewitness to a historical event (for example, someone present at the Battle of Batoche).

3. Your research must be based on at least two sources, including both print and multimedia formats. A bibliography must be included in the written interview turned in after the presentation.

4. Presentation
   a. Introduce the interviewee and briefly tell why this person is important or interesting.
   b. Your questions must stay within your time frame. You can't ask Louis Riel if he wants to be premier of Manitoba, since the office doesn't exist yet. You may ask him if he would like Manitoba to be part of Confederation in the future.
   c. The interviewee's answers must be reasonable and based on historical facts from your research.
   d. You are encouraged to include visual aids: websites, pictures, cartoons, maps, props, and costumes.
   e. The interview should last no less than four minutes and no more than 10 minutes.

Here is a list of possible subjects, or you may choose your own.

Louis Riel	General Strange	John A. Macdonald
Marguerite Riel	Colonel Otter	Inspector Samuel Steele
Marie Anne Lagimodiere	Big Bear (Mistahimaskwa)	Superintendent Lief Crozier
Gabriel Dumont	Poundmaker (Petocahhanawawin)	Lawrence Clark
Madelaine Dumont		W. J. McLean
Thomas Scott	Wandering Spirit	Helen McLean
General Middleton	(Kapapamachahkwet)	Kitty McLean

Someone present at the military encounter of your choice (for example, Batoche, Frog Lake, Seven Oaks, Duck Lake, Frenchman's Butte)

A Métis land-holder, one of Lord Selkirk's settlers, a member of a local Cree band, a banker living in Toronto, or a member of a Catholic religious order in Winnipeg reading and responding to the Metis Bill of Rights (1869)

LOOKING BACK, LOOKING FORWARD

Content area teachers can plan instruction that will lead to active text learning. Students must act on ideas in print and also interact with one another when learning with texts. The instructional framework and the thematic unit provide the structure for bringing learners and texts together in content areas.

The instructional framework makes provisions for prereading, reading, and postreading instruction for core text lessons. This particular lesson structure helps teachers imagine the kinds of activity to use before, during, and after reading. A unit helps the teacher organize instructional activities around multiple texts. Unit planning gives you much more latitude to coordinate resource materials and activities. Unit activities can be organized for the whole class, small groups, or individuals. The emphasis, however, should be on inquiry-centred research projects.

The next chapter begins Part 2, Instructional Strategies. It examines the relationships between the vocabulary of a content area—its special and technical terms—and its concepts. How can a teacher help students to interact with the language of a content area and, in the process, show them how to define, clarify, and extend their conceptual knowledge?

MINDS-ON

1. You have probably seen some variation of the bumper sticker "If you can read this, thank a teacher." In a small group, sitting in a circle, discuss how you feel about this sticker and what you think it means. Select one member of your group to act as an observer, and use the questions that follow to record group interactions. Allow 10 to 15 minutes for discussion, and then ask the observer to share her or his list of questions and answers with the group. Observer's questions:

   a. Who raised questions during group discussion?
   b. Could most of the questions be answered yes or no, true or false?
   c. Who answered the questions?
   d. Who decided who would answer and when they would answer?
   e. Who kept the group on task?
   f. Did your seating arrangement change before or after the discussion?

   As a group, discuss the following:

   a. Did the discussion process described by the observer involve the sharing of ideas by group members with no one person asking or answering all the questions?

   b. What were the advantages and disadvantages of having the discussion progress without the rigid protocol of one person deciding who would answer and when?

   c. How would you contrast the effect of the seating in rows used in lecture question-and-answer sessions with the effect of the circle seating used in this discussion?

2. Join together with four or five other individuals who either teach or are planning to teach at approximately the same grade level. Imagine that you have just attended a cooperative learning workshop and you plan to incorporate what you learned into your teaching. What do you consider the single best cooperative activity for your grade level and why? Discuss how you would implement this approach with a selected topic. List any problems you expect might arise, and explain how you would solve them.

3. Recognizing that students with different abilities and interests learn differently, to what extent should a teacher attempt to organize a class so that all the students in the class will learn the same concepts and information? Would your answer be the same for a grade 6 science class and a secondary school advanced physics class? What general guidelines can you develop as a group to help a new teacher organize learning to balance course content with individual differences? Also, what type of physical classroom design do you think would best facilitate your philosophy?

HANDS-ON

1. Try the following experiment. Roll a standard $8\frac{1}{2}$-by-11-inch sheet of paper into a tube 11 inches or 28 cm long and approximately 1 inch or 3 cm in diameter. Then hold the tube in your left hand and, keeping both eyes open, look through the tube with your left eye. Next, place your right hand, palm toward your face, against the side of the tube approximately half the distance from your eye to the end of the tube. Angle the tube slightly so that the far end of the tube is behind your palm, and a hole should appear in your hand.

   With a small group or individually, brainstorm how you might use this experiment as a prereading activity for a science lesson on the eye.

2. Team up with two other individuals. Designate one member of your group "observer," one "reader," and one "artist." The observer's task will be to make a written record of the actions of the reader and the artist. The artist will draw a triangle described by the reader in the following instructions:

   Draw a triangle so that one side is twice as long as one of the other two. Use one of the small sides as the base, and construct the triangle so that the longest side faces the left side of the paper. Design your triangle so that the longest side is 10 cm long. Make it exactly 10 cm if you have a ruler available, or estimate the length if you do not. Finally, assign the letters a, b, and c to each side of the triangle, designating the longest side as c.

   After the reader and the artist have completed the drawing, review the notes by the observer, and develop a written record of the intentions or reasons for each action previously recorded. For example, if the observer recorded that the reader turned back to reread the instructions, you might explain that the artist had forgotten a fact that he or she needed to understand.

   Finally, compare observations, make a class list of the learning strategies used by each group, and discuss which are successful approaches for a number of people. From this activity, what conclusions can you draw about the role of metacognition in reading to learn?

3. Bring your favourite book, magazine, poem, or drama to class. Develop a prereading activity that would provide the rationale for using this material, and introduce this piece. (This activity can be done in small groups of five or six or with the entire class.)

   Before your presentation, plan a series of entry questions and comments to match what you think others will say in response. Also, because you are introducing this material with a purpose in mind, the discussion should lead your small group to a particular point from which the next activity might begin.

   Be prepared to reach that departure point by a number of alternate routes. Prereading activities and discussions often remain detached from the reading/content activity, so that a novice is tempted to say, "That's enough talking. Let's get to the real lesson." The discussion or activity must be integral to the "real" lesson.

Here is the complete passage from the exercise at the conclusion of Chapter 1 on page 27:

> We have gathered from coast to coast to coast, from one ocean to another, united in our grief, to say goodbye.
>
> But this is not the end. He left politics in '84. But he came back for Meech. He came back for Charlottetown. He came back to remind us of who we are and what we're all capable of.
>
> But he won't be coming back anymore. It's all up to us, all of us, now.
>
> The woods are lovely, dark and deep. He has kept his promises and earned his sleep.
>
> Je t'aime Papa.

SUGGESTED READINGS

Aschbacher, P. R. (1991). Humanitas: A thematic curriculum. *Educational Leadership, 49*(2), 16–19.

Davies, A., Politano, C., & Cameron, C. (1993). *Making themes work: Building connections.* Winnipeg: Peguis Publishing.

Fogarty, R. (1994, March). Thinking about themes: Hundreds of themes. *Middle School Journal, 25,* 30–31.

Jacobs, H. H. (Ed.). (1989). *Interdisciplinary curriculum: Design and implementation.* Alexandria, VA: Association for Supervision and Curriculum Development.

Katz, L. G., & Chard, S. C. (1990). *Engaging children's minds: The project approach.* Norwood, NJ: Ablex.

Leu, Jr., D. J., & Leu, D. D. (2000). *Teaching with the internet: Lesson from the classroom.* Norwood, MA: Christopher-Gordon.

Lounsbury, J. H. (Ed.). (1992). *Connecting the curriculum through interdisciplinary instruction.* Columbus, OH: National Middle School Association.

Luongo-Orlando, K. (2001). *A project approach to language learning: Linking literary genres and themes in elementary classrooms.* Markham, ON: Pembroke Publishing.

Manning, M., Manning, G., & Long, R. (1994). *Theme immersion: Inquiry-based curriculum in elementary and middle schools.* Portsmouth, NH: Heinemann.

Meinbach, A. M., Rothlein, L., & Fredericks, A. D. (1995). *The complete guide to thematic units: Creating the integrated curriculum.* Norwood, MA: Christopher-Gordon.

The Metropolitan Toronto School Board. *Getting it all together: Curriculum integration in the transition years.* Markham, ON: Pembroke Publishers.

Moss, J. F. (1994). *Using literature in the middle grades: A thematic approach.* Norwood, MA: Christopher-Gordon.

Short, K. G., & Armstrong, J. (1993). Moving toward inquiry: Integrating literature into science curriculum. *The New Advocate, 6,* 183–199.

Stevenson, C., & Carr, J. F. (Eds.). (1993). *Integrated studies in the middle grades: "Dancing through walls."* New York: Teachers College Press.

Vars, G. F. (1993). *Interdisciplinary teaching in the middle grades: Why and how.* Columbus, OH: National Middle School Association.

Weaver, C., Chaston, J., & Peterson, S. (1995). *Theme exploration: A voyage of discovery.* Portsmouth, NH: Heinemann.

part two

Instructional Strategies

chapter five

Vocabulary and Concepts

*I am a Bear of Very Little Brain
and long words Bother me.*

–A. A. Milne, from *Winnie-the-Pooh*

ORGANIZING PRINCIPLE

There is a strong connection between vocabulary knowledge and reading comprehension. If students are not familiar with most words they meet in print, they will undoubtedly have trouble understanding what they read. Long words bothered Pooh, probably as much as technical vocabulary—words unique to a content area—bother students who are not familiar with the content they are studying in an academic discipline. The more experience students have with unfamiliar words and the more exposure they have to them, the more meaningful (and less bothersome) the words will become.

Vocabulary is as unique to a content area as fingerprints are to a human being. A content area is distinguishable by its language, particularly the technical terms that label the concepts undergirding the subject matter. Teachers know they must do something with the language of their content areas, but they often have trouble with what that something should be. Consequently, they reduce instruction to routines that have withstood time and teacher-centred practice, directing students to look up, define, memorize, and use content-specific words in sentences. Such practices divorce the study of vocabulary from an exploration of the subject matter. Learning vocabulary becomes an activity in itself—a separate one—rather than an integral part of learning academic content. The result is lack of awareness of the strong relationship between word knowledge and reading comprehension. Content area vocabulary must be taught well enough to remove potential barriers to students' understanding of texts as well as to promote a long-term acquisition of the language of a content area. The organizing principle underscores the main premise of the chapter: **teaching words well means giving students multiple opportunities to learn how words are conceptually related to one another in the material they are studying.**

Study the chapter overview to get a sense of the major relationships among the key concepts and strategies that we develop in this chapter. Try to verbalize these relationships by thinking aloud. What do you predict this chapter will be about? What ideas and strategies in the chapter are familiar to you? Somewhat familiar?

Also, take the time to put yourself in a frame of mind that will enable you to approach the chapter purposefully. The "Frame of Mind" questions raise expectations of the content presented in the chapter and will help guide your search for information.

CHAPTER OVERVIEW

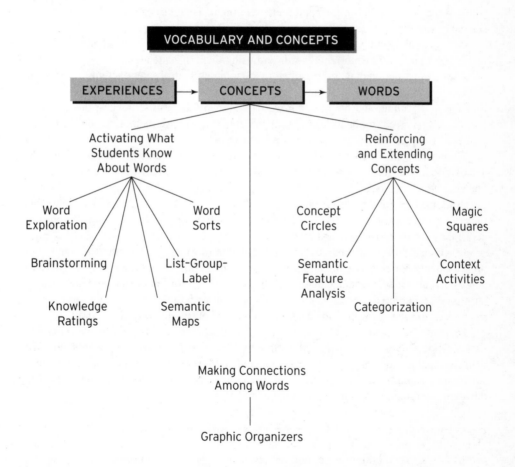

VOCABULARY AND CONCEPTS

EXPERIENCES → CONCEPTS → WORDS

Activating What Students Know About Words

Reinforcing and Extending Concepts

Word Exploration

Word Sorts

Concept Circles

Magic Squares

Brainstorming

List-Group-Label

Semantic Feature Analysis

Context Activities

Knowledge Ratings

Semantic Maps

Categorization

Making Connections Among Words

Graphic Organizers

FRAME OF MIND

1. Why should the language of an academic discipline be taught within the context of concept development?

2. What are the relationships among experiences, concepts, and words?

3. How can a teacher activate what students know about words and help them make connections among related words?

4. How do activities for vocabulary extension help students refine their conceptual knowledge of special and technical vocabulary?

5. How do magic squares for vocabulary reinforcement help students associate words and definitions?

Fridays always seemed to be set aside for quizzes when we were students. And one of the quizzes most frequently given was the vocabulary test: "Look up these words for the week. Write out their definitions and memorize them. Then use each word in a complete sentence. You'll be tested on these terms on Friday."

Our vocabulary study seemed consistently to revolve around the dull routines of looking up, defining, and memorizing words and using them in sentences.

Such an instructional pattern resulted in meaningless, purposeless activity—an end in itself, rather than a means to an end. Although there was nothing inherently wrong with looking up, defining, and memorizing words and using them in sentences, the approach itself was too narrow for us to learn words in depth. Instead, we memorized definitions to pass the Friday quiz—and forgot them on Saturday.

Having students learn lists of words is based on the ill-founded conclusion that the acquisition of vocabulary is separate from the development of ideas and concepts in a content area. Teaching vocabulary often means assigning a corpus of words rather than exploring word meanings and relationships that contribute to students' conceptual awareness and understanding of a subject. Once teachers clarify the relationship between words and concepts, they are receptive to instructional alternatives.

Teaching words well removes potential barriers to reading comprehension and supports students' long-term acquisition of language in a content area. Teaching words well entails helping students make connections between their prior knowledge and the vocabulary to be encountered in the text and providing them with multiple opportunities to clarify and extend their knowledge of words and concepts during the course of study.

To begin, let's explore the connections that link direct experience to concepts and words. Understanding these connections lays the groundwork for teaching words, with the emphasis on learning concepts. As Anderson and Freebody (1981) suggest, "Every serious student of reading recognizes that the significant aspect of vocabulary development is in the learning of concepts, not just words" (p. 87).

EXPERIENCES, CONCEPTS, AND WORDS

Words are labels—nothing more, nothing less—for concepts. A single concept, however, represents much more than the meaning of a single word. It may take thousands of words to explain a concept. However, answers to the question, "What does it mean to know a word?" depend on how well we understand the relationships among personal experiences, concepts, and words.

Concepts are learned through our acting on and interacting with the environment. Students learn concepts best through direct, purposeful experiences. Learning is much more intense and meaningful when it is firsthand. However, in place of using direct experience (which is not always possible), we develop and learn concepts through various levels of contrived or vicarious experience. According to Dale (1969), learning a concept through oral or written language is especially difficult because this kind of learning is so far removed from direct experience.

Concepts create mental images, which may represent anything that can be grouped together by common features or similar criteria: objects, symbols, ideas, processes, or events. In this respect, concepts are similar to schemata. A concept hardly ever stands alone; instead, it is bound by a hierarchy of relationships. As a result, "most concepts do not represent a unique object or event but rather a general class linked by a common element or relationship" (Johnson & Pearson 1984, p. 33).

Bruner, Goodnow, and Austin (1977) suggest that we would be overwhelmed by the complexity of our environment if we were to respond to each object or event that we encountered as unique. Therefore, we invent categories (or form concepts) to reduce the complexity of our environment and the necessity for constant learning. For example, every feline need not have a different name; each is known as a *cat*. Although cats vary greatly, their common characteristics cause them to be referred to by the same general term. Thus to facilitate communication, we invent words to name concepts.

Consider your concept for the word *ostrich*. What picture comes to mind? Your image of an ostrich might differ from ours, depending on your prior knowledge of the ostrich or the larger class to which it belongs, known as *land birds*. Moreover, your direct or vicarious experiences with birds may differ significantly from someone else's. Nevertheless, for any concept, we organize all our experiences and background knowledge into conceptual hierarchies according to *class*, *example*, and *attribute* relations.

The concept *ostrich* is part of a more inclusive class or category called *land birds*, which is in turn subsumed under an even larger class of animals known as *warm-blooded vertebrates*. These class relations are depicted in Figure 5.1 on page 144.

In any conceptual network, class relationships are organized in a hierarchy consisting of superordinate and subordinate concepts. In Figure 5.1, the superordinate concept is *animal kingdom*. *Vertebrates* and *invertebrates* are two classes within the animal kingdom; they are in a subordinate position in this hierarchy. *Vertebrates*, however—divided into two classes, *warm-blooded* and *cold-blooded*—are superordinate to *mammals*, *birds*, *fish*, and *amphibians*, which are types or subclasses of vertebrates. The concept *land birds*, subordinate to *birds* but superordinate to *ostrich*, completes the hierarchy.

For every concept, there are examples. An *example* is a member of any concept being considered. Class-example relations are complementary: Vertebrates and invertebrates are examples within the *animal kingdom*; mammals, birds, fish, and amphibians are examples of *vertebrates*; land birds are one example of *birds*; and so on.

Let's make *land birds* our target concept. What are some other examples of land birds in addition to the ostrich? *Penguin*, *emu*, and *rhea* are a few, as shown in Figure 5.2 on page 144. We could have listed more examples of land birds. Instead, we now ask, "What do the ostrich, penguin, emu, and rhea have in common?" This question allows us to focus on their *relevant attributes*, the features, traits, properties, or characteristics common to every

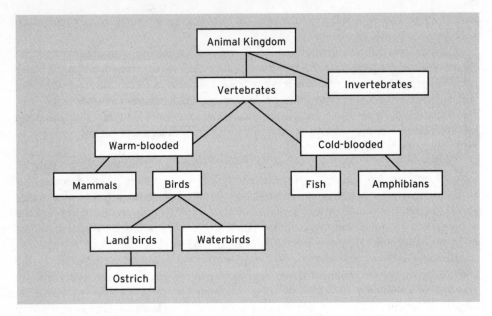

FIGURE 5.1 **Semantic Map Based on Class Relations**

example of a particular group. In this case, the relevant attributes of land birds are the characteristics that determine whether the ostrich, penguin, emu, and rhea belong to the class of birds called *land birds*. An attribute is said to be *critical* if it is a characteristic that is necessary to class membership. An attribute is said to be *variable* if it is shared by some but not all examples of the class.

Thus we recognize that certain physical and social characteristics are shared by all land birds but that not every land bird has each feature. Virtually all land birds have feathers, wings, and beaks. They hatch from an egg and have two legs. They differ in colour, size, habitat, and size of feet. Some land birds fly, and others, with small wings that cannot support their bodies in the air, do not. In what ways is the ostrich similar to other land birds? How is the ostrich different?

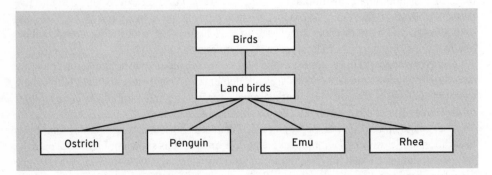

FIGURE 5.2 **Class-Example Relations of the Target Concept *Land Birds***

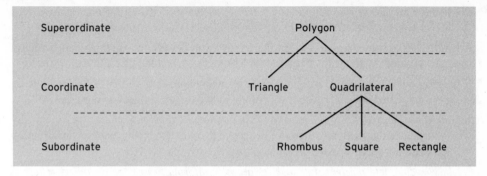

FIGURE 5.3 A Hierarchical Arrangement of Mathematical Concepts with Similar Attributes

Source: From Thelen, Judith N. (1982, March), "Preparing Students for Content Area Reading Assignments." *Journal of Reading, 25*(6), 544–549. Copyright © 1982 by the International Reading Association. All rights reserved. Used by permission of the author and the International Reading Association.

This brief discussion illustrates an important principle: **teachers can help students build conceptual knowledge of content area terms by teaching and reinforcing the concept words in relation to other concept words.** This key instructional principle plays itself out in content area classrooms whenever students are actively making connections among the keywords in a lesson or unit of study.

MAKING CONNECTIONS AMONG KEY CONCEPTS

At the start of each chapter, we have asked you to organize your thoughts around the main ideas in the text. These ideas are presented within the framework of a *graphic organizer*, a chart that uses content vocabulary to help students anticipate concepts and their relationships to one another in the reading material. These concepts are displayed in an arrangement of key technical terms relevant to the important concepts to be learned.

Graphic organizers may vary in format. One commonly used format to depict the hierarchical relationships among concept words is a tree diagram. For example, study the hierarchical arrangement of mathematical concepts having similar attributes and characteristics in Figure 5.3. The concept *quadrilateral* is subordinate to *polygon*, coordinate to *triangle*, and superordinate to *rhombus*, *square*, and *rectangle*. *Polygon* is the most inclusive concept and subsumes all of the others (Thelen 1982).

Keep in mind, the graphic organizer always shows concepts in relation to other concepts. Let's take a closer look at its construction and application in the classroom.

Constructing Graphic Organizers

Barron (1969) suggests the following steps for developing the graphic organizer and introducing the vocabulary diagram to students:

1. *Analyze the vocabulary of the learning task.* List all the words that you believe are important for the students to understand.

2. *Arrange the list of words until you have a scheme that shows the interrelationships among the concepts particular to the learning task.*

3. *Add to the scheme vocabulary.* Add terms that you believe the students understand in order to show relationships between the learning task and the discipline as a whole.

4. *Evaluate the organizer.* Have you clearly shown major relationships? Can the organizer be simplified and still effectively communicate the idea you consider crucial?

5. *Introduce the students to the learning task by showing them the scheme.* Tell them why you arranged the terms as you did. Encourage them to contribute as much information as possible to the discussion of the organizer.

6. *As you complete the learning task, relate new information to the organizer where it seems appropriate.*

Suppose you were to develop a graphic organizer for a text chapter in a secondary school psychology course. Let's walk through the steps involved.

1. *Analyze the vocabulary, and list the important words.* The chapter yields these words:

hebephrenia	neurosis	personality disorders
psychosis	schizophrenia	catatonia
abnormality	mental retardation	phobias

2. *Arrange the list of words.* Choose the word that represents the most inclusive concept, the one superordinate to all the others. Then choose the words classified immediately under the superordinate concept, and coordinate them with one another. Then choose the terms subordinate to the coordinate concepts. Your diagram may look like Figure 5.4.

3. *Add terms to the scheme vocabulary that you believe the students understand.* You add the following terms: *antisocial, anxiety, intellectual deficit, Walter Mitty, depression, paranoia.* Where would you place these words on the diagram?

4. *Evaluate the organizer.* The interrelationships among the key terms may look like Figure 5.5 once you evaluate the vocabulary arrangement.

5. *Introduce the students to the learning task.* As you present the vocabulary relationships shown on the graphic organizer, create as much discussion as possible. Draw on stu-

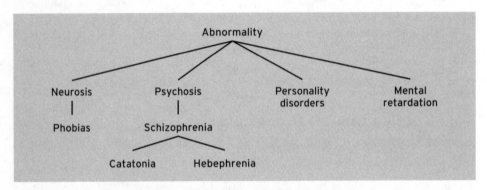

FIGURE 5.4 **Arrangement of Words in a Psychology Text**

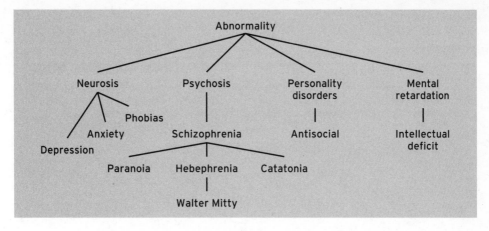

FIGURE 5.5 **Arrangement of Psychology Words After Evaluation of Organizer**

dents' understanding of and experience with the concepts that the terms label. You might have students relate previous study to the terms. For example, *Walter Mitty* is subsumed under *hebephrenia*. Students who are familiar with James Thurber's short story "The Secret Life of Walter Mitty" would have little trouble bringing meaning to *hebephrenia*: a schizophrenic condition characterized by excessive daydreaming and delusions. The discussion might also lead to a recognition of the implicit comparison-and-contrast pattern of the four types of abnormality explained in the text. What better opportunity to provide direction during reading than to have students visualize the pattern? The discussions you will stimulate with the organizer will be worth the time it takes to construct it.

6. *As you complete the learning task, relate new information to the organizer.* This step is particularly useful as a study and review technique. The organizer becomes a study guide that can be referred to throughout the discussion of the material. Students should be encouraged to add information to flesh out the organizer as they develop concepts more fully.

Use a graphic organizer to show the relationships in a thematic unit in a chapter or in a subsection of a chapter. Notice how the graphic organizer in Figure 5.6 on page 148, developed for a secondary school class in data processing, introduced students to the different terms of data processing, delineating causes and effects.

An art teacher used Figure 5.7 on page 148 to show relationships among types of media used in art. She used an artist's palette rather than a tree diagram. After completing the entries for paint and ceramics herself, the teacher challenged her students to brainstorm other media that they had already used or knew about and to provide examples and used the open areas on the palette to record students' associations.

Graphic organizers are easily adapted to learning situations in the elementary grades. For class presentation, elementary teachers often construct organizers on large sheets of chart paper or on bulletin boards. Other teachers introduce vocabulary for content units by

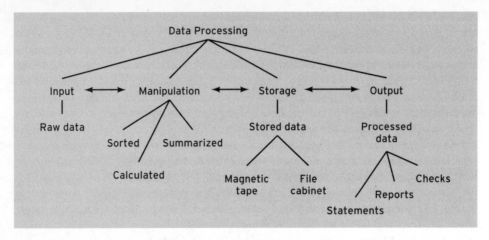

FIGURE 5.6   **A Graphic Organizer for Data Processing**

constructing mobiles they hang from the ceiling. Hanging mobiles are an interest-riveting way to attract students' attention to the hierarchical relationships among the words they will encounter. Still other elementary teachers draw pictures with words that illustrate the key concepts under study.

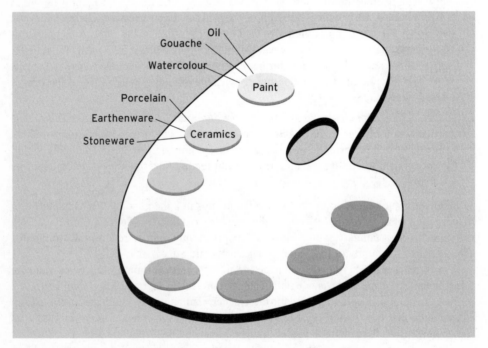

FIGURE 5.7   **A Graphic Organizer for Types of Media in Art**

Showing Students How to Make Their Own Connections

Graphic organizers may be used by teachers to build a frame of reference for students as they approach new material. However, in a more student-centred adaptation of the graphic organizer, the students work in cooperative groups and organize important concepts into their own graphic representations.

To make connections effectively, students must have some familiarity with the concepts in advance of their study of the material. In addition, student-constructed graphic organizers presume that the students are aware of the idea behind a graphic organizer. If they are not, you will need to give them a rationale and then model the construction of an organizer. Exposure to teacher-constructed graphic organizers from past lessons also creates awareness and builds the students' schema for the technique.

To introduce students to the process of making their own graphic organizers, follow these steps, adapted from Barron and Stone (1973):

1. *Type the keywords and make photocopies for students.*
2. *Have them form small groups of two or three students each.*
3. *Distribute the list of terms and a packet of 3-by-5-inch index cards to each group.*
4. *Have the students write each word from the list on a card.* Then have them work together to decide on a spatial arrangement of the cards that depicts the major relationships among the words.
5. *As students work, provide assistance as needed.*
6. *Initiate a discussion of the constructed organizer.*

Before actually assigning a graphic organizer to students, you should prepare for the activity by carefully analyzing the vocabulary of the material to be learned. List all the terms that are essential for students to understand. Then add relevant terms that you believe the students already understand and will help them relate what they know to the new material. Finally, construct your own organizer.

The form of the student-constructed graphic organizer will undoubtedly differ from the teacher's arrangement. However, this difference in and of itself should not be a major source of concern. According to Herber (1978),

> Form is not the issue; substance is, and that is demonstrated by a clear portrayal of the implicit relationships among key words.... Students will see things differently [from] teachers and from one another. It is good ... for the teacher to have thought through his or her own arrangement of the words for purposes of comparison, clarification, and confirmation. (p. 149)

What is important, then, is that the graphic organizer support students' ability to anticipate connections through the key vocabulary terms in content materials.

Seniors in a calculus course participated in the construction of graphic organizers as a way of becoming familiar with key terms in a chapter on logarithmic and exponential functions, and they were encouraged to make anticipated connections among the terms. The terms included the following:

integration	logarithmic properties
logarithmic differentiation	differentiation

natural exponential function	constructive theorem
log rule	definite integral as a function
logarithmic and exponential functions	mean value theorem for integrals
natural logarithmic function	inverse functions
second fundamental theorem of calculus	

The teacher had the students work in pairs to create a graphic display, assuring them that there were no "right answers." The students had to rely on their prior knowledge of logarithmic and exponential functions to anticipate connections.

ACTIVATING WHAT STUDENTS KNOW ABOUT WORDS

Graphic organizers activate students' prior knowledge of the vocabulary words in a text selection or unit of study. From a strategy perspective, students need to learn how to ask the question, "What do I know about these words?" When you use graphic organizers prior to reading or talking about key concepts, help the students build strategy awareness by exploring key terms before reading or discussion. In addition to graphic organizers, there are several instructional activities that you can use to scaffold students' exploration of words.

Word Exploration

Word exploration is a *writing-to-learn* strategy that works well as a vocabulary activity. Before asking students to make connections between the words and their prior knowledge, a biology teacher asked them to explore what they knew about the concept of *natural selection* by writing in their learning logs.

A word exploration activity invites students to write quickly and spontaneously, a technique called *freewriting*, for no more than five minutes, without undue concern about spelling, neatness, grammar, or punctuation. The purpose of freewriting is to get down on paper everything that students know about the topic or target concept. Students write freely for themselves, not for an audience, so the mechanical, surface features of language, such as spelling, are not important.

Word explorations activate schemata and jog long-term memory, allowing students to dig deep into the recesses of their minds to gather thoughts about a topic. Examine one of the word explorations for the target concept *natural selection*:

> Natural selection means that nature selects—kills off—does away with the weak so only the strong make it. Like we were studying in class last time things get so competive even among us for grades and jobs etc. The homeless are having trouble living with no place to call home except the street and nothing to eat. That's as good an example of natural selection as I can think of for now.

The teacher has several of the students share their word explorations with the class, either reading them verbatim or talking through what they have written, and notes similarities and differences in the students' concepts. The teacher then relates their initial associations to the concept and asks the students to make further connections: "How does your personal understanding of the idea of *natural selection* fit in with some of the relationships that you see?"

Brainstorming

An alternative to word exploration, brainstorming is a procedure that quickly allows students to generate what they know about a key concept. In brainstorming, the students can access their prior knowledge in relation to the target concept. Brainstorming involves two basic steps that can be adapted easily to content objectives: (1) The teacher identifies a key concept that reflects one of the main topics to be studied in the text, and (2) students work in small groups to generate a list of words related to the concept in a given number of seconds.

These two steps help you discover almost instantly what your students know about the topic they are going to study. Furthermore, Herber (1978) suggests,

> The device of having students produce lists of related words is a useful way to guide review. It helps them become instantly aware of how much they know, individually and collectively, about the topic. They discover quickly that there are no right or wrong answers.... Until the students reach the point in the lesson where they must read the passage and judge whether their predictions are accurate, the entire lesson is based on their own knowledge, experience, and opinion. This captivates their interest much more than the more traditional, perfunctory review. (p. 179)

List-Group-Label

Hilda Taba (1967) suggests an extension of brainstorming that she calls "list–group–label." When the brainstorming activity is over, and *lists* of words have been generated by the students, have the class form learning teams to *group* the words into logical arrangements. Then invite the teams to *label* each arrangement. Once the list–group–label activity is completed, ask the students to make predictions about the content to be studied. You might ask, "Given the list of words and groupings that you have developed, what do you think we will be reading and studying about? How does the title of the text (or the thematic unit) relate to your groups of words? Why do you think so?"

A teacher initiated a brainstorming activity with a class of middle school students. The students, working in small groups, were asked to list in two minutes as many words as possible that were related to the early history of Canada. Then the groups shared their lists of words. The teacher then created a master list on the board from the individual entries of the groups. He also wrote three categories on the board—"English," "French," and "Aboriginal"—and asked the groups to classify each word from the master list under one of the categories. Here's how one group responded:

English	French	Aboriginal
Upper Canada	Lower Canada	Mi'kmaq
John A. Macdonald	Jesuits	Iroquois
Toronto	Quebec City	reserves
Queen	Roman Catholic	medicinal herbs
Anglican	Montcalm	quillwork
Wolfe	Jacques Cartier	Poundmaker

Note that in this example, the teacher provided the categories. He recognized that students needed the additional structure to be successful with this particular task. The activity led to a good deal of discussion and debate. Students were put in the position of "authority," sharing what they knew and believed already with other class members. As a result of the activity, they were asked to raise questions about the early history of Canada that they wanted to have answered through reading and class discussion.

Semantic Word Maps

Semantic word maps may be used to depict spatial relationships among words. In addition, the use of semantic word maps includes brainstorming and the use of collaborative small groups, and it allows students to cluster words belonging to categories and to distinguish relationships among words.

Here's how semantic mapping works:

1. *The teacher or the students decide on a key concept to be explored.*
2. *Students suggest related terms and phrases.* Once the key concept is determined, the students, depending on what they have been studying and on their background knowledge and experiences, offer as many words or phrases as possible related to the concept term. These are recorded by the teacher on the board.

Once the list of terms is generated, the teacher may form small groups of students to create semantic maps and then to share their constructions in class discussion. Such was the case in an industrial arts class exploring the concept of *solvents* in relation to choosing different kinds of wood finishes. The semantic map created by one of the small groups in the class is shown in Figure 5.8.

Teachers will need to model the construction of semantic maps once or twice so that students will get a feel for how to develop their own in small groups or individually. In Chapter 9, we expand on the use of semantic maps as a postreading learning strategy used by students to outline content material as they study texts.

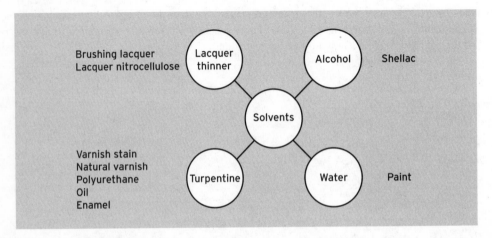

FIGURE 5.8 **Semantic Map for Solvents**

Word Sorts

Like brainstorming, word sorts require students to classify words into categories based on their prior knowledge. However, unlike in brainstorming, students do not generate a list of words for a target concept. Instead, the teacher identifies the keywords from the unit of study and invites the students to sort them into logical arrangements of two or more.

A word sort is a simple yet valuable activity. Individually or in small groups, students literally sort out technical terms that are written on cards or listed on an exercise sheet. The object of word sorting is to group words into different categories by looking for shared features among their meanings. According to Gillet and Kita (1979), a word sort gives students the opportunity "to teach and learn from each other while discussing and examining words together" (pp. 541–542).

Gillet and Kita (1979) also explain that there are two types of word sorts: the open sort and the closed sort. Both are easily adapted to any content area. In the closed sort, students know in advance of sorting what the main categories are. In other words, the criterion that the words in a group must share is stated. In a middle-grade music class, students were studying the qualities of various "instrumental families" of the orchestra. The music teacher assigned the class to work in pairs to sort musical instruments into four categories representing the major orchestral families: strings, woodwinds, brass, and percussion. Figure 5.9 represents the closed sort developed by one collaborative "think–pair–share" group.

Open sorts prompt divergent and inductive reasoning. No category or criterion for grouping is known in advance of sorting. Students must search for meanings and discover relationships among technical terms without the benefit of any structure.

On page 154, study how an art teacher activated what students knew about words associated with pottery making by using the open word sort strategy. She asked the secondary school students to work in collaborative pairs to arrange the following words into possible groups and to predict the concept categories in which the words would be classified:

Strings (Bow or Struck)	Woodwinds (Single or Double Reed)	Brass (Lips Vibrate in Mouthpiece)	Percussion (Sounds by Striking)
Violin	Flute	Trumpet	Timpani
Viola	Piccolo	Trombone	Bass drum
Cello	Oboe	French horn	Chimes
Harp	Clarinet		Xylophone
	Saxophone		Bells
	Bassoon		Triangle
			Snare drum

FIGURE 5.9 **Closed Sort for Musical Instruments**

jordan	lead	Cornwall stone
ball	chrome	cone
antimony	slip	wheel
cobalt	scale	bisque
mortar	kaolin	stoneware
sgraffito	leather	oxidation
roka	hard	

Three categories that students formed were *types of clay*, *pottery tools*, and *colouring agents*.

Open word sorts can be used before or after reading. Before reading, a word sort serves as an activation strategy to help learners make predictive connections among the words. After reading, word sorts enable students to clarify and extend their understanding of the conceptual relationships.

Knowledge Ratings

Knowledge ratings get readers to analyze what they know about a topic. Blachowicz (1986) recommends that the teacher present students with a list of vocabulary in a survey-like format and ask them to analyze each word individually, as in the two examples in Figure 5.10.

A follow-up discussion might revolve around questions such as these: Which are the hardest words? Which do you think most of the class doesn't know? Which are the easiest ones? Which do most of us know? Students should be encouraged within the context of the discussion to share what they know about the words. In this way, the teacher can get some idea of the knowledge the class brings to the text reading or a larger unit of study.

These procedures are all part of prereading preparation. Naturally, it would be foolhardy to use all of these procedures at one time, but one or two in combination set the stage for students to read with some confidence in their competence with the language of the text.

REINFORCING AND EXTENDING VOCABULARY KNOWLEDGE AND CONCEPTS

When students manipulate technical terms in relation to other terms, they are thinking critically. Vocabulary activities can be designed to give a class the experience of *thinking about*, *thinking through*, and *thinking with* the technical vocabulary of a subject.

Students need many experiences, real and vicarious, to develop word meanings and concepts. They need to use, test, and manipulate technical terms in instructional situations that capitalize on reading, writing, speaking, and listening. In having students do these things, you create the kind of natural language environment that is needed to extend vocabulary and concept development.

As a rule of thumb, reinforcing and extending vocabulary should be completed individually by students and then discussed either in small groups or in the class as a whole. The oral interaction in team learning gives more students a chance to use terms. Students can exchange ideas, share insights, and justify responses in a nonthreatening situation. Barron and Earle (1973) suggest the following procedures for small-group discussion of reinforcement activities:

1. *End small-group discussion only after the group has discussed each answer.* Every member of the group should understand the reasons for each answer.

2. *Encourage the active participation of all group members.* A student who has trouble with a particular exercise can still make a valuable contribution by asking questions or asking someone to explain answers.

3. *Limit talk to the particular exercise or to related questions.*

4. *Students should use the words and their meanings in discussing the answers.* They should not use letters and numbers (for example, avoid "I think the answer to number 1 is *c*").

"How much do you know about these words?"

From a unit on quadratic functions and systems of equations in a secondary school math class:

	Can Define	Have Seen/Heard	?
Exponent	X		
Intersection	X		
Domain			X
Intercept			X
Slope		X	
Parabola			X
Origin		X	
Vertex		X	
Irrationals	X		
Union		X	
Coefficient		X	

From a newspaper unit in a middle school language arts class:

	A Lot!	Some	Not Much
Wire service		X	
AP		X	
Copy		X	
Dateline	X		
Byline	X		
Caption	X		
Masthead			X
Jumpline			X
Column	X		

FIGURE 5.10 **Two Examples of Knowledge Ratings**

Semantic Feature Analysis (SFA)

Semantic feature analysis (SFA) establishes a meaningful link between students' prior knowledge and words that are conceptually related to one another. The strategy requires that you develop a chart or grid to help students analyze similarities and differences among the related concepts. As the SFA grid in Figure 5.11 illustrates, a topic or category (in this case, properties of quadrilaterals) is selected, words related to that category are written across the top of the grid, and features or properties shared by some of the words in the column are listed down the left side of the grid.

Students analyze each word, feature by feature, writing Y (yes) or N (no) in each cell of the grid to indicate whether the feature is associated with the word. Students may write a question mark (?) if they are uncertain about a particular feature.

As a teaching activity, SFA is easily suited to prereading or postreading. If you used it for prereading to activate what students know about words, recognize that they can return to the SFA after reading to clarify and reformulate some of their initial responses on the SFA grid.

Categorization Activities

Vocabulary extension exercises involving categorization require students to determine relationships among technical terms much as word sorts do. Students are usually given four to six words per grouping and asked to do something with them. That something depends on the format used in the exercise. For example, you can give students sets of words and ask them to circle the word in each set that includes the others. This exercise demands that students perceive common attributes or examples in relation to a more inclusive concept and to distinguish superordinate from subordinate terms. The following is an example from a grade 8 social studies class.

Directions: Determine which of these properties are found in the four quadrilaterals listed. Mark "Y" or "N" in each box.

	Parallelogram	Rectangle	Rhombus	Square
Diagonals bisect each other.				
Diagonals are congruent.				
Each diagonal bisects a pair of opposite angles.				
Diagonals form two pairs of congruent triangles.				
Diagonals form four congruent triangles.				
Diagonals are perpendicular to each other.				

FIGURE 5.11 **An SFA for Geometry**

Directions: Circle the word in each group that includes the others.

1. government
   council
   judges
   premier

2. throne
   coronation
   crown
   church

A variation on this format directs students to cross out the word that does not belong and then to explain in a word or phrase the relationship that exists among the common items, as illustrated in the following example.

Directions: Cross out the word in each set that does not belong. On the line above the set, write the word or phrase that explains the relationship among the remaining three words.

1. _____
   drama
   comedy
   epic
   tragedy

2. _____
   time
   character
   place
   action

Concept Circles

One of the most versatile activities we have observed at a wide range of grade levels is the concept circle. Concept circles provide still another format and opportunity for studying words critically—for students to relate words conceptually to one another. A concept circle may simply involve putting words or phrases in the sections of a circle and directing students to describe or name the concept relationship among the sections. The example in Figure 5.12 is from a middle-grade science lesson.

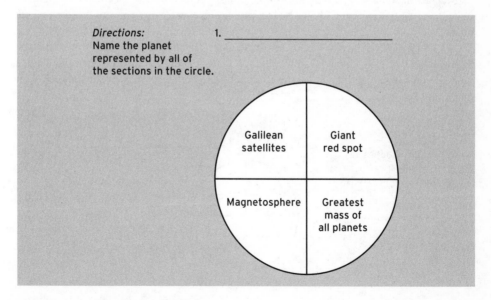

FIGURE 5.12 **The Concept Circle**

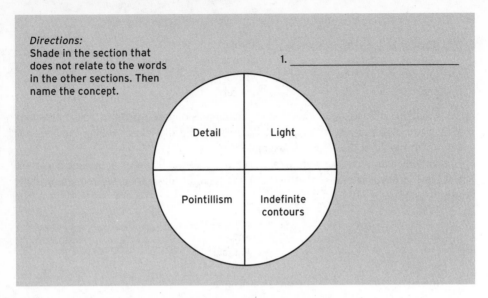

Directions:
Shade in the section that does not relate to the words in the other sections. Then name the concept.

1. _____

Detail | Light

Pointillism | Indefinite contours

FIGURE 5.13   A Variation on the Concept Circle

In addition, you might direct students to shade in the section of a concept circle containing a word or phrase that *does not relate* to the words or phrases in the other sections of the circle and then identify the concept relationships that exist among the remaining sections (see Figure 5.13).

Finally, you can modify a concept circle by leaving one or two sections of the circle empty, as in Figure 5.14. Direct students to fill in the empty section with a word or two that relates in some way to the terms in the other sections of the concept circle. Students must then justify their word choice by identifying the overarching concept depicted by the circle.

As you can see, concept circles serve the same function as categorization activities. However, students respond positively to the visual aspect of manipulating the sections in a circle. Whereas categorization exercises sometimes seem like tests to students, concept circles are fun to do.

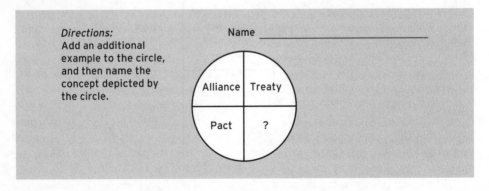

Directions:
Add an additional example to the circle, and then name the concept depicted by the circle.

Name _____

Alliance | Treaty

Pact | ?

FIGURE 5.14   Another Variation on the Concept Circle

Context- and Definition-Related Activities

Artley (1975) captured the role that context plays in vocabulary learning: "It is the context in which the word is embedded rather than the dictionary that gives it its unique flavor" (p. 1072). Readers who build and use contextual knowledge are able to recognize fine shades of meaning in the way words are used. They know the concept behind the word well enough to use that concept in different contexts. First, we suggest several ways to reinforce and extend a student's contextual knowledge of content area terms. Then we move on to techniques to help students inquire into the meaning of an unknown word by using its context.

Modified Cloze Passages Cloze passages (discussed in Chapter 3) can be created to reinforce technical vocabulary. However, the teacher usually modifies the procedure for teaching purposes. Every nth word, for example, needn't be deleted. The modified cloze passage will vary in length. Typically, a 200- to 500-word text segment yields sufficient technical vocabulary to make the activity worthwhile.

Should you consider developing a modified cloze passage on a segment of text from a reading assignment, make sure that the text passage is one of the most important parts of the assignment. Depending on your objectives, students can supply the missing words either before or after reading the entire assignment. If they work on the cloze activity before reading, use the subsequent discussion to build meaning for key terms and to raise expectations for the assignment as a whole. If you assign the cloze passage after reading, it will reinforce concepts attained through reading.

On completing a short lecture on why Newfoundland joined Confederation, a Canadian history teacher assigned a cloze passage before students read the entire introduction for homework. See how well you fare on the first part of the exercise.

> What caused Newfoundland to join Canada? Was this joining inevitable? What role did economics play? To what extent did Joey Smallwood influence the process? Which were more decisive—the intellectual or the emotional issues?
>
> > At the convention, Joey Smallwood emerged as the principal proponent of joining (1). Journalist, trade unionist, and farmer, the colourful Smallwood promised (2) from the old dominion politics and a better material (3) within (4). Not only would (5) with Canada—which had grown dramatically during the (6)—continue to expand, but also economic uncertainty would be forever banished by the social safety net provided by family (7), unemployment insurance, and old age (8). St. John's merchants presented a rather different picture of the Confederation option, suggesting that the (9) and trade policies of the once-proud dominion would be controlled by foreign (10). (Finkel & Conrad 1998, p. 343)

> (Answers can be found at the end of this chapter on page 164.)

OPIN OPIN is a meaning-extending vocabulary strategy developed by Frank Greene of McGill University. OPIN provides another example of context-based reinforcement and extension. *OPIN* stands for *opinion* and also plays on the term *cloze*.

Here's how OPIN works. Divide the class into groups of three. Distribute exercise sentences, one to each student. Each student must complete each exercise sentence individually. Then each group member must convince the other two members that his or her word choice is the best. If no agreement is reached on the best word for each sentence, each member of the group can speak to the class for his or her individual choice. When all groups have finished, have the class discuss each group's choices. The only rule of discussion is that each choice must be accompanied by a reasonable defence or justification. Answers like "Because ours is best" are not acceptable.

OPIN exercise sentences can be constructed for any content area. Here are sample sentences from science, social studies, and health and home ecology:

SCIENCE

1. A plant's _____ go into the soil.
2. The earth gets heat and _____ from the sun.
3. Some animals, such as birds and _____, are nibblers.

SOCIAL STUDIES

1. We cannot talk about _____ in Canada without discussing the welfare system.
2. Some form of _____ or rebellion would be necessary because the Métis would fight to hold on to their land.
3. Charts and graphs are used to _____ information.

HEALTH AND HOME ECOLOGY

1. Vitamin C is _____ from the small intestine and circulates to every tissue.
2. Washing time for cottons and linens is 8 to 10 minutes unless the clothes are badly _____.

(Answers can be found at the end of the chapter on page 165.)

OPIN encourages differing opinions about which word should be inserted in a blank space. In one sense, the exercise is open to discussion, and as a result, it reinforces the role of prior knowledge and experiences in the decisions that each group makes. The opportunity to "argue" one's responses in the group leads not only to continued motivation but also to a discussion of word meanings and variations.

Magic Squares The magic square activity is by no means new or novel, yet it has a way of reviving even the most mundane matching exercise. We have seen the magic square used successfully in elementary and secondary grades as well as in graduate courses. Here's how a magic square works. An activity sheet has two columns, one for content area terms and one for definitions or other distinguishing statements such as characteristics or examples (see Figure 5.15). Direct students to match terms with definitions. In doing so, they must take into account the letters signalling the terms and the numbers signalling the definitions. The students then put the number of a definition in the proper space (denoted by the letter of the term) in the "magic square answer box." If their matchups are correct, they will form a magic square. That is, the numerical total will be the same for each row across and each column down the answer box. This total forms the puzzle's "magic number." Students need to add up the rows and columns to check if they're coming up with the same number each time. If not, they should go back to the terms and definitions to re-evaluate their answers.

Directions: Select the best answer for each of the laundering terms from the numbered definitions. Put the number in the proper space in the magic square box. If the total of the numbers are the same both across and down, you have found the magic number!

Terms

A. Durable press
B. Soil release
C. Water repellent
D. Flame retardant
E. Knitted fabrics
F. Simulated suede leather
G. Pretreating
H. Sorting
I. Care labelling

Definitions

1. Textile Labelling Act makes this practice voluntary in Canada.
2. Fabric must maintain finish for up to 50 machine washings.
3. Ability to protect against redeposition of soil on fabrics.
4. Turn inside out to avoid snags.
5. Resists stains, rain, and dampness.
6. Special treatment of spots and stains before washing.
7. Resists wrinkling during wear and laundering.
8. Separate clothes into suitable washloads.
9. Washable suedelike fabric made from polyester.

Answer Box

A	B	C
D	E	F
G	H	I

Magic number = _____

FIGURE 5.15 **Magic Square on Care of Clothing**

The magic square exercise in Figure 5.15 is from a family and consumer studies class. Try it. Its magic number is 15. Analyze the mental manoeuvres that you went through to determine the correct number combinations. In some cases, you undoubtedly knew the answers outright. You may have made several educated guesses on others. Did you try to beat the number system? Imagine the possibilities for small-group interaction.

Many teachers are intrigued by the possibilities offered by the magic square, but they remain wary of its construction: "I can't spend hours figuring out number combinations." This is a legitimate concern. Luckily, the eight combinations in Figure 5.16 on page 162 make magic square activities easy to construct. You can generate many more combinations from the eight patterns simply by rearranging rows or columns (see Figure 5.17 on page 162).

7	3	5
2	4	9
6	8	1

0*   15**

10	8	6
2	9	13
12	7	5

4*   24**

7	11	8
10	12	4
9	3	14

5*   26**

9	2	7
4	6	8
5	10	3

1*   18**

9	7	5
1	8	12
11	6	4

3*   21**

16	2	3	13
5	11	10	8
9	7	6	12
4	14	15	1

0*   34**

19	2	15	23	6
25	8	16	4	12
1	14	22	10	18
7	20	3	11	24
13	21	9	17	5

0*   65**

2	7	18	12
8	5	11	15
13	17	6	3
16	10	4	9

0*   39**

* Foils needed in answer column
**Magic number

FIGURE 5.16   **A Model of Magic Square Combinations**

Notice that the single asterisk in Figure 5.16 denotes the number of foils needed so that several of the combinations can be completed. For example, the magic number combination of 18 requires one foil in the number 1 slot that will not match with any of the corresponding items in the matching exercise. To complete the combination, the number 10 is added. Therefore, when you develop a matching activity for combination 18, there will be 10 items in one column and nine in the other, with item 1 being the foil.

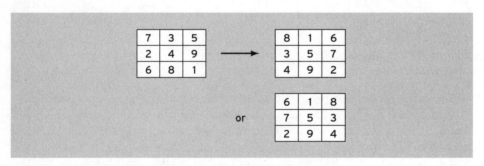

FIGURE 5.17   **Variations on Magic Square Combinations**

LOOKING BACK, LOOKING FORWARD

A strong relationship exists between vocabulary knowledge and reading comprehension. In this chapter, we provided numerous examples of what it means to teach words well: giving students multiple opportunities to build vocabulary knowledge, to learn how words are conceptually related to one another, and to learn how they are defined contextually in the material that students are studying. Vocabulary activities provide students the multiple experiences they need to use and manipulate words in differing situations. Conceptual and definitional activities provide the framework needed to study words critically. Various types of concept extension activities, such as semantic feature analysis, semantic maps, concept of definition, word sorts, categories, concept circles, word puzzles, and magic squares, reinforce and extend students' abilities to perceive relationships among the words they are studying.

In the next chapter, our emphasis turns to kindling student interest in text assignments and preparing them to think positively about what they will read. The importance of the role of prereading preparation in learning from text has often been neglected or underestimated in the content area classroom. Yet prereading activity is in many ways as important to the text learner as warm-up preparation is to the athlete. Let's find out why.

MINDS-ON

1. A few of your students come to you and ask why they aren't using dictionaries to help them learn vocabulary words as they did last year. What is your response? Justify your response.
2. Each of the following statements should be randomly assigned to members of your group. Your task with your drawn statement is to play the "devil's advocate." Imagine that you are in a conference with other teachers, all of whom have the same child in their classes. One member of the teaching team, represented by the other members of your discussion group, makes the statement you've selected, and you totally disagree. Argue to these teachers why you feel this statement is false. Members of the teaching team must respond with counterarguments, using classroom examples for support whenever possible.

    a. Students who interested and enthusiastic are more likely to learn the vocabulary of a content area subject.
    b. Students need to know how to inquire into the meanings of unknown words by using context analysis and dictionary skills.
    c. An atmosphere for vocabulary reinforcement is created by activities involving speaking, listening, writing, and reading.
    d. Vocabulary reinforcement provides opportunities for students to increase their knowledge of the technical vocabulary of a subject.
    e. Vocabulary taught and reinforced within the framework of concept development enhances reading comprehension.
    f. Vocabulary knowledge and reading comprehension have a strong relationship.

    Were there any statements that you had difficulty defending? If so, pose these to the class as a whole, and solicit perspectives from other groups.

3. Your principal notices that your history class spends a lot of time working in pairs and groups on vocabulary, and she doesn't understand why this is necessary "just to learn words." As a group, compose a letter to her explaining the importance of student inter-action in learning the vocabulary of any content area.

HANDS-ON

1. The class should be organized into four groups. Two groups will represent alien life forms, and two will represent human beings. Each group meets for 15 to 20 minutes. Working separately, each alien group will create five or six statements in their own "alien" language. The humans will organize strategies for decoding the messages they will receive.

   After the time has elapsed, each alien group meets with a human group, and the aliens make their statements. If possible, the aliens will attempt to respond to the humans' questions with keywords or phrases. Next, with the alien and human groups switched, the process is repeated. Finally, as a whole class, discuss your success or lack of success in translating in relation to what you have learned about vocabulary and concepts.

2. Examine the following list of vocabulary words taken from this chapter:

general vocabulary	comprehension
technical vocabulary	conceptual level
special vocabulary	concept circles
concept	OPIN
word sorts (open, closed)	word puzzles
brainstorming	magic squares
semantic word maps	prior knowledge
knowledge ratings	target concept
syntactic and semantic contextual aids	cognitive operations
semantic feature analysis	joining
freewriting	excluding
modified cloze passages	selecting
context	implying

   Team with three other members of the class, and with this list of words, each cre-ate one of the following:

   a. Two conceptually related activities such as a set of concept circles and a closed word sort
   b. A context activity that presents the key concept words in meaningful sentence con-texts
   c. A semantic word map or a semantic feature analysis

   Follow this activity with a discussion of the advantages and disadvantages of each approach and of the appropriate time during a unit to use each.

   Answers to cloze passage: 1. Canada, 2. escape, 3. life, 4. Confederation, 5. trade, 6. war, 7. allowance, 8. pensions, 9. fisheries, 10. politicians.

Possible answers to OPIN exercises: Science: 1. roots, 2. radiation, 3. rodents; Social Studies: 1. poverty, 2. violence, 3. organize; Health and Home Ecology: 1. absorbed, 2. soiled.

SUGGESTED READINGS

Baumann, J., & Kameenui, E. (1991). Research on vocabulary instruction: Ode to Voltaire. In J. Flood, J. M. Jensen, D. Lapp, & J. R. Squire (Eds.), *Handbook of research on teaching the English language arts.* New York: Macmillan.

Blachowicz, C. L. Z. (1991). Vocabulary instruction in content classes for special needs learners: Why and how? *Reading, Writing, and Learning Disabilities, 7,* 297–308.

Blachowicz, C. L. Z., & Fisher, P. J. L. (1994). Vocabulary instruction: In A. C. Purves, *Encyclopedia of English studies and language arts.* New York: Scholastic.

Blachowicz, C. L. Z., & Fisher, P. J. L. (1996). *Teaching vocabulary in all classrooms.* Columbus, OH: Merrill.

Buikema, J., & Graves, M. (1993). Teaching students to use context clues to infer work meanings. *Journal of Reading, 36,* 450–457.

Gordon, C., Sheridan, M., & Paul, W. (1998). Reading and writing to enhance vocabulary development. In *Content literacy for secondary teachers* (pp. 165–208). Toronto: Harcourt Brace.

Graves, M. F., & Slater, W. (1996). Vocabulary instruction in content areas. In D. Lapp, J. Flood, & N. Farnan (Eds.), *Content area reading and learning: Instructional strategies.* Boston, MA: Allyn & Bacon.

Heimlich, J. E., & Pittelman, S. D. (1986). *Semantic mapping: Classroom applications.* Newark, DE: International Reading Association.

Kibbey, M. (1995). The organization and teaching of things and the words that signify them. *Journal of Adolescent and Adult Literacy, 39,* 208–223.

Marzano, R., & Marzano, J. (1988). *A cluster approach to elementary vocabulary instruction.* Newark, DE: International Reading Association.

McKeown, M. (1985). The acquisition of word meaning from context by children of high and low ability. *Reading Research Quarterly, 20,* 482–496.

McKeown, M., Beck, I., Omanson, R., & Pople, M. (1985). Some effects of the nature and frequency of vocabulary instruction on the knowledge and use of words. *Reading Research Quarterly, 20,* 222–235.

Nagy, W. E. (1988). *Teaching vocabulary to improve reading comprehension.* Newark, DE: International Reading Association.

Ruddell, M. R. (1994). Vocabulary knowledge and comprehension: A comprehension-process view of complex literacy relationships. In R. B. Ruddell, M. R. Ruddell, & H. Singer (Eds.), *Theoretical models and processes of reading* (4th ed.). Newark, DE: International Reading Association.

Ryder, R. (1985). Student-activated vocabulary instruction. *Journal of Reading, 28,* 254–259.

Scott, J. A., & Nagy, W. E. (1994). Vocabulary development. In A. C. Purves, *Encyclopedia of English studies and language arts.* New York: Scholastic.

Stahl, S. (1986). Three principles of effective vocabulary instruction. *Journal of Reading, 29,* 662–668.

chapter six

Prereading
Strategies

> *When the student is ready,*
> *the teacher appears.*
>
> –Anonymous

ORGANIZING PRINCIPLE

More often than not, content area teachers are perplexed by the behaviour of learners who are capable of acquiring content through lecture, discussion, and other modes of classroom presentation but appear neither ready nor willing to learn with print texts. The wisdom in the saying, "When the student is ready, the teacher appears" is self-evident, yet teachers who want to use texts often find themselves wondering, "*When* are my students ready?"

Certainly, preparing students for the language of a content area, as we discussed in Chapter 5, readies them for learning with texts. The more learners connect what they know to the vocabulary of a content area, the more familiar and confident they are likely to be with the material being studied. To be ready is surely a state of mind, a mental preparation for learning, a psychological predisposition but content area teachers know that readiness also entails an emotional stake in the ideas under scrutiny and a willingness on the part of the students to *want* to engage in learning. Most students, we believe, would like to use reading to learn but don't believe that they have much chance of success. So some find any excuse to avoid reading. Others go through the motions—reading the assigned material purposelessly—to satisfy the teacher's requirements rather than their own as learners.

Students *will* want to read when they have developed a sense of confidence with texts. Ability alone is no guarantee that students will use reading to learn. Neither is knowledge of the subject. As Virgil, the ancient Roman poet, affirmed, all things are within the realm of human possibility when people have confidence in their ability to succeed. "They can," Virgil mused, "because they think they can."

Confident readers think and learn with texts, and they also think positively about the process of learning with texts. They generate interest in the task at hand; their goals are in front of them. If there is an imperative in this chapter, it is to kindle student interest in text assignments and prepare them to think positively about what they will read.

Preparing students to read (and listen and view) can easily be neglected in a teacher's rush to cover the content of the curriculum. Yet prereading (or prelistening or previewing) strategies, as suggested in the organizing principle of the chapter, will make your efforts worthwhile: **piquing interest in and raising expectations about the meaning of texts create a context in which students will read, listen, and view with purpose and anticipation.**

Explanations of reading tend to be complex. Yet as intricate a process as reading may be, it's surely just as magical and mysterious to most of us. After all, who ever really knows a covert process—one that takes place in the head?

We believe an element of mystery will always be a part of reading, even though it appears to be second nature to many of us. For most teachers, reading just happens, particularly when there is a strong purpose or a need to read in the first place. However, a great deal of uncertainty pervades reading for many students. The reading process remains a mystery, a lot of hocus-pocus, to students who believe they have limited control over their chances of success with a reading assignment.

CHAPTER OVERVIEW

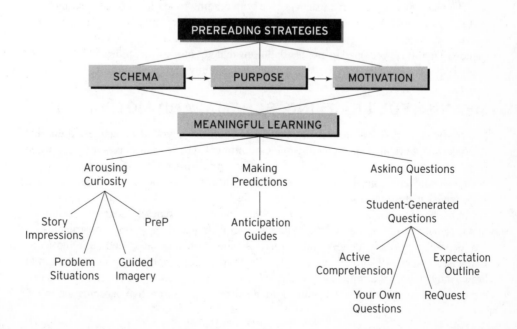

FRAME OF MIND

1. Why do prereading strategies that activate prior knowledge and raise interest in the subject prepare students to approach texts in a critical frame of mind?

2. How can meaningful learning be achieved with content area reading?

3. What are the relationships among curiosity arousal, conceptual conflict, and motivation?

4. How and why does a prediction strategy such as use of an anticipation guide facilitate comprehension?

5. What is the value of student-generated questions, and how might teachers help students ask questions as they read, listen, and view?

6. Which prereading strategies seem to be the most useful in your content area? Least useful? Why?

As a result, some students resort to a special kind of "magic" to achieve control over the information and concepts communicated in a print text. Magic, in this case, often involves bypassing the text altogether. In its place, students may resort to memorizing class notes, reading Cliffs Notes summaries, or hoping for an easy exam that doesn't require reading.

You can do a great deal to reduce the lack of control and the uncertainty that students bring to learning situations. You can take the mystery out of learning by generating students' interest in what they are reading, listening to, or viewing; convincing them that they know more about the subject under study than they think they do; helping them actively connect what they do know to the content of the text; and making them aware of the strategies they need in order to construct meaning.

The challenge content area teachers face with reading to learn is not necessarily related to students' inability to handle the conceptual and stylistic demands of academic texts. What students can do and what they choose to do are related but different instructional matters. Therefore, you need to create conditions that not only allow students to read effectively but also motivate them to want to read purposefully and meaningfully.

MEANINGFUL LEARNING, SCHEMA, AND MOTIVATION

Jerome Bruner (1970), a pioneer in the field of cognitive psychology, suggested that the mind doesn't work apart from feeling and commitment. The learner makes meaning when he or she exhibits an "inherent passion" for what is to be learned. That is to say, *if* knowledge is to be constructed, it must be put into a context of action and commitment. Willingness is the key; action, the instrument for learning.

In his book *Acts of Meaning*, Bruner (1990) champions a renewed cognitive revolution that is sensitive to meaning-making within a cultural context. How people construct meaning depends on their beliefs, mental states, intentions, desires, and commitments. Likewise, Eisner (1991) calls us to celebrate thinking in schools by reminding us that brains may be born, but minds are made. Schools do not pay enough attention to students' curiosity and imagination. As a result, students disengage from active participation in the academic life of the classroom because there is little satisfaction to be gained from it. Unless the student receives satisfaction from schoolwork, Eisner argues, there is little reason or motive to continue to pursue learning: "Thinking ... should be prized not only because it leads to attractive destinations but because the journey itself is satisfying" (p. 40).

In exploring matters of the mind, cognitive activity cannot be divorced from emotional involvement. Schema and motivation are intertwined with students' reasons for reading. Meaningful learning with texts occurs when students reap satisfaction and a sense of accomplishment from texts.

Two of the most appropriate questions that students can ask about a reading, listening, or viewing selection are, "What do I need to know?" and "How well do I already know it?" "What do I need to know?" prompts readers to activate their prior knowledge to make predictions and set purposes. It gets them thinking positively about the reading material. "How well do I already know it?" helps readers search their experience and knowledge to give support to tentative predictions and to help make plans for comprehending.

As simple as these two questions may seem on the surface, maturing learners rarely know enough about the reading process to ask them. "What do I need to know?" and "How well do I already know it?" require *metacognitive awareness* on the part of learners. However, these two questions, when consciously raised and reflected on, put students on the road to regulating and monitoring their own learning behaviour. It is never too early (or too late) to begin showing students how to set purposes by raising questions about the text.

In Chapter 1, we underscored the important role that schema plays in meaningful learning, so we won't belabour the point here, other than to reaffirm that prior knowledge activation is inescapably bound to one's purposes for reading and learning. As students ready themselves to learn with texts, they need to approach upcoming material in a critical frame of mind for potentially meaningful but new material that they will encounter while reading. Instructional scaffolding should make readers receptive to meaningful learning by creating a reference point for connecting the given (what one knows) with the new (the material to be learned). A frame of reference signals the connections students must make between the given and the new. They need to recognize how new material fits into the conceptual frameworks they already have.

Conceptual conflicts are the key to creating motivational conditions in the classroom (Berlyne 1965). Should students be presented with prereading situations that take the form of puzzlement, doubt, surprise, perplexity, contradiction, or ambiguity, they will be motivated to seek resolution. Why? The need within the learner is to resolve the conflict. As a result, the search for knowledge becomes a driving motivational force. When a question begins to gnaw at a learner, searching behaviour is stimulated; learning occurs as the conceptual conflict resolves itself.

AROUSING CURIOSITY

Arousing curiosity and activating prior knowledge are closely related instructional activities. Curiosity arousal gives students the chance to consider what they know already about the material to be read. Through your guidance, they are encouraged to make connections and to relate their knowledge to the text assignment. And further, they will recognize that there are problems—conceptual conflicts—to be resolved through reading. Arousing curiosity helps students raise questions that they can answer only by giving thought to what they read.

Creating Story Impressions

Story impressions is a prereading strategy that arouses curiosity and allows students to anticipate what stories might be about. Although teachers use story impressions with narrative text, this technique may also be used to create "text impressions" in content areas other than English language arts.

As a prereading activity, this strategy uses clue words associated with the setting, characters, and events in the story (the story impressions) to help readers write their own versions of the story prior to reading. McGinley and Denner (1987), originators of the strategy, describe it this way: "Story impressions get readers to predict the events of the story that will be read, by providing them with fragments of the actual content. After reading the set of clues, the students are asked to render them comprehensible by using them to compose a story of their own in advance of reading the actual tale" (p. 249).

Fragments from the story, in the form of clue words, enable readers to form an overall impression of how the characters and events interact in the story. This strategy can also be used with listening texts (for example, from a storyteller) or for a film. The clue words are selected directly from the story and are sequenced with arrows or lines to form a descriptive chain. The chain of clue words triggers impressions of what the story may be about. Students then write a "story guess" that predicts the events in the story.

Study the story impressions example in Figure 6.1. It is based on *Sarah and the People of Sand River* by W. G. Valgardson. The book was used as a read-aloud to introduce middle school learners to a unit on "supernatural happenings."

McGinley and Denner (1987) explain, "The object, of course, is not for the student to guess the details or the exact relations among the events and characters of the story, but to simply compare his or her own story guess to the author's actual account" (p. 250). They suggest the following steps to introduce story impressions to the class for the first time:

1. *Introduce the strategy.* Say to the students, "Today we're going to make up what we think this story *could* be about."

2. *Use large newsprint, a transparency, or a chalkboard to show students the story chain.* (see the left side of Figure 6.1 for an example). Say, "Here are some clues about the story we're going to read." Explain that the students will use the clues to write their own version of the story and that after reading, they will compare what they wrote with the actual story.

3. *Read the clues together, and explain how the arrows link one clue to another in a logical order.* Then brainstorm story ideas that connect all of the clues in the order that they are presented saying, "What do we think this story could be about?"

4. *Demonstrate how to write a story guess.* Use the ideas generated to write a class-composed story that links all of the clues. Use newsprint, the chalkboard, or a transparency for this purpose. Read the story prediction aloud with the students.

5. *Invite the students to read the actual story silently, or initiate a shared reading experience.* Afterward, discuss how the class-composed version is similar to and different from the author's story.

Story Chain	Story Impression
New Iceland ↓ LAke Winnipeg ↓ Sarah, father ↓ Cree pendant ↓ Winnipeg ↓ Mrs. Simpson ↓ boarder ↓ slave ↓ raven ↓ Cree woman, mittens ↓ Cree man, moccasins ↓ lost pendant ↓ returned pendant ↓ runaway ↓ snowstorm ↓ ghostly figures ↓ raven ↓ boy ↓ rescue ↓ New Iceland	The trek from New Iceland to the shores of Lake Winnipeg was a long one, but Sarah and her father were determined to retrieve the Cree pendant. Upon their arrival in Winnipeg they were met by Mrs. Simpson, who took them to the house where she herself was a boarder. The slave who worked in the kitchen told them of a good omen she had seen in a raven which had settled in the tree opposite the house. The next day they ventured to the open market, where they spoke to a Cree woman selling mittens, and a Cree man selling moccasins, and described the lost pendant. The returned pendant was found in its leather pouch by a runaway boy who had struggled through a snowstorm to follow the ghostly figures that had lured him away from their villages, and was led by a raven to shelter. The boy, grateful for his rescue, gave them the pendant and all three returned to New Iceland.

FIGURE 6.1   Story Impression for *Sarah and the People of Sand River*

6. *For subsequent stories, use story impressions to have students write individual story predictions.* Or have them work in cooperative teams to write a group-composed story guess.

Notice in Figure 6.2 how a science teacher adapted story impressions to have students predict events leading up to the patent for insulin. In the space provided for a "text prediction," try writing what you think the text will be about. Compare your prediction with the one appearing at the end of this chapter on page 186.

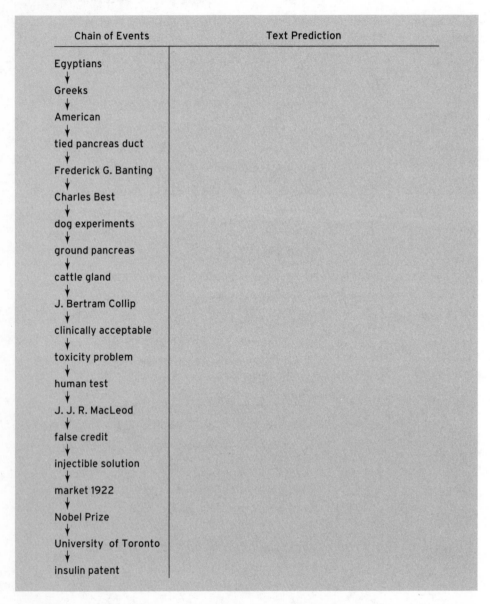

Chain of Events	Text Prediction
Egyptians	
↓	
Greeks	
↓	
American	
↓	
tied pancreas duct	
↓	
Frederick G. Banting	
↓	
Charles Best	
↓	
dog experiments	
↓	
ground pancreas	
↓	
cattle gland	
↓	
J. Bertram Collip	
↓	
clinically acceptable	
↓	
toxicity problem	
↓	
human test	
↓	
J. J. R. MacLeod	
↓	
false credit	
↓	
injectible solution	
↓	
market 1922	
↓	
Nobel Prize	
↓	
University of Toronto	
↓	
insulin patent	

FIGURE 6.2   Chain of Events Leading to the Patent for Insulin

Establishing Problematic Perspectives

Creating problems to be solved or perspectives from which readers approach text material provides an imaginative entry into a text selection. For example, the teacher's role in creating problematic perspectives is (1) providing the time to discuss the problem, raising questions, and seeking possible solutions before reading and then (2) assigning the reading material that will help lead to resolution and conceptual development.

A social studies teacher and her students were exploring the development of early settlements in a unit on pioneer Canadian life. She presented the problem situation to her students as shown in Figure 6.3. The series of questions promoted an interest-filled discussion, putting students in a situation in which they had to rely on prior knowledge for responses.

Asking the students in the social studies class to approach reading by imagining that they were early European settlers placed them in a particular role. With the role came a perspective. Creating such a perspective has its underpinnings in a schema-theoretical view of the reading process.

One of the early studies of the Center for the Study of Reading at the University of Illinois pointed to the powerful role of perspective in comprehending text (Pichert & Anderson 1977). The researchers showed just how important the reader's perspective can be. Two groups of readers were asked to read a passage about a house from one of two perspectives: a burglar or a house buyer. When readers who held the perspective of a house burglar read the story about going through the house, they recalled different information from those readers who approached the story from the perspective of a house buyer.

Creating a perspective (a role) for the student is one way to get into reading. Students in these roles find themselves solving problems that force them to use their knowledge and experience.

In Figure 6.4 on page 174, a secondary school teacher created a perspective for students before assigning a reading selection from an auto mechanics manual.

In preparation for reading the short story "Alas Babylon," an English teacher set up a perspective in which students' curiosity was aroused and their expectations of the story raised:

> The time is 1840 and the place is Upper Canada. Imagine that you are early European settlers. You will want to try to think as you believe they may have thought and act as they might have acted. Divide into two groups. One group has purchased a number of 40 hectare lots to use as farms. The other group decides to provide services in a village and in the surrounding area. What businesses will you build first? Later? (Examples might include grist mill, lumber mill, general store, post office, doctor's office, and school.) As proprietors, would you treat yourselves differently from those who work for you? Why? How would you run the government?

FIGURE 6.3   **A Problem Situation in a Canadian History Class**

You are the only mechanic on duty when a four-wheel-drive truck with a V-8 engine pulls in for repair. The truck has high mileage, and it appears that the problem may be a worn clutch disk. What tools do you think you will need? What procedures would you follow? Put your answers to these questions under the two following headings.

Tools Needed   **Procedures**

_____   _____

_____   _____

_____   _____

_____   _____

FIGURE 6.4   **Creating a Perspective in an Auto Mechanics Class**

The year is 2015. We are on the verge of a nuclear disaster. Through inside sources, you hear that the attack will occur within five days. What preparations will you consider making before the nuclear attack occurs?

The class considered the orienting question. After some discussion, the teacher initiated the activity in Figure 6.5. The students formed small groups, and each group was directed to come to a consensus on the 12 activities they would choose. Those items were chosen from the list in Figure 6.5.

From the small-group discussions came the recognition that the values, beliefs, and attitudes readers bring to a text shape their perspective as much as their background knowledge of a topic. For this reason, we suggest that building the motivation for a text that is to be read take into account, where appropriate, an examination of values, attitudes, and controversial issues related to the subject matter.

Guided Imagery

Guided imagery allows students to explore concepts visually. Samples (1977) recommends guided imagery, among other things, as a means of

- Building an experience base for inquiry, discussion, and group work
- Exploring and stretching concepts
- Solving and clarifying problems
- Exploring history and the future
- Exploring other lands and worlds

Read the example in Figure 6.6 on page 176; then close your eyes and do what it says.

You may wish to have students discuss their "trips," which, of course, should parallel in some way the content of the reading selection to be assigned. In the classroom where this example was devised, students in a literature class participated in the imagery discus-

Assuming that your town and house will not be destroyed by the bomb and that you have enough time to prepare for the attack, which 12 activities from the following list will you choose?

_____ 1. Buy a gun and ammunition to protect against looters.

_____ 2. Cash in all mutual funds and take all the money out of your chequing and savings accounts.

_____ 3. Build a fireplace in your house.

_____ 4. Buy firewood and charcoal.

_____ 5. Buy extra tanks of gasoline and fill up your car.

_____ 6. Purchase antibiotics and other medicines.

_____ 7. Dig a latrine.

_____ 8. Buy lumber, nails, and various other supplies.

_____ 9. Plant fruit trees.

_____ 10. Notify all your friends and relatives of the coming nuclear attack.

_____ 11. Invest in books on canning and making candles and soap.

_____ 12. Buy a few head of livestock from a farmer.

_____ 13. Buy fishing equipment and a boat.

_____ 14. Buy seeds of several different kinds of vegetables for a garden.

_____ 15. Make friends with a farmer who has a horse and wagon.

_____ 16. Shop at antiques stores for kerosene lamps and large cooking pots.

_____ 17. Buy a safe in which to hide your money.

_____ 18. Buy foodstuffs.

FIGURE 6.5 **Creating a Perspective in an English Class**

sion before reading a short story on space travel. Discussion questions included, "How did you feel just before entering the space capsule? What were the reactions of your companions? Where did your exploration take you? Were there things that surprised you on the trip? Colours? Sounds?"

Some teachers will find themselves uncomfortable using guided imagery as a prereading strategy; others will not. However, it gives you an additional instructional option

Close your eyes... tell all your muscles to relax. You are entering a space capsule 10 minutes before takeoff. Soon you feel it lift off ... you look over at your companions and check their reactions. Now you are ready to take a reading of the instrument panel. As you relay the information to ground control, it is 11 minutes into the flight ... You settle back into your chair and tell your fellow astronauts about your thoughts ... about what you hope to see when the vehicle lands ... about what you might touch and hear as you explore your destination. Finally, you drift off to sleep ... picturing yourself returning to earth ... seeing once again your friends and relations. You are back where you started ... tell your muscles to move ... open your eyes.

FIGURE 6.6   **A Guided Imagery Illustration**

that will help students connect, in this case, what they "see" in their mind's eye to what they will read.

PreP

Brainstorming is a key feature of the prereading plan (PreP), which may be used to generate interest in content area reading and to estimate the levels of background knowledge that students bring to the text assignments. Judith Langer (1981) recommends PreP as an assessment and instructional activity that fosters group discussion and an awareness of the topics to be covered. She suggests that PreP works best with groups of about 10 students.

Before beginning the PreP activity, the teacher should examine the text material for keywords (which represent major concepts to be developed), phrases, or pictures and then introduce the topic that is to be read, following the three-phase plan that Langer (1981, p. 154) outlines:

1. *Initial associations with the concept.* In this first phase the teacher says, "Tell anything that comes to mind when ... " (e.g., " ... you hear the word *Senate*"). As each student tells what ideas initially came to mind, the teacher jots each response on the board. During this phase, the students have their first opportunity to find associations between the key concept and their prior knowledge. When this activity was carried out in a middle school class, one student, Bill, said, "Important people." Another student, Danette, said, "Ottawa."

2. *Reflections on initial associations.* During the second phase of PreP, the students are asked, "What made you think of ... [the response given by a student]?" This phase helps the students develop awareness of their network of associations. They also have an opportunity to listen to each other's explanations, to interact, and to become aware of their changing ideas. Through this procedure, they may weigh, reject, accept, revise, and integrate some of the ideas that came to mind. When Bill was asked what made him think of important people, he said, "I saw them in the newspaper." When Danette was asked what made her think of Ottawa, she said, "Senate is there."

3. *Reformulation of knowledge.* In this phase, the teacher says, "Based on our discussion and before we read the text, have you any new ideas about ... [e.g., Senate]?" This phase allows students to verbalize associations that have been elaborated or changed through the discussion. Because they have had a chance to probe their memories to elaborate on their prior knowledge, the responses elicited during the third phase are often more refined than those from the first. This time, Bill said, "Government of Canada," and Danette said, "Canadian government part that reviews the laws."

Through observation and listening during PreP, content area teachers will find their students' knowledge can be divided into three broad levels. On one level are students who have *much* prior knowledge about the concept. These students are often able to define and draw analogies, make conceptual links, and think categorically. On the second level are students who may have *some* prior knowledge. These students can give examples and cite characteristics of the content but may be unable to see relationships or make connections between what they know and the new material. On the third level are students who have *little* background knowledge. They often respond to the PreP activity with words that sound like the concept word and may attempt to make simple associations, often misassociating with the topic.

MAKING PREDICTIONS

Prediction strategies activate thought about the content before reading. Students must rely on what they know through previous study and experience to make educated guesses about the material to be read.

Why an educated guess? Smith (1988) defines *predicting* as the prior elimination of unlikely alternatives. He suggests:

> Readers do not normally attend to print with their minds blank, with no prior purpose and with no expectation of what they might find in the text.... The way readers look for meaning is not to consider all possibilities, nor to make reckless guesses about just one, but rather to predict within the most likely range of alternatives.... Readers can derive meaning from text because they bring expectations about meaning to text. (p. 163)

You can facilitate student-centred purposes by creating anticipation about the meaning of what will be read.

ANTICIPATION GUIDES

An *anticipation guide* is a series of statements to which students must respond individually before reading the text. Their value lies in the discussion that takes place after the exercise. The teacher's role during discussion is to activate and agitate thought. As students connect their knowledge of the world to the prediction task, you must remain open to a wide range of responses. Draw on what students bring to the task, but remain nondirective in order to keep the discussion moving.

Anticipation guides may vary in format but not in purpose. In each case, the readers' expectations about meaning are raised before they read the text. Keep these guidelines in mind in constructing and using an anticipation guide:

1. *Analyze the material to be read.* Determine the major ideas—implicit and explicit—with which students will interact.

2. *Write those ideas in short, clear declarative statements.* These statements should in some way reflect the world in which the students live or about which they know. Therefore, avoid abstractions whenever possible.

3. *Put these statements in a format that will elicit anticipation and prediction.*

4. *Discuss the students' predictions and anticipations before they read the text selection.*

5. *Assign the text selection.* Have the students evaluate the statements in light of the author's intent and purpose.

6. *Contrast the readers' predictions with the author's intended meaning.*

A middle school social studies teacher prepared students for a reading assignment that contrasted the characteristics of French and English Canadians in the early twentieth century. She began by writing "French" and "English" in separate columns on the board. She asked students to think about what they already knew about the two groups: "How do you think they were alike? How were they different?" After some discussion, the teacher invited the students to participate in the anticipation activity in Figure 6.7.

French and English Canadians were the two biggest groups in early twentieth century Canada. You will be reading about some of their basic differences in your textbook. What do you think those differences will be? Before reading your assignment, place the initials FC in front of the phrases that you think best describe French Canadians. Place the initials EC in front of the statements that best describe English Canadians. Do not mark statements common to both.

_____   1. More likely to be Roman Catholic.

_____   2. More likely to be from a rural setting.

_____   3. More likely to vote Conservative.

_____   4. More likely to belong to a labour union.

_____   5. More likely to oppose conscription into the army.

_____   6. More likely to join a socialist party.

_____   7. More likely to belong to a religious order.

_____   8. More likely to be a suffragist.

_____   9. More likely to be from a large family.

_____ 10. More likely to work in a factory.

FIGURE 6.7   Anticipation Guide for a Canadian History Lesson

180

Of course, each of the points highlighted in the statements was devel_ selection. Not only did the students get a sense of the major ideas they woulc the text selection, but they also read to see how well they had predicted which more accurately represented members of the French Canadian and English _ communities.

A science teacher began a weather unit by introducing a series of popular clichés a the weather. He asked his students to anticipate whether the clichés had a scientific basis (see Figure 6.8).

The prereading discussion led the students to review and expand their concepts of scientific truth. Throughout different parts of the unit, the teacher returned to one or two of the clichés in the anticipation guide and suggested to the class that the textbook assignment would explain whether there was a scientific basis for each saying. Students were then directed to read to find out what the explanations were.

A health education teacher raised expectations and created anticipation for a chapter on the human immunodeficiency virus (HIV) and AIDS. Rather than prepare written statements, she conducted the anticipatory lesson as part of an introductory class discussion.

Directions: Put a check under "Likely" if you believe that the weather saying has any scientific basis; put a check under "Unlikely" if you believe that it has no scientific basis. Be ready to explain your choice.

Likely   Unlikely

_____   _____   1. Red sky at night, sailors delight; red sky at morning, sailors take warning.

_____   _____   2. If you see a sunspot, there is going to be bad weather.

_____   _____   3. When the leaves turn under, it is going to storm.

_____   _____   4. If you see a hornet's nest high in a tree, a harsh winter is coming.

_____   _____   5. Aching bones mean a cold and rainy forecast.

_____   _____   6. If a groundhog sees his shadow, six more weeks of winter.

_____   _____   7. Rain before seven, sun by eleven.

_____   _____   8. If a cow lies down in a pasture, it is going to rain soon.

_____   _____   9. Sea gull, sea gull, sitting on the sand; it's never good weather while you're on land.

FIGURE 6.8   Anticipation Guide for Clichés About Weather

She raised curiosity about the topic by asking students to participate in a strategy known as the "every-pupil response." She told the students that she would ask several questions about becoming infected with HIV. Every student was to respond to each question by giving a "thumbs up" if they agreed or a "thumbs down" if they disagreed. The class had to participate in unison and keep their thumbs up or down. After each question, the students shared their reasons for responding thumbs up or thumbs down.

The questions were framed as follows: "Is it true that you can contract HIV by

- Having unprotected sex with an infected partner?"
- Kissing someone with HIV?"
- Sharing needles with an HIV-infected drug user?"
- Sharing a locker with an infected person?"
- Using a telephone after someone with HIV has used it?"
- Being bitten by a mosquito?"

The "oral anticipation guide" created lively discussion as students discussed some of their preconceived notions and misconceptions about HIV and AIDS.

Mathematics teachers also have been successful in their use of anticipation guides. In a precalculus class, the teacher introduced the activity in Figure 6.9 to begin the trigonometry section of the textbook. She created the anticipation guide to help students address

Directions: Put a check under "Likely" if you believe that the statement has any mathematical truth. Put a check under "Unlikely" if you believe that it has no mathematical truth. Be ready to explain your choices.

Likely   Unlikely

_____   _____   1. Trigonometry deals with circles.

_____   _____   2. Angles have little importance in trigonometry.

_____   _____   3. Sailors use trigonometry in navigation.

_____   _____   4. Angles can be measured only in degrees.

_____   _____   5. Calculators are useless in trigonometry.

_____   _____   6. Trigonometry deals with triangles.

_____   _____   7. Trigonometry has no application in the real world.

_____   _____   8. Radians are used in measuring central angles.

_____   _____   9. Trigonometry has scientific uses.

_____   _____   10. Radians can be converted to degrees.

FIGURE 6.9   Anticipation Guide for Preconceived Notions About Trigonometry

their own knowledge about trigonometry and to create conceptual conflict for some of the more difficult sections of the chapter they would be studying.

STUDENT-GENERATED QUESTIONS

Teaching students to generate their own questions about material to be read is an important prereading instructional goal. Harry Singer (1978) contends that whenever readers are involved in asking questions, they are engaged in "active comprehension." Teachers can use an active comprehension strategy when they *ask questions that beget questions in return*. You might, for example, focus attention on a picture or an illustration from a story or book and ask a question that induces student questions in response, "What would you like to know about the picture?" In return, invite the students to generate questions that focus on the details in the picture or its overarching message.

Or you might decide to read to students an opening paragraph or two from a text selection, enough to whet their appetite for the selection. Then ask, "What else would you like to know about _____?" Complete the question by focusing attention on some aspect of the selection that is pivotal to students' comprehension. It may be the main character of a story or the main topic of an expository text.

Active comprehension questions not only arouse interest and curiosity but also draw learners into the material. As a result, students will read to satisfy purposes and resolve conceptual conflicts that they have identified through their own questions. Let us examine several additional instructional strategies for engaging students in asking questions for reading.

ReQuest

ReQuest was originally devised as a one-on-one procedure involving the student and the teacher. Yet this strategy can easily be adapted to content area classrooms to help students think as they read. ReQuest encourages students to ask their own questions about the content material under study. Self-declared questions are forceful. They help students establish reasonable purposes for their reading. Betts (1950) describes a "highly desirable learning situation" as one in which the student does the questioning: "That is, the learner asks the questions, and sets up the problems to be solved during the reading activity" (p. 450).

ReQuest fosters an active search for meaning. Manzo (1969) describes the rules for ReQuest:

> The purpose of this lesson is to improve your understanding of what you read. We will each read silently the first sentence. Then we will take turns asking questions about the sentence and what it means. You will ask questions first, then I will ask questions. Try to ask the kind of questions a teacher might ask, in the way a teacher might ask them. You may ask me as many questions as you wish. When you are asking me questions, I will close my book (or pass the book to you if there is only one between us). When I ask questions, you close your book.... Any question asked deserves to be answered as fully and honestly as possible. It is cheating for a teacher to withhold information or play dumb to draw out the student. It is unacceptable for a student to answer with "I don't know," since he can at least attempt to explain why he cannot answer. If questions are unclear to either party, requests for rephrasing or clarification are in order. The responder should be ready (and make it a practice) to justify his answer by reference back to the text or to expand on background that was used to build or to limit an answer. Whenever possible, if there is uncer-

tainty about an answer, the respondent should check ... [the] answer against the text. (pp. 124–125)

Although the rules for ReQuest were devised for one-on-one instruction, they can be adapted for the content area classroom. If you decide to use ReQuest in your class, consider these steps:

1. *Both the students and the teacher silently read the same segment of the text.* Manzo recommends one sentence at a time for students who have trouble comprehending what they read. However, text passages of varying length are suitable in classroom applications. For example, both teacher and students may begin by reading a paragraph or two.

2. *The teacher closes the book and is questioned about the passage by the students.*

3. *Next, there is an exchange of roles.* The teacher queries the students about the material.

4. *On completion of the student–teacher exchange, the class and the teacher read the next segment of text.* Steps 2 and 3 are repeated.

5. *Stop questioning and begin predicting.* At a suitable point in the text, when the students have processed enough information to make predictions about the remainder of the assignment, the exchange of questions stops. The teacher then asks prediction questions, "What do you think the rest of the assignment is about? Why do you think so?" Speculation is encouraged.

6. *Students are then assigned the remaining portion of the selection to read silently.*

7. *The teacher facilitates a follow-up discussion of the material.*

You can modify the ReQuest procedure to good advantage. For example, consider alternating the role of questioner after each question. By doing so, you will probably involve more students in the activity. Once students sense the types of questions that can be asked about a text passage, you might also try forming ReQuest teams. A ReQuest team composed of three or four students is pitted against another ReQuest team. Your role is to facilitate the multiple action resulting from the small-group formations.

Our own experiences with ReQuest suggest that students may consistently ask factual questions to stump the teacher or other students. Such questions succeed brilliantly because you are subject to the same restrictions imposed by short-term memory as the students. That you miss an answer or two is actually healthy—after all, to err is human.

However, when students ask only verbatim questions because they don't know how to ask any others, the situation is unhealthy. The sad fact is that some students don't know how to ask questions that will stimulate interpretive or applied levels of thinking. Therefore, your role as a good questioner during ReQuest is to provide a model from which students will learn. Over time, you will notice the difference in the quality of the student questions formulated.

Expectation Outlines

Spiegel (1981) suggests the development of an expectation outline to help students ask questions about text. She recommends the expectation outline for factual material, but the strategy can be adapted to narrative studies as well. The expectation outline is developed on the chalkboard or an overhead projector transparency as students simply tell what they expect to learn from a reading selection.

If students are reading a factual selection, you may have them first take several minutes to preview the material. Then ask, "What do you think your assignment is going to be about?" Ask students to state their expectations in the form of questions. As they suggest questions, group related questions on the chalkboard or transparency. You also have the opportunity to ask students what prompted them to ask these questions in the first place. At this point, students may be encouraged to refer to the text to support their questions.

Once questions have been asked and grouped, the class labels each set of questions. Through discussion, students begin to see the major topics that will emerge from the reading. Help them to recognize that gaps may exist in the expectation outline of the assignment. For example, you may add a topic or two to the outline about which no questions were raised. On completion of the expectation outline, students read to answer the questions generated.

For narrative materials, students may formulate their questions from the title of the selection or pictures or keywords and phrases in the selection. For example, direct students to preview a story by skimming through it quickly, studying the pictures and illustrations (if any), and jotting down 5 to 10 keywords or phrases that appear to indicate the main direction of the story. As students suggest keywords and phrases, write them on the board and categorize them. Then ask students to state what they expect to find out from the story. Have them raise questions about its title, setting, characters, plot, and theme. As an alternative to questions, students may summarize their expectations by writing a paragraph about the story using the keywords and phrases that were jotted down and categorized.

A variation on the expectation outline is a strategy called "asking your own questions." Here's how it works:

1. Have students listen to or read a portion of the text from the beginning of a selection.
2. Ask students to write 5 to 10 questions that they think will be answered by the remainder of the selection.
3. Discuss some of the questions asked by the students before reading. Write the questions on the board.
4. Have students read to determine whether the questions are answered.
5. After reading, ask the students to explain which questions were answered, which weren't, and why not.

Strategies such as an expectation outline or asking your own questions teach students how to approach reading material with an inquisitive mind. These instructional strategies and the others presented in this chapter form a bridge between teacher-initiated guidance and independent learning behaviour by students.

 ## LOOKING BACK, LOOKING FORWARD

Meaningful learning with texts occurs when students experience a sense of satisfaction with text and a feeling of accomplishment. In this chapter, the role that commitment and motivation play in purposeful learning was emphasized. Although some students may be skilled in reading and knowledgeable about the subject, they may not bring that skill and knowledge to bear in learning situations. It takes motivation, a sense of direction and purpose, and a teacher who knows how to create conditions in the classroom that allow students to establish their own motives for reading. One way to arouse curiosity about reading material is to encourage students to make connections among the key concepts to be studied. Another is to create conceptual conflict. Students will read to resolve conflicts arising from problem situations and perspectives and will use guided imagery to explore the ideas to be encountered during reading.

To reduce any uncertainty that students bring to reading material, you can help them raise questions and anticipate meaning by showing them how to connect what they already know to the new ideas presented in the text. The questions students raise as a result of predicting will guide them into the reading material and keep them on course. Anticipation guides, ReQuest, expectation outlines, and self-questioning are strategies for stimulating predictions and anticipation about the content.

In the next chapter, we explore the powerful role of talk in the curriculum. Talking to learn occurs in social collaboration—through cooperative effort. Students' interactions with one another permit them to pool knowledge, compare understandings, and share and negotiate meanings. A classroom context that encourages talk brings learners and texts together to explore and construct meaning.

 ## MINDS-ON

1. Suppose you go to the library looking for a good book to read. You see a cart with a sign: "Current Best-Sellers." Because you have little familiarity with any of the books, how will you make a selection? How will you anticipate which book is for you? Because students rarely have the opportunity to select their course textbook, what can teachers do to help students make the book "fit?"

2. Divide your discussion group into two subgroups: individuals who are willing to take the position that all of the following statements are correct and those willing to argue that all of the statements are inaccurate. Discuss the pros and cons of each topic for five minutes. After you have finished, bring any items to the class as a whole that you believe could truly have been defended from either view, and be prepared to explain why or under what circumstances.

   a. Students are not qualified to ask their own questions about difficult content material.

   b. The old but still common practice of assigning reading in preparation for a discussion is, unfortunately, backward.

   c. Just as athletes need to warm up before a contest, readers (or listeners or viewers) need to warm up to get ready for text.

   d. Analyzing content vocabulary before reading, listening, or viewing is a sound instructional practice.

   e. Having students get information from a variety of materials on the subject matter will only confuse them.

   f. It is pointless to discuss most subjects with students before they read the text because the varied social and economic backgrounds of the students make it possible for only a few to connect any relevant personal experience to the subject.

3. Eliot Eisner believes that brains are born but minds are made. What do you believe is the teacher's role in a classroom filled with 25 brains waiting to be made into minds? Is the teacher the moulder, shaper, and maker—that is, the only active partner? Is the teacher to serve as a model learner, a guide through knowledge, or a facilitator—that is, an equal or superior partner? Or do you see some happy medium? In your group, attempt to reach a consensus on what you consider the best role for a teacher to be in relation to these prompts.

HANDS-ON

1. Try the following science experiment to activate prior knowledge and to stimulate interest in reading an explanation of the formula, *force equals pressure times area*. Bring the following materials to class: 90-L garbage bag, duct tape, and a dozen straws. Flatten the trash bag on a table large enough for a volunteer to lie on with his or her upper body resting on the bag. Cut four small holes about 25 cm along each of the edges of the two sides of the flattened bag that are perpendicular to the open end. Insert one straw in each opening. Next, tape each hole airtight. Tape the open end of the bag airtight as well. Ask a volunteer to lie on his or her back on top of the garbage bag on the table.

    Next, have eight individuals each select one straw, and explain that they will be attempting to lift the volunteer by blowing through the straws into the sealed bag. Before proceeding, however, invite the group to pose questions, draw on their prior knowledge, and anticipate why this experiment may succeed or fail. After the group has theorized about and discussed the problem, mention that the bag will break at a pressure of 454 g per 2.54 cm^2, and ask if that fact changes their predictions. Finally, have the eight individuals attempt to inflate the bag by blowing into the straws simultaneously. As they do, be sure that someone stabilizes the volunteer so that he or she does not roll off the bag.

    If the experiment works, the volunteer should rise several centimetres from the table. Break into small groups of five or six, and imagine that a science instructor has just used this experiment as an introduction to a chapter on the relationship between air pressure, force, and surface area. How motivated are the group members to read this chapter? As a group, discuss how science experiments may be used with anticipation guides, ReQuest, expectation outlines, and graphic organizers.

2. Team with a group of four or five other students. Before the next class, each member should collect three political cartoons, each using a different newspaper, magazine, or book. These cartoons may represent current or historical political issues.

    When you return to class, share the cartoons you found, and discuss the knowledge the reader must already have in order to understand the humour. Select the one cartoon you found most enjoyable, and list the background knowledge needed to understand it. When all groups have finished discussing and selecting, have each group read and explain its favourite cartoon to the whole class. As a large group, discuss how this activity illustrates the concept of prior knowledge when reading text. If there are art majors in the class, ask them to share the role of prior knowledge in viewing works of art.

3. Bring to class a nonfiction book or magazine article on a subject you enjoy. With a partner, practise the ReQuest strategy. On completion of the activity, join with two other pairs, and as a small group, discuss the effectiveness of the questioning, the successfulness of the learning that occurred, and your perceptions of the usefulness of this activity in a content area classroom.

Text prediction for story impressions activity in Figure 6.2 on page 172

Diabetes has been recognized since the days of the ancient Egyptians and Greeks. American attempts to cure the disease in the early twentieth century were unsuccessful. Experimentation on dogs with a tied pancreas duct yielded results for researchers Frederick G. Banting and Charles Best, who conducted dog experiments using insulin derived from ground pancreas, and eventually from cattle glands. J. Bertram Collip joined them in developing an insulin that was clinically acceptable; however, a toxicity problem developed in a human test. J. J. R. McLeod provided people to do the research and was initially given false credit as the actual discoverer of insulin. An injectable solution was on the market in 1922. The Nobel Prize was awarded to Banting and Best, and the University of Toronto obtained the insulin patent.

SUGGESTED READINGS

Anderson, R. C. (1994). Role of the reader's schema in comprehension, learning and memory. In R. B. Ruddell, M. R. Ruddell, & H. Singer (Eds.), *Theoretical models and processes of reading* (4th ed.). Newark, DE: International Reading Association.

Ash, B. H. (1992). Student-made questions: One way into a literary text. *English Journal, 81*(5), 61–64.

Bransford, J. W. (1983). Schema activation–schema acquisition. In R. C. Anderson, J. Osborn, & R. J. Tierney (Eds.), *Learning to read in American schools.* Hillsdale, NJ: Erlbaum.

Crapse, L. (1995). Helping students construct meaning through their own questions. *Journal of Reading, 38,* 389–390.

Dufflemeyer, F. (1994). Effective anticipation guide statements for learning from expository prose. *Journal of Reading, 37,* 452–457.

Dufflemeyer, F., & Baum, D. (1992). The extended anticipation guide revisited. *Journal of Reading, 35,* 654–656.

Gillespie, C. (1990). Questions about student-generated questions. *Journal of Reading, 34,* 250–257.

Herber, H. L. (1978). Prediction as motivation and an aid to comprehension. In *Teaching reading in content areas* (2nd ed.). Upper Saddle River, NJ: Prentice Hall.

Langer, J. A. (1982). Facilitating text processing: The elaboration of prior knowledge. In J. A. Langer & M. T. Smith-Burke (Eds.), *Reader meets author: Bridging the gap.* Newark, DE: International Reading Association.

Mathiason, C. (1989). Stimulating and sustaining student interest in content area reading. *Reading Research and Instruction, 28,* 76–83.

Moore, D. W., Readence, J. E., & Rickelman, R. (2000). *Prereading activities for content area reading* (3rd ed.). Newark, DE: International Reading Association.

Ruddell, M. R. (1996). Engaging students' interest and willing participation in subject area and learning. In D. Lapp, J. Flood, & N. Farnan (Eds.), *Content area reading and learning: Instructional strategies* (2nd ed.). Boston, MA: Allyn & Bacon.

Stipek, D. (1988). *Motivation to learn: From theory to practice.* Upper Saddle River, NJ: Prentice Hall.

chapter seven

Talking to Learn

Talk is the sea upon which all else floats.

–James Britton

ORGANIZING PRINCIPLE

Talk is the primary means by which teachers and students communicate. Talk saturates the classroom environment. It is, to use Britton's metaphor, "the sea upon which all else floats." Without talk, it's difficult to imagine how teachers would ply their craft and how students would engage in meaningful learning. Yet talking is so much a part of our lives that we (and our students) often take for granted the role that talk plays in learning. Donald Rubin (1990), for example, compares classroom talk to the parable about fish in water: just as fish are the least likely creatures ever to become aware of water, teachers and students hardly recognize the power of talk as a medium for learning. Because talk surrounds us and constitutes so much of what we do in the classroom, Rubin suggests that it is invisible to us much of the time. As a result, the potential to use talking to learn often goes untapped in content area classrooms.

As teachers, we can make strong connections between literacy and learning when we link talking to reading and writing. Talk is a bridge to literacy and learning across the curriculum. Through the power of talk—that is to say, authentic classroom discussion—students are able to transcend the information encountered in text, and in doing so, they are in a better position to transform knowledge and make it their own. Making talk more visible in our classrooms, however, isn't an easy task. The predominant type of talk in content area classrooms usually revolves around question–answer exchanges known as *recitations*, in which students take turns answering questions with bits and pieces of information. In these exchanges, the social and psychological context for learning is dominated by teacher talk, with little opportunity for students to explore and clarify ideas, think critically and creatively, and reflect on what they are learning. In this chapter, we examine ways in which teachers can scaffold *text-talk* so that students engage in lively discussions about ideas they encounter in text.

Teachers who make talk visible in their classrooms recognize that students need opportunities to talk spontaneously and to respond personally and critically to ideas they are encountering in text. Over 35 years ago, the London Association for the Teaching of English prepared a seminal policy document on the uses of language across the curriculum (Barnes, Britton, & Rosen 1969). The association's policy statement underscores the power of talk not only to shape a student's ideas but also to modify them by listening to others. Informal, collaborative classroom talk allows students to question; plan; express doubt, difficulty, and confusion; and experiment with new language as they connect literacy to learning. The organizing principle of this chapter highlights the connections students make: **talking to learn helps students explore, clarify, and think about ideas and concepts they encounter in reading and writing, listening and speaking, and viewing and representing.**

CHAPTER OVERVIEW

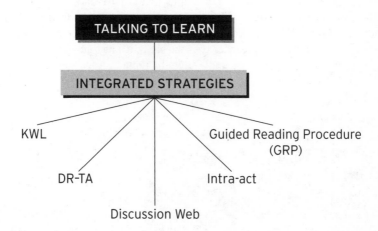

FRAME OF MIND

1. What is the importance of talk as a medium for literacy and learning?
2. How is recitation different from discussion as a type of classroom talk?
3. How can teachers plan discussions so that students actively respond to texts?
4. Why and how do various instructional strategies guide reader-text interactions and encourage talking to learn?

Most students, regardless of ability, bring an important but underused resource to their classrooms, a resource that they have been developing throughout their lives to negotiate meaning and make sense of the world about them: they know how to talk. Young people talk easily and freely for a variety of aims and purposes, most of them social: to communicate, to persuade, to entertain, to inform, to learn about the world in which they live. Observe students in school corridors, on the playground, or in a mall on weekends as they mingle with friends and interact with one another. Talk is something they do all the time.

Teachers are in a position to orchestrate a full range of instructional activities that promote meaningful classroom talk. Gambrell (1996) illustrates how various types of talk fall on a continuum from informal to formal modes of interaction. The model in Figure 7.1 depicts the types of informal and formal talk in relation to the range of audiences with whom individuals interact. At one end of the continuum, the most informal type of talk is inner speech (talking to oneself), and at the other end is the most formal mode of large-audience communication, broadcasting, where talk is technologically mediated, as for a radio talk show or a newscast on television.

In classrooms, instructional conversations and discussions with one or more students represent less formal modes of interaction. Recitations, by contrast, are a more formal type of classroom communication. Because they are formal and directed to large groups, recitations tend to silence student voices and limit responses to one- or two-word answers.

As Douglas Barnes (1995) explains, "The kinds of participation in the classroom conversation that are supported and encouraged by a teacher signal to students what learning is required of them" (p. 2). If student talk is limited by recitations in which teachers do most of the talking, ask mostly factual questions that require one- or two-word answers, and control who takes turns answering questions, students will take their proper role to be passive nonparticipants. Lou, a student, describes what it is like to be in classrooms where teachers dominate talk: "When a teacher runs the show, it's just, just kind of up to him. He has like a lecture written out and, you know, point by point.... A teacher kind of intimidates

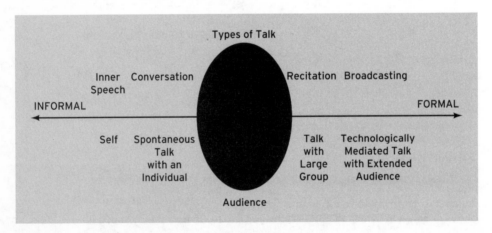

FIGURE 7.1   **A Model of the Continuum of Talk**

Source: From Linda B. Gambrell, "What Research Reveals About Discussion." In Linda B. Gambrell and Janet F. Almasi (Eds.), *Lively Discussions! Fostering Engaged Reading* (Newark, DE: International Reading Association 1996), p. 28. Reprinted with permission of Linda B. Gambrell and the International Reading Association.

the students. 'Cause he's up there, you know, talking, making these complicated points and, you know, [students] just taking notes or something" (Knoeller 1994, p. 578).

Sometimes we unwittingly put students on the spot with the questions we ask during a recitation. Do you recall ever being put on the spot by a question? In that interminable second or two between question and answer, between pounding heart and short gasps for air, do you remember asking yourself, "What's *the* right answer—the one this instructor expects?" When questions are used to foster a right-answer-only atmosphere in class, they will not focus thinking about what has been read, nor will they prompt the processes by which students construct knowledge. They make the correct answer the all-important concern.

When students are on the spot, they often resort to guessing what is inside the teacher's head. One need only read Judy Blume's devastating parody of a music teacher's question to her class in Box 7.1 on page 192 to appreciate how nonproductive that guessing game is.

Seeking right answers only, putting students on the spot, and reinforcing "guess what's in my head" behaviour are tied to what some consider the prevalent instructional practice in North American schooling, *turn taking* (Duffy 1983). Turn taking occurs whenever the teacher asks a question or assigns a turn, the student responds, and the teacher gives feedback by correcting or reinforcing the response. Teachers often depend on turn taking to "discuss" topics under study. Yet what results is hardly a discussion at all. During turn-taking routines, questions usually forestall or frustrate classroom talk. Question–answer exchanges are brief, usually three to five seconds in duration, sometimes less, sometimes more. Rather than characterize these question–answer exchanges as discussion, it is more appropriate to view them as recitation.

The striking feature of recitation is that the teacher's talk consists of questions. To illustrate this point, the following transcript might illustrate a typical recitation conducted by a secondary school teacher of Canadian history:

Teacher:	Okay, so we've covered the early events of Canada's involvement in World War I. What was a famous Canadian battle in this war? Anyone?
Student:	Juno Beach?
Teacher:	That's a famous battle, but it was in World War II. Someone else?
Student:	Vimy Ridge?
Teacher:	Right! And why is it famous? I mean, we won the battle but what else?
Student:	Lots of guys died?
Teacher:	Okay ... how many?
Student:	A thousand?
Teacher:	No, more ...
Student:	A hundred thousand?
Teacher:	Ten thousand. And what year was this?
Student:	1940?
Teacher:	Come on now, people, World War I ...

In these exchanges, the students take turns answering questions about the success of the Canadian army in World War I. The six question–answer exchanges lasted a little more than 30 seconds, or four to five seconds per exchange. Each student addressed a response to the

BOX 7.1	**Guess What's in My Head**

When she finished her song she was right next to Wendy. "Wendy ... can you tell me what was coming out of my mouth as I sang?"

"Out of your mouth?" Wendy asked.

"That's right," Miss Rothbelle told her.

"Well ... it wasm ... um ... words?"

"No ... no ... no," Miss Rothbelle said.

Wendy was surprised. She can always give teachers the answers they want.

Miss Rothbelle moved on. "Do you know, Caroline?"

"Was it sound?"

"Wrong!" Miss Rothbelle said, turning. "Donna Davidson, can you tell me?"

"It was a song," Donna said.

"Really Donna ... we all know that!" Miss Rothbelle looked around. "Linda Fischer, do you know what was coming out of my mouth as I sang to the class?"

Linda didn't say anything.

"Well, Linda ... " Miss Rothbelle said.

"I think it was air," Linda finally told her. "Either that or breath."

Miss Rothbelle walked over to Linda's desk. "That was not the correct answer. Weren't you paying attention?" She pulled a few strands of Linda's hair....

She walked up and down the aisles until she stopped at my desk....

"We'll see if you've been paying attention ... suppose you tell me the answer to my question."

I had no idea what Miss Rothbelle wanted me to say. There was just one thing left that could have been coming out of her mouth as she sang, so I said, "It was spit."

"What?" Miss Rothbelle glared at me.

"I mean, it was saliva," I told her.

Miss Rothbelle banged her fist on my desk. "That was a very rude thing to say. You can sit in the corner for the rest of the period." ...

At the end of the music period Robby Winters called out, "Miss Rothbelle ... Miss Rothbelle ... "

"What is it?" she asked.

"You never told us what was coming out of your mouth when you sang."

"That's right," Miss Rothbelle said. "I didn't."

"What was it?" Robby asked.

"It was melody," Miss Rothbelle said. Then she spelled it. "M-e-l-o-d-y. And every one of you should have known." She blew her pitchpipe at us and walked out of the room.

teacher, not to other students. The nature of turn taking is such that it is forbidden for another student to jump into the exchange unless first recognized by the teacher to take a turn.

Our language and actions signal to students what their roles are to be within a lesson. Although recitation may serve legitimate educational purposes (quizzing, reviewing), it may negatively affect students' cognitive, affective, and expressive processes. Given the rules that operate during turn taking, teachers may very well increase student passivity and dependency. Furthermore, turn taking leads to a limited construction of meaning with text. Because the pace of questions is often rapid, readers hardly have the time to think about or to clarify or explore their understanding of the text. When we ask predominantly "quiz show" questions, students soon engage in fact finding rather than in thinking about the ideas the author communicates. The inherent danger to text learners is subtle but devastating: mistaken signals may be telegraphed to students about what it means to comprehend text and what their role is as comprehenders. Finding bits and pieces of information becomes the end-all and be-all of reading.

In the remainder of this chapter, we show how you can use talk as a bridge to literacy and learning. Through instructional frameworks and strategies that support talk, you lay the groundwork for thinking and learning with text.

ENCOURAGING TEXT-TALK THROUGH INTEGRATED STRATEGIES

In Chapter 4, we examined the prereading, reading, and postreading stages of instructional lessons involving text-related learning. Although some instructional strategies—for example, the prereading strategies discussed in the previous chapter—may focus only on certain stages, there are other instructional strategies that cut across the prereading, reading, and postreading stages of a text-centred lesson. These "integrated strategies" allow teachers to connect literacy and learning before, during, and after reading.

The KWL Strategy

KWL is an integrated strategy that engages students in active text learning. The strategy begins with what students *know* about the topic to be studied, moves to what the students *want to know* as they generate questions about the topic, and leads to a record of what students *learn* as a result of their engagement in the strategy. Follow-up activities to KWL include discussion, the construction of graphic organizers, and summary writing to clarify and internalize what has been read.

KWL may be initiated with small groups of students or the whole class. When they develop confidence and competence with the KWL strategy, students may begin to use it for independent learning. KWL uses a strategy sheet, such as the one in Figure 7.2 on page 194. The steps in KWL revolve around the completion of the strategy sheet as part of the dynamics of student response and discussion.

Steps in the KWL Strategy Here's how the KWL strategy works.

1. *Introduce the KWL strategy in conjunction with a new topic or text selection.* Before assigning a text, explain the strategy. Donna Ogle (1992), the originator of KWL, suggests that dialogue begin with the teacher saying:

K–What I Know	W–What I Want to Know	L–What I Learned and Still Need to Learn

Categories of Information I Expect to Use

A.   E.

B.   F.

C.   G.

D.

FIGURE 7.2   **A KWL Strategy Sheet**

Source: From Donna M. Ogle, "K-W-L: A Teaching Model That Develops Active Reading in Expository Text" (February 1986). *The Reading Teacher, 39*(6), 564–570. Copyright © 1986 by the International Reading Association. All rights reserved. Used by permission of the author and International Reading Association.

It is important to first find out what we think we know about this topic. Then we want to anticipate how an author is likely to present and organize the information. From this assignment we can generate good questions to focus on reading and study. Our level of knowledge will determine to some extent how we will study. Then as we read we will make notes of questions that get answered and other new and important information we learn. During this process some new questions will probably occur to us; these we should also note so we can get clarification later. (p. 271)

In the process of explaining KWL, be sure that students understand *what* their role involves and *why* it is important for learners to examine what they know and to ask questions about topics that they will be reading and studying.

The next several steps allow you to model the KWL strategy with a group of learners or the entire class. Some students will find it difficult to complete the KWL strategy sheet on their own. Others will avoid taking risks or revealing what they know or don't know about a topic. Others simply won't be positively motivated. Modelling the KWL strategy lessens the initial risk and creates a willingness to engage in the process. Students who experience the modelling of the strategy quickly recognize its value as a learning tool.

2. *Identify what students think they know about the topic.* Engage the class in brainstorming, writing their ideas on the board or on an overhead transparency. Use the format of the KWL strategy sheet as you record students' ideas on the board or transparency. It's important to record everything that the students *think* they know about the topic, including their misconceptions. The key in this step is to get the class actively involved in making associations with the topic, not to evaluate the rightness or wrongness of the associations. Students will sometimes challenge one another's knowledge base. The teacher's role is to help learners recognize that differences exist in what they think they know. These differences can be used to help students frame questions.

3. *Generate a list of student questions.* Ask, "What do you want to know more about? What are you most interested in learning about?" As you write their questions on the board or transparency, recognize that you are again modelling for students what their role as learners should be: to ask questions about material to be studied.

When you have completed modelling the brainstorming and question-generation phases of KWL, have the students use their own strategy sheets to make decisions about what they personally think they know and what they want to know more about. Students, especially those who may be at risk in academic situations, may refer to the board or the overhead transparency to decide what to record in the first two columns.

4. *Anticipate the organization and structure of ideas that the author is likely to use in the text selection.* As part of preparation for reading, have students next use their knowledge and their questions to make predictions about the organization of the text. What major categories of information is the author likely to use to organize his or her ideas?

The teacher might ask, "How do you think the author of a text or article on _____ is likely to organize the information?" Have students focus on the ideas they have brainstormed and the questions they have raised to predict possible categories of information. As students make their predictions, record these on the board or transparency in the area suggested by the KWL strategy sheet. Then have students make individual choices on their own strategy sheets.

5. *Read the text selection to answer the questions.* As they engage in interactions with the text, the students write answers to their questions and make notes for new ideas and information in the L column of their strategy sheets. Again, the teacher's modelling is crucial to the success of this phase of KWL. Students may need a demonstration or two to understand how to record information in the L column.

Debrief students after they have read the text and have completed writing responses in the L column. First, invite them to share answers, recording these on the board or transparency. Then ask, "What new ideas did you come across that you didn't think you would find in the text?" Record and discuss the responses.

6. *Engage students in follow-up activities to clarify and extend learning.* Use KWL as a springboard into postreading activities to internalize student learning. Activities may include the construction of graphic organizers to clarify and retain ideas encountered during reading or the development of written summaries.

A KWL Illustration In Zahida Mitha's history class, students were beginning a study of World War II. Zahida realized that her students would have some, if not much, prior knowledge of and attitudes toward the war, because it has remained a strong part of our national consciousness. The students, in fact, were acutely aware of the war from recent popular movies and also from grandfathers and other relatives who had participated in it.

However, Zahida realized that although students might know something about World War II, they had probably had little opportunity to study it from the perspective of historians. This, then, was Zahida's objective as a teacher of history: to help students approach the study of World War II—and understand the social, economic, and political forces surrounding it—from a historian's perspective.

Therefore, Zahida believed that the KWL strategy would be an appropriate way to begin the unit. She believed that it would help students get in touch with what they knew (and didn't know) about the war and raise questions that would guide their interactions with the materials that they would be studying.

Zahida began KWL knowing that her students were familiar with its procedures, having participated in the strategy on several previous occasions in the class. Following the six steps, the class as a whole participated in brainstorming what they knew about the war and what they wanted to know. Zahida recorded their ideas and questions on an overhead transparency and encouraged students' participation by asking such questions as, "What else do you know? Who had a relative who was in the war? What did he or she say about it? Who has read about World War II or seen a movie about it? What did you learn?"

As ideas and questions were recorded on the transparency, Zahida asked the students to study the K column to anticipate categories of information that they might study in their textbook and other information sources that they would be using: "Do some of these ideas fit together to form major categories we might be studying?" She also asked the students to think about other wars they had studied—War of 1812, World War I, the Korean War: "When we study wars, are there underlying categories of information on which historians tend to focus?"

On completion of the whole-class activity, Zahida invited her students to complete their strategy sheets, recording what they knew, what they wanted to find out more about, and what categories of information they expected to use.

Then, for homework, she assigned several sections from a textbook covering World War II and asked students to work on the L column on their own. Figure 7.3 shows how one student, Clayton, completed his strategy sheet.

As part of the next day's class, Zahida asked the students to work in groups of four to share what they had found out about the war. They focused on the questions they had raised, as well as on new ideas they had not anticipated. When the groups completed their work, Zahida brought the class together. She directed them to open their learning logs and write a summary of what they had learned from participating in KWL. Students used the L column on their strategy sheets to compose the summary. Clayton's summary is shown in Figure 7.4 on page 198.

In Zahida's class, the learning logs serve as a history notebook, where students can record what they are learning, using a variety of writing-to-learn activities. (We explain learning logs and their uses more fully in Chapter 8.)

A secondary school mathematics teacher adapted the KWL strategy to support his students' study of the Fibonacci numbers. Fibonacci numbers (a famous sequence of numbers that has been shown to occur in nature) are the direct result of a problem posed by a thirteenth century mathematician, Leonardo of Pisa, on the regeneration of rabbits. The teacher used a mathematics text from an enrichment unit to clarify and extend students'

K—What I Know	W—What I Want to Know	L—What I Learned and Still Need to Learn
Allies, which included Canada, won the war The Allies fought the Germans and the Japanese Many battles at sea in the Atlantic and south Pacific POWs World's top scientists developed a nuclear bomb Major battle on D-Day in France Japanese bombed by Allies' atomic bomb	What/Who instigated the war? If the Allies were called the Allies, what were Germany and Japan called together as a collective? What countries were not involved in World War II? How many Canadians lost their lives? Who was the prime minister during the war? How many soldiers were transported across the oceans by ships and by planes?	In 1939 Canada officially declared war on Germany. Italy was on Germany's side. Germany, Italy, and Japan signed the Tripartite (Axis) Pact and were known as the Axis power. 1940—Conscription in Canada during WWII. Bacterial warfare research conducted in Canada. Germany first bombed Britain two days before Britain bombed Berlin. 34 000 Canadian soldiers died in World War II. King, William Lyon Mackenzie was prime minister of Canada during WWII. (1935.10.23–1948.11.14)

Categories of Information I Expect to Use

A. cause   E.

B. results   F.

C. Canadian involvement   G.

D. type of fighting

FIGURE 7.3   Clayton's KWL Strategy Sheet on World War II

understanding of the Fibonacci numbers. The text selection, "Mathematics in Nature," illustrates the properties of the Fibonacci numbers and requires students to determine the relationships between these numbers and various phenomena in nature—for example, the leaves on a plant, the bracts on a pine cone, the curves on a seashell, or the spirals on a pineapple.

Before initiating the KWL strategy, the teacher used three props (a toy rabbit, a plant, and a pineapple) to arouse students' curiosity and to trigger their responses to the question, "What do these items have to do with mathematics?" After some exploratory talk, he then asked students, "What do you know about mathematics and nature?" The strategy sheet in Figure 7.5 o page 198 illustrates the reader–text interactions that occurred as the teacher guided students through the steps in KWL.

Canada and the other Allies fought the aggressive Axis of Germany, Italy, and Japan in World War II. The Canadian government led by prime minister William Lyon Mackenzie King put conscription into place and carried out nuclear and bacterial weapons research. Canada officially entered the war in 1939 and fought until the Axis finally surrendered in 1945. A total of 34 000 Canadians lost their lives during the war.

FIGURE 7.4 Clayton's Summary in the Learning Log

K–What I Know	W–What I Want to Know	L–What I Learned and Still Need to Learn

planetary motion
spirals
4 seasons
landscaping
geometric designs
multiplying
  populations
phases of the moon
	What does a
	  pineapple have to
	  do with math?
	How are growth
	  patterns in plants
	  related to math?
	How is mathematics
	  specifically related
	  to nature?
	Where do bees fit?
		Pineapples have hexagons
		  on the surface that are
		  arranged in sets of
		  spirals.
		These spirals are related
		  to Fibonacci numbers.
		Fibonacci numbers are found
		  in leaf arrangements
		  on plants.
		The rate that bees
		  regenerate males is
		  related to Fibonacci
		  numbers.
		Who is this Fibonacci guy?
		What's the big deal about
		  the "golden ratio"?

Categories of Information **I Expect to Use** 1. Animals 2. Plants 3. Solar System 4. Laws of Nature		

FIGURE 7.5 A KWL Strategy Sheet in a Mathematics Class

Directed Reading–Thinking Activity

The directed reading–thinking activity (DR–TA) fosters critical awareness by moving students through a process that involves prediction, verification, judgment, and ultimately extension of thought. The teacher guides reading and stimulates thinking through the judicious use of questions. These questions will prompt response through interpretation, clarification, and application.

The atmosphere created during a DR–TA is paramount in the strategy's success. You must be supportive and encouraging so as not to inhibit students' free participation. Never refute any predictions that students make; to do so is comparable to pulling the rug out from under them.

Think time is again important. When you pose an open-ended question, is it reasonable to pause no more than two, three, five, or even ten seconds for a response? If silence pervades the room for several seconds or more after a question has been asked, simply wait a few more seconds. Too often, the tendency is to slice the original question into smaller parts. Sometimes a teacher starts slicing too quickly out of a sense of frustration or anxiousness (after all, three seconds of lapsed time can seem an eternity in the midst of a questioning foray) rather than because of the students' inability to respond. Silence may very well be an indication that hypothesis formation or other cognitive activities are taking place in the students' heads. So wait—and see what happens.

To prepare for a DR–TA with an informational text, analyze the material for its superordinate and subordinate concepts. What are the relevant concepts, ideas, relationships, and information in the material? The content analysis will help you decide on logical stopping points as you direct students through the reading.

For short stories and other narrative material, determine the key elements of the story: the *setting* (time and place, major characters) and the *events in the plot* (the initiating events or problem-generating situation, the protagonist's reaction to the event and his or her goal to resolve the problem, the set of attempts to achieve the goal, outcomes related to the protagonist's attempts to achieve the goal and resolve the problem, the character's reaction).

Once these elements have been identified, the teacher has a framework for deciding on logical stopping points within the story. In Figure 7.6, we indicate a general plan that may be followed or adapted for specific story lines. Notice that the suggested stopping points come at key junctures in a causal chain of events in the story line. Each juncture suggests

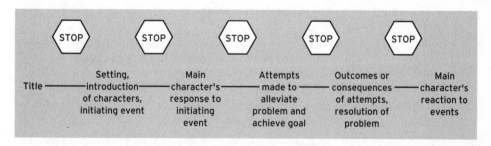

FIGURE 7.6 **Potential Stopping Points in a DR-TA for a Story Line with One Episode**

a logical stopping point in that it assumes that the reader has enough information from at least one preceding event to predict a future happening or event.

Steps in the DR-TA Set the climate and guide the DR–TA by the frequent use of three questions:

"What do you think?" (or "What do you think will happen next?")

"Why do you think so?" (or "What part of the story gave you a clue?")

"Can you prove it?" (or "What else might happen?")

The following may be considered general steps in the DR–TA:

1. *Begin with the title of the narrative or with a quick survey of the title, subheads, illustrations, and other expository material.* Ask, "What do you think this story (or section) will be about?" Encourage predictions. Ask, "Why do you think so?"

2. *Ask students to read silently to a predetermined logical stopping point in the text.* Have students use a 5-by-8-inch index card or a blank sheet of paper placed on the page to mark the place to which they are reading. This will also slow down those who want to read on before answering the questions.

3. *Repeat questions as suggested in step 1.* Some predictions will be refined; new ones will be formulated. Ask, "How do you know?" to encourage clarification or verification. Redirect questions.

4. *Continue silent reading to another suitable point.* Ask similar questions.

5. *Continue in this way to the end of the material.* A note of caution: too frequent interruption of reading may detract from the focus of attention, which needs to be on larger concepts. As readers move through the DR–TA process, encourage reflection and thoughtful responses to the text.

How do you apply DR–TA to informational texts? The following steps specify the procedures.

1. *Set the purposes for reading.* Individual or group purposes are set by students based on some limited clues in material and their own background of experience.

    a. "From reading just the chapter title (subtitles, charts, maps, etc.), what do you think the author will present in this chapter (passage, next pages, etc.)?"
    b. Record speculations on the board and augment them by the query, "Why do you think so?"
    c. Encourage a guided discussion. If speculations and statements of proof yield an inaccurate or weak knowledge base, review through discussion. Frequently, terminology will be introduced by students (especially those who are more knowledgeable) in their predictions. The teacher may choose to capitalize on such situations by further clarifying significant concepts in a way that enhances pupil discussion and inquiry through discovery techniques.
    d. A poll can be taken to intensify the predictive process, and a debate may naturally ensue. Additional proof may be needed from available reference books.

2. *Adjust the rate to the purposes and the material.* The teacher should adjust the amount of reading, depending on the purposes, nature, and difficulty of the reading material; skimming, scanning, and studying are involved. Students are told, "Read to find out if your predictions were correct." The reading task may be several pages, a few passages, or some other amount of the text. If the teacher designates numerous stopping points within the reading task, the same procedures as in step 1 should be executed at each stopping point.

3. *Observe the reading.* The teacher observes the reading by assisting students who request help and noting abilities to adjust rate to purpose and material, to comprehend material, and to use word recognition strategies.

4. *Guide reader–text interactions.* Students check the purposes by accepting, rejecting, or redefining them. This can be accomplished during discussion time after students have read a predetermined number of pages or by encouraging students to rework their predictions as they read, by noting down their revised predictions and hypotheses.

5. *Extend learning through discussion, further reading, additional study, or writing.* Students and teacher identify these needs throughout the strategy.

    a. After reading, students should be asked (1) if their predictions were inaccurate, (2) if they needed to revise or reject any predictions as they read, (3) how they knew revision was necessary, and (4) what their new predictions were.

    b. Discussion in small groups is most useful in this step. A recorder, appointed by the group, can share the groups' reading–thinking processes with the total class. These should be compared with original predictions.

    c. The teacher should ask open-ended questions that encourage generalization and application relevant to students' predictions and the significant concepts presented. In any follow-up discussion or questioning, proof should always be required: "How do you know that? Why did you think so? What made you think that way?" Encourage students to share passages, sentences, and so on for further proof (Homer 1979).

A DR-TA Illustration In a grade 8 science class, students were engaged in a study of a textbook chapter about the light spectrum (Davidson & Wilkerson 1988). Using a DR–TA framework, the teacher guided the students' interactions with the text material. Study an excerpt of the transcript from the beginning cycle of the DR–TA in Box 7.2.

As you examine the transcript, note that teacher–student interactions are recorded in the left column of the box. The teacher's questions and comments are printed in italics, followed by the students' responses. An analysis of the DR–TA lesson as it evolved is printed in the right column.

The transcript shows how the students used prior knowledge to anticipate the information that the text would reveal. As they shared what they expected to find, the students engaged in analyzing their pooled ideas. Their interactions with the teacher illustrate how a DR–TA instructional framework creates a need to know and helps readers declare purposes through anticipation and prediction making.

Once the purposes were established, the teacher assigned a section of the text chapter to be read. According to Davidson and Wilkerson (1988), two observers of the lesson:

| BOX 7.2 | **Excerpt of a DR-TA Transcript from a Science Lesson on the Light Spectrum** |

TEACHER–STUDENT INTERACTIONS

I'D LIKE FOR YOU TO BEGIN BY JUST READING THIS ACTIVITY IN THIS SECTION. THEN TELL ME WHAT YOU EXPECT TO FIND IN THIS PASSAGE. YOU KNOW IT'S ABOUT LIGHT AND COLOUR AND SPECTRUMS. WHAT ELSE DO YOU EXPECT THAT YOU WILL FIND?

s: Heat

WHY DO YOU SAY HEAT?

s: Well, some of the colours are cooler.

DO YOU KNOW WHICH ONES WILL BE COOLER?

s: I think the darker ones.

WHY DO YOU SAY THAT?

s: They look cooler.

THEY LOOK COOLER? OKAY.

WHAT ELSE? DO YOU AGREE OR DISAGREE?

s: Well, I agree with her on infrared and ultraviolet. They are probably the hottest colours you can get of the spectrum.

ALL RIGHT. ANYBODY ELSE?

s: I think he is wrong.

WHY?

s: Because whenever you melt steel, steel always turns red before it turns white. When it turns white, it melts completely.

OKAY.

s: You can't see infrared.

AND HOW WOULD THAT MAKE A DIFFERENCE IN WHAT HE JUST SAID?

s: Well, he just said that it turned red before it turned white. And you can't see white, it's just a shade. Infrared you can't see—which would be just like sunlight. You can't see sunlight. So, I think it would be hotter.

YOU THINK IT WOULD BE HOTTER?

OKAY.

ANYBODY ELSE?

WELL, LET ME GIVE YOU THIS WHOLE FIRST PARAGRAPH. I WANT YOU TO READ TO THE BOTTOM OF THE PAGE AND THEN I WANT YOU TO GO TO THE TOP OF THE NEXT PAGE. IT WILL BE THE VERY TOP PARAGRAPH. COVER UP WHAT'S BELOW IT WITH YOUR PAPER. READ THAT FAR AND THEN STOP.

(Students read silently.)

ANALYSIS OF LESSON

The teacher directs students to read a description of an activity designed to produce a sun's spectrum with a prism. The activity includes holding a thermometer in the spectrum produced, placing a fluorite substance near the spectrum, and anticipating changes.

The student's response is based on prior knowledge, which she judges will be relevant.

The teacher encourages the student to extend the response.

Teacher asks for justification.

Teacher accepts response, recognizing that the student has, in fact, generated a question to be answered in reading the text.

The teacher encourages other students to analyze this hypothesis or generate a different one.

The student's response shows that he is evaluating the other student's response. Also, he uses specific vocabulary from his prior knowledge to extend the prediction.

The teacher does not make a judgment about the validity of the predictions, since that is the responsibility of the students as they read and discuss.

A student disagrees.

Teacher asks for justification.

The student analyzes the prior student's prediction and explains in terms of his own experience.

As stated, the student's response is a literal statement.

The teacher assumes that there is a connection with the discussion and asks for an explanation.

In his extended response, the student disagrees with the prior student's conclusion and explanation and uses an illustration from his prior knowledge, which he feels is relevant to "prove" his point.

The teacher does not point out the validity or lack of validity of either student's logic. She recognizes that both students are thinking critically and that they and others in the group will read to find clues to justify the concepts they are hypothesizing. She is consistent in her role as a facilitator of student discussion.

Source: Reprinted with permission of Jane L. Davidson and Bonnie C. Wilkerson.

When students read the portion of the text they were directed to read, they read that infrared waves are invisible and that they are heat waves. Discussion, involving text ideas, students' previous ideas, and their reasoning abilities, showed that they discovered that infrared light is *not* one of the hottest colors because it is not a color. They also discovered that infrared waves are hot, since they are heat waves. The text supplied literal information. The discussion facilitated concept development and critical thinking. (p. 37)

Although the students' predictions were amiss in the initial cycle of questioning, the teacher chose not to evaluate or judge the predictions. She recognized that as readers interact with the text, more often than not they are able to clarify their misconceptions for themselves.

Discussion Webs

Discussion webs encourage students to engage the text and each other in thoughtful discussion by creating a framework for students to explore texts and consider different sides of an issue in discussion before drawing conclusions. Donna Alvermann (1991) recommends discussion webs as an alternative to teacher-dominated discussions.

The strategy uses cooperative learning principles that follow a "think–pair–share" discussion cycle (McTighe & Lyman 1988). The discussion cycle begins with students thinking about the ideas they want to contribute to the discussion based on their interactions with the text. Then they meet in dyads to discuss their ideas with a partner. Partners then team with a different set of partners to resolve differences in perspective and to work toward a consensus about the issue under discussion. In the final phase of the discussion cycle, the two sets of partners, working as a foursome, select a spokesperson to share their ideas with the entire class.

The discussion web strategy uses a graphic display to scaffold students' thinking about the ideas they want to contribute to the discussion based on what they have read. The graphic display takes the shape of a web, as illustrated in Figure 7.7. In the centre of the web is a question or statement. It is posed in such a way that it reflects more than one point of view. Students explore the pros and cons in the "no" and "yes" columns of the web—in pairs, and then in groups of four. The main goal of the four-member teams is to draw a conclusion based on their discussion of the web.

Steps in the Discussion Web Strategy Alvermann (1991) suggests an integrated lesson structure for the discussion web strategy that includes the following steps:

1. *Prepare your students for reading by activating prior knowledge, raising questions, and making predictions about the text.*

2. *Assign students to read the selection and then introduce the discussion web by having the students work in pairs to generate pro and con responses to the question.* The partners work on the same discussion web and take turns jotting down their reasons in the "Yes" and "No" columns. Students may use keywords and phrases to express their ideas and need not fill all of the lines. They should try to list an equal number of pro and con reasons on the web.

3. *Combine partners into groups of four to compare responses, work toward consensus, and reach a conclusion as a group.* Explain to your students that it is okay to disagree with other members of the group, but they should all try to keep an open mind as they

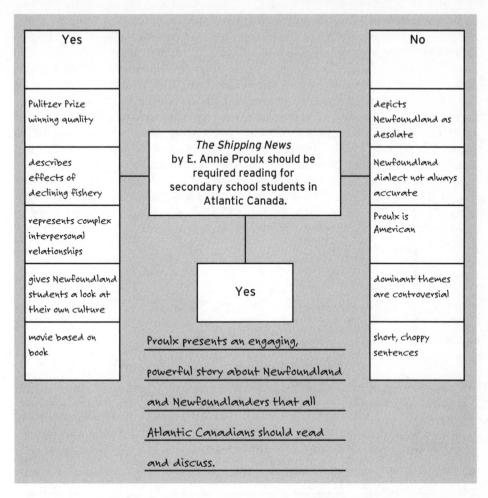

Yes	No

The Shipping News by E. Annie Proulx should be required reading for secondary school students in Atlantic Canada.

Pulitzer Prize winning quality

describes effects of declining fishery

represents complex interpersonal relationships

gives Newfoundland students a look at their own culture

movie based on book

depicts Newfoundland as desolate

Newfoundland dialect not always accurate

Proulx is American

dominant themes are controversial

short, choppy sentences

Yes

Proulx presents an engaging, powerful story about Newfoundland and Newfoundlanders that all Atlantic Canadians should read and discuss.

FIGURE 7.7   A Discussion Web for *The Shipping News* by E. Annie Proulx

listen to others during the discussion. Dissenting views may be aired during the whole-class discussion.

4. *Give each group three minutes to decide which of all the reasons given best supports the group's conclusion.* Each group selects a spokesperson to report to the whole class.

5. *Have your students follow up the whole-class discussion by individually writing their responses to the discussion web question.* Display the students' responses to the question in a prominent place in the room so that they can be read by others.

The level of participation in discussion web lessons is usually high. The strategy privileges students' individual interpretations of what they are reading and also allows them to formulate and refine their own interpretations of a text in light of the points of view of others. As a result, students are eager to hear how other groups reached a consensus and drew conclusions during whole-class sharing. The strategy works well with informational or narrative texts and can be adapted to the goals and purposes of most content area subjects.

A Discussion Web Illustration Donna Mitchell, a music teacher, introduced her middle-grade students to components of an opera by having them listen to Wagner's *The Flying Dutchman*. In Chapter 4, we discussed Mrs. Mitchell's lesson in detail. In the discussion, she activated students' prior knowledge of opera using a playbill that she constructed in the form of a modified cloze activity. As part of the lesson, Mrs. Mitchell also had students listen to the overture of the opera to set a mood and read portions of the story to them over several days. At the conclusion of the read-alouds, students entered the postreading stage of the lesson as they engaged in a discussion web activity. Study the discussion web in Figure 7.8 completed by one group of students in her class as they grappled with the question, " Did Senta need to throw herself off the cliff into the sea?"

Mathematics teachers might also use the discussion web to help students consider relevant and irrelevant information in story problems. Study the discussion web in Figure 7.9, noting the adaptations the teacher made. In this illustration, the students worked in pairs to distinguish relevant and irrelevant information in the story problem. They then formed groups of four to solve the problem.

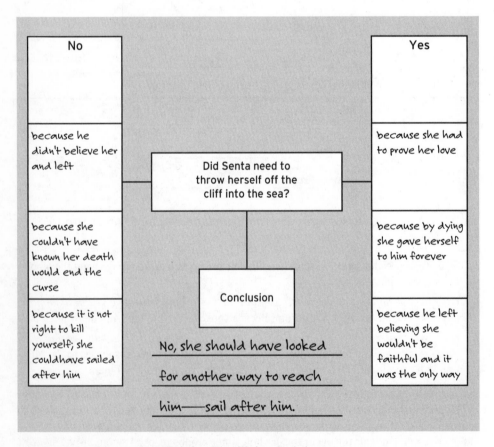

FIGURE 7.8 **Discussion Web for** *The Flying Dutchman*

Source: Donna Kowallek Mitchell © 2000. Printed with permission.

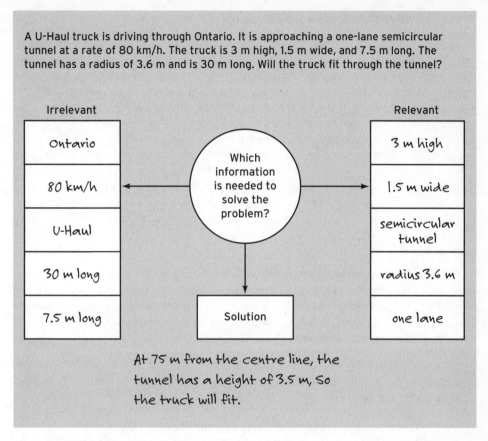

A U-Haul truck is driving through Ontario. It is approaching a one-lane semicircular tunnel at a rate of 80 km/h. The truck is 3 m high, 1.5 m wide, and 7.5 m long. The tunnel has a radius of 3.6 m and is 30 m long. Will the truck fit through the tunnel?

Irrelevant

Ontario

80 km/h

U-Haul

30 m long

7.5 m long

Which information is needed to solve the problem?

Solution

Relevant

3 m high

1.5 m wide

semicircular tunnel

radius 3.6 m

one lane

At 75 m from the centre line, the tunnel has a height of 3.5 m, so the truck will fit.

FIGURE 7.9   Discussion Web for a Story Problem

Intra-Act

Intra-act lays the groundwork for reflective discussion. Pivotal to the intra-act strategy is the notion that students engage in a process of valuing as they reflect on what they have read. Hoffman (1979) suggests intra-act to provide readers with "the opportunity to experience rather than just talk about critical reading" (p. 608). According to Hoffman, students are more likely to read critically when they engage in a process of valuing. The valuing process allows students to respond actively to a text selection with thought and feeling.

The intra-act procedure can be used with a variety of reading materials—content area text assignments, historical documents, newspaper and magazine articles, narrative, and poetic material. The procedure requires the use of small groups whose members are asked to react to value statements based on the content of the text selection. There are four phases in the intra-act procedure: (1) *comprehension* (understanding of the topic under discussion), (2) *relating* (connecting what has been learned about the topic to what students already know and believe), (3) *valuation* (expressing personal values and feelings related to the topic), and (4) *reflection* (reflecting on the values and feelings just experienced).

Steps in Intra-Act   Here's how intra-act works.

1. *Comprehension.* The comprehension phase promotes an understanding of the reading material to be learned. To begin this phase, the teacher follows effective prereading procedures by introducing the text reading, activating and building background knowledge for the ideas to be encountered during reading, and inviting students to make predictions and speculate on the nature of the content to be learned. Building a frame of reference for upcoming text information is crucial to the overall success of the intra-act procedure.

Prereading preparation paves the way for readers to interact with the text. Before inviting students to read the selection individually, the teacher forms small groups—intra-act teams—of four to six members. Assign a student from each group to serve as the team leader. The comprehension phase depends on the team leader's ability to initiate and sustain a discussion of the text. The team leader's responsibility is to lead a discussion by first summarizing what was read. The group members may contribute additional information about the selection or ask questions that seek clarification of the main ideas of the selection. The comprehension phase of the group discussion should be limited to 7 to 10 minutes.

2. *Relating.* The team leader is next responsible for shifting the discussion from the important ideas in the selection to the group's personal reactions and values related to the topic. Many times, this shift occurs naturally. However, if this is not the case, members should be encouraged by the team leader to contribute their own impressions and opinions. Discussion should again be limited to 7 to 10 minutes.

3. *Valuation.* Once group members have shared their personal reactions to the material, they are ready to participate in the valuation phase of the discussion. The teacher or team leader for each group distributes a game sheet. This game sheet contains a valuing exercise—a set of four declarative statements based on the selection's content. These value statements reflect opinions about the text selection and draw insights and fresh ideas from it. The purpose of the valuing exercise is to have students come to grips with what the material means to them by either agreeing (A) or disagreeing (D) with each statement. Figure 7.10 shows such a game sheet.

Study the game sheet in Figure 7.10. Note that students must first indicate on the game sheet their own reactions to the four value statements. Then, based on the previous discussion, they must predict how each of the other members of their group would respond. In the example of Figure 7.10, Joe disagreed with three of the statements. His predictions as to how other team members would respond are indicated by the circled letters underneath the individual names. Once the responding is complete, the students are ready for the reflective phase of the intra-act procedure.

4. *Reflection.* Begin the reflection phase of intra-act by scoring the game sheet. Group members take turns revealing how each responded to the four statements. As each member tells how he or she responded, the other members check whether their predictions agreed with that member's actual responses. During this phase, the teacher acts as a facilitator, noting how students responded but refraining from imposing a particular point of view on students. Instead, encourage students to reflect on what they have learned. According to Hoffman (1979), "It is very important that during this period students be allowed ample time to discuss, challenge, support and question one another's response. This interaction serves to separate opinions quickly arrived at from sound evaluative thinking" (p. 607).

Name_____
Date_____
Total Score_____
Percentage
of Correct Predictions_____

Names	Joe	Olga	Ranjit	Katie
1. Tobacco companies should be held responsible for the deaths of smokers from heart attacks and lung cancer.	A (D)	(A) + D	A + (D)	(A) − D
2. Smokers should be able to quit. They just need to really want to.	(A) D	(A) + D	(A) + D	A + (D)
3. The sale of cigarettes should be illegal just like the sale of cocaine or heroin.	A (D)	(A) + D	A + (D)	(A) + D
4. The government should spend money on programs to help people stop smoking.	A (D)	(A) − D	A + (D)	A − (D)

+: Joe's predictions were correct.
−: Joe's predictions were incorrect.

FIGURE 7.10 **Joe's Game Sheet**

Intra-act will require several classroom applications before students become accustomed to their roles during discussion. Repeated and extensive participation in intra-act will help students become fully aware of the task demands of the procedure. In the beginning, we recommend that on completion of an intra-act discussion, students engage in a whole-class discussion of the process in which they participated. Help students debrief: "What did we learn from our participation in intra-act? Why must all members of a group participate? How might discussion improve the next time we use intra-act?" Questions such as these make students sensitive to the purpose of the intra-act procedure (problem solving) and the role of each reader (critical analysis).

An Intra-Act Illustration After students in a health education class read the article "Getting Hooked on Tobacco," four students, Joe, Olga, Ranjit, and Katie, met as a group to discuss their impressions. Joe, who was the group's team leader, began with a summary of the article and then gave his own reactions. Here's how Joe summarized the article's main ideas: "Well, basically the article says that the government says that tobacco makes you, you know, a drug addict, or something like that. It's like using cocaine or heroin. They say that people can't quit and they need more and more, so cigarettes should be like liquor and you have to get a licence to sell them. The cigarette companies don't agree. Me too. I don't think a guy is going to go out and rob people just to get cigarettes. I mean, if he is that hard up, he would just quit."

After some clarifying discussion of what the article was about, the discussion shifted gears into the relating phase. Olga reacted to the article this way: "Well, I don't think that a company should be allowed to sell stuff that kills people. And if all the people quit, the company would go out of business anyway, so it should just go out of business now because of a law."

Ranjit entered the conversation: "I think the guy was right that said if cigarettes were illegal the gangs would have gang wars to see who would get to sell them—just like they do with crack and cocaine right now. Besides, if people really want to kill themselves with smoking, they should be allowed. And if they don't, they should just quit. There's a warning right on the pack."

Katie replied, "It ain't so easy to quit. My dad tried, like, five times, and he finally had to get hypnotized to quit. And he wouldn't have started if he had to buy them from some gang or something. You get them from a store, and nobody ever asks you how old you are. Besides, who reads the warnings?"

When time for discussion was over, the valuation phase was initiated. Students were given a game sheet with these four value statements:

1. Tobacco companies should be held responsible for the deaths of smokers from heart attacks and lung cancer.
2. Smokers should be able to quit. They just need to really want to.
3. The sale of cigarettes should be illegal just like the sale of cocaine or heroin.
4. The government should spend money on programs to help people stop smoking.

Each student was asked to respond individually to the statements and then predict whether the other members of the group would agree or disagree with each statement. Joe's sheet is reproduced in Figure 7.10. From the discussion, he was pretty sure that Olga would agree with the first statement because she had said that they "shouldn't be allowed to kill people." Similarly, he thought Ranjit would disagree because he thought people should "just quit." He was also pretty sure that Katie would agree because she seemed to think it was bad that you could just go into a store and buy cigarettes. He used similar reasons to predict the group members' reactions to the other statements.

As part of the reflection phase of intra-act, the group members shared what they had learned. Joe found that most of his predictions were correct. He was surprised to find out that Katie did not agree with statement 1, but she explained that, "It's not the companies' fault that they sold something that's not illegal. First, they should make it illegal; then it's the companies' fault." Other members argued that her reasoning "didn't make sense" because the tobacco companies know that cigarettes are harmful. That debate was typical of the discussion that went on in all the groups as students worked out the ways in which the ideas presented in the text fit in with their own attitudes and beliefs.

Guided Reading Procedure (GRP)

The guided reading procedure (GRP) emphasizes close reading (Manzo 1975). It requires that students gather information and organize it around important ideas, and it places a premium on accuracy as students reconstruct the author's message. With a strong factual base, students will work from a common and clear frame of reference. They will then be in a position to elaborate thoughtfully on the text and its implications.

STEPS IN THE GRP. The GRP is a highly structured activity and, therefore, should be used sparingly as a training strategy—perhaps once a week at most. These steps are suggested:

1. *Prepare students for reading.* Clarify key concepts; determine what students know and don't know about the particular content to be studied, build appropriate background; give direction to reading.

2. *Assign a reading selection.* Assign 500 to 900 words in the middle grades (approximately five to seven minutes of silent reading); 1000 to 2000 words for secondary school (approximately 10 minutes). Provide general purpose to direct reading behaviour. *Direction*: Read to remember all you can.

3. *As students finish reading, have them turn books face down.* Ask them to tell what they remember. Record it on the board in the fashion in which it is remembered.

4. *Help students recognize that there is much that they have not remembered or have represented incorrectly.* Simply, there are implicit inconsistencies that need correction and further information to be considered.

5. *Redirect students into their books and review the selection to correct inconsistencies and add further information.*

6. *Organize recorded remembrances into some kind of an outline.* Ask guiding, nonspecific questions: "What were the important ideas in the assigned reading? Which came first? What facts on the board support it? What important point was brought up next? What details followed?"

7. *Extend questioning to stimulate an analysis of the material and a synthesis of the ideas with previous learnings.*

8. *Provide immediate feedback, such as a short quiz, as a reinforcement of short-term memory.*

A GRP Illustration Grade 8 students were assigned a reading selection from the music education magazine *Pipeline*. The selection, "Percussion—Solid as Rock," concerns the development and uses of percussion instruments from ancient to modern times.

The teacher introduced the selection by giving some background. She then began a guided discussion by asking students to remember as much as they could as they read the assignment silently. The teacher recorded the collective memories of her students on a transparency, projecting responses onto an overhead screen. Then she asked, "Did you leave out any information that might be important?" Students were directed to review the selection to determine if essential information was missing from the list on the screen. The teacher also asked, "Did you mix up some of the facts on the list? Did you misrepresent any of the information in the author's message?"

These two questions are extremely important to the overall GRP procedure. The first question—"Did you leave out any information that might be important?"—encourages a review of the material. Students sense that some facts are more important than others. Further questioning at this point will help them distinguish essential from nonessential information. The second question—"Did you mix up some of the facts on the list?"—reinforces the importance of selective rereading and rehearsal because of the limitations imposed by short-term memory.

Next the teacher asked the class to study the information recorded on the screen. The teacher requested the students to form pairs and then assigned the following task: "Which facts on the overhead can be grouped together? Organize the information around the important ideas in the selection. You have five minutes to complete the task."

On completion of the task the teacher encouraged students to share their work in whole-group discussion. Their groupings of facts were compared, refined, and extended. The teacher served as a facilitator, keeping the discussion moving, asking clarifying questions, provoking thought. She then initiated the next task: "Let's organize the important ideas and related information. Let's make a map." Figure 7.11 shows what the students produced.

Outlining the mass of information will make students aware of the text relationships developed by the author. In Chapter 9 we explore several outlining procedures, such as semantic mapping, which help students produce the author's main ideas in relation to one another. Producing the author's organizational structure leads to more efficient recall at a later time and lays the groundwork for interpreting and applying the author's message. Once this common framework is developed, your questioning should lead to more divergent and abstract responding by the students.

The discussion "took off" after the outline was completed. The teacher asked several reflective questions that helped students associate their previous experiences and beliefs about drumming to the content under discussion. Cognitive performance centred on evaluation and application as students linked what they knew to what they were studying.

The final suggested step in the GRP is a short quiz—mainly to demonstrate in a dramatic way how successful the students can be with the reading material. The quiz should

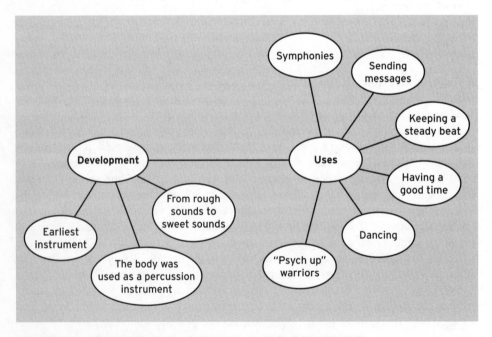

FIGURE 7.11 **Semantic Map of "Percussion–Solid as Rock"**

be viewed as positive reinforcement, not an interrogation check. Most of the students in this class earned perfect or near-perfect scores on the quiz—and this is as it should be.

LOOKING BACK, LOOKING FORWARD

Teachers connect literacy and learning when they weave together talking, listening, reading, and writing. Talking to learn is an expressive and exploratory form of classroom communication. Strategies that facilitate talking to learn help students explore, clarify, and extend ideas they encounter in text. Although classroom talk is the main medium by which students and teachers communicate, the potential for talk as a tool for learning is rarely realized in classrooms. Too often, teachers rely on a type of talk called *recitation*, expecting students to recite answers to questions. Recitation is a limiting form of oral interaction because teachers dominate classroom talk when they overuse recitation. The danger of recitation lies in signalling to students that reading is a disjointed search for bits and pieces of information.

When readers are not able to handle difficult texts on their own, a teacher supports their efforts to make meaning by *scaffolding* their interactions with texts. Various kinds of integrated strategies may be used to guide reader–text interactions. These strategies provide a structure through which students can actively engage in text response and discussion. In this chapter, several strategies that prepare students for reading, guide their interaction with texts, and help them clarify and extend meaning were described.

KWL is a meaning-making strategy that engages students in active text learning and may be used with small groups of students or with the whole class. KWL comprises several steps that help students examine what they know, what they want to know more about, and what they have learned from reading. The directed reading–thinking activity was also described. DR–TA revolves around three guiding questions: (1) What do you think? (2) Why do you think so? (3) Can you prove it? The guided reading procedure (GRP) encourages close reading of difficult text, whereas the discussion web and intra-act strategies are based on the notion that students engage in a process of consensus building and valuing as they reflect on what they have read. The GRP, the discussion web, and intra-act lay the groundwork for reflective discussion following the reading of text material.

In the next chapter we underscore the interrelationships among reading, thinking, and writing processes as we explore the role of writing in content area learning. The ideas presented in the chapter are intended to show how writing activity can and must go beyond "mechanical uses" in the content classroom.

MINDS-ON

1. Think of the concept of "class discussion." Try to recall an example of a prior classroom situation in which enjoyable, lively "discussions" occurred. Freeze-frame this scene in your mind. Look closely at it, and jot down as many descriptive or sensory words as you can that paint this picture and make it seem real.

   Now, try to recall a prior classroom situation that was not conducive to meaningful or enjoyable class discussions. Again, freeze-frame this scene in your mind and look at it closely. Jot down as many descriptive or sensory words as you can that paint this picture and make it seem real.

Why and how will the instructional frameworks that you have studied help you facilitate a good environment for a class discussion?

2. With a small group, create an intra-act guide sheet for this chapter. After you have finished, discuss any insights into reading gained from this activity.

HANDS-ON

1. Without sharing perceptions, each member of your group should read this short paragraph and follow the directions that follow it.

> An artist was talking enthusiastically about one of her favourite paintings to several people visiting the gallery when a woman approached her and offered to purchase the work. The owner of the gallery removed the painting from the wall. The painting was snatched from her hands, and the woman bolted through the front door into a waiting van, which sped down the street through a nearby red light and vanished into the night.

Using the paragraph as a reference, respond to each of the following statements, in the order presented, by circling T (for true), F (for false), or ? (for unable to determine from the paragraph). Once you have characterized a statement as true, false, or questionable, you cannot change your answer.

a. The artist talked about one of her paintings. T F ?
b. The thief was a woman. T F ?
c. The crime appeared to be premeditated. T F ?
d. This type of theft seems unlikely. T F ?
e. The owner removed the painting from the wall. T F ?
f. The owner was the artist. T F ?
g. The woman who bolted through the door stole the painting. T F ?
h. The person who snatched the painting from the owner's hands was the artist. T F ?
i. A robbery didn't occur. T F ?

Discuss the variety of possible answers based on your responses.

2. Select a short informational article in a magazine or book, and make photocopies for each member of your group. Have each member of the group create at random one of the following instructional strategies: (1) KWL (What do you *know*? About what do you *want to know* more? What did you *learn*?), (2) a directed reading–thinking activity (DR–TA), (3) intra-act, and (4) a discussion web. If there are more than four members in your group, duplicate strategies as needed.

Using the same article, design a lesson around the strategy you have created, and make copies to share with the members of the group. As you review the four different lessons prepared by your colleagues, what comparisons and contrasts can you make between these instructional frameworks?

SUGGESTED READINGS

Alvermann, D. E. (1996). Peer-led discussions: Whose interests are served? *Journal of Adolescent and Adult Literacy, 39,* 282–289.

Alvermann, D. E., Dillon, D. R., & O'Brien, D. G. (1988). *Using discussion to promote reading comprehension.* Newark, DE: International Reading Association.

Alvermann, D. E., O'Brien, D. G., & Dillon, D. R. (1990). What teachers do when they say they're having discussions of content reading assignments: A qualitative analysis. *Reading Research Quarterly, 25,* 296–322.

Bainbridge, J., & Malicky, G. (2000). *Constructing meaning: Balancing elementary language arts.* Toronto: Harcourt.

Barton, J. (1995). Conducting effective classroom discussions. *Journal of Reading, 38,* 346–350.

Bayer, C. S. (1990). *Collaborative-apprenticeship learning: Language and thinking across the curriculum, K–12.* Mountain View, CA: Mayfield.

Calfee, R. C., Dunlap, K. L., & Wat, A. Y. (1994). Authentic discussion of texts in middle grade schooling: An analytic-narrative approach. *Journal of Reading, 37,* 546–556.

Carlsen, W. S. (1991). Questioning in classrooms: A sociolinguistic perspective. *Review of Educational Research, 61,* 157–178.

Carr, E. G., & Ogle, D. M. (1987). K-W-L plus: A strategy for comprehension and summarization. *Journal of Reading, 30,* 626–631.

Dillon, J. T., (1983). *Teaching and the art of questioning.* Bloomington, IN: Phi Delta Kappa.

Dillon, J. T. (1984). Research on question and discussion. *Educational Leadership, 42,* 50–56.

Dillon, J. T. (1985). Using questions to foil discussion. *Teaching and Teacher Education,* 109–121.

Gambrell, L. B., & Almasi, J. F. (Eds.). (1996). *Lively discussions! Fostering engaged reading.* Newark, DE: International Reading Association.

Gaskins, I. W., Satlow, E., Hyson, D., Ostertag, J., & Six, L. (1994). Classroom talk about text: Learning in science class. *Journal of Reading, 37,* 558–565.

Greabell, L. C., & Anderson, N. (1992). Applying strategies from the directed reading-thinking activity to a directed mathematics activity. *School Science and Mathematics, 92,* 42–44.

Johnson, D. W., Johnson, R. T., & Holubec, E. J. (1994). *The new circles of literacy: Cooperation in the classroom and school.* Alexandria, VA: Association for Supervision and Curriculum Development.

Kletzien, S. B., & Baloche, L. (1994). The shifting muffled sound of the pick: Facilitating student-to-student discussion. *Journal of Reading, 37,* 540–545.

Preece, A. (1995). Talking about learning: Making reflection meaningful in elementary classroom. *English Quarterly, 23*(4), 18–21.

Slavin, R. E. (1995). *Cooperative learning: Theory, research, and practice* (2nd ed.). Boston, MA: Allyn and Bacon.

Vacca, J. L., Vacca, R. T., & Gove, M. K. (1995). *Reading and learning to read* (3rd ed.). New York: HarperCollins.

Vogt, M. E. (1996). Creating a response-centered curriculum with discussion groups. In L. B. Gambrell & J. F. Almasi (Eds.), *Lively discussions! Fostering engaged reading.* Newark, DE: International Reading Association.

chapter eight

Writing to Learn

We do not write in order to be understood; we write in order to understand.

–C. Day Lewis

ORGANIZING PRINCIPLE

Writing is not without its rewards and surprises. The surprises come from discovering what you want to say about a subject; the rewards lie in knowing that you crafted to satisfaction what you wanted to say. C. Day Lewis didn't sit down at his desk to write about things that were already clear in his mind. If he had, there would have been little incentive to write. Lewis used writing first to discover and clarify meaning—*to understand*—and second, to communicate meaning to others—*to be understood*.

Some of you may find it surprising to find a separate chapter in this book on the role that writing plays in content literacy and learning. In other chapters, we recommend various kinds of writing activities to scaffold students' interactions with texts. In this chapter, however, our intent is to highlight and reaffirm the powerful learning opportunities that arise whenever teachers link reading and writing in the instructional lessons that they create.

A classroom environment that supports reading and writing invites students to explore ideas, clarify meaning, and construct knowledge. When reading and writing are taught in tandem, the union influences content learning in ways not possible when students read without writing or write without reading. When teachers invite a class to write before or after reading, they help students use writing to think about what they will read and to explore and think more deeply about the ideas they have read.

Reading and writing have been taught in most classrooms as if they bear little relationship to each other. The result has often been to sever the powerful bonds for meaning-making that exist between reading and writing. There's little to be gained from teaching reading apart from writing. The organizing principle reflects this notion: **writing facilitates learning by helping students explore, clarify, and think deeply about the ideas and concepts they encounter in reading, viewing, and listening.**

CHAPTER OVERVIEW

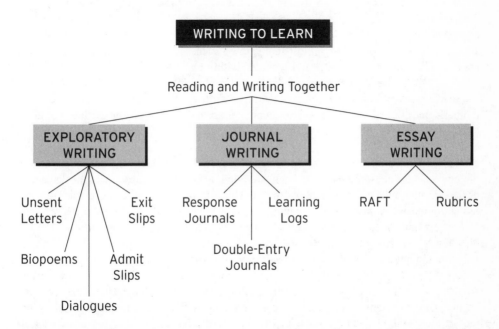

FRAME OF MIND

1. Why emphasize writing to learn in content areas?
2. Why teach writing and reading together?
3. How might teachers create occasions for students to write to read and to read to write?
4. How can teachers use exploratory writing activities to connect reading and writing?
5. How can teachers use journals to connect writing and reading?
6. How can teachers develop and evaluate essay-writing assignments?

Margaret Atwood, a winner of both the Giller and Booker Prizes for literature, says, "A word after a word after a word is power." Microcomputers and word processors notwithstanding, writing isn't easy for most people. Yet for those who are successful, the process of writing—sweat and all—is enormously challenging, rewarding, and powerful.

Perhaps for this reason, Chin's mother was a bit perplexed by her daughter's writing. Chin was 13 years old and, by all accounts, a bright student. Yet her mother was bewildered by her daughter's writing activities both in and out of school: "She'll spend hours email-ing friends all over the world but reluctantly writes skimpy, simple-minded paragraphs for school assignments." When Chin was questioned about the discrepancy in her writing, her reply was all the more confusing: "But, Mom, that's what my teachers want."

Chin may never win a prize for literature, but she does have a need to write. Most chil-dren and adolescents do. Often, just out of sight of teachers, students will write continual-ly to other students during the course of a school day—about classmates, teachers, intrigues, problems, parents, or anything else that happens to be on their minds. The top-ics may not be academically oriented, but they are both real and immediate to students.

In Chin's case, writing to a distant friend was so important that she was willing to struggle with a blank screen to keep in touch. However, as far as school writing was con-cerned, she had probably psyched out what her teachers expected from her. She knew what she needed to do to get by and, most likely, to be successful. Chin intuitively understood the role of writing in her classes and operated within that context.

Although students often engage in some form of writing in content area classrooms, few teachers use writing to its fullest potential as a tool for learning. Chin's response to her mother's question reflects what researchers such as Judith Langer and Arthur Applebee (1987) have consistently observed to be the role of writing in content classrooms: it is mainly restricted to short responses to study questions or to taking notes in class. For example, examine the worksheet responses in Figure 8.1 of a student in a secondary school biology class. The students have been studying a unit on viruses. The worksheet is designed to have the class think about the life characteristics of viruses in relation to other living organisms. Notice how the spacing on the worksheet restricts the student's respons-es to short one- or two-sentence answers. The student provides accurate information but only enough to satisfy the requirements of the assignment.

Even though the purpose of the worksheet writing may be legitimate, students need var-ied and frequent experiences with writing as a tool for learning. According to Langer and Applebee (1987), "Put simply, in the whole range of academic course work, [...] children do not write frequently enough, and the reading and writing tasks they are given do not require them to think deeply enough" (p. 4). There are at least three good reasons for teach-ers to take a second look at the role of writing in their classrooms. First, writing improves thinking. Second, it facilitates learning. Third, writing is intimately related to reading.

Content area teachers usually have second thoughts about assigning writing in their classrooms because of preconceived notions of what the teaching of writing may entail. Writing isn't generally thought of as basic to thinking and learning about content fields. Nancie Atwell (1990) is quick to point out that although the role of language arts teachers is to guide students' development as writers, teachers of every discipline share in the responsibility of showing students how to think and write as scientists, historians, mathe-maticians, and literary critics do. When students engage in writing as a way of knowing, they are thinking on paper.

READING AND WRITING TOGETHER

There is no better way to think about a subject than to have the occasion to read and write about it. However, reading and writing don't necessarily guarantee improved thinking or

Characteristics of Life

1. CELLS: All living things are composed of cells.
    VIRUSES: Viruses are constructed of compounds usually associated with cells, but they are not considered cells.

2. ORGANIZATION: All organisms are organized at both the molecular and the cellular level. They take in substances from the environment and organize them in complex ways.
    VIRUSES: No, they aren't organized because they don't take in substances from the environment. They just replicate, using a host cell.

3. ENERGY USE: All organisms use energy for growth and maintenance.
    VIRUSES: Viruses don't use energy until they are in a cell; they do not grow; they use host cells for energy.

4. RESPONSE TO THE ENVIRONMENT: All organisms respond to a stimulus. A complex set of responses is called a behaviour.
    VIRUSES: They respond only when they are affecting a cell.

5. GROWTH: All living things grow. Growth occurs through cell division and cell enlargement.
    VIRUSES: They don't grow.

6. REPRODUCTION: All species of organisms have the ability to reproduce on their own.
    VIRUSES: They require a host cell to reproduce.

FIGURE 8.1   A Biology Student's Written Responses on a Worksheet

learning. Students can go through the motions of reading and writing, lacking purpose and commitment, or they can work thoughtfully to construct meaning, make discoveries, and think deeply about a subject. A classroom environment for reading and writing is one that lends encouragement to students who are maturing as readers and writers and that provides instructional support so that readers and writers can play with ideas, explore concepts, clarify meaning, and elaborate on what they are learning.

Reading and writing are acts of composing, because readers and writers are involved in an ongoing, dynamic process of constructing meaning (Tierney & Pearson 1983). Composing processes are more obvious in writing than in reading: the writer, initially facing a blank page or screen, constructs a text. The text is a visible entity and reflects the writer's thinking on paper. Less obvious is the "text"—the configuration of meanings—that students compose or construct in their own minds as they read.

Think of reading and writing as two sides of the same coin. Whereas the writer works to make a text sensible, the reader works to make sense from a text. As a result, the two processes, rooted in language, are intertwined and share common cognitive and sociocultural characteristics. Both reading and writing, for example, involve purpose, commitment, schema activation, planning, working with ideas, revision and rethinking, and monitoring. Both processes occur within a social, communicative context. Skilled writers are mindful of their content (the subject about which they are writing) and also of their audiences (the readers for whom they write). Skilled readers are mindful of a text's content and are also aware that they engage in transactions with its author.

The relationships between reading and writing have been a source of inquiry by language researchers since the mid-1970s (Tierney & Shanahan 1991). Several broad conclusions about the links between reading and writing can be drawn: good readers are often good writers, and vice versa; students who write well tend to read more than those who do not write well; wide reading improves writing; and students who are good readers and writers perceive themselves as such and are more likely to engage in reading and writing on their own.

Why connect reading and writing in instructional contexts? According to Shanahan (1990), the combination of reading and writing in a classroom improves achievement and instructional efficiency. From a content area perspective, writing about ideas and concepts encountered in texts will improve students' acquisition of content more than simply reading without writing. When reading and writing are taught in concert, the union fosters communication, enhances problem solving, and makes learning more powerful than if reading or writing is engaged in separately.

When teachers integrate writing and reading, they help students use writing to *think about what they will read* and to *understand what they have read*. Writing may be used to catapult students into reading. It is also one of the most effective ways for students to understand something they have read. Teachers can put students into writing-to-read or reading-to-write situations, since the writing process is a powerful tool for exploring and clarifying meaning.

Donald Murray (1980) explains that writers engage in a process of exploration and clarification as they go about the task of making meaning. In Figure 8.2, Murray suggests that writers progress from exploring meaning to clarifying it as they continue to draft and shape a piece of writing. A writer's first draft is an initial attempt to think on paper or screen. The more writers work with ideas put on paper or screen, the more they are able to revise, rethink, and clarify what they have to say about a subject.

Santa and Havens (1991) illustrate the power of writing before and after reading with an example from a biology class. Before reading a textbook assignment on flower reproduction, students wrote before-reading entries in *learning logs* (a student resource we explain shortly), telling what they knew about the subject they would be reading and studying. Here's an example of a student's entry:

> In this chapter I am going to learn about flower reproduction. I know that flowers have male and female parts. I think that these parts are in the inside of the flower. To see them you have to pull aside the petals. I think petals probably protect the reproductive parts, but I am not sure. I remember something about separate flowers for male and females, but I think many flowers have both parts on the same flower. I'm pretty sure you need to have at least two plants before they can reproduce. (p. 124)

In the biology class, students also had an occasion to write about flower reproduction after reading. In an after-reading entry, writing helps the students continue to explore and clarify meaning by focusing on what they learned and noting their misconceptions in their before-reading entries. Study the after-reading entry written by the same student:

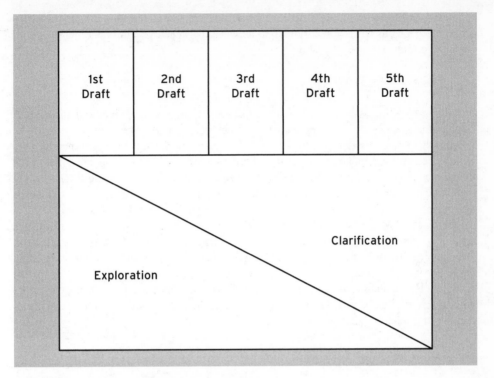

FIGURE 8.2 Exploration and Clarification

Source: From "Writing as Process: How Writing Finds Its Own Meaning," by Donald M. Murray in *Eight Approaches to Teaching Composition*, Donovan and McClelland (Eds.). Copyright © 1980 by the National Council of Teachers of English. Reprinted with permission.q

I learned that stamens are the male parts of the flower. The stamen produces the pollen. The female part is the pistil. At the bottom of the pistil is the ovary. Plants have eggs just like humans. The eggs are kept in the ovary. I still am not sure how pollen gets to the female part. Do bees do all this work, or are there other ways to pollinate? I was right, sometimes male and female parts are on separate flowers. These are called incomplete flowers. Complete flowers have both male and female parts on the same flower. I also learned that with complete flowers just one plant can reproduce itself. So, I was partially wrong thinking it always took two plants to reproduce. (p. 124)

Occasions to write on content subjects, such as the before-reading and after-reading entries just shown, create powerful opportunities to learn content in concert with reading. Students who experience the integration of writing and reading are likely to learn more content, to understand it better, and to remember it longer. This is the case because writing, whether before or after reading, promotes thinking, but in different ways. Writing a summary after reading (see Chapter 9), for example, is likely to result in greater understanding and retention of important information. However, another type of writing—let's say an essay—may trigger the analysis, synthesis, and elaboration of ideas encountered in reading and class discussion.

Because writing promotes different types of learning, students should have many different occasions to write. Let's look at some ways that teachers can create occasions for students to think and learn by writing.

EXPLORATORY WRITING

Exploratory writing is first-draft writing. Often, it is messy, tentative, and unfinished. Exploration of ideas and concepts may be pursued before or after reading. Writing activities that help students tap into their storehouse of memories—their prior knowledge— make excellent springboards into reading. Exploratory writing helps students collect what they know and connect it to what they will be reading. For example, some teachers combine brainstorming on a topic to be studied with five or so minutes of spontaneous freewriting in which students tell what they know about the subject to be studied.

Gere (1985) describes exploratory writing as unfinished. In her words, unfinished writing is "writing that evinces thought but does not merit the careful scrutiny which a finished piece of writing deserves" (p. 4). There is value in planning unfinished writing activity in the content area classroom. The excellent monograph she edited, *Roots in the Sawdust* (1985), shows how teachers from various disciplines use and adapt exploratory writing activities in their classrooms. We have found the following to be quite useful in elementary or secondary classes.

Unsent Letters

The writing-to-learn activity known as *unsent letters* establishes a role-play situation in which students are asked to write letters in response to the material they are studying. The activity requires the use of imagination and often demands that students engage in interpretive and evaluative thinking. The following is Dan's unsent letter to the prime minister of Canada, written after he studied Canada's involvement in slavery in his social studies text and then read a novel on the same topic. It reflects both personal and informative writing.

> Dear Mr. Prime Minister,
>
> How is life on Sussex Drive? In school we have been studying the novel *Underground to Canada* by Barbara Smucker. The book is about an African American born into slavery in the American South who escaped to freedom in Canada. I was surprised to learn in my social studies class that Canada once permitted slavery. However, I am also proud that our country ended up being the safe haven for many American slaves. There is still much social injustice in the world, and I hope that Canada will continue to lend support to those in need as we did through the Underground Railway in the 1800s.

Unsent letters direct students' thinking with particular audiences in mind. Students can also send their letters, either by conventional surface mail or by email. Biopoems, by contrast, require students to play with ideas using precise language in a poetic framework.

Biopoems

A *biopoem* allows students to reflect on large amounts of material within a poetic form. The biopoem follows a pattern that enables writers to synthesize what they have learned about a person, place, thing, concept, or event under study. For example, study the pattern suggested by Gere (1985) for a person or character:

Line 1. First name

Line 2. Four traits that describe character

Line 3. Relative ("brother," "sister," "daughter," etc.) of _____

Line 4. Lover of _____ (list three things or people)

Line 5. Who feels _____ (three items)

Line 6. Who needs _____ (three items)

Line 7. Who fears _____ (three items)

Line 8. Who gives _____ (three items)

Line 9. Who would like to see _____ (three items)

Line 10. Resident of _____

Line 11. Last name

Notice how a physical education teacher adapted the preceding pattern to a writing activity in her course. The lesson was part of a unit on controversial topics in health such as HIV and AIDS awareness and the use of performance enhancing drugs. After the class spent several days studying the topic, the teacher introduced the biopoem strategy and explained how it could be useful in learning. She shared several biopoems from previous years that students had written on various topics. She then discussed the biopoem format and clarified any questions that students might have about writing a biopoem. She invited the students to write a biopoem using what they learned about controversial health issues. They could apply what they learned to a person they "invented" or to a real-life person who had HIV or who had used drugs to enhance performance.

Here are two of the biopoems the students wrote. The first deals with an invented person; the second, with Ben Johnson, who lost his gold medal for winning the 100-m sprint in the 1988 Olympics when he tested positive for steroid use.

Valerie,
Thin, tired, sad, confused.
She asks: "Why me?"
        "How will I deal with this?"
        "Will I be alone?"

Valerie,
She needs love,
        support,
        care,
        and advice.

Valerie,
She fears dying,
      being alone,
      feeling rejected.

Valerie,
She would like to see a cure,
             Her family's approval,
             Friends who care.

Valerie,
Your neighbour next door
A resident of Anywhere, The World.
Valerie

Big Ben

Ben Johnson
Born December 30, 1961, in Jamaica
Strong, brave, outspoken—a Canadian hero
Why you?
You were Big Ben! But how do you feel now?
Embarrassed? Confused? Lonely?
Even Ben Johnson needs love, support, family.
How do you want to be remembered
By athletes?
By the world?
One of the fastest men
Ben Johnson
You are still Big Ben!

Dialogues

In a dialogue activity, students are asked to create an exchange between two or more persons, historical figures, or characters being studied. Beaman (1985), a secondary school social studies teacher, illustrated the use of dialogue as a writing-to-learn assignment. He asked his students to write a dialogue between themselves and a "friend" who wanted them to do something they were opposed to but were unsure of how to respond to because of peer pressure. Beaman suggested that students write about awkward teenage situations of peer pressure. Here's a sample dialogue between Mary and Betty:

> **Mary:** Let's skip class and go out on the parking lot. I have some awesome dope and a new disk by the Scorpions.
>
> **Betty:** I can't. I've skipped second period one too many times, and I really want to graduate. Contemporary Problems is required, and I'm afraid I may fail.
>
> **Mary:** Get serious, one class missed is not going to get you an F. You need the relaxation, and besides, the Scorpions ...

Betty:	I wish I could say "yes" to you.
Mary:	Say "yes" then, or are you turning into a real "school" girl?
Betty:	You are pressuring me, Mary!
Mary:	No pressure, just fun, come on ...
Betty:	No, I'm going to class, I do want to graduate. You can go, but I'm going to class. (Beaman 1985, p. 63)

A dialogue such as this one permits writers to think about conflicts and possible solutions. As an unfinished writing activity, a dialogue also provides an opportunity for students to react to ideas and to extend their thinking about the material being studied.

Foreign-language teachers adapt the use of dialogues to help their students converse in writing and then to role-play their conversations in front of the class. In the dialogue that follows, secondary school French students wrote a dialogue about a concert they would like to see. The teacher gave them the option of working in pairs or groups of three. As part of the dialogue writing, each student had to contribute at least four lines to the conversation. The teacher also directed the students to use at least three new verbs in their dialogue and at least 10 new vocabulary words. The students practised reading their dialogues to each other while working in their groups. The teacher evaluated students on their pronunciation during the role-play of the dialogues (individual accountability) and on originality, sentence structure, and grammar usage in the written dialogue (group accountability). The dialogue, as drafted by the students, follows:

Margaux:	Salut, Antoine, tu vas bien?
Antoine:	Oui je vais très bien! J'ai gagné deux billets pour le concert de Avril Lavigne!
Margaux:	OH, tu as de la chance! Est-ce que je peux y aller avec toi?
Sophie:	Et bonjour, les amis. Savez-vous qu'Avril Lavigne vient à Québec pour un concert?
Antoine:	Oui, j'ai déjà deux billets.
Sophie:	Quelle chance, moi aussi, j'y vais.
Antoine:	J'ai une super idée. Je peux donc inviter Margaux!
Margaux:	Antoine, tu es extra! J'ai hâte d'y aller. Quel jour est-ce?
Sophie:	C'est samedi soir.
Antoine:	A quelle heure, ça commence?
Sophie:	A huit heures.
Margaux:	Alors, allons manger ensemble avant.
Antoine:	Excellente idée, à samedi les filles! Je m'en vais, j'ai un cours de français dans deux minutes.
Sophie:	Au revoir, à samedi!

Admit Slips and Exit Slips

Admit slips and exit slips involve anonymous writing and, therefore, shouldn't be part of the permanent record of learning that builds over time in students' learning logs. Thus, these activities should be introduced as a separate assignment and not as part of a learning-log entry.

Admit slips are brief comments written by students on index cards or half-sheets of paper at the very beginning of class. Gere (1985) recommends that these written responses be collected as tickets of admission to class. The purpose of the admit slip is to have students react to what they are studying or to what's happening in class. Students are asked to respond to questions such as

What's confusing you about _____?

What problems did you have with your text assignment?

What would you like to get off your chest?

What do you like (dislike) about _____?

The admit slips are collected by the teacher and read aloud (with no indication of the authorship of individual comments) as a way of beginning class discussion. Admit slips build a trusting relationship between teacher and students and contribute to a sense of community in the classroom.

In an advanced algebra class, where students had been studying complex numbers, the teacher asked the class to use admit slips to explain difficulties students had with one of their homework assignments. One student wrote, "I didn't know where to start." Several other students made similar comments. The teacher was able to use the written feedback to address some of the problems that students had with the assignment.

An *exit slip*, as you might anticipate, is a variation on the admit slip. Toward the end of class, the teacher asks students for exit slips as a way of bringing closure to what was learned. An exit slip question might require students to summarize, synthesize, evaluate, or project.

In the advanced algebra class, exit slips were used toward the end of the class to introduce a new unit on imaginary numbers. The teacher asked students to write for several minutes as they reflected on the question, "Why do you think we are studying imaginary numbers after we studied the discriminant?" One student wrote, "Because the discriminant can be negative and I didn't know what kind of a number $\sqrt{-1}$ was. I guessing [*sic*] it must be imaginary. Right?" The teacher was able to sort through the exit slip responses and use them to introduce the new unit.

The several minutes devoted to exit-slip writing are often quite revealing of the day's lesson and establish a direction for the next class.

Brainstorming and Clustering

Brainstorming and clustering are related instructional strategies that permit students to examine ideas as rehearsal for reading and writing. Brainstorming and clustering are exploratory strategies for prereading or prewriting, since they help students to establish purpose as they think about ideas and concepts to be studied. Teachers usually begin a brainstorming session by presenting an idea or concept to students based on some aspect of the subject they will be studying. A time limit is then set for brainstorming, which involves listing as many ideas as possible about the topic.

Clustering may be viewed as both a variation and an extension of brainstorming. Rather than list ideas, students "cluster" them around a nucleus word or concept, as in the accompanying diagram. When introducing clustering to students, first model the strategy by writing a key or nucleus word on the board or overhead transparency and then surround it with other associated words that are offered by the students. In this way, students not only gather ideas for writing but also connect the ideas within categories of information. Teacher-led clustering provides students with opportunities to practise the strategy. As they become aware of the strategy and how to use it, students will be able to cluster ideas quickly on their own.

Notice in Figure 8.3 on page 228 how a teacher used brainstorming and clustering to help her students explore the topic of "railway workers" as part of a unit on the building of the Canadian National Railway. As part of their study, students explored issues such as the settlement of western Canada and the contributions of early Asian immigrants. One of the learning experiences for the chapter concerned a writing activity designed to help students examine some of the important ideas that they had studied. The teacher began the lesson with a lead-in: "Using any information that you can recall from your text or class discussion, think about what might have been some of the problems or concerns of Chinese workers during the building of the railway. Let's do some brainstorming." As the students offered ideas related to prejudice, isolation, and dangerous working conditions, the teacher listed them on the board.

Getting ideas out in the open through brainstorming was the first step in the lesson. The second step was to cluster the words into meaningful associations based on student suggestions. The teacher modelled the activity by choosing as the keyword the concept of *Chinese railway workers*. She then drew a line to the upper right corner of the chalkboard and connected the keyword to the word *problems*. She connected some of the words generated by students during brainstorming to the cluster. The teacher then asked what some

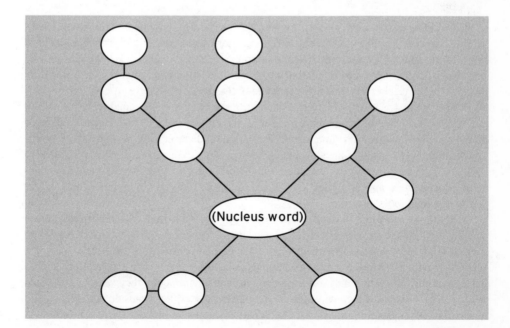

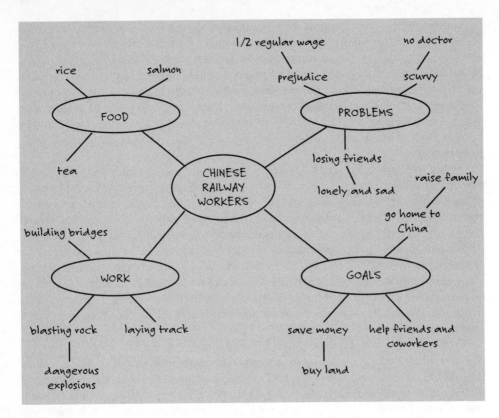

FIGURE 8.3 Cluster on the Lives of Chinese Railway Workers

of the results of the workers' problems would be. One student volunteered the word *scurvy*. The teacher wrote *scurvy* in the upper right corner of the cluster and asked students to brainstorm some more examples. These examples were then connected to the cluster. The remainder of the class session centred on discussion. Figure 8.3 depicts the completed cluster that the teacher and students produced on the board.

With the cluster as a frame of reference, the students were assigned to write what it would have been like to be a Chinese worker on the railway in the 1800s. Because the textbook presented a variety of primary sources (including diary entries, newspaper clippings, and death notices), many of the students decided to write in one of those forms (see Figure 8.4). One member of the class became so involved in the activity that he wanted his historical document to appear authentic by aging the paper. This he did by burning the edges so that it would look "historic."

Students should begin to develop their own clusters for writing as soon as they understand how to use the strategy effectively. They should feel comfortable enough to start with a basic concept or topic—written in the centre of a sheet of paper or on the computer screen—and then to let go by making as many connections as possible. Connections should develop rapidly, "radiating outward from the center in any direction they want to go" (Rico 1983, p. 35). Because there is no right or wrong way to develop a cluster, students should be encouraged to play with ideas based on what they are studying and learning in class.

> May 3, 1883
>
> My name is Tingmin. I work in the Fraser Canyon helping to build the railway. I came to Canada because I wanted to make enough money to go home to China and buy some land.
>
> I know that I make only half the wages non-Chinese workers would make. I was desperate in China because I was a landless peasant. I worried that my wife and five children would starve.
>
> But now I find that life here in what we called Gum San, Gold Mountain, has no gold for people like me. Today I have started writing a diary because I am sick. I think I have scurvy because all we have to eat is rice, salmon, and tea. If only I could get some vegetables. I know that there will be no doctor called. The other Chinese workers will try to help me, but I am afraid.
>
> Today my friend Lin died. There was an accident when a dynamite blast went off before it was supposed to. Six other men died too. We see that only the Chinese workers are given these dangerous jobs. I think that the boss does not like us. We pay so much for room and board that I have nothing to send home. I worry that I will never see my family again.

FIGURE 8.4   A Student's Writing Sample on What It Would Be Like to Be a Chinese Railway Worker

JOURNAL WRITING

Because journals serve a variety of real-life purposes, not the least of which is to write about things that are important to us, they have withstood the test of time. Artists, scientists, novelists, historical figures, mathematicians, dancers, politicians, teachers, children, athletes—all kinds of people—have kept journals "to record the everyday events of their lives and the issues that concern them" (Tompkins 1990). Some journals—diaries, for example—are meant to be private and are not intended to be read by anyone but the writer. Sometimes, however, a diary makes its way into the public domain and affects readers in powerful ways. Anne Frank, probably the world's most famous child diarist, kept a personal journal of her innermost thoughts, fears, hopes, and experiences while hiding from the Nazis during World War II. Having read her diary, who hasn't been moved to think and feel more deeply about the tragic consequences of the Holocaust?

Other journals are more work-related than personal in that writers record observations and experiences that will be useful, insightful, or instructive. In more than 40 notebooks, Leonardo da Vinci recorded artistic ideas, detailed sketches of the human anatomy, elaborate plans for flying machines, and even his dreams. Novelists throughout literary history have used journals to record ideas, happenings, and conversations that have served to stimulate their imaginations and provide material for their writing. Even in a professional sport such as baseball, it is not unusual for hitters to keep a log of their at-bats: who the pitcher was, what the situation was (e.g., runner on base or bases empty), what types of pitches were thrown, and what the outcome of each at-bat was.

Academic journals also serve a variety of purposes. They help students generate ideas, create a record of thoughts and feelings in response to what they are reading, and explore their own lives and concerns in relation to what they are reading and learning. Academic journals create a context for learning in which students interact with information personally as they explore and clarify ideas, issues, and concepts under study. Students can be encouraged to draw and sketch as well as write in their journals. These visual/verbal journals may be used as springboards for class discussion or as mind stretchers that extend thinking, solve problems, or stimulate imagination. All forms of writing, representing, and written or visual expression can be incorporated into academic journal writing, from doodles and sketches to poems and letters to comments, explanations, and reactions.

Three types of journals in particular have made a difference in content literacy situations: *response journals*, *double-entry journals*, and *learning logs*. Each of these can be used in an instructional context to help students explore literary and informational texts. Teachers who use academic journals in their classes encourage students to use everyday, expressive language to write about what they are studying, in the same way that they encourage students to use talk to explore ideas during discussion. When expressive or exploratory language is missing from students' journal writing, the students do not experience the kind of internal talk that allows them to explore and clarify meaning in ways that are personal and crucial to thinking on paper (Britton 1970) or on screen.

When writing in academic journals, students need not attempt to sound "academic," even though they are writing about ideas and information of importance in various disciplines. Like the exploratory writing activities previously discussed in this chapter, journal entries need to be judged on the writer's ability to communicate and explore ideas, not on the quality of handwriting or the number of spelling and grammatical errors in the writing. Journal writing underscores informal learning. It relieves teachers of the burden of correction so that they can focus on students' thinking, and it creates a nonthreatening situation for students who may be hesitant to take risks because they are overly concerned about the mechanics of writing (e.g., handwriting, neatness, spelling, and punctuation).

Response Journals

Response journals create a permanent record of what readers are feeling and thinking as they interact with literary or informational texts. A response journal allows students to record their thoughts about texts and emotional reactions to them. Teachers may use prompts to trigger students' feelings and thoughts about a subject or may invite students to respond freely to what they are reading and doing in class. Prompts may include questions, visual stimuli, read-alouds, or situations created to stimulate thinking. An earth science teacher, for example, might ask students to place themselves in the role of a water molecule as they describe what it's like to travel through the water cycle. Examine how Mathieu, a low-achieving grade 9 student who didn't like to write, responded in his journal entry:

> My name is Moe, its short for Molecule. I was born in a cloud when I was condensed on a dust particle. My neverending life story goes like this.
>
> During Moes life he had a great time boncing into his friends. He grew up in the cloud and became bigger and heavier. Moe became so heavy that one night lightning struck and he fell out of his cloud as a raindrop. He landed in a farmers field where this leavy plant sucked him up. Moe became a small section of a leave on the plant and their he absorbed sunlight and other things. One day a cow came by and ate Moes leave. He was now part of the cow.
>
> Well you can guess the rest. The farmer ate the cow and Moe became part of the farmer. One day the farmer was working in the field, he started sweating and thats when Moe escaped. He transpirated into the air as a molecule again. Free at last he rejoined a group of new friends in a cloud and the cycle went on.

The teacher was pleased by this journal entry, mechanical errors and all. On homework questions, Mathieu usually wrote short, incoherent answers. In this entry, however, he interacted playfully with the information in the text and demonstrated his understanding of the water cycle.

Role playing is an excellent prompt for response journal writing. A history teacher may invite students to assume the role of a historical character and to view events and happenings from the character's perspective. In one Canadian history class, students keep a journal of events that take place in Canadian history from the perspective of a fictitious historical family that each student creates. The families witness all of the events that take place in Canadian history and write their reactions to these events. The teacher scaffolds the journal writing assignment with the guidesheet in Figure 8.5 on page 232.

A secondary school art teacher, Ken Gessford, incorporates a sketchbook into his courses to guide students' thinking and responses to what they are learning and studying in class. As an introduction to the sketchbook, the class discusses reasons for keeping a sketchbook, which Gessford adapted from a model used by McIntosh (1991):

- *What should you include in your sketchbook?*

  New ideas, sketches, concepts, designs, redesigns, words, notes from class, drawings to show understanding, reflections on the class, questions that you have, and new things you've learned.

- *When should you include entries in your sketchbook?*

  (1) After each class; (2) anytime an insight or a design idea or question hits you; (3) anytime, so keep the sketchbook handy and visible in your work area.

To help you develop your historical character, use the information that you have gained about Upper Canada and your own background knowledge.

Who is your character?

1. What is your character's name? How old is your character? Is he or she married? (*Note:* How old were people when they married during his time?)
   _____
   _____

2. Who else is in your character's family? How old is each of these people? (*Note*: What happened to a lot of children during this time?)
   _____
   _____

3. Where does your character live?
   _____
   _____

4. What does your character do for a living? Is he or she rich or poor?
   _____
   _____

5. What religion is your character? What attitude does he or she have toward religion?
   _____
   _____

6. How much education does your character have?
   _____
   _____

7. Was your character born in Canada, Europe, the United States, or elsewhere? Specify in which country he or she was born.
   _____
   _____

8. How does your character feel about people who are "different" in skin colour, religion, social or economic class, or nationality?
   a. Skin colour? (*Note:* This may depend on where he or she lives.)
   _____
   b. Religion?
   _____
   c. Social or economic class?
   _____
   d. Nationality?
   _____

9. How does your character feel about living in Canada?
   _____
   _____

FIGURE 8.5 **A Guidesheet for Historical Character Journals**

■ *Why should you draw and write in your sketchbook?*

(1) It will record ideas you might otherwise forget; (2) it will record and note your growth; (3) it will facilitate your learning, problem solving, idea forming, research, reading, and discussion in class.

■ *How should you write and draw entries in your sketchbook?*

You can express yourself in sketches and drawings; in single words, questions, or short phrases; in long, flowing sentences; in designs and redesigns; in diagrams, graphs, and overlays; or in colours.

■ *Remember, the sketchbook is yours, and it reflects how perceptive you are with your ideas and how creative you are in your thought processes!*

Examine several of the students' sketchbook entries in Figure 8.6 on page 234.

Mathematics teachers use response journals in a variety of ways. They may invite students to write a "math autobiography" in which they describe their feelings and prior experiences as mathematics learners. Rose (1989) suggests the following prompt for a biographical narrative in mathematics:

Write about any mathematical experiences you have had. The narratives should be told as stories, with as much detail and description as possible. Include your thoughts, reactions, and feelings about the entire experience. (p. 24)

If students need more scaffolding than the prompt, Rose recommends having them complete and write elaborations on sentences, such as

My most positive experience with mathematics was _____

My background in mathematics is _____

I liked mathematics until _____

Mathematics makes me feel _____

If I were a mathematics teacher, I'd _____

The content of mathematics journals may also include exploratory writing activities, summaries, letters, student-constructed word problems and theorem definitions, descriptions of mathematical processes, calculations and solutions to problems, and feelings about the course. Examine, for example, the journal entries in Figures 8.7 and 8.8 on page 235.

In addition to prompts, consider having students engage in freewriting in their journals. Hancock (1993) provides a set of guidelines for writing freely in response journals in literature. These guidelines, with some modification, can easily be adapted to informational text. Some of the guidelines for students to consider when using response journals are the following:

■ *Write your innermost feelings, opinions, thoughts, likes, and dislikes.* This is your journal. In it, feel the freedom to express yourself and your personal responses to reading.

■ *Write down anything that you are thinking about while you read.* The journal is a way of recording those fleeting thoughts that pass through your mind as you interact with the book.

<u>Van Gogh vs. Gauguin</u>

——I like Van Gogh much better

——Gauguin is nice but too showy

——I like the elegance of Van Gogh

——Self-portraits are really challenging

——Van Gogh——master directionalist

——Unbelievable that he (Van Gogh) had no training!

——I like looking at different artists. Even though I know these people are masters, I love their work.

——I could never do that without lots of training!!

<u>Impressionists</u>

——Pretty

——Watercoloury

——Really masterful handling of paint (watercolour)

<u>Question</u>

When am I going to work larger?

I liked what we did in Photoshop——hope I get a chance to work with it again.

<u>Questions</u>

Why is it that I always draw late at night or early in the morning?

Shouldn't I start thinking about painting?

Will I ever understand colour mixing?

Will I ever understand doing pencil directions?

Will I learn to stretch a canvas?

<u>Looking to the future</u>

——I don't use this sketchbook to do sketches——I like it more as a log

——Paint!! (probably a final problem)

FIGURE 8.6   **Entries from a Sketchbook**

October 7

When I look at something I have to prove, the answer is always so obvious to me, I don't know what to write. This confuses me more because then I just write down one thing. Even though I understand it, no one else could. I don't use postulates & theorems because I have no idea which is which. So if you gave me a proof, I could probably prove it, but just not mathematically using big words.

FIGURE 8.7   Journal Entry in Response to the Prompt, "What Goes Through Your Mind When You Do a Proof?"

9/4

How to Draw a Bisected Angle

Make an acute angle. Label it $\angle ABC$—making Point A on one ray, B at the vertex, or point where rays meet, and C on the other ray. Now, with a compass, draw an arc of any measurement that will cross both rays. Next, use your compass to measure the distance between the two points you made by making the arc and keep the measurement locked on your protractor. Now, put the point of your compass on one of the arc points and make a slash in the middle of the angle. Do the same from the other dot on the other ray. The slash marks should cross in the centre. Make a point where the slashes cross. Label it Point D.   Draw a ray starting at Point B going through Point D. $\overrightarrow{BD}$ now bisects $\angle ABC$.

FIGURE 8.8   Journal Entry in Response to the Prompt, "Explain to Someone How to Bisect an Angle"

- *Don't worry about the accuracy of spelling and mechanics in the journal.* The content and expression of your personal thoughts should be your primary concern.
- *Record the number of the page you were reading when you wrote your response.* You might want to look back to reread and verify your thoughts.
- *Write on only one side per page of your spiral notebook.* Expect to read occasional interested comments from your teacher or another student on the other side.
- Relate what you are reading to your own experiences.
- *Ask questions while reading.* This will help you make sense of the story or characters.
- *Make predictions about what you think will happen as the plot unfolds.* Validate or change those predictions as you proceed in the text. Don't worry about being wrong.
- Praise or criticize the book, the author, the style.
- *Talk to the characters as you begin to know them.* Give them advice to help them. Put yourself in their place and tell them how you would act in a similar situation.
- There is no limit to the type of responses you can write. These guidelines are meant to trigger, not limit, the kinds of things you write.

Teachers often make students aware of how and why they can use response journals through metacognitive discussions and demonstrations. One way to demonstrate how to write an effective entry is to share with the class some past students' responses of different types. Use these demonstrations to build confidence and procedural knowledge in the use of the journal.

Double-Entry Journals

A double-entry journal is a versatile adaptation of the response journal. As the name implies, the double-entry journal allows students to record dual entries that are conceptually related. In doing so, students juxtapose their thoughts and feelings according to the prompts they are given for making the entries. To create a two-column format for the double-entry journal, have students divide sheets of notebook paper in half lengthwise. As an alternative, younger writers may need more room to write their entries than a divided page allows. They find that it is easier to use the entire left page of a notebook as one column and the right page as the other column.

Double-entry journals serve a variety of functions. In the left column of the journal, students may be prompted to select words, short quotes, or passages from the text that interest them or evoke a strong response. In this column, they write the word, quote, or passage verbatim or use their own words to describe what is said in the text. In the right column, the students record their reactions, interpretations, and responses to the text segments they have selected. As part of a science unit on the solar system, for example, middle-level students used double-entry journals as an occasion to explore their own personal meanings for the concept of the solar system. In the left column, they responded to the question, "What is it?" In the right column, the students reflected on the question, "What does it mean to you?" Study the entries that three of the students wrote in the "What is it?" column. Then compare the three corresponding entries from the right column, "What does it mean to you?"

"WHAT IS THE SOLAR SYSTEM?"	**"WHAT DOES IT MEAN TO YOU?"**
It is nine planets, along with asteroid belts, stars, black holes, and so on.	The solar system is a mystery to me. I know the planets and stuff, but how did it come into being? Galileo had something to do with the solar system, but I'm not sure exactly what. I would like to find out more about it.
It is planets and stars. Earth is the third planet from the sun. It is the only planet with water. Stars are huge. Many are much greater than the sun in size.	The solar system reminds me of a white-haired scientist who is always studying the big vast opening in the sky. When I look at the sky at night I see tiny twinkling lights. People tell me that they're planets but I think they're stars. I see constellations, but I don't recognize them. I am not a white-haired scientist yet.
The nine planets are not very interesting to me and I won't bother to go through them. But I did memorize the order of the planets by this sentence. *My very eager mother just served us nine pizzas.* Take the beginning letters to remind you of each planet.	When I think about what the solar system means to me, I think about an unknown universe, which could be much larger than we think it is. I start to think about science fiction stories that I have read, alien beings and creatures that are in the universe some place.

In a grade 8 language arts class, Harry Noden and his students were engaged in a unit on the Yukon and Jack London's *Call of the Wild* (Noden & Vacca 1994). As part of the core book study of London's classic novel about the adventures of a sled dog named Buck, Noden arranged for a sled-dog-team demonstration by a group of local residents who participate in dog sledding as a hobby. His class was excited by the demonstration, which took place on the school's grounds. The next day, the class used double-entry journals to reflect on the experience. In the left column, they responded to the question, "What did you learn from the demonstration?" In the right column, they reflected on the question, "How did the demonstration help you better understand the novel?" Examine some of the students' entries in Figure 8.9 on page 238.

Mathematics teachers have also been encouraged to use double-entry journals to help students solve word problems (Tobias 1989). In the left column, a teacher might direct students to engage in "thinking out loud" as they work on a word problem. In the right column, the students go about solving the problem, providing a layout of their sketches and calculations. Tobias noticed that as students began to use the two-column format to think about their problem-solving processes, they focused on posing two kinds of questions: What is making the problem difficult for me? And what could I do to make it easier for myself? Here is one student's "thinking out loud" entry in response to this problem: *a car goes 30 000 km on a long trip, rotating its five tires (including the spare) regularly and frequently. How many kilometres will any one tire have driven on the road?*

What did you learn from the demonstration?	How did the demonstration help you better understand the novel?
I learned that although dogs just look big and cuddly they really can work. When people take the time they can teach their dog anything. Yet that saying also applies to life. **[Alex]**	I never realized how hard it was for Buck to pull the sled. It takes a lot of work.
It was excellent. I learned that the owners and the dogs were a family and extremely hard workers. I learned how hard a race could be and the risk involved. I'm glad I got to see the dogs and their personalities. **[Marcus]**	It proved to me how Buck needed to be treated with praise and discipline and equality. That way you get a wonderful dog and a companion for life.
I learned about how they trained their dogs and that they need as much or more love and attention as they do discipline. **[Jennifer]**	It helped me understand the book better because it showed how unique Buck is compared to the other dogs. Also what a dog sled looks like and what Buck might have looked like. It made the story come alive more.

FIGURE 8.9   Entries from a Double-Entry Journal Assignment for *The Call of the Wild*

I assume there is a formula for solving this problem, but I have forgotten (if I ever knew) what it is.

I am being confused by the word "rotate." Simply by driving, we cause our tires to turn or "rotate" on the road. But "rotate" means something else in this problem. I had better concentrate on that.

I wonder how many kilometres each tire will have gone while in the trunk? Is this a useful approach? Let me try. (p. 52)

Tobias explains that using this unorthodox approach, trying to find the number of kilometres that any one tire will have travelled in the trunk of the car, is a productive way to solve the problem. In the right column, the student calculated the correct answer by dividing 5 tires into 30 000 miles to get 6000 km per tire in the trunk. He then subtracted 6000 km from the total 30 000 km driven, yielding the correct answer: Each tire, rotated onto the four on-road positions, travelled a total of 24 000 km.

Learning Logs

Learning logs add still another dimension to personal learning in content area classrooms. The strategy is simple to implement but must be used regularly to be effective. As is the case with response and double-entry journals, students keep an ongoing record of learning *as it happens* in a notebook or loose-leaf binder. They write in their own language, not necessarily for others to read but to themselves, about what they are learning. Entries in logs influence learning by revealing problems and concerns.

There is no one way to use learning logs, although teachers often prefer allowing 5 or 10 minutes at the end of a period for students to respond to process questions such as, "What did I understand about the work we did in class today? What didn't I understand? At what point in the lesson did I get confused? What did I like or dislike about class today?" The logs can be kept in a box and stored in the classroom. The teacher then reviews them during or after school to see what the students are learning and to recognize their concerns and problems. Let's take a look at how several teachers integrate logs into their instructional contexts.

Two mathematics teachers report using learning logs with much success in their classrooms. Kennedy (1985), a middle school teacher, has designed what he calls a "writing in math" program in which learning logs are a key feature. In addition to the preceding process questions, he likes to ask students about what they're wondering. What specific questions do they have about the material being studied? He also finds that logs are effective for "making notes." According to Kennedy, the distinction between *taking* and *making* notes is central to the use of learning logs: "Taking notes is copying someone else's information; *making notes* is writing interpretive comments and personal reminders such as 'Ask about this' or just 'Why?'" (p. 61).

A secondary school algebra teacher introduces learning logs to her class this way:

From time to time, I'll be asking you to write down in your logs how you went about learning a particular topic in this class. In other words, can you capture that moment when things finally made sense to you and how you felt? And can you express the frustration that might have preceded this moment? (Pradl & Mayher 1985, p. 5)

Students may at first be tentative about writing and unsure of what to say or reveal—after all, journal writing is reflective and personal. It takes a trusting atmosphere to open up to the teacher. However, to win the trust of students, teachers, such as the algebra teacher, refrain from making judgmental or evaluative comments when students admit a lack of understanding of what's happening in class. If a trusting relationship exists, students will soon recognize the value of logs, although perhaps not as enthusiastically as one secondary school student:

> This journal has got to be the best thing that's hit this chemistry class. For once the teacher has direct communication with every member of the class. No matter how shy the student is they can get their lack of understanding across to the teacher.... These journals act as a "hot line" to and from the teacher. I feel this journal has helped me and everyone that I know in class. The only thing wrong is we should have started these on the first day of school!! In every class! (Pradl & Mayher 1985, p. 6)

The algebra teacher's students probably feel the same way about their algebra class. Here are some of the things that they do in their logs. For starters, the teacher likes to introduce a new topic by asking students to jot down their predictions and expectations of what the topic may involve. She also has her students write down their understanding of any new theorem that is introduced. After students believe that they have learned a theorem well, they use their logs to imagine how they might explain the theorem to another, less well-informed person, such as a younger sister or brother.

Both Kennedy and the algebra teacher use logs to have students create word problems that are then used to challenge other members of the class. Kennedy (1985) likes to have students write different kinds of word problems in their learning logs: "Sometimes I have them supply the data (for example, 'Write a problem involving the use of percent'); other times I supply the data (for example, 'Write a problem using the numbers 200, 400, and 600')" (p. 61).

Most journal activities require thinking but do not demand a finished product. Students soon learn to write without the fear of making errors. However, there are times when students should know in advance that their journal entries will be read aloud in class. According to Levine (1985), this is when students often produce their best writing because they are composing for an audience of peers. Josh, for example, a grade 8 student, wrote about a lab experiment this way:

> Today in class we did a demo to try and find effective ways of recovering the solute from a solution.
>
> Several people came up with ideas as to how we could do this. A few people suggested filtering the solution, and others thought heating the solution so it evaporated would bring the solute back.
>
> First we tried filtering a copper sulfate solution but found that process didn't work. Evidently the crystals had dissolved to such an extent, that they were too small to be gathered by the filter paper.
>
> We then heated the solution and found we were far more successful than in our first try. Approximately thirteen minutes after we began heating the solution, a ring of copper sulfate crystals appeared in the bowl where the solution was. Eventually all the liquid evaporated leaving only the crystals. Quite obviously I learned that to recover the solute from a solution you can heat the solution. I also learned not to bother trying to filter the solution. (p. 45)

Journal writing allows students such as Josh to express what's on their minds honestly and without pretense.

ESSAY WRITING

As useful as exploratory and journal writing are, they represent informal tools to help students explore content that they will be or are reading and studying in class. Essay writing, by contrast, is more formal and finished. When students engage in essay writing, they become immersed in the content and are able to think more deeply about the subject they are exploring and clarifying. The purpose of writing essays, then, is to create a context in which students discover, analyze, and synthesize ideas through the process of writing.

Whereas exploratory and journal writing involves expressive, loosely written explorations of a subject, essays engage students in longer, more considered pieces of writing. Traditionally, essays have been the province of English teachers, whose students sometimes become more preoccupied with the form and organization of the essay—learning how to write a three-paragraph or five-paragraph paper—than with the exploration of content and the analysis and synthesis of ideas.

Essays have been shown to be effective writing-to-learn tools (1) when content exploration and synthesis, not form and organization, become the primary motives for the writing assignment; (2) when writing involves reading more than a single text source; and (3) when students engage in the writing process.

When students combine reading with writing essays, they think more deeply about the subject they are studying. Spivey (1984), for example, found that when writers read more than a single text source in order to write essays, they are immersed in organizing, selecting, and connecting content. Newell (1984) discovered that students who engage in essay-type writing acquire more content knowledge than students who take notes or answer study questions. Langer and Applebee (1987) concluded that when reading is combined with analytic writing, students are able to think more deeply about the key ideas and concepts they encounter during reading.

What the research on writing to learn demonstrates is that students who read to write engage in a range of reasoning processes. Essay writing creates occasions for students to discover, analyze, and synthesize ideas from multiple sources of information. The key to thoughtful student writing is to design good essay assignments. The teacher's primary concern should be how to make a writing prompt *explicit* without stifling interest or the spirit of inquiry. A prompt should provide more than a subject on which to write.

RAFT: Creating Writing Prompts for Essays

RAFT is an acronym that stands for *r*ole, *a*udience, *f*orm, and *t*opic. RAFT allows teachers to create writing prompts for essay writing assignments (Holston & Santa 1985). What constitutes an effective writing prompt for academic assignments? Suppose you were assigned one of the following topics to write on, based on text readings and class discussion:

Batiking

The role of the laser beam in the future

Victims of crime

No doubt, some of you would probably begin writing on one of the topics without hesitation. Perhaps you already know a great deal about the subject, have strong feelings about it, and can change the direction of the discourse without much difficulty. Others, however, may resist or even resent the activity. Your questions might echo the following concerns: "Why do I want to write about any of these topics in the first place? For whom am I writing? Will I write a paragraph? A book?" The most experienced writer must come to grips with questions such as these, and with even more complicated ones: "How will I treat my subject? What role will I take?" If anything, the questions raise to awareness the *rhetorical context*—the *writer's role*, the *audience*, the *form* of the writing, and the writer's *topic*—that most writing assignments should provide. A context for writing allows students to assess the writer's relationship to the subject of the writing (the topic) and to the reader (the audience for whom the writing is intended). Lindemann (1982) suggests a *communications triangle* to show how the context can be defined. Some of the questions raised by the relationships among writer, subject, and reader in the communications triangle are depicted in Figure 8.10.

The writer plans a response to the assignment by asking questions such as, "For whom am I writing this? What do I know about my subject? How do I feel about it? What role or perspective can I take in treating the topic?" A good writing prompt, then, *situates* students in the writing task. Instead of assigning an essay on how to batik, give students a RAFT prompt:

> To show that you understand how batiking works, imagine that you are giving a demonstration at an arts-and-crafts show. Describe the steps and procedures involved in the process of batiking to a group of onlookers, recognizing that they know little about the process but are curious enough to find out more.

This example creates a context for writing. It suggests the writer's role (the student providing a batiking demonstration), the writer's audience (observers of the demonstration), the form of the writing (a how-to demonstration), and the topic (the process of batiking).

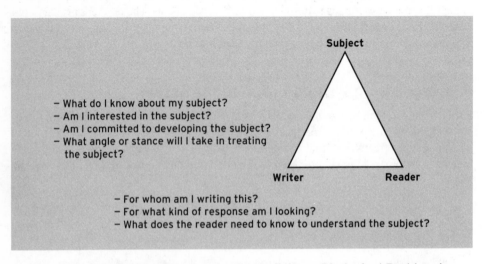

FIGURE 8.10 **A Communications Triangle: Defining a Rhetorical Problem in Writing**

RAFT writing prompts contrived situations and audiences in the context of what is being read or studied. However, they are far from trivial, nonacademic, or inconsequential. Instead, when students "become" someone else, they must look at situations in a nontraditional way. After writing, they can compare different perspectives on the same issue and examine the validity of the viewpoints that were taken.

Although some RAFT writing assignments may contrive situations and audiences, others should reflect real situations and audiences outside the classroom. For example, letters to the editor of the local newspaper and to political leaders, authors, and scientists can be an important part of classroom study. Furthermore, a variety of writing forms can be easily incorporated into RAFT writing assignments. In Table 8.1 on page 244, Tchudi and Yates (1983) provide a representative listing of some of these forms for content area writing.

Evaluating and Grading Essays

The paper load in classrooms where essay writing happens regularly is a persistent matter of concern for teachers. They often blanch at the prospect of grading 125 or more papers. A science teacher reacted to us in a workshop this way: "The quickest way to squelch my interest in writing to learn is to sock me with six sets of papers to correct at once." We couldn't agree more—weekends weren't made for drowning in a sea of ink or printout.

Yet the notion of what it means to evaluate written work must be examined. "Correcting papers" may be an inappropriate concept. It suggests that the teacher's role is primarily one of detecting errors in papers. Overemphasis on error detection often telegraphs to students that correctness rather than the discovery and communication of meaning is what writing is all about. Content area teachers who view their job as an error hunt soon become, and understandably so, reluctant to devote hours to reading and "grading" papers.

The types of errors that often take the most time to detect and correct are those that involve various elements of language such as punctuation, spelling, and grammar. These elements, sometimes referred to as the *mechanics* or *form* of writing, must take a back seat to other features of writing, mainly *content* and *organization*. It's not that linguistic elements should be ignored or left unattended. However, they must be put into perspective. As Pearce (1983) explains, "If writing is to serve as a catalyst for gaining insight into course material, then content—not form—needs to be emphasized.... If a paper has poor content, then no amount of correcting elements of form will transform it into a good piece of writing" (p. 214). Ideas, and how they are logically and coherently developed in a paper, must receive top priority when one is evaluating and grading writing in content area classrooms.

Once writing is thought of and taught as a process, teachers can begin to deal effectively with the paper load. Although the volume of papers will inevitably increase, it is likely to become more manageable. For one thing, when provisions are made for active student responses to writing, much of the feedback that a student writer needs will come while writing is still occurring. Guiding and channelling feedback as students progress with their drafts is a type of *formative* evaluation. In contrast, a *summative* evaluation takes place during the postwriting stage, usually after students have shared their finished products with one another.

Summative evaluations are often *holistic* so that a teacher can quickly and accurately judge a piece of writing based on an impression of its overall effectiveness. Thus, a holis-

TABLE 8.1	Some Discourse Forms for Content Area Writing

Journals and diaries (real or imaginary)
Biographical sketches
Anecdotes and stories:
    From experience
    As told by others
Thumbnail sketches:
    Of famous people
    Of places
    Of content ideas
    Of historical events
Guess who/what descriptions

Letters:
    Personal reactions
    Observations
    Public/informational
    Persuasive:
        To the editor
        To public officials
    To imaginary people
    From imaginary places
Requests
Case studies:
    School problems
    Local issues
    National concerns
    Historical problems
    Scientific issues
Songs and ballads
Demonstrations
Poster displays

Reviews:
    Books (including textbooks)
    Films
    Outside reading
    Television programs
    Documentaries

Historical "you are there" scenes

Science notes:
    Observations
    Science notebook
    Reading reports
    Lab reports
Written debates

Taking a stand:
    School issues
    Family problems
    Provincial or national issues
    Moral questions

Books and booklets
Informational monographs
Radio scripts
TV scenarios and scripts
Dramatic scripts
Notes for improvised drama
Cartoons and cartoon strips
Slide show scripts
Puzzles and word searches
Prophecy and predictions
Photos and captions
Collage, montage, mobile, sculpture
Applications
Memos
Résumés and summaries
Poems
Plays
Stories
Fantasy
Adventure
Science fiction
Historical stories

Dialogues and conversations
Children's books
Telegrams
Editorials
Commentaries
Responses and rebuttals
Newspaper "fillers"
Fact books or fact sheets
School newspaper stories
Stories or essays for local papers
Proposals

Mathematics:
    Story problems
    Solutions to problems
    Record books
    Notes and observations
Responses to literature
Utopian proposals
Practical proposals

Interviews:
    Actual
    Imaginary

Directions:
    How-to
    School or neighbourhood guide
    Survival manual
Dictionaries and lexicons
Technical reports
Future options, notes on:
    Careers, employment
    School and training
    Military/public service

Source: From *Teaching Writing in the Content Areas: Senior High School* by Stephen Tchudi and JoAnne Yates. Copyright © 1983, National Education Association. Reprinted with permission.

Paper topic: Expulsion of the Acadians

High-quality papers contain:

An overview of French–English relations before the expulsion in 1755, with three specific examples.

A statement defining the Canadian government's stance with regard to the presence of French Canadians in Acadia, with a cause-and-effect list of five events leading to the expulsion, including the role of Governor Charles Lawrence.

Two or more other approaches to resolving conflicts between French and English settlers in Canada, with specific examples, and a comparison of these approaches with the Acadian expulsion that illustrates differences or similarities in at least two ways.

Good organization, well-developed arguments, few mechanical errors (sentence fragments, grammatical errors, spelling errors).

Medium-quality papers contain:

An overview of French–English relations, with two specific examples.

A statement defining the Canadian government's stance with regard to the presence of French Canadians in Acadia, with a cause-and-effect list of three events leading to the expulsion, including the role of Governor Lawrence.

One other approach to resolving conflicts between French and English settlers, with specific examples, and a comparison of this approach with the Acadian expulsion that illustrates differences or similarities in at least two ways.

Good organization, moderately developed arguments, few mechanical errors.

Lower-quality papers contain:

A general statement defining the Canadian government's stance with regard to the presence of French Canadians in Acadia and at least one example.

One other approach to resolving French–English relations and how it differed from the Acadian expulsion.

Fair organization and development, some mechanical errors.

Lowest-quality papers contain:

A general statement on what the Acadian expulsion was or a general statement on French–English relations.

A list of points, poor organization, many mechanical errors.

FIGURE 8.11 A Rubric for Grading

tic evaluation permits teachers to sort, rank, and grade written pieces rather efficiently and effectively. Holistic scoring is organized around the principle that a written composition is judged on how successfully it communicates a message, rather than on the strengths and weaknesses of its individual features. The whole of a composition, if you will, is greater than the sum of its parts. In other words, teachers don't have to spend inordinate amounts of time enumerating and counting errors in a paper. Instead, the paper is judged for its total effect on a rater.

One type of holistic measure, *primary trait scoring*, is of particular value in content area writing situations. Primary trait scoring is tied directly to a specific writing assignment. Primary trait scoring helps the teacher decide how well students completed the writing task.

As a result, primary trait scoring focuses on the characteristics in a paper that are crucial to task completion. How successfully did students handle the assignment in relation to purpose, audience, subject, or role? Papers should be evaluated for these primary traits or characteristics: (1) accurate content in support of a position, (2) a logical and coherent set of ideas in support of a position, and (3) a position statement that is convincing and persuasive when aimed at an audience of fellow students.

Pearce (1983) recommends that teachers develop a *rubric* based on the primary traits exhibited in student papers. A rubric is a scoring guide. It provides a summary listing of the characteristics that distinguish high-quality from low-quality compositions.

Study the rubric in Figure 8.11 on page 245 for the following assignment: *You are a newspaper reporter who covered the Acadian expulsion. Write a time capsule document analyzing Governor Lawrence's approach to dealing with French inhabitants of Acadia in the early 1750s. Compare this approach to one taken by other Canadian leaders.* For this assignment, papers were evaluated for the following traits: (1) accurate and adequate content about French–English relations, (2) a comparison of Lawrence's approach with at least one other approach, and (3) a logical and organized presentation that provides evidence for any generalization made.

LOOKING BACK, LOOKING FORWARD

In this chapter, we focused on writing to emphasize the powerful bonds between reading and writing. Content area learning, in fact, is more within the reach of students when writing and reading are integrated throughout the curriculum. The two processes, both rooted in language, are intertwined and share common cognitive and sociocultural characteristics. The combination of reading and writing in a classroom improves achievement and instructional efficiency. When students write to learn in content area classrooms, they are involved in a process of manipulating, clarifying, discovering, and synthesizing ideas. The writing process is a powerful strategy for helping students gain insight into course objectives.

The uses of writing have been noticeably limited in content area classrooms. Writing has often been restricted to noncomposing activities such as filling in the blanks on worksheets and practice exercises, writing one-paragraph-or-less responses to study questions, or taking notes. The role of writing in content areas should be broadened because of its potentially powerful effect on thinking and learning.

Because writing promotes different types of learning, students should have many different occasions to write. Students should participate in exploratory writing activities, keeping journals, and writing essays. Exploratory writing activities, such as the unsent or sent letter/email, place students in an authentic role-playing situation in which they are asked to write letters about the material being studied. Additional activities include biopoems, dialogues, and admit and exit slips. Journals, one of the most versatile writing-to-learn strategies, entail students' responding to text as they keep an ongoing record of learning while it happens, in a notebook or loose-leaf binder. When students use response journals, double-entry journals, character journals, or learning logs, they soon learn to write without the fear of making mechanical errors. Students can also be assigned essays for exploratory-centred writing that is task-explicit. An explicit assignment helps students determine the role, the audience, the form of the writing, as well as the topic. Rubrics were recommended as a means of evaluating and grading essays.

The next chapter examines what it means to study. Studying texts requires students to engage in purposeful independent learning activities. Organizing information, summarizing chunks of information, taking notes, and conducting and reporting inquiry-centred research are examples of learner-directed strategies.

MINDS-ON

1. Each member of your group should select one of the following roles to play: (a) a language arts teacher who believes that correct mechanics are the heart of good writing, (b) a science teacher who assigns students a variety of "writing-to-learn" projects, (c) a history teacher who believes that writing is the job of the language arts department, (d) a mathematics teacher who uses mathematics journals to aid in students' comprehension, and (e) an administrator who lacks a philosophical view and is listening to form an opinion.

    Imagine that this group is eating lunch in the staff room at a middle school where you teach. The language arts teacher turns to the science teacher and says, "My students were telling me that in the writing assignment you gave, you told them not to worry about mechanics, that you were interested mainly in their content and form. I wish you wouldn't make statements like that. After all, I'm trying to teach these kids to write correctly." Continue the discussion in each of your roles.

2. What strategies do you believe would be most useful in making writing assignments meaningful for learning?

3. Your group should divide into two teams, one pro and one con. Review each of the following five statements, and discuss from your assigned view the pros and cons of each issue. After you have discussed all five statements, take an "agree" or "disagree" vote on each statement, and discuss what you really believe about the issue.

    a. We write to discover meaning (to understand) and to communicate meaning to others (to be understood).
    b. Writing is an incidental tool in learning and relatively unconnected to reading.
    c. Writing to learn is a catalyst for reading and studying course material.
    d. Students need to know the writer's role, audience, and form, and topic for a writing assignment.
    e. A word after a word after a word is power.

4. At the start of the chapter, we wrote, "When reading and writing are taught in tandem, the union influences content learning in ways not possible when students read without

writing or write without reading." Drawing on your experience and the text, discuss some specific examples that support this thesis.

HANDS-ON

1. In the centre of a blank sheet of paper, write the name of the first colour that comes to your mind. Circle that colour. Let your mind wander, and quickly write down all descriptive words or phrases that come to your mind that are related to that colour word. Connect the words logically, creating clusters. Next, see what images these relationships suggest to you. Write a piece (a poem, a story, or an essay) and/or draw a sketch based on your clusters. Exchange papers, and in pairs, comment on

    a. The best phrase/image in your partner's piece
    b. What needs explanation or clarification
    c. The central idea of the piece

    With your partner, discuss how this exercise illustrates the characteristics of writing to learn.

2. Work with a partner. Your task is to observe the other during the following activity and to record the characteristics of the other's approach to composing. For example, you might describe the writer pausing, sighing, gazing off, writing hurriedly, scratching out, and erasing. At the end of the activity, share your written description with the partner you observed to see if your observations match the writer's own perceptions.

    For this activity, write down seven pairs of rhyming words, and then recopy the pairs, alternating words (e.g., *hot, see, not, me*). Next, give your list of rhymes to your partner, and have him or her write lines of poetry, using each word on the list as the final word in a line of the poem.

    What did you learn from both observing and being observed as a writer?

3. Take part in the following activities:

    a. Brainstorm by clustering associations with the topic "writing in school."
    b. Use this cluster to write a first draft of your experiences with writing in school.
    c. Meet with a small group. Share your draft by reading it aloud to your group. Receive formative evaluation on your piece, and respond to the writing presented by others in your group. Make notes about possible changes that might be made in a second draft of your piece.
    d. Revise your draft.
    e. Describe for the entire class your experiences during this activity. Was this a helpful process? Discuss implications for your own teaching.

4. With a small group, create a rubric for primary trait scoring of the "writing in school" assignment in activity 3. Score your written piece using this rubric.

SUGGESTED READINGS

Applebee, A. N. (1981). *Writing in the secondary school: English and the content areas*. Urbana, IL: National Council of Teachers of English.

Asselin, M. (2001). Grade 6 research process instruction: An observation study. *Alberta Journal of Educational Research, 47*(2), 123–140.

Atwell, N. (1989). *Coming to know: Writing to learn in the intermediate grades.* Portsmouth, NH: Heinemann.

Azzolino, A. (1990). Writing as a tool for teaching mathematics: The silent revolution. In T. Cooney, & E. Hirsh (Eds.), *Teaching and learning mathematics in the 1990's.* Reston, VA: National Council of Teachers of Mathematics.

Begoray, D. (1996). The borrowers: Issues in using previously composed text. *English Quarterly, 28*(2&3), 60–69.

Bright, R. (1995). *Writing instruction in the intermediate grades: What is said, what is done, what is understood.* Newark, DE: International Reading Association.

Bromley, K. (1993). *Journaling: Engagements in reading, writing, and thinking.* New York: Scholastic.

Countryman, J. (1992). *Writing to learn mathematics: Strategies that work, K–12.* Portsmouth, NH: Heinemann.

Fazio, B. (1992). Students as historians—writing their school's history. *The Social Studies, 83,* 64–67.

Fulwiler, T. (1987). *Teaching with writing.* Portsmouth, NH: Boynton/Cook.

Gere, A. R. (Ed.). (1985). *Roots in the sawdust: Writing to learn across the curriculum.* Urbana, IL: National Council of Teachers of English.

Gunnery, S. (1998). *Just write! Ten practical workshops for successful student writing.* Markham, ON: Pembroke Publishers.

Irwin, J. W., & Doyle, M. A. (1992). *Reading/writing connections: Learning from research.* Newark, DE: International Reading Association.

Langer, J. A. (1986). Learning through writing: Study skills in the content areas. *Journal of Reading, 29,* 400–406.

Macrorie, K. (1980). *Searching writing.* Rochelle Park, NJ: Hayden.

Martin, N., D'Arcy, P., Newton, B., & Parker, R. (1976). *Writing and learning across the curriculum.* Montclair, NJ: Boynton/Cook.

Maxwell, R. (1996). *Writing across the curriculum in middle and high schools.* Boston: Allyn and Bacon.

Murray, D. (1982). *Learning by teaching.* Montclair, NJ: Boynton/Cook.

Myers, J. (1984). *Writing to learn across the curriculum.* Bloomington, IN: Phi Delta Kappa.

Parsons, L. (1994). Expanding response journals in all subject areas. Markham, Ontario: Pembroke Publishers.

Santa, C., Havens, L., & Harrison, S. (1996). Teaching secondary science through reading, writing, studying, and problem-solving. In D. Lapp, J. Flood, & N. Farnan (Eds.), *Content area reading and learning: Instructional practices* (2nd ed., pp. 165–180). Boston: Allyn and Bacon.

Tchudi, S., & Huerta, M. (1983). *Teaching writing in the content areas: Middle school/junior high.* Washington, DC: National Education Association.

Tchudi, S., & Tchudi, S. (1983). *Teaching writing in the content areas: Elementary school.* Washington, DC: National Education Association.

Tchudi, S., & Yates, J. (1983). *Teaching writing in the content areas: Senior high school.* Washington, DC: National Education Association.

Willinsky, J. (1990). *The new literacy: Redefining reading and writing in the schools.* New York: Routledge.

Wills, H. (1993). *Writing is learning: Strategies for math, science, social studies and language arts.* Bloomington, IN: Edinfo Press.

Wollman-Bonilla, J. (1991). *Response journals.* New York: Scholastic.

chapter nine

Study Strategies

> *The process of reading is not a half-sleep,*
> *but in the highest sense, an exercise, a*
> *gymnast's struggle; that the reader is to do*
> *something for himself, must be on the alert,*
> *must himself or herself construct*
> *[meaning]—the text furnishing the hints,*
> *the clues, the start or framework.*

—Walt Whitman

ORGANIZING PRINCIPLE

Poet Walt Whitman says in a few words what we have been illustrating throughout this book: learning with text is as demanding mentally as gymnastics are physically. Processing text is not a passive activity, a "half-sleep," but an active process, an exercise that takes place inside the head. The mental gymnastics that students engage in help them use text to construct meaning. A student who works with a text is as skillful as a gymnast who works on a balance beam or the parallel bars.

Students who study texts—whether oral, print, visual, or multimedia—are self-directed, deliberate in their plans and actions, and conscious of their goals. They have reasons for studying, whether their purposes involve acquiring, organizing, summarizing, or using information and ideas. Studying a text is hard work, just as building the body through gymnastic activity is hard work. It requires readers to be disciplined and patient. But because they are deliberate in their plans and actions and conscious of their goals, students who study texts not only know how to work hard but also know how to work smart.

To work smart, students need to develop strategies for studying. Putting study strategies to good use is directly related to students' knowledge and awareness of what it means to study. As they become more aware of studying texts, students look for *struc-*

ture—how the important information and ideas are organized in text—in everything they read. Common sense tells us that most texts should have structure, because authors have nothing to gain and much to lose by presenting ideas aimlessly. Whitman put it well: the text furnishes "the hints, the clues, the start or framework." Good students know how to study more effectively by using the hints and clues provided by authors and the framework of ideas embodied in the structure of the text. They use study strategies to raise questions and make plans for reading; to comprehend, make connections among the important ideas, and remember information; to summarize what they have read; and to take and make notes. The organizing principle suggests that one important aspect of helping students study more effectively is to show them how to use the framework of ideas in text to their advantage: **looking for and using text structure helps students "do something" with texts in order to process and think more deeply about ideas encountered during reading.**

CHAPTER OVERVIEW

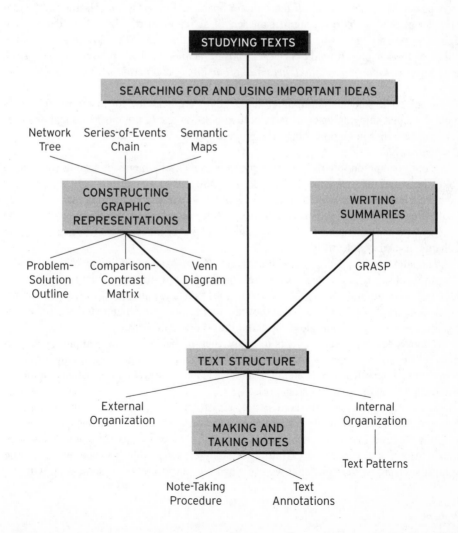

FRAME OF MIND

1. What does it mean to study?

2. How are *textually* important ideas different from *contextually* important ideas?

3. How is internal text structure different from external text structure and story structure?

4. What are text patterns?

5. How do graphic representations (a mix of visual and print texts) help students make connections among important ideas?

6. How can you show students how to summarize information?

7. How can you show students how to take and make notes?

A poster had just gone up on the bulletin board in Julie Meyer's classroom. "School Daze: From A to Z" defined significant school activities in the lives of students, each beginning with a letter of the alphabet. The entry for the letter *S* just happened to be the subject of this chapter. It read, "STUDY: *Those precious moments between soap operas, movies, sports, video games, food, personal grooming, and general lollygagging when one opens one's school books—and falls asleep.*"

Though some students might agree that study is a quick cure for insomnia, few of us would deny that studying texts, especially textbooks, is one of the most frequent and predominant activities in schools today. The older students become, the more they are expected to learn with texts.

It's not uncommon to find a teacher prefacing text assignments by urging students to "study the material." And some students do. They are able to study effectively because they know what it means to *approach* a text assignment: to *analyze* the reading task at hand, to *make plans* for reading, and then to *use strategies* to suit their purposes for studying. Students who approach texts in this way achieve a level of independence because they are in charge of their own learning.

Other students, less skilled in reading and studying, wage a continual battle with texts. Some probably wonder why teachers make a big deal out of studying in the first place. For them, the exhortation to "study the material" goes in one ear and out the other. Others try to cope with the demands of study. Yet they are apt to equate studying texts with rote memorization, cramming "meaningless" material into short-term memory.

Whenever teachers urge students to study, they probably have something definite in mind. Whatever that something is, it shouldn't remain an ambiguous or unattainable classroom goal. All too often, the problem for students is that they aren't aware of what it means to study, let alone to use study strategies.

What better context than the content area classroom to teach learners what it means to be a student? The term *student*, derived from Latin, means "one who pursues knowledge."

Studying is an intentional act. Students need to establish goals for studying. Nila B. Smith's (1959) straightforward definition of study captures what it means to study. She explains *studying* as strategies that we use when our purpose is to do something with the content we have read. "Doing something" means putting strategies to good use by applying them toward purposeful ends.

Students will tell you that they study to pass tests. Fair enough. They are quick to associate studying with memorizing information. A concept of study that includes retention has merit. But too many students spend too much time using up too much energy on what often becomes their only strategy: rote memorization. Rote memorizing leads to short-lived recall of unrelated bits and pieces of information. Alternatives to rote memorization should be taught and reinforced when and where they count the most: in a content area classroom.

Studying is an unhurried and reflective process. A lack of discipline and patience with print is probably one reason why so few adolescents and young adults study effectively on their own in middle and secondary schools or in college. A sociology instructor once met with students who were doing poorly in his class during their first semester in college. The purpose of the meeting was to discuss ways to study sociology. The students, however, soon turned the meeting into a battleground, venting their own frustrations with the course. The sociologist finally reached his own boiling point: "Listen, the bottom line is this: studying is hard work. You can't read sociological material once and expect to 'get it.' You should 'work' the material. Read it. And reread it. First, get the important ideas straight in your head. Make connections. And eventually you will make them a part of you."

We find ourselves agreeing with the college instructor's analysis. Studying text *is* hard work. Cultivating a repertoire of study strategies to "get the important ideas straight in your head" is essential. Showing students how to distinguish important from less important ideas is one of the key aspects of studying texts effectively.

TEXTUALLY AND CONTEXTUALLY IMPORTANT IDEAS

To make information accessible, authors organize ideas in text. Some ideas, of course, are more important than others. Suppose you were reading a magazine article and came across the passage in Box 9.1 on page 254. Read the passage; then, in the space provided, write what you think is the most important idea and why.

If you were to compare your response with others' responses, what each of you wrote as the most important idea would vary. You may have written something to the effect that "standards guide the decisions we make," whereas someone else may have responded, "One should try not to lose one's head in an emergency." Why is there a difference? Why not a single main idea?

In their research, Moore and Cunningham (1986) classify the main ideas produced by readers according to the similarity in their responses. As a result, the researchers were able to identify nine types of main-idea responses. They concluded that the term *main idea* serves as an umbrella for a *wide range of tasks* that readers engage in when they search for main ideas in a text. No wonder Pearson (1981) characterizes the concept "main idea" as an abstraction, "a polyglot of tasks and relations among ideas" (p. 124).

What a reader identifies as the main idea may *not* be what the author intended as the main idea. The reader's purpose and the perspective that he or she brings to the text often determines the relative importance attached to what the author is saying. In this respect, the important ideas in text may vary from reader to reader and text situation to text situation (Winograd & Bridge 1986).

BOX 9.1	**What's the Most Important Idea in This Passage?**

Standards are essential as reference points. Wise living depends upon finding a standard against which values may be measured. Consider, for example, the story about a fellow who was riding his motorcycle on a cold day. The zipper on his jacket was broken, so the rider stopped and put the jacket on backwards to shield him from the wind. A bit later, the rider had an accident and was knocked unconscious. He stayed in the hospital for weeks. The doctors said the boy wasn't hurt much in the wreck, but he was severely injured when the policeman tried to turn his head around to match his jacket. You see, a coat is supposed to zip up the front and the policeman made his judgment against that standard, which just goes to show you: if the standard is wrong, then the resulting decision will be wrong.

What is the most important idea in the passage?

_____

_____

_____

Why do you think so?

_____

_____

_____

Source: Passage from "Things Worth Keeping," by Bishop Ernest A. Fitzgerald, *Pace Magazine,* December 1987. Reprinted by permission of Ernest A. Fitzgerald.

The distinction between *contextually* important information and *textually* important information helps the teacher understand where students are coming from when they respond to main-idea questions during discussion or writing activity. Van Dijk (1979) explains that textually important information is considered central to the text by the author. As a result, authors often showcase textually important ideas in the text organization they use.

Contextually important information, by contrast, is information that the reader considers important. In earlier chapters, we explored strategies that encourage students to use what they know to respond to text—in effect, to construct meaning that is personally or contextually important. But throughout this book, we also underscore the importance of grasping an author's intended meaning. On the road to reading maturity, students must develop flexibility in distinguishing what is textually important from what is contextually important in the texts that they read.

Authors impose structure—an organization among ideas—on their writing. Perceiving structure in text material improves learning and retention. When students are shown how to see relationships among concepts and bits of essential information, they are in a better position to respond to meaning and to distinguish important from less important ideas.

SEARCHING FOR AND USING TEXT STRUCTURE

Educational psychologists from Thorndike (1917) to Kintsch (1977) and Meyer and Rice (1984) have shown that text structure is a crucial variable in learning and memory. Likewise, for more than 50 years, reading educators have underscored the recognition and use of organization as essential processes underlying comprehension and retention (Salisbury 1934; Smith 1964; Niles 1965; Herber 1978).

The primary purpose of many content area texts is to provide users with information. To make information readily accessible, authors use external and internal structural features. *External text structure* is characterized by a text's overall instructional design—its format features. Its *internal text structure* is reflected by the interrelationships among ideas in the text as well as by the subordination of some ideas to others.

External Text Structure

Printed and electronic texts contain certain format features—organizational aids—that are built into the text to facilitate reading. This book, for example, contains a *table of contents*, a *preface*, *appendixes*, a *bibliography*, and *indexes*. These aids, along with the *title page* and *dedication*, are called the *front matter* and *end matter* of a book. Of course, textbooks vary in the amount of front and end matter they contain. These aids can be valuable tools for prospective users of a textbook. Yet the novice reader hardly acknowledges their presence in texts, let alone uses them to advantage.

In addition, each chapter of a textbook usually has *introductory or summary statements*, *headings*, *graphs*, *charts*, *illustrations*, and *guide questions*.

Organizational aids, whether in electronic or printed texts, are potentially valuable—if they are not skipped or glossed over by readers. Headings, for example, are inserted in the text to divide it into logical units. Headings strategically placed in a text should guide the reader by highlighting major ideas.

Within a text, authors use an internal structure to connect ideas logically in a coherent whole. Internal text structure might vary from passage to passage, depending on the author's purpose. These structures, or patterns of organization, within a text are closely associated with informational writing.

Internal Text Structure

Content area texts are written to inform. This is why exposition is the primary mode of discourse found in informational texts. This is not to say that some authors don't, at times, attempt to persuade or entertain their readers. They may. However, their primary business is to *tell*, *show*, *describe*, or *explain*. It stands to reason that the more logically connected one idea is to another, depending on the author's informative purpose, the more coherent the description or explanation is.

Skilled readers search for structure in a text and can readily differentiate the important ideas from less important ideas in the material. Research has shown that good readers know how to look for major thought relationships (Meyer, Brandt, & Bluth 1980; Taylor 1980). They approach a reading assignment looking for a predominant *text pattern* or organization that will tie together the ideas contained throughout the text passage.

Text patterns represent the different types of logical connections among the important and less important ideas in informational material. A case can be made for five text patterns that seem to predominate in informational writing: *description, sequence, comparison and contrast, cause and effect,* and *problem and solution.*

Here are descriptions and examples of these text structures.

1. *Description.* Providing information about a topic, concept, event, object, person, idea, and so on (facts, characteristics, traits, features), usually qualifying the listing by criteria such as size or importance. This pattern connects ideas through description by listing the important characteristics or attributes of the topic under consideration. Niles (1965) and Bartlett (1978) found the description pattern to be the most common way of organizing texts. Here is an example:

> Nineteenth-century Ottawa was a very unhealthy place to live. One problem was disease carried by flies, rats, and mosquitoes. Another was the extremes of temperature. A third problem was the lack of proper sewers.

2. *Sequence.* Putting facts, events, or concepts into a sequence. The author traces the development of the topic or gives the steps in the process. Time reference may be explicit or implicit, but a sequence is evident in the pattern. The following paragraph illustrates the pattern:

> Wilfrid Laurier was a promising young lawyer who lacked ambition and drive. Then he met Emilie Lavergne, the wife of his partner. They developed an intellectual relationship, and some scholars attribute Laurier's growing determination and sense of purpose during his parliamentary years to their friendship.

3. *Comparison and contrast.* Pointing out likenesses (comparison) and/or differences (contrast) among facts, people, events, concepts, and so on. Study this example:

> Castles were built for defence, not comfort. In spite of some books and movies that have made them attractive, castles were cold, dark, gloomy places to live. Rooms were small and not the least bit charming. Except for the great central hall or the kitchen, there were no fires to keep the rooms heated. Not only was there a lack of furniture, but what there was was uncomfortable.

4. *Cause and effect.* Showing how facts, events, or concepts (effects) happen or come into being because of other facts, events, or concepts (causes). Examine this paragraph for causes and effects:

> The fire was started by sparks from a campfire left by a careless camper. Thousands of acres of important watershed burned before the fire was brought under control. As a result of the fire, trees and the grasslands on the slopes of the valley were gone. Smoking black stumps were all that remained of tall pine trees.

5. *Problem and solution.* Showing the development of a problem and one or more solutions to the problem. Consider the following example:

The skyrocketing price of oil in the 1970s created a serious problem. The oil companies responded to the high cost of purchasing oil by searching for new oil supplies. This resulted in new deposits being found in some Third World nations, such as Nigeria. Oil companies also began drilling for oil on the ocean floor, and scientists discovered ways to extract oil from a rock known as *oil shale*.

Authors often showcase text patterns by giving readers clues or signals to help them figure out the structure being used. Readers usually become aware of the pattern if they are looking for the signals. A signal may be a word or a phrase that helps the reader follow the writer's thoughts. Linguists call these words *connectives*, or *ties*, because they connect one idea to another (Halliday & Hasan 1976).

Figure 9.1 shows connectives that authors use to call attention to the organizational patterns just defined.

Awareness of the pattern of *long stretches* of text is especially helpful in planning reading assignments. In selecting from a passage of several paragraphs or several pages, teachers first need to determine whether a predominant text pattern is contained in the material. This is no easy task.

Informational writing is complex. Authors do not write in neat, perfectly identifiable patterns. Within the individual paragraphs of a text assignment, several kinds of thought relationships often exist. Suppose an author begins a passage by stating a problem. In telling about the development of the problem, the author *describes* a set of events that contributed to the problem. Or perhaps the author *compares* or *contrasts* the problem under consideration with another problem. In subsequent paragraphs, the *solutions* or attempts at solutions to the problem are stated. In presenting the solutions, the author uses heavy

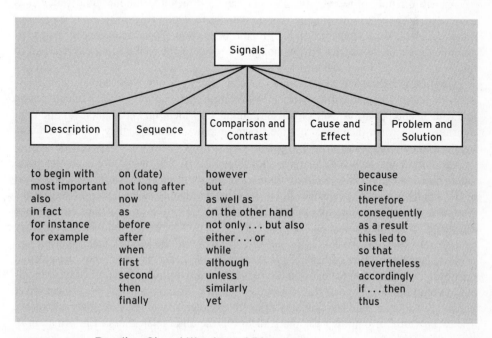

FIGURE 9.1   **Reading Signal Words and Phrases**

description and explanation. These descriptions and explanations are logically organized in a *sequence*.

The difficulty that teachers face is analyzing the overall text pattern, even though several types of thought relationships are probably embedded in the material. Analyzing a text for a predominant pattern depends in part on how clearly an author represents the relationships in the text.

Several guidelines follow for analyzing text patterns. First, survey the text for the most important idea in the selection. Are there any explicit signal words that indicate a pattern that will tie together the ideas throughout the passage? Second, study the content of the text for additional important ideas. Are these ideas logically connected to the most important idea? Is a pattern evident? Third, outline or diagram the relationships among the superordinate and subordinate ideas in the selection. Use the diagram to specify the major relationships contained in the text structure and to sort out the important from the less important ideas.

Students must learn how to recognize and use the explicit and implicit relations in the text patterns that an author uses to structure content. When readers perceive and interact with text organization, they are in a better position to comprehend and retain information.

GRAPHIC REPRESENTATIONS

Graphic or visual representations help learners comprehend and retain *textually important information*. When students learn how to use and construct graphic representations, they are in control of a study strategy that allows them to identify what parts of a text are important, how the ideas and concepts encountered in the text are related, and where they can find specific information to support more important ideas.

An entire family of teacher-directed and learner-directed techniques and strategies is associated with the use of graphic representations to depict relationships in text: word maps, semantic maps, semantic webs, graphic organizers, flowcharts, concept matrices, and tree diagrams, to name a few. Although it is easy to get confused by the plethora of labels, a rose by any other name is still a rose.

What these techniques and strategies have in common is that they help students interact with and outline textually important information. For example, when students read a text with an appropriate graphic organizer in mind, they focus on important ideas and relationships. And when they construct their own graphic organizers, they become actively involved in outlining those ideas and relationships.

Outlining helps students clarify relationships. Developing an outline is analogous to fitting together the pieces in a puzzle. Think of a puzzle piece as a separate idea and a text as the whole. A completed puzzle shows the separate identity of each idea as well as the part each idea plays in the total picture (Hansell 1978). Outlining strategies can be used effectively to facilitate a careful analysis and synthesis of the relationships in a text. They can form the basis for critical discussion and evaluation of the author's main points.

Problems arise when students are restricted by the means by which they must depict relationships spatially on paper or on a screen. The word *outlining* for most of us immediately conjures up an image of the "correct" or "classic" format that we have all learned at one time or another but have probably failed to use regularly in real-life study situations. The classic form of outlining has the student represent the relatedness of information in linear form:

I. Main Idea
    A. Idea supporting I
        1. Detail supporting A
        2. Detail supporting A
           a. Detail supporting 2
           b. Detail supporting 2

    B. Idea supporting I
        1. Detail supporting B
        2. Detail supporting B

II. Main Idea

This conventional format represents a hierarchical ordering of ideas at different levels of subordination. Roman numerals signal the major or superordinate concepts in a text section; capital letters, the supporting or coordinate concepts; Arabic numbers, the supporting or subordinate details; and lowercase letters, the subsubordinate details.

Some readers have trouble using a restricted form of outlining. Initially, at least, they need a more visual display than the one offered by the conventional format. And this is where graphic representations can play a critical role in the development of independent learners.

To show students how to use and construct graphic representations, begin by assessing how students usually outline text material. Do they have a sense of subordination among ideas? Do they have strategies for connecting major and minor concepts? Do they use alternatives to the conventional format? Make them aware of the rationale for organizing information through outlining. The jigsaw puzzle analogy—fitting pieces of information together into a coherent whole—works well for this purpose. Assessment and building awareness set the stage for illustrating, modelling, and applying the strategies.

To introduce students to various kinds of graphic representations that may be applicable to texts in your content area, Jones, Pierce, and Hunter (1988–1989) suggest some of the following steps:

1. *Present an example of a graphic representation that corresponds to the type of outline you plan to teach.* For example, suppose that a text students will read is organized around a cause and effect text pattern. First, preview the text with the students. Help them discover features of the text that may signal the pattern. Make students aware that the title, subheads, and signal words provide them with clues to the structure of the text. Then ask questions that are pertinent to the pattern—for example, "What happens in this reading? What causes it to happen? What are the important factors that cause these effects?"

2. *Demonstrate how to construct a graphic outline.* Suppose that mathematics students have completed reading about the differences between isosceles triangles and isosceles trapezoids. Show them how to construct a *Venn diagram* to map how they are alike and different. Next, refer to the comparison and contrast questions you raised in the preview. Walk students through the procedures that lead to the development of the Venn diagram: First, on an overhead transparency, present an example of a partially completed Venn graphic. Second, have students review the text and offer suggestions to help complete the graphic. Figure 9.2 shows a class-constructed rendering of the Venn diagram. Third, develop procedural knowledge by discussing when to use the Venn graphic and why.

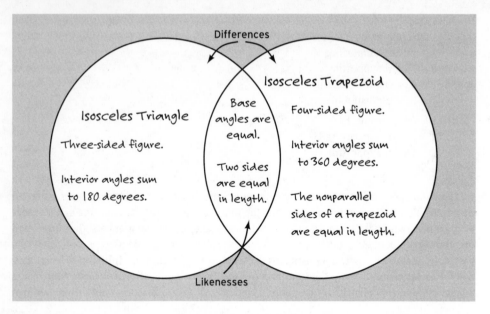

FIGURE 9.2   Venn Diagram for Isosceles Triangle and Isosceles Trapezoid

3. *Coach students in the use of the graphic outline and give them opportunities to prac-tise.* If other texts represent a particular text pattern that you have already demonstrated with the class, encourage students individually or in teams to construct their own graphic outlines and to use their constructions as the basis for class discussion.

Semantic (Cognitive) Mapping

A popular graphic representation, often called a *semantic map* or a *cognitive map*, helps students identify important ideas and shows how these ideas fit together. Teachers avoid the problem of teaching a restricted, conventional outline format. Instead, the students are responsible for creating a logical arrangement among keywords or phrases that connect main ideas to subordinate information. When maps are used, instruction should proceed from teacher-guided modelling and illustration to student-generated productions.

A semantic map has three basic components:

1. *Core question or concept.* The question or concept (stated as a keyword or phrase) that establishes the main focus of the map. All the ideas generated for the map by the stu-dents are related in some way to the core question or concept.

2. *Strands.* The subordinate ideas generated by the students that help clarify the question or explain the concept.

3. *Supports.* The details, inferences, and generalizations that are related to each strand. These supports clarify the strands and distinguish one strand from another.

Students use the semantic map as an organization tool that visually illustrates the cat-egories and relationships associated with the core question or concept under study. To model and illustrate the use of a semantic map, a middle school social studies teacher walked students through the process. The class began a unit on Nova Scotia's non-aboriginal early settlements. As part of the prereading discussion, four questions were raised for the class to ponder: What do you think were the three most important non-aboriginal early settlements in Nova Scotia? What do you think these settlements had in common? How were they different? In what ways might the location of a settlement be important to the survival of the settlers? Predictions were made and discussed and led naturally to the text assignment.

The teacher assigned the material, directing the students to read with the purpose of confirming or modifying their predictions about the early settlements.

After reading, the students formed small groups. Each group listed everything its members could remember about the settlements on index cards, with one piece of information per card.

In the centre of the chalkboard, the teacher wrote "The First Non-Aboriginal Nova Scotia Settlements" and circled the phrase. She then asked students to provide the main strands that helped answer the question, "What were Nova Scotia's most important non-aboriginal early settlements?" The students responded by contrasting their predictions to the explanations in the text assignment. The teacher began to build the semantic map on the board by explaining how strands help students answer the questions and understand the main concept.

Next, she asked the students to work in their groups to sort the cards that had been compiled according to each of the settlements depicted on the semantic map. Through discussion, questioning, and think-aloud probes, the class completed the semantic map depicted in Figure 9.3.

Some teachers prefer to distinguish strands from supports through the use of lines. Notice that in Figure 9.3, a double line connects the strands to the core concept. Supports are linked to each web strand by single lines. With younger students, some teachers also recommend using different-coloured chalk to distinguish one strand from another.

With appropriate modelling, explanation, and experience, students soon understand the why, what, and how of semantic maps and can begin to develop maps by themselves. We suggest that the teacher begin by providing the core question or concept. Students can then compare and contrast their individual productions in a follow-up discussion. Of course, text assignments should also be given in which students identify the core concept on their own and then generate the structures that support and explain it.

Using Graphic Representations to Reflect Text Patterns

Students can be shown how to construct maps and other types of graphic representations to reflect the text patterns authors use to organize ideas. According to Jones et al. (1988–1989), "A fundamental rule in constructing graphic representations is that the structure of the graphic should reflect the structure of the text it represents" (p. 21). For example, the semantic map of the first Nova Scotia settlements reflects a predominantly descriptive text pattern, but in describing the settlement of each city, the text lends itself to comparison and contrast. The teacher invites students to reorganize the heavily descriptive text into a comparison and contrast pattern through the use of the class-constructed semantic map. To make explicit connections that tie together how the settlements were alike and dif-

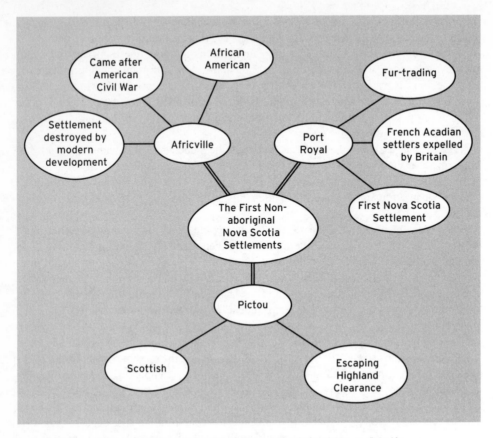

FIGURE 9.3   Semantic Map: The First Non-aboriginal Nova Scotia
Settlements

ferent, she asks guiding questions, such as, "What did Africville and Pictou have in common?" or "How were Port Royal and Pictou different?"

Jones and her colleagues recommend a variety of possible graphic representations that
reflect different text patterns. These "generic" outlines are illustrated in Appendix B. What
follows are classroom examples of how some of these outlines might be developed in content area classrooms.

Comparison and Contrast Matrix In addition to the Venn diagram and semantic map
graphic displays, a teacher can show students how a comparison and contrast pattern
serves to organize ideas in a text through the use of a matrix outline. A comparison and
contrast matrix shows similarities and differences between two or more things (people,
places, events, concepts, processes, etc.). Readers compare and contrast the target concepts
listed across the top of the matrix according to attributes, properties, or characteristics listed along the left side. Study the two examples of a comparison and contrast matrix in
Figure 9.4 on pages 264 and 265. Secondary school students used the biology example to
outline the likenesses and differences of fungi and algae. Precalculus students used the
matrix outline to compare and contrast conic sections (parabola, ellipse, and hyperbola).

Problem and Solution Outline This graphic representation depicts a problem, attempted solutions, the results or outcomes associated with the attempted solutions, and the end result. It works equally well with narrative or informational texts to display the central problem in a story or the problem and solution text pattern. Noden and Vacca (1994) show how a world history teacher used the problem and solution outline in conjunction with a text assignment related to Wat Tyler's Rebellion, which took place in England in 1381. Wat Tyler's Rebellion was one of the first popular English movements for freedom and equality. The teacher introduced the outline in Figure 9.5 on page 266 as a tool for organizing the information in the text relevant to the problem. Students first worked in pairs to complete the outline and then shared their work with the whole class. The completed outline in Figure 9.5 illustrates the thinking of two "study buddies."

Network Tree The network tree is based on the same principle as the graphic organizers introduced in Chapter 9 and used in the chapter overviews in this book. That is to say, it represents the network of relationships that exists between superordinate concepts and subordinate concepts. It can be used to show causal information or to describe a central idea in relation to its attributes and examples. Notice how mathematics students explored relationships in the quadratic formula by using the network tree illustrated in Figure 9.6 on page 267.

Series-of-Events Chain The series-of-events chain may be used with narrative material to show the chain of events that lead to the resolution of conflict in a story. It may also be used with informational text to reflect the sequence pattern in a text. It may include any sequence of events, including the steps in a linear procedure, the chain of events (effects) caused by some event, or the stages of something. Science and historical texts are often organized in a sequence pattern and lend themselves well to this type of graphic display. A science class, for example, might be asked to map the sequence of steps in the scientific method by using a series-of-events chain. After reading about the scientific method, students might make an outline similar to the one in Figure 9.7 on page 267.

In an English class integrated with a science class, students read an excerpt from *The Origin* by Irving Stone. Stone writes about the life of Charles Darwin. The teacher assigned an excerpt to be read in class and then divided the students into learning circles (four-member teams) to work through the sequence of events that led Darwin to write his last book. The series-of-events chain in Figure 9.8 on page 268 illustrates the work of one of the learning circles.

Appendix B illustrates additional types of graphic representations that may be adapted to different content areas. Closely associated with the use of graphic representations is an instructional scaffold that involves questioning.

Using Questions with Graphic Representations

Graphic representations are closely associated with key questions that parallel the text patterns used by authors (Armbruster & Anderson 1985). Skilled readers are aware of these key questions, and they study texts with the expectation that the authors have organized the content within the text patterns that are associated with a content area.

Along with the graphic representations, introduce students to the key questions associated with each of the major text patterns. Beuhl (1991), for example, lists the types of

	Fungi	Algae
Body structure		
Food source		
Method of reproduction		
Living environment		

(a)

FIGURE 9.4 Comparison and Contrast Matrices for Biology (a) and Precalculus (b)

	Parabola	Ellipse	Hyperbola
Sketch two examples			
Equation in standard form			
Special characteristics			
Foci (focal points)			
Line(s) of symmetry			

(b)

Problem

Who has the problem?

Peasants of England

What was the problem?

Unfair taxes and harsh labour laws

Why was it a problem?

Peasants were treated as serfs and were the lowest class of people in England.

Solutions

Attempted Solutions	Outcomes
1. Riots	1. Property destroyed People killed
2. Protest march on London to force a meeting with king	2. King's advisers desert him; king agrees to protesters' demands
3. Tyler refuses to give in —makes more demands	3. Tyler killed by mayor of London

End Result

King broke his promises

Peasants' demands forgotten, but the rebellion inspired other popular movements for freedom and equality

FIGURE 9.5   Problem and Solution Outline for Wat Tyler's Rebellion

Source: From Harry Noden and Richard Vacca, *Whole Language in Middle and Secondary Classrooms.* Copyright © 1994 by Allyn & Bacon. Reprinted by permission.

questions associated with the problem and solution, cause and effect, and comparison and contrast patterns.

PROBLEM AND SOLUTION

1. What is the problem?
2. Who has the problem?
3. What is causing the problem?
4. What are the effects of the problem?
5. Who is trying to solve the problem?
6. What solutions are attempted?

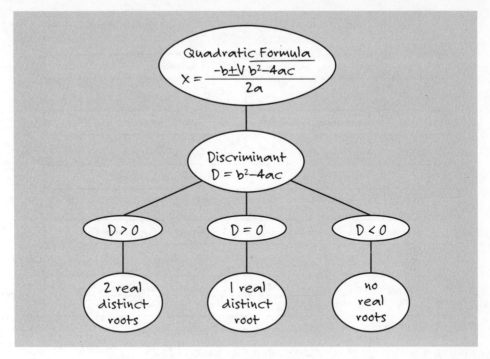

FIGURE 9.6   **Network Tree for the Quadratic Formula**

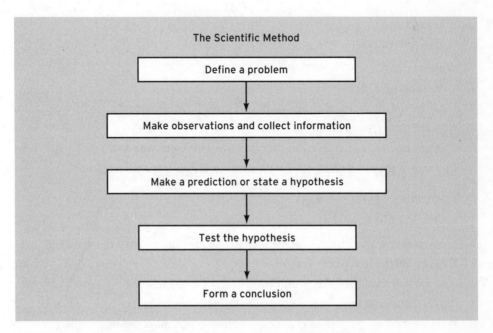

FIGURE 9.7   **Series-of-Events Chain for the Scientific Method**

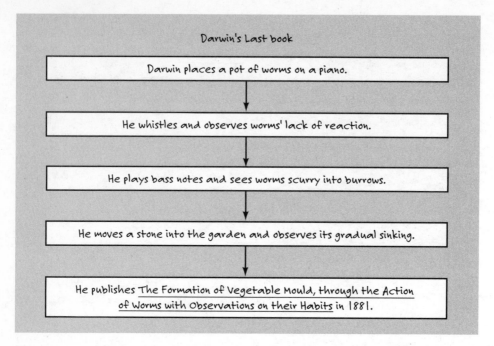

FIGURE 9.8   **Series-of-Events Chain for an Excerpt from *The Origin***

7. What are the results of these solutions?
8. Is the problem solved? Do any new problems develop because of the solutions?

CAUSE AND EFFECT

1. What happens?
2. What causes it to happen?
3. What are the important elements or factors that cause this effect?
4. How are these factors or elements interrelated?
5. Will this result always happen from these causes? Why or why not?
6. How would the result change if the elements or factors were different?

COMPARISON AND CONTRAST

1. What items are being compared and contrasted?
2. What categories of attributes can be used to compare and contrast the items?
3. How are the items alike or similar?
4. How are the items not alike or different?
5. What are the most important qualities or attributes that make the items similar?
6. What are the most important qualities or attributes that make the items different?

7. In terms of the qualities that are most important, are the items more alike or more different?

Additional questions are provided in Appendix B. There are many benefits to learning how to use and construct graphic representations, not the least of which is that they make it easier for students to find and reorganize important ideas and information in the text.

In addition to using graphic outlines, teachers can scaffold students' writing of summaries to distinguish important ideas from less important ideas. Let's explore how summaries support students' interactions with text.

WRITING SUMMARIES

Summarizing involves reducing a text to its main points. To become adept at summary writing, students must be able to discern and analyze text structure. If they are insensitive to the organization of ideas and events in expository or narrative writing, students will find it difficult to distinguish important from less important information. Good summarizers, therefore, guard against including information that is not important in the text passage being condensed. Immature text learners, by contrast, tend to *retell* rather than condense information, often including in their summaries interesting but inessential tidbits from the passage. Good summarizers write in their own words but are careful to maintain the author's point of view and to stick closely to the sequence of ideas or events as presented in the reading selection. When important ideas are not explicitly stated in the material, good summary writers create their own topic sentences to reflect textually implicit main ideas.

Kintsch and van Dijk (1978) were among the first to formulate a set of basic rules for summarization based on analyses of how people summarize effectively. Others have modified and adapted these rules, but generally, students should follow these procedures:

1. *Include no unnecessary detail.* In preparing a summary, students must learn to delete trivial and repetitious information from a text passage.

2. *Collapse lists.* When a text passage includes examples, details, actions, or traits, students must learn how to condense these into broader categories of information. With frequent exposure to instructional activities, such as graphic organizers, vocabulary categorization exercises, and outlining strategies, students soon become aware that similar items of information can be encompassed by more inclusive concepts. They must learn to summarize information by collapsing a list of details and thinking of a keyword or phrase that names its concept. Study the examples that Hare and Borchardt (1984) give: "If you saw a list like eyes, ears, neck, arms, and legs, you could say 'body parts.' Or, if you saw a list like ice skating, skiing, or sledding, you could say 'winter sports'" (p. 66).

3. *Use topic sentences.* Expository text sometimes contains explicit topic sentences that preview a paragraph. However, if a paragraph doesn't have a topic sentence, students must learn to create their own for a summary. This is probably the most difficult demand placed on maturing learners.

4. *Integrate information.* Summarizers must learn how to use keywords, phrases, and explicit and invented topic sentences to compose a summary. The first three rules help

students do the basic work of summarizing. In other words, the rules *prepare* students for writing the summary. Yet when they actually put ideas into words, they must integrate the information into a coherent piece of writing.

5. *Polish the summary.* Because writing often follows a composing process, students must learn to revise a *draft* of a summary into a more organized, natural-sounding piece of writing. While rethinking a summary, students will get a firmer grasp on the main points of the material and will state them clearly.

Using GRASP to Write a Summary

Teachers can show students how to summarize information through the guided reading procedure (GRP) as explained in Chapter 7. After students have read a text passage, they turn the books face down and try to remember everything that was important in the passage. What they recall is recorded by the teacher on the board. Seize this opportune moment to show students how to delete trivial and repetitious information from the list of ideas on the board. As part of the procedure, the students are given a chance to return to the passage, review it, and make sure that the list contains all of the information germane to the text.

When this step is completed, the teacher then guides the students to organize the information using a graphic outline format. Here is where students can be shown how to collapse individual pieces of information from a list into conceptual categories. These categories can be the bases for identifying or creating topic sentences. The students can then integrate the main points into a summary.

Hayes (1989) shows how to adapt the GRP to summarizing information. As part of his instructional framework, he modelled the development and writing of an effective summary by guiding students through a procedure he labelled GRASP (guided reading and summarizing procedure). After following the initial steps of the GRP, Hayes illustrates, in Figure 9.9, the information that his students remembered based on their first recollections after reading an article on the Rosetta Stone and their additions and corrections after rereading.

The students then organized the information into the following categories: importance of the Rosetta Stone, its discovery, its description, its decipherment, and the result of having made the discovery. These categories, along with the subordinate information associated with each, became the basis for writing the summary. Hayes walked the students through the summary-writing process as a whole class. First, he asked students to contribute sentences to the summary based on the outline of information that was organized on the board. Then he invited their suggestions for revising the summary into a coherent message. Figure 9.10 on page 272 displays the completed summary, as revised by the class.

Polishing a Summary

As you can see from the revised summary in Figure 9.10, a good summary often reflects a process of writing *and* rewriting. Teaching students how to write a polished summary is often a neglected aspect of instruction. When students reduce large segments of text, the condensation is often stilted. It sounds unnatural. We are convinced that students will learn

Students' First Recollections	Additions and Corrections
Found by an officer in Napoleon's (army)	Engineering corps
1799	Taken to British Museum, where it is today
Key to language of Egypt	Ancient
Forgotten language of Egypt	Champollion published a pamphlet
Found in mud near Rosetta	The pamphlet, a tool scholars use to translate ancient Egyptian literature
Black basalt	Ancient language of Egypt had been a riddle for hundreds of years
3' 9" tall	The stone half buried in mud
Inscriptions in hieroglyphics	Demotic, the popular Egyptian language at the time
	Written with Greek letters
Jean Champollion deciphered the inscription	Champollion knew Coptic
Compared Greek (words) with Egyptian words in same position	Proper names
Coptic was the Egyptian language	Coptic was last stage of Egyptian language
Decree to commemorate (birth) of an Egyptian king	Crowning
2' 4½" wide	Carved by Egyptian priests
He knew Greek	Ptolemy V Epiphanes 203-181 B.C.

FIGURE 9.9 **Details Remembered from an Article on the Rosetta Stone**

and understand the main points better and retain them longer when they attempt to create a more natural-sounding summary that communicates the selection's main ideas to an audience—for example, the teacher or other students. Rewriting in a classroom is often preceded by *response* to a draft by peers and teacher. We dealt in much more detail with responding and revising in Chapter 8. Here, however, let us suggest the following:

The Rosetta Stone provided the key for reading the ancient ~~language of Egypt. The~~

~~ancient~~ Egyptian language , which had been a riddle for hundreds of years. An officer in

Napoleon's engineering corps found was found in 1799 the Rosetta Stone ~~half buried in the~~

~~mud~~ the Egyptian city of near Rosetta by . The black basalt stone bore inscriptions in ancient Egyptian

hieroglyphics, in Demotic, and in Greek. The inscriptions were deciphered by Jean

Champollion, who with knowledge of Greek and Coptic (the last stage of the Egyptian

language) compared ~~Greek~~ words in the Greek text with ~~Egyptian~~ words in the Egyptian texts . The inscription ~~were~~ had been carved

by Egyptian priests to commemorate the crowning of Egyptian king Ptolemy Epiphanes,

203–181 B.C. In 1822 Champollion described the decipherment in a pamphlet which

has since been used as a tool for translating ancient Egyptian literature. The Rosetta

Stone is preserved ~~kept~~ in the British Museum.

FIGURE 9.10 The Completed Rosetta Stone Summary, as Revised

■ Compare a well-developed summary that the teacher has written with the summaries written by the students. Contrasting the teacher's version with the student productions leads to valuable process discussions on such subjects as the use of introductory and concluding statements; the value of connectives, such as *and* and *because*, to show how ideas can be linked; and the need to paraphrase—that is, to put ideas into one's own words to convey the author's main points.

■ Present the class with three summaries: One is good in that it contains all the main points and flows smoothly. The second is OK; it contains most of the main points but is somewhat stilted in its writing. The third is poor in content and form. Let the class rate and discuss the three summaries.

■ Team students in pairs or triads, and let them read their summaries to one another. Student response groups are one of the most effective means of obtaining feedback on writing in progress.

■ In lieu of response groups, ask the whole class to respond. With prior permission from several students, discuss their summaries. What are the merits of each one, and how could they be improved in content and form?

The real learning potential of summary writing lies in students' using their own language to convey the author's main ideas.

MAKING NOTES

An effective study activity for acting on and remembering material is to annotate what is read in the form of notes. Notes can be put on study cards (index cards) or in a learning log that is kept expressly for the purpose of compiling written reactions to and reflections on text readings.

Note making should avoid verbatim text reproductions. Instead, notes can be used to paraphrase, summarize, react critically, question, or respond personally to what is read. Whatever the form notes take, students need to become aware of the different types of notes that can be written and should then be shown how to write them.

Eanet and Manzo (1976) underscore the importance of making notes as a means of helping students learn what they read. They describe the different kinds of notes students can write. Several are particularly appropriate for middle-grade and secondary school students. For example, read the passage in Box 9.2. Then study each of the notes made by a secondary school student, shown in Figures 9.11 through 9.14.

BOX 9.2	**Efforts to Stem Bear Gall Bladder Trade**

The Canadian director of the World Society for the Protection of Animals (WSPA) says authorities are to be congratulated on recent efforts to stem the illegal trade in bear gall bladders and other bear parts but says more needs to be done.

Says WSPA Director Silia Smith: "We are pleased to see attention being given to the illegal trade in bear parts. Recent arrests in Quebec and Ontario are a testament to the good that can come when authorities share information across jurisdictions. They are also evidence of a growing trade in bear parts."

[On Friday February 14, 2003], charges were laid against three family members in Toronto. According to a story in the Canadian Press, the three individuals face 84 separate charges under federal and provincial statutes involving illegal possession, transport, export, and trafficking of 368 gall bladders and two sets of black bear paws.

The charges stem from a massive sting operation this past November aimed at dismantling a network of more than 100 hunters, trappers, taxidermists, furriers, and smugglers. This operation, the largest of its kind in recent memory, was coordinated by the Canadian Wildlife Service and involved provincial conservation officers in Quebec and Ontario, along with members of the Toronto Police Service.

The Toronto arrests are notable, according to WSPA, as they involve an attempt to advertise and sell gall bladders over the internet. This tactic, fairly common in some Asian countries such as Japan, is not known to be widespread in North America.

Source: "WSPA Applauds Law Enforcement Efforts to Stem Bear Gall Trade but Says Trade Is Increasing." (2003). Retrieved February 20, 2004, from http://www.wspa.ca/press/2003/0203/180203_1.html.

> The illegal trading of bear parts is growing. The Canadian Wildlife Service, provincial conservation officers, and police are cooperating to arrest traders, some of whom are now using the internet.

FIGURE 9.11   A Summary Note

As part of a growing understanding of the different types of notes, students should be able to tell a well-written note from a poorly written one. Have the class read a short passage, followed by several examples of a certain type of note, one well written and the others flawed in some way. For example, a discussion of critical notes may include one illustration of a good critical note, one that lacks the note maker's position, and another that fails to defend or develop the position taken.

Modelling and practice should follow naturally from awareness and knowledge building. Teachers should walk students through the process of making different types of notes by sharing their thought processes. Show how a note is written and revised to satisfaction through think-aloud procedures. Then have students practise note making individually and in peer groups of two or three. Peer-group interaction is nonthreatening and leads to productions that can be duplicated or put on the board, compared, and evaluated by the class with teacher direction.

The *summary note*, as you might surmise, condenses the main ideas of a text selection into a concise statement. Summary notes are characterized by their brevity, clarity, and conciseness. When a note summarizes expository material, it should clearly distinguish the important ideas from supporting information and detail. When the summary note involves narrative material, such as a story, it should include a synopsis containing the major story elements. Examine the example of a summary note from a student's note card in Figure 9.11.

> Illegal trade in bear parts is opposed by government officials but continues to grow, therefore more should be done.

FIGURE 9.12   A Thesis Note

The *thesis note* answers the question, "What is the main point the composition has tried to get across to the reader?" The thesis note has a telegram-like character. It is incisively stated yet unambiguous in its identification of the main proposition. The thesis note for a story identifies its theme. Study the example in Figure 9.12 on page 274.

The *critical note* captures the reader's reaction or response to the thesis. It answers the question, "So what?" In writing critical notes, the reader should first state the thesis, then state the reader's position in relation to the thesis, and finally, defend or expand on the position taken (see Figure 9.13 on page 275).

The *question note* raises a significant issue in the form of a question. The question is the result of what the reader thinks is the most germane or significant aspect of what he or she has read (see Figure 9.14 on page 275).

Showing students how to write different types of notes begins with assessment; leads to awareness and knowledge building, modelling, and practice; and culminates in application. First, assign a text selection and ask students to make whatever notes they wish. Second, have the class analyze the assessment, share student notes, and discuss difficulties in making notes. Use the assessment discussion to make students aware of the importance of making notes as a strategy for learning and retention.

Third, build students' knowledge for note making by helping them recognize and define the various kinds of text notes that can be written. Eanet and Manzo (1976) recommend the following strategy: assign a short selection to be read in class; then write a certain type of note on the board. Ask students how what they read on the board relates to the passage that was assigned. Through discussion, formulate the definition and concept of the note under discussion.

To facilitate application to classroom reading tasks, we suggest that students write notes regularly in a learning log, on study cards, or on their computers. Save note making activities in learning logs for the latter half of a class period. The next class period then begins with a review or a sharing of notes, followed by discussion and clarification of the text material.

Notes written on study cards are an alternative to the learning log. Direct students to make study cards based on text readings. One tactic is to write questions on one side of the cards and responses to the questions on the other side. For example, ask students to convert the major subheadings of a text selection into questions, writing one question per card. The responses will probably lend themselves to summary or critical notes, depending on the questions posed. Later, students can use the study cards to prepare for a test. As part of test preparation, a student can read the question, recite the response aloud, and then review the note written earlier.

Lester (1984) offers the following tips for making notes on cards:

1. *Use ink.* Pencilled notes smudge easily with repeated shuffling of the cards.
2. *Use index cards.* Index cards are more durable and can be rearranged and organized more easily than large sheets of paper.
3. *Jot down only one item per card.* Don't overload a card with more than one type of note or one piece of information.
4. *Write on one side of the card.* Material on the back of a card may be overlooked during study. (One exception is question-and-response cards.)

The trading of bear parts is a threat to our wildlife. The lure of big money and lack of risk in this illrgal activity will cause it to grow. The use of the internet to advertise and sell bear parts further increases the ease of trade. All of these challenges will have to be opposed strongly by better informed and equipped government officers.

FIGURE 9.13   A Critical Note

(Given that the illegal trade in bear parts is growing despite efforts to stop it, should it be ignored?) The Canadian Director of the World Society for the Protection of Animals says more needs to be done. Massive arrests can help, but the use of the internet in illegal trading needs to be examined before it becomes too well established. If we ignore this trade, it will grown and threaten our bear population.

FIGURE 9.14   A Question Note

TAKING NOTES

Walter Pauk's response to the question, "Why take notes?" is profound in its simplicity: because we forget (1978). More than 50 percent of the material read or heard in class is forgotten in a matter of minutes. A system for taking and making notes triggers recall and overcomes forgetting.

Labels	Notes
	Our eyes, ears, nose, tongue, and skin pick up messages and send them to the brain.
	1. The lens of the eye focuses light on the retina, and neurons change it into a message that's carried by the optic nerves.
Neurons are detectors that signal messages to the brain	2. The tongue and nose work together to detect chemicals and send a message to the brain.
	—tongue has areas for sweet, salty, sour, bitter
	—each area has neurons
	3. The skin has neurons that detect pain, pressure, touch.

FIGURE 9.15 **Note-Taking Procedure That Uses Labels and Notes**

A popular note-taking procedure, suggested by Palmatier (1973), involves the following steps: First, have students use only one side of an $8\frac{1}{2}$-by-11-inch sheet of loose-leaf paper with a legal-width margin (if necessary, the student should add a margin line 3 inches from the left side of the paper). Second, have the students take lecture notes to the right of the margin. Although no specific format for taking notes is required, students should develop a format that uses subordination and space to illustrate the organization of the material; for example, they can indent to show continuation of ideas or enumerate to show series of details. Third, have the students put labels in the left margin that correspond to units of information recorded in the notes. The labels help organize the welter of information in the right column and give students the chance to fill in gaps in the notes. The labelling process should be completed as quickly as possible following the original taking of notes (see Figure 9.15 on page 277).

Once notes are taken and the labelling task is completed, students can use their notes to study for exams. For example, in preparing for a test, the student can spread out the note pages for review. One excellent strategy is to show students how to spread the pages, in order, in such a way that the lecture notes are hidden by succeeding pages and only the left-margin labels show. The labels can then be used as question stems to recall information—for example, "What do I need to know about (label)?" Accuracy of recall, of course, can be checked by referring to the original notes, which were concealed by overlapping the pages.

Students need to learn how to become text-smart. Being text-smart is comparable to being street-smart. It's knowing how to stay out of trouble; it's knowing when and when not to take shortcuts; it's knowing how to survive and triumph over the everyday cognitive demands that are a natural part of classroom life.

Becoming a student requires time and patience. Studying is a process that is learned inductively through trial and error and the repeated use of different strategies in different learning situations. This is where teachers have a role to play. Through the instructional support you provide, students discover that some strategies work better for them than others in different learning situations.

LOOKING BACK, LOOKING FORWARD

Teaching students how to study texts involves showing them how to become independent learners. In this chapter, we used the role that text structure plays to illustrate how you can teach students to use learner-directed strategies that involve constructing graphic representations, writing summaries, and making and taking notes.

How authors organize their ideas is a powerful factor in learning with texts. Because authors write to communicate, they organize ideas to make them accessible to readers. A well-organized text is a considerate one. The text patterns that authors use to organize their ideas revolve around description, sequence, comparison and contrast, cause and effect, and problem and solution. The more students perceive text patterns, the more likely they are to remember and interpret the ideas they encounter in reading.

Graphic representations help students outline important information that is reflected in the text patterns that authors use to organize ideas. The construction of graphic representations allows students to map the relationships that exist among the ideas presented in text. This strategy is a valuable tool for comprehending and retaining information.

Students who engage in summarizing what they have read often gain greater understanding and retention of the main ideas in text. Students need to become aware of summarization rules and to receive instruction in how to use these rules to write and polish a summary.

Notes are part of another useful strategy for studying text. Making notes allows students to reflect on and react to important ideas in text.

In the next chapter, we examine the role that study guides play in content literacy. A study guide is teacher-developed and provides instructional support for content understanding of text material.

MINDS-ON

1. A member of the board of education has been quoted as saying that she is opposed to "spoon-feeding" secondary school students. After a board meeting one evening, you have an opportunity to talk with her. You explain that there is a difference between "spoon-feeding" students and scaffolding instruction. As a group, discuss how you might justify supporting students' studying through the use of techniques such as graphic representations, summaries, and note taking.

2. Following an in-service program on using graphic representations, you notice that some teachers in your building are preparing a semantic map or graphic organizer for every assignment, whereas others, who say they don't have time, never use them. Your principal asks you, as a member of a team, to prepare a one-page sheet of guidelines for the use of graphic representations in which you suggest when, why, and how various graphic displays should be used. What would you include in this guide?

3. Imagine that your group is team-teaching an interdisciplinary unit on Canada during the Depression of the 1930s. Each member of your group should select (a) a content area and (b) one of the text patterns described in this chapter (sequence, comparison and contrast, problem and solution, cause and effect, or description). After reviewing some materials on the art, history, music, politics, science, mathematics, and literature of the Depression years, discuss how you might make use of a selected text pattern to teach a concept.

4. As part of an effort to improve school achievement in content area subjects, the curriculum director of your school system has suggested implementing a mandatory study skills course for all secondary school first-year students. As a team, compose a memo explaining why and how studying can be effectively taught when content area teachers are also involved in the delivery of instruction.

HANDS-ON

1. Design a semantic map for a science lesson on evolution. Create what you consider the most effective design for that specific content.

2. Using either problem and solution, cause and effect, or comparison and contrast, construct a graphic for a passage from an informational text. Share your representation with members of your group, and discuss how some topics seem appropriate for one specific organizational pattern whereas others might be organized in a variety of ways.

3. Distribute one card to each member of the class. Ask the students to write down the name of an individual they believe has made a significant contribution to society. Emphasize that the contribution may be in either a specific area of knowledge (art, music, science, literature, politics) or a nonspecific area such as acts of humanitarianism or environmental activism.

   Next, announce that the task of the class will be to create clusters of cards with names that have a common focus. Give each student in the class three minutes to find one partner whose card name relates to his or her own. Then have each team of partners locate another team whose names can be classified together. Explain that, if necessary, groups may redefine their common focus to create clusters. As a whole class, share the focus categories developed by each group.

   Finally, repeat the process, but do not allow any group to use the same common focus. Discuss how this activity relates to the process of outlining.

4. Imagine that one of your colleagues asks students to write summaries of what they are reading in class but does not provide explicit instruction on how to summarize a text effectively. You have observed that many of your colleague's students are frustrated by the task or are simply copying summaries written by other students. With a member of your group, create a dialogue in which you discuss some instructional alternatives that will lead to students' writing summaries effectively. As a group, discuss the suggestions you found effective and recommend some others that might have been included.

5. In a small group, read a short selection from a current news story, magazine article, textbook, or electronic media source. Write examples of the different kinds of notes that can be made from the text. Compare your group's notes with those of other groups, and discuss the different thinking tasks each type of note required, as well as the further use of each note in a classroom teaching situation.

6. In a small group, compile a list of study strategies that the group members use as well as the purposes for which they are used. Categorize the strategies into different groupings according to their perceived purposes. Display the strategies on an overhead or a chalkboard for a discussion of commonalities and suggestions for studying texts.

SUGGESTED READINGS

Anderson, T. H., & Armbruster, B. B. (1991). The value of taking notes during lectures. In R. F. Flippo & D. C. Cacverly (Eds.), *Teaching reading and study strategies at the college level.* Newark, DE: International Reading Association.

Anderson, V., & Hidi, S. (1998–1989). Teaching students to summarize. *Educational Leadership, 4,* 26–29.

Armbruster, B. B., & Anderson, R. C. (1981). Research synthesis on study skills. *Educational Leadership, 19,* 154–156.

Armbruster, B. B., Anderson, T. H., & Ostertag, J. (1987). Does text structure/summarization instruction facilitate learning from expository text? *Reading Research Quarterly, 22,* 331–346.

Boudreau, R., Wood, E., Willoughby, T., & Specht, J. (1999). Evaluating the efficacy of elaborative strategies for remembering expository text. *Alberta Journal of Educational Research, 25*(2), 170–183.

Devine, T. G. (1991). Studying: Skills, strategies, and systems. In J. Flood, J. M. Jensen, D. Lapp, & J. R. Squire (Eds.), *Handbook of research on teaching the English language arts.* New York: Macmillan.

Garner, R., & Gillingham, M. (1987). Students' knowledge of text structure. *Journal of Reading Behavior, 29,* 247–259.

Gordon, C., Sheridan, M., & Paul, W. (1998). Strategic learning for life: Learning to learn. *In Content literacy for secondary teachers.* Toronto: Harcourt Brace.

Heimlich, J. E., & Pittleman, S. D. (1986). *Semantic mapping: Classroom applications.* Newark, DE: International Reading Association.

Hill, M. (1991). Writing summaries promotes thinking and learning across the curriculum—but why are they so difficult to write? *Journal of Reading, 34,* 536–539.

Hoffman, J. (1992). Critical reading/thinking across the curriculum: Using I-charts to support learning. *Language Arts, 69,* 121–127.

Jackson, F. R., & Cunningham, J. W. (1994). Investigating secondary content teachers' and preservice teachers' conceptions of study strategy instruction. *Reading Research and Instruction, 34,* 111–135.

Jones, B. F., Palincsar, A. S., Ogle, D. M., & Carr, E. G. (1987). *Strategic teaching and learning: Cognitive instruction in content areas.* Alexandria, VA: Association of Supervision and Curriculum Development.

Jones, B. F., Pierce, J., & Hunter, B. (1988–1989). Teaching students to construct graphic representations. *Educational Leadership, 46,* 20–25.

Pearson, J. W., & Santa, C. M. (1995). Students as researchers of their own learning. *Journal of Reading, 38,* 462–469.

Peresich, M. L., Meadows, J. D., & Sinatra, R. (1990). Content area cognitive mapping for reading and writing proficiency. *Journal of Reading, 34,* 424–432.

Santa, C. M. (1988). *Content reading including study systems.* Dubuque, IA: Kendall/Hunt.

Simpson, M. L. (1984). The status of study strategy instruction: Implications for classroom teachers. *Journal of Reading, 28,* 136–142.

Wade, S. E., Trathen, W., & Schraw, G. (1990). An analysis of spontaneous study strategies. *Reading Research Quarterly, 25,* 147–166.

Winograd, P. N. (1984). Strategic difficulties in summarizing text. *Reading Research Quarterly, 19,* 404–425.

chapter ten

Study Guides

*There's no limit to how
complicated things can get.*

—E. B. White

ORGANIZING PRINCIPLE

Growth *in* reading. Growth *through* reading. These are two themes that run throughout this book. From the very first day that a child picks up a book, he or she is reading to learn and learning to read. It's a two-way street from the beginning and a dual process that never ends. When the famous German author and philosopher Johann Wolfgang von Goethe was in his eighties, he is attributed with having said, "The dear people do not know how long it takes to learn to read. I have been at it all my life and cannot say that I have reached the goal." Reading is an act of maturity. And every teacher that a student encounters has the potential to contribute in a significant way to the reading maturity of students within the context of subject matter instruction.

As children read to learn and learn to read, they become more fluent, and their ability to handle the mechanics of the process becomes more automatic. But that doesn't necessarily mean that learning with texts gets easier as readers grow older. To paraphrase E. B. White, there's no limit to how complicated reading can get. This is particularly so if the ideas we encounter are beyond our knowledge or experience.

Teachers can contribute to literacy and learning as they teach subject matter. Although the raison d'être of content area literacy is to show students how to learn with texts independently, many students may have trouble handling the conceptual demands inherent in difficult texts. This is often the case, for example, when they have difficulty responding to and thinking about what they're reading at high levels of comprehension. Our task, then, is to help students experience what it is to respond to difficult texts. The organizing principle of this chapter reflects one of the most basic approaches to scaffolding difficult material: **study guides provide the kind of instructional support that allows students to interact with and respond to difficult texts in meaningful ways.**

As the chapter overview shows, you will learn about several types of study guides. The first type, a *three-level guide*, reflects the concept of levels of comprehension. *Pattern guides* and *concept guides* are similar to three-level guides but make a concerted effort to help students recognize the organizational and conceptual structure underlying the author's text. The *selective reading guide* models the way a strategic reader responds to text that is difficult to read. You can devise other types of reading guides to scaffold students' learning; the ones that you read about in this chapter reflect some of the possibilities for guided instruction.

CHAPTER OVERVIEW

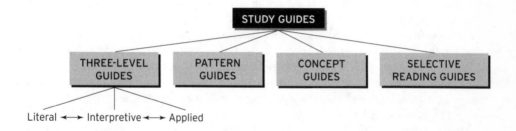

FRAME OF MIND

1. Why and when should you use study guides?

2. What is a three-level guide?

3. What is a pattern guide, and how is it similar to and different from a three-level guide?

4. What is a concept guide, and how is it similar to and different from three-level and pattern guides?

5. What is a selective reading guide, and how can you use it to model flexible reading?

6. How can you use and adapt different kinds of study guides in your content area?

Study guides simplify difficult text for students. As a result, study guides, used appropriately, can make learning with texts easier for students. That doesn't mean less challenging, however; just the opposite is intended. You should use study guides precisely because the text material is difficult and important enough to warrant scaffolding.

Why will the judicious use of study guides make learning easier? The conceptual load of academic texts is often greater than the levels of reading that students bring to the reading task. As a result, students experience difficulty comprehending what they read. The whole idea of a study guide is to provide enough instructional support and direction for students to learn with texts. In the process of doing so, they will gain confidence. Over time, study guides contribute to the development of strategies that lead to independent reading and learning.

Some teachers consider the use of study guides tantamount to spoon-feeding. Maybe it is. However, spoon-feeding doesn't necessarily mean that you are giving away the content. It means that you simplify the tough sledding that is ahead for students when the information in text appears too overwhelming to read on their own. Without some simplification, students' only alternative is often to avoid textbooks altogether.

What exactly is a study guide? It has sometimes been likened to a "worksheet"—something students complete after reading, usually as homework. But study guides do more than give students work to do. As the name implies, a study guide scaffolds students' understanding of academic content *and* the literacy and thinking processes needed to comprehend and learn with texts. Guides, like worksheets, may consist of questions and activities related to the instructional material under study. The difference is that students respond to the questions and activities in the study guide *as* they read the text, not after. Because a study guide accompanies reading, it provides instructional support as students need it. Moreover, a well-developed study guide not only influences content acquisition but also prompts higher-order thinking.

Study guides are firmly grounded in the here and now, helping students comprehend texts better than they would if left to their own resources. Over time, however, text learners should be weaned from this type of scaffolding as they develop the maturity and the learning strategies to interact with difficult texts without guide material. With this *caveat* in mind, let's explore the use of study guides that scaffold learning at different levels of understanding.

THREE-LEVEL GUIDES

Because reading is a thoughtful process, it embraces the idea of levels of comprehension. Readers respond to meaning at various levels of abstraction and conceptual difficulty. Figure 10.1 shows the different levels of comprehension.

At the *literal level*, students *read the lines* of the content material. They stay with print sufficiently to get the gist of the author's message. In simple terms, a literal recognition of that message determines what the author says. Searching for important literal information isn't an easy chore, particularly if readers haven't matured enough to know how to make the search or, even worse, haven't determined why they are searching in the first place. Most students can and will profit greatly from being shown how to recognize the essential information in the text.

Knowing what the author says is necessary but not sufficient in constructing meaning with text. Good readers search for conceptual complexity in material. They read at the

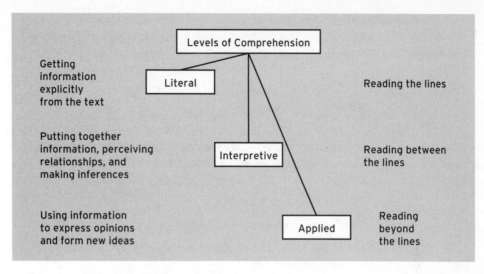

FIGURE 10.1 **Levels of Comprehension**

interpretive level—between the lines. They focus not only on what authors say but also on what authors mean by what they say. Herber (1978) clarifies the difference between the literal and interpretive levels this way: "At the literal level readers identify the important information. At the interpretive level readers perceive the relationships that exist in that information, conceptualizing the ideas formulated by those relationships" (p. 45).

The interpretive level delves into the author's intended meaning. How readers conceptualize implied ideas by integrating information into what they already know is part of the interpretive process. Recognizing the thought relationships that the author weaves together helps readers make inferences that are implicit in the material.

From time to time throughout the book, you have probably been trying to read us—not our words but us. And in the process of responding to our messages, you probably raised questions similar to these: "So what? What does this information mean to me? Does it make sense? Can I use these ideas for content instruction?" Your attempt to seek significance or relevance in what we say and mean is one signal that you are reading at the *applied level*. You are reading *beyond the lines*.

Reading at the applied level is undoubtedly akin to discovery. It underscores the constructive nature of reading comprehension. Bruner (1961) explains that discovery "is in its essence a matter of rearranging or transforming evidence in such a way that one is enabled to go beyond the evidence so reassembled to additional new insights" (p. 21). When students respond to text at the applied level, they know how to synthesize information—and to lay that synthesis alongside what they know already—to express opinions about and to draw additional insights and fresh ideas from content material.

The levels-of-comprehension model lends itself well to the preparation of guide material to scaffold reader–text interactions. A three-level guide provides the scaffold from which students can interact with difficult texts at different levels. One of the best ways to become familiar with the three-level guide as an instructional scaffold is to experience one. Therefore, we invite your participation in the following demonstration.

Preview the three-level guide in Figure 10.2; next, read "The Case of the Missing Ancestor" (p. 287), which originally appeared in *Silver Burdett Biology* (1986). Then complete the three-level guide as you read the text or after reading.

I. *Directions:* Check the statements that you believe say what the author says. Sometimes, the exact words are used; at other times, other words may be used.

_____ 1. The Germans discovered the fossilized remnants of the Neanderthal man and the Heidelberg man.

_____ 2. Charles Dawson found a human skull in a gravel pit in Piltdown Common, Sussex.

_____ 3. Charles Dawson was a professional archaeologist.

_____ 4. The fossil, labelled *Eoanthropus dawsoni*, became known as the Piltdown man.

_____ 5. The discovery of the Piltdown man was acclaimed as an important archaeological find.

_____ 6. Dental evidence regarding the Piltdown man was ignored.

II. *Directions:* Check the statements that you believe represent the author's *intended* meaning.

_____ 1. The English scientific community felt left out, because important fossils had been found in other countries.

_____ 2. Good scientific practices were ignored by the people working with the Piltdown fossils.

_____ 3. Many scientists said that Piltdown was important, because they wanted England to be important.

_____ 4. Dawson wanted to make himself famous, so he constructed a hoax.

III. *Directions:* Check the statements you agree with, and be ready to support your choices with ideas from the text and your own knowledge and beliefs.

_____ 1. Competition in scientific research may be dangerous.

_____ 2. Scientists, even good ones, can be fooled by poorly constructed hoaxes.

_____ 3. People often see only what they want to see.

_____ 4. A scientific "fact" is not always correct simply because many scientists believe strongly in it; theories are always open to question.

FIGURE 10.2 **Three-Level Guide**

Source: From *Silver Burdett Biology* by Alexander, 1986.

THE CASE OF THE MISSING ANCESTOR

From the mid-1800s to the early 1900s, Europeans were actively searching for early ancestors. The Germans dug up the fossilized remnants of Neanderthal man and Heidelberg man. The French discovered not only ancient bones but also cave paintings done by early humans.

England, Charles Darwin's home, had no evidence of ancient ancestors. English scientists—both professionals and amateurs—began searching for fossils. Scarcely a cave was left unexplored, scarcely a stone was left unturned. Many scientists asked workers in gravel pits to watch for fossils.

In 1912, Charles Dawson, a part-time collector of fossils for the British Museum, wrote to Dr. Arthur Smith Woodward, keeper of the Natural History Department at the British Museum. Dawson claimed that a human skull he had found in a gravel pit in Piltdown Common, Sussex, "would rival Heidelberg man." Soon Woodward was digging in the gravel pit with Dawson and other eager volunteers. They found a separate jaw that, though apelike, included a canine tooth and two molars, worn down as if by human-type chewing. Flints and nonhuman fossils found at the same dig indicated that the finds were very old.

Despite arguments by some scientists that the jaw came from a chimpanzee or an orangutan, the discoverers reconstructed the skull and connected the jaw to it. They named the fossil *Eoanthropus dawsoni,* Dawson's "Dawn man," and said that it was much older than Neanderthal man. The find came to be known as Piltdown man.

The finds were X-rayed. One dental authority was suspicious of the canine; he said it was too young a tooth to show such wear. However, such contrary evidence was ignored in the general surge of enthusiasm. So the Piltdown man was acclaimed as an important find, a human in which the brain had evolved more quickly than the jaw.

Beginning in the 1940s, the bones were subjected to modern tests. It is now believed that the skull was from a modern human and the jaw was from a modern ape, probably an orangutan. The animal fossils and flints were found to be very old but not the types that have been found in England. Apparently, they had been placed in the gravel pit to make the finds more convincing. Why were the scientists and others fooled so easily? Perhaps the desire to find an "ancestor" may have interfered with careful scientific observation.

Several comments are in order on your participation in the three-level guide demonstration. First of all, note that the three-level format gave you a "conscious experience" with comprehension levels as a process (Herber 1978). Note also that as you walked through the process, you responded to and manipulated the important explicit and implicit ideas in the material. You may have sensed the relatedness of ideas as you moved within and among the levels.

Why did we direct you first to preview the guide and then to read the material? Because surveying helps create a predisposition to read the material. Previewing helps reduce the reader's uncertainty about the material to be read. You know what is coming. When we asked you to read the guide first, we hoped to raise your expectations about the author's message. By encountering some of the ideas before reading, you are in a better position to direct your search for information in the reading material that may be relevant.

You probably noted also that the declarative statements did not require you to produce answers to questions. Rather, you had to make decisions among likely alternatives; it's easier to recognize possible answers than to produce them.

Notice, too, that in a very positive way, the statements can serve as springboards for discussion and conversation about the content. Were students to react to guides *without* the opportunity to discuss and debate responses, the instructional material would soon deteriorate into busywork and paper shuffling.

A final comment: your maturity as a reader is probably such that you didn't need structured guidance for this selection, particularly at levels I and II. If you make the decision that certain segments of your text can be handled without reading guidance, don't construct guide material. A three-level guide is a means to growth in reading and growth through reading. It is not an end in itself.

Constructing Three-Level Guides

Don't be misled by the apparent discreteness of comprehension levels. Don't, as Dale (1969) pronounced, suffer from "hardening of the categories." The term *levels* implies a cognitive hierarchy that may be more apocryphal than real. A reader doesn't necessarily read first for literal recognition, then interpretation, and finally application—although that may appear to be a logical sequence. Many readers, for instance, read text for overarching concepts and generalizations first and then search for evidence to support their inferences.

It is very important to recognize that in reading, levels are probably interactive and inseparable. Nevertheless, the classroom teacher attempts to have students experience each aspect of the comprehension process as they read content material. In doing so, students adapt strategies as they interact with the material. They get a feel for the component processes within reading comprehension. They come to sense in an instructional setting what it means to make inferences, to use information as the basis for those inferences, and to rearrange or transform acquired understandings into what they know already in order to construct knowledge.

If the study guide were to be used with every text assignment every day, it would become counterproductive. One mathematics teacher's evaluation of a three-level guide crystallizes this point: "The students said the guide actually helped them organize the author's ideas in their minds and helped them understand the material. I think the guide was successful, but I would not use it all the time because many of the assignments don't lend themselves to this type of activity." The three-level guide is only one instructional aid that helps students grow toward mature reading and independent learning.

Merlin the magician doesn't wave his magic wand to ensure the effectiveness of three-level guides. They are facilitative only when students know how to work in groups and know how to apply techniques that have been taught clearly. The heart of the matter is what the teacher does to make guided reading work.

Finally, we urge you also to consider guides as tools, not tests. Think of each statement in a study guide as a prompt that will initiate student discussion and reinforce the quality of the reader's response to meaning in text material.

There is no set of procedures for constructing three-level guides. Before constructing a guide, however, the teacher has to decide the following: What important ideas should be emphasized? What are the students' competencies? What depth of understanding are the students expected to achieve? What is the difficulty of the material? Having made these decisions, you may wish to consider these guidelines:

1. *Begin construction of the guide at level II, the interpretive level.* Analyze the text selection, asking yourself, "What does the author mean?" Write down in your own words all inferences that make sense to you and that fit your content objectives. Make sure your statements are written simply and clearly. (After all, you don't want to construct a guide to read the guide.)

2. *Next, search the text for the propositions and explicit pieces of information needed to support the inferences you have chosen for level II.* Put these into statement form. You now have level I, the literal level.

3. *Decide whether you want to add a distractor or two to levels I and II.* We have found that a distractor maintains an active response to the information search, mainly because students sense that they cannot indiscriminately check every item and, therefore, must focus their information search more carefully.

4. *Develop statements for level III, the applied level.* Such statements represent additional insights or principles that can be drawn when relationships established by the author are combined with other ideas outside the text selection itself but inside the heads of your students. In other words, help students connect what they know already to what they read.

5. *Be flexible and adaptive.* Develop a format that will appeal to you and your students. Try to avoid crowding too much print on the study guide.

Using Three-Level Guides

The format of the three-level guide should vary. The classroom examples that follow serve only as models. As you study them, think of ways that you will be able to adapt and apply the three-level construct to your content materials.

Guides are extremely useful adjuncts in the study of literature. A three-level guide can be easily adapted to dramatic, narrative, and poetic forms of literature. For example, note in Figure 10.3 on pages 290 and 291 how a grade 9 English teacher used a three-level guide for Shakespeare's *Romeo and Juliet*. The class was at the tail end of its study of the play, and the guide helped students pull together some of the important points related to the climactic action of the final act. Moreover, the statements at levels II and III of the guide helped students reflect on possible inferences and themes that emerge from the action.

The simplicity of Figure 10.4 on page 292 speaks for itself. A middle-grade teacher constructed it as part of a health unit. Notice how she uses Question-Answer Relationships (QARs) as cues to direct students' responses. Students completed the guide individually and then discussed their responses in small groups.

As we have shown, one important way to guide comprehension is through three-level guides, which a teacher constructs to bridge the gap between students' competencies and the difficulty of the text material. As you consider adapting three-level guides to content area materials, keep these summarizing points in mind. First, the three-level guide stimulates an active response to meaning at the literal, interpretive, and applied levels. It helps

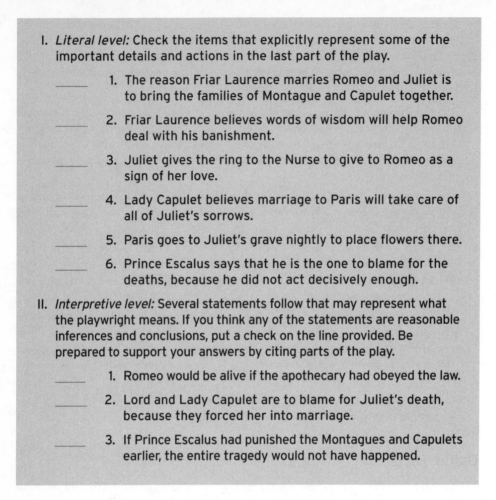

I. *Literal level:* Check the items that explicitly represent some of the important details and actions in the last part of the play.

_____ 1. The reason Friar Laurence marries Romeo and Juliet is to bring the families of Montague and Capulet together.

_____ 2. Friar Laurence believes words of wisdom will help Romeo deal with his banishment.

_____ 3. Juliet gives the ring to the Nurse to give to Romeo as a sign of her love.

_____ 4. Lady Capulet believes marriage to Paris will take care of all of Juliet's sorrows.

_____ 5. Paris goes to Juliet's grave nightly to place flowers there.

_____ 6. Prince Escalus says that he is the one to blame for the deaths, because he did not act decisively enough.

II. *Interpretive level:* Several statements follow that may represent what the playwright means. If you think any of the statements are reasonable inferences and conclusions, put a check on the line provided. Be prepared to support your answers by citing parts of the play.

_____ 1. Romeo would be alive if the apothecary had obeyed the law.

_____ 2. Lord and Lady Capulet are to blame for Juliet's death, because they forced her into marriage.

_____ 3. If Prince Escalus had punished the Montagues and Capulets earlier, the entire tragedy would not have happened.

FIGURE 10.3 Three-Level Guide for *Romeo and Juliet*

readers acquire and construct knowledge from content material that might otherwise be too difficult for them to read. Second, levels of comprehension interact during reading; in all probability, the levels are inseparable in mature readers. Nevertheless, for instructional purposes, it is beneficial to have students experience each level in order to get a feel for the component processes involved in comprehending. And third, three-level guides will help students develop a good sense of the conceptual complexity of text material.

In the next section, we consider another type of study guide: pattern guides.

PATTERN GUIDES

Text patterns, as we explained in Chapter 9, are difficult for maturing readers to discern, but once students become aware of the importance of organization and learn how to search for relationships in text, they are in a better position to use information more effectively and to comprehend material more thoroughly.

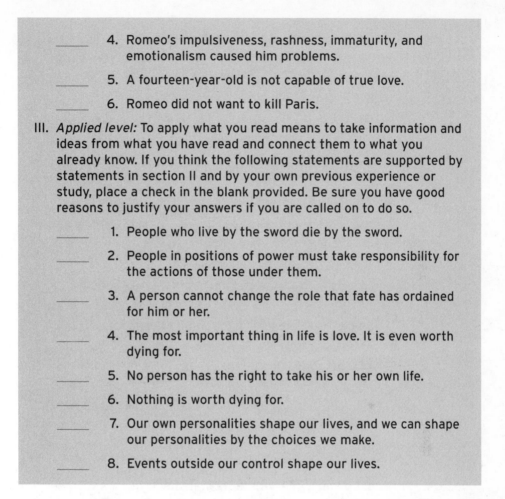

_____ 4. Romeo's impulsiveness, rashness, immaturity, and emotionalism caused him problems.

_____ 5. A fourteen-year-old is not capable of true love.

_____ 6. Romeo did not want to kill Paris.

III. *Applied level:* To apply what you read means to take information and ideas from what you have read and connect them to what you already know. If you think the following statements are supported by statements in section II and by your own previous experience or study, place a check in the blank provided. Be sure you have good reasons to justify your answers if you are called on to do so.

_____ 1. People who live by the sword die by the sword.

_____ 2. People in positions of power must take responsibility for the actions of those under them.

_____ 3. A person cannot change the role that fate has ordained for him or her.

_____ 4. The most important thing in life is love. It is even worth dying for.

_____ 5. No person has the right to take his or her own life.

_____ 6. Nothing is worth dying for.

_____ 7. Our own personalities shape our lives, and we can shape our personalities by the choices we make.

_____ 8. Events outside our control shape our lives.

A pattern guide helps students perceive and use the major text relationships that predominate in the reading material. Although the three-level guide focuses on a recognition of the relevant information in the material, text organization is implicit.

For example, a grade 8 social studies class read a text assignment, "Today's Stone Age Elephant Hunters" (Beebe 1968), as part of a unit on primitive cultures in the modern world. The text explains how pigmy hunters from the western Congo hunt and kill elephants for food as well as for cultural rituals associated with young hunters' rights of passage into manhood. To get a feel for how a text pattern guide scaffolds the reader's recognition of text relationships, read the excerpt from "Today's Stone Age Elephant Hunters" on page 294 and then complete the text pattern guide in Figure 10.5 on page 298.

Notice how part I of the guide helps you recognize the temporal sequence of events associated with the elephant hunt. The sequence then forms the basis for the interpretive and applied levels of comprehension. The guide helps the reader focus not only on explicit text relationships but also on important ideas implicit in the text.

How, then, might you scaffold the search for text patterns in reading materials as you teach your content? First, you should try to keep to a minimum the number of patterns that

I. Right There! What did the author say?

Directions: Place a check on the line in front of the number if you think a statement can be found in the pages you read.

_____ 1. Every human being has feelings or emotions.

_____ 2. Research workers are studying the effects on the body of repeated use of marijuana.

_____ 3. You should try hard to hide your strong emotions such as fear or anger.

_____ 4. Your feelings affect the way the body works.

_____ 5. You are likely to get angry at your parents or brothers or sisters more often than at other people.

II. Think and Search! What did the author mean?

Directions: Check the following statements that state what the author was trying to say in the pages you read.

_____ 1. Sometimes you act in a different way because of your mood.

_____ 2. Your emotional growth has been a continuing process since the day you were born.

_____ 3. The fact that marijuana hasn't been proved to be harmful means that it is safe to use.

_____ 4. Each time you successfully control angry or upset feelings, you grow a little.

III. On Your Own! Do you agree with these statements?

Directions: Check each statement that you can defend.

_____ 1. Escaping from problems does not solve them.

_____ 2. Decisions should be made on facts, not fantasies.

_____ 3. Getting drunk is a good way to have fun.

FIGURE 10.4 Three-Level Guide for a Health Lesson

students are to identify and use. Second, your goal should be to guide students to recognize a single pattern that predominates over long stretches of text, even though you recognize that individual paragraphs and sentences are apt to reflect different thought relationships within the text selection.

TODAY'S STONE AGE ELEPHANT HUNTERS
B. F. Beebe

Some pigmies of the western Congo use a system of concealing their scent when hunting elephants. Few of these little jungle dwellers hunt elephants but those that do have chosen about the most dangerous way to secure food in today's world.

Hunting is done by a single man using a spear with a large metal spearhead and thick shaft. After taking the trail behind an elephant herd the hunter pauses frequently to coat his skin with fresh elephant droppings for several days until he had lost all human scent.

Closing on the herd the pigmy selects his prey, usually a young adult. He watches this animal until he is aware of its distinctive habits—how often it dozes, eats, turns, wanders out of the herd, and other individual behavior.

Then he moves toward his prey, usually at midday when the herd is dozing while standing. The little hunter moves silently between the elephant's legs, braces himself and drives the spear up into the stomach area for several feet. The elephant snaps to alertness, screaming and trying to reach his diminutive attacker. Many pigmy hunters have lost their lives at this moment, but if the little hunter is fast enough he pulls out the spear to facilitate bleeding and ducks for safety.

Death does not come for several days and the hunter must follow his wounded prey until it stops. When the elephant falls the pigmy cuts off the tail as proof of his kill and sets off for his village, which may be several days away by now.

Source: From *African Elephants* by B. F. Beebe, 1968.

mation *per se*, you can create guide material that allows them to experience how the information fits together. Research and experience (Vacca 1975, 1977; Herber 1978) indicate that the following teaching sequence works well in content area classes:

1. *Examine a reading selection.* Decide on the predominant pattern used by the author.
2. *Make students aware of the pattern.* Explain how to interpret the author's meaning as part of the total lesson.
3. *Provide guidance.* Students may have trouble perceiving organization through a pattern guide. Small-group or whole-class discussion may help them see the pattern.
4. *Provide assistance.* Students may have unresolved problems concerning the process or the content under discussion.

This sequence is deductive. Once you decide that a particular text selection has a predominant pattern, share your insights with the class. Perceiving text organization is undoubtedly one of the most sophisticated activities in which readers engage. Chances are that most readers will have trouble recognizing text organization independently. By dis-

I. What is the sequence?

Directions: The pigmy hunter follows ten steps in hunting and killing an elephant. Some of the steps are given to you. Decide which steps are missing, and write them in the spaces provided. The pigmy hunter

1. takes the trail of an elephant herd.

2. _____

3. selects the elephant he will kill.

4. _____

5. moves in for the kill.

6. _____

7. _____

8. pulls out the spear.

9. _____

10. cuts off _____

II. What did the author mean?

Directions: Check the statements that you think suggest what the author was trying to say.

_____   1. The pigmy hunter is smart.

_____   2. The pigmy hunter uses instinct much as an animal does.

_____   3. The pigmy hunter is a coward.

III. How can we use meanings?

Directions: Based on what you read and what you know, check the statements with which you agree.

_____   1. A person's ingenuity ensures survival.

_____   2. Where there's a will, there's a way.

_____   3. There are few differences between primitive and civilized people.

FIGURE 10.5 Pattern Guide for "Today's Stone Age Elephant Hunters"

Constructing Pattern Guides

As you can see, a pattern guide is a variation of the three-level guide. The difference between the two lies in the literal level: rather than have students respond to relevant infor-

cussing the pattern before they read, students will develop a frame of reference that they can apply during reading. From a metacognitive point of view, discussing the pattern and why the reader should search for relationships is a crucial part of the lesson.

The pattern guide itself tears the text organization apart. The students' task, then, is really to piece together the relationships that exist within the predominant pattern. Interaction among class members as they discuss the guide heightens their awareness of the pattern and how the author has used it to structure information. Students learn from one another as they share their perceptions of the relationships in the reading selection.

The final step in the teaching sequence should not be neglected. As students work on or discuss a pattern guide, provide feedback that will keep them going, will clarify and aid in rethinking the structure of the material, and will get students back into the material. Combining information is an important intellectual act requiring analysis followed by synthesis. It isn't enough, in most cases, to exhort students to "read for cause and effect" or "study the sequence." You must show them how to perceive organization over long stretches of text. Pattern guides help you do this. As you consider developing a pattern guide, you may find it useful to follow these three steps:

1. *Read through the text selection.* Identify a predominant pattern.

2. *Develop an exercise in which students can react to the structure of the relationships represented by the pattern.*

3. *Decide on how much guidance you want to provide in the pattern guide.* If it suits your purposes, you may develop sections of the guide for the interpretive and applied levels. Or you may decide that these levels can be handled adequately through questioning and discussion once students have sensed the author's organization through the guided reading activity.

Pattern guides help students follow relationships among ideas. Pattern guides are most suitable for informational materials, where a predominant pattern of organization is likely to be apparent.

Using Pattern Guides

Note the variations in the following first two classroom examples of pattern guides. Each was developed by a teacher to help students recognize the cause and effect pattern. In presenting the guides to their classes, the teachers followed the four-step teaching sequence previously outlined. Study each illustration as a model for preparing your own guides based on causes and effects.

The students in an auto mechanics' class were described by the teacher as "nonreaders." Most activities in the course were hands-on, as you might expect, and although the students had a textbook, they seldom used it.

But the auto mechanics teacher believed that the textbook section on transmissions warranted reading because of the relevance of the material. To help the students follow the author's ideas about causes and effects, the teacher constructed the pattern guide in Figure 10.6 on page 296.

The students worked in pairs to complete the guide. When some had trouble locating certain effects in the assignment, the teacher told them what page to study. The teacher believed that as a result of the guided recognition of cause and effect the students would be better able to handle interpretation and application through class discussion followed by a hands-on activity.

Directions: In your reading assignment on transmissions, find the causes that led to the effects listed. Write each cause in the space provided.

1. Cause: _____

   Effect: Grinding occurs when gears are shifted.

2. Cause: _____

   Effect: Car speed increases but engine speed remains constant while torque
   is decreasing.

3. Cause: _____

   Effect: Car makers changed over to synchronizing mechanisms.

4. Cause: _____

   Effect: Helical gears are superior to spur gears.

5. Cause: _____

   Effect: Some cars cannot operate correctly with three-speed transmissions
   and require extra speeds.

6. Cause: _____

   Effect: Most manuals have an idler gear.

7. Cause: _____

   Effect: All cars require some type of transmission.

FIGURE 10.6 **Pattern Guide for Power Mechanics**

A middle school teacher prepared a matching activity to illustrate the cause and effect pattern for students who were studying a unit titled "First Nations: A Search for Identity." One reading selection from the unit material dealt with Crowfoot, a Blackfoot chief who helped his people ada   pt to a new way of life after European contact.

The teacher asked, "Why did Crowfoot urge the Blackfoot to keep the peace?" The question led to prereading discussion. The students offered several predictions. The teacher then suggested that the reading assignment was written in a predominantly cause and effect pattern. He discussed this type of pattern, and the students contributed several examples. Then he gave them the pattern guide in Figure 10.7 to complete as they read the selection.

The class read for two purposes: to see whether their predictions were accurate and to follow the cause and effect relationships in the material. First, the students read the selection silently; then they worked in groups of four to complete the pattern guide.

A final example, the comparison and contrast pattern guide in Figure 10.8, shows how the format of a guide will differ with the nature of the material (in this case, narrative) and the teacher's objectives. In Figure 10.8, grade 10 students in an English class used the pattern guide to discuss changes in character in Jeanette C. Armstrong's story "Blue Against White."

Adapt pattern guide formats to match the major organizational structures in your content materials. If you do so, students will begin to develop the habit of searching for organization in everything they read.

CONCEPT GUIDES

Concept guides extend and reinforce the notion that concepts are hierarchically ordered in informational material and that some ideas are subordinate to others.

Main idea–detail relationships can be described as a distinct pattern of organization. Herber (1978) explained the main idea pattern this way:

Directions: Select from the causes column at the left the cause that led to each effect in the effects column at the right. Put the letter of each effect next to its cause in the space provided.

Causes

_____ 1. Indian Act requires that aboriginal people farm reserves.
_____ 2. Settlers and hunters kill buffalo in vast numbers.
_____ 3. Blackfoot have no resistance to European diseases.
_____ 4. Railway construction moves westward.
_____ 5. Crowfoot wants to stop conflict between Blackfoot and Cree tribes.
_____ 6. Aboriginal groups lose battles in United States.
_____ 7. Whiskey trade threatens peace between Blackfoot and settlers.
_____ 8. Eleven treaties signed between 1871 and 1921.
_____ 9. Crowfoot uses power as speaker and leader to keep peace.

Effects

a. 800 members of Blackfoot tribe die from smallpox in 1870.
b. Crowfoot seeks peace instead of battles with settlers.
c. Aboriginal people can no longer pursue nomadic life.
d. Canada gains 2 million square kilometres from aboriginal peoples.
e. Buffalo herds almost wiped out.
f. Blackfoot refuse to join Northwest Rebellion in 1885.
g. More settlers arrive in Calgary, Regina, Moose Jaw.
h. Crowfoot welcomes North West Mounted Police to deal with illegal trade.
i. Crowfoot, a Blackfoot, adopts a Cree boy to ensure peace between tribes.

FIGURE 10.7 **Pattern Guide for "First Nations: A Search for Identity"**

Directions: Consider Lena's attitude (how she feels) about the following characters and concepts at the beginning of the story and at the end. Record quotations from the story to support your ideas.

Characters and Concepts	Lena's Attitude at the Beginning of the Story	Lena's Attitude at the End of the Story
Blue door City Reserve Freeway Her father Her mother Herself		

FIGURE 10.8 **Pattern Guide for "Blue Against White"**

"Main idea" is sometimes identified as an additional organizational pattern. True, it is a pattern, but ... its construct is so broad that it subsumes each of the other patterns. For example, a *cause* might be the "main idea" of a paragraph and the *effects*, the "details"; or a *comparison* might be the "main idea" and the *contrasts*, the "details"; or a stated objective might be the "main idea" and the *enumeration* of steps leading to that objective, the "details." (p. 78)

The point, of course, is that in any pattern of organization, there are likely to be certain concepts that are more important than others.

This is why students need to be shown how to distinguish important information (the main ideas of a passage) from less important information (the details). Three-level guides and pattern guides do this to some degree. The concept guide also serves this purpose.

Baker (1977) claimed that concept guides help students associate and categorize subordinate information under major concepts. Therefore, the first step in constructing a concept guide is to analyze the text material for the main ideas, and then identify less inclusive concepts and relevant propositions that support each main idea.

Figure 10.9 presents an example of a concept guide. Part I of the concept guide is similar to the literal-level task in a three-level guide. In part II of the guide, however, students are required to categorize information under coordinate concepts related to the main topic (in this case, India's economy), which makes them aware that some ideas are more important than others. The reader associates specific pieces of information and then groups them together to aid conceptual learning and retention. The culmination of this activity leads to part III in the concept guide. Students are asked to support major ideas (superordinate concepts) that are integral to the content material.

There are many modifications that you can make in developing concept guides for your content area. Here two sample guides are described.

A secondary school photography instructor wanted his students to distinguish between two important concepts related to picture composition: the rules of composition and the techniques of composition. Note how the concept guide in Figure 10.10 on page 300 achieves this purpose.

Figure 10.11 on page 301 shows how a grade 7 social studies teacher modified the concept guide to fit his content objectives. This guide provoked a good deal of discussion among the students. The teacher extended students' thinking after they discussed their responses to the guide by asking them to circle the numbers of the concepts in part II that they believed described life in North America today. Students worked in small groups and had to support their decisions with specific reasons; thus, the concept guide became a springboard for thoughtful conversation and discussion. Comprehension processes will develop in situations that require not only active responding but also interaction among the respondents.

SELECTIVE READING GUIDES

Selective reading guides show students how to think with print. The effective use of questions combined with signalling techniques helps model how readers interact with text when reading and studying.

Cunningham and Shablak (1975) were among the first to discuss the importance of guiding students to respond selectively to text. They indicate that content area teachers can impart tremendous insight into *how* to acquire text information through a selective reading guide:

INDIA'S ECONOMY

I. *Directions:* Check each of the following statements that you think is true, based on what you have learned from your textbook reading, outside reading, class discussions, and lectures.

_____ 1. Approximately 10 percent of India's people are *subsistence farmers* enjoying *private land ownership.*

_____ 2. One of India's *government programs* is the attempt to increase agriculture production.

_____ 3. Since India became independent in 1947, *land reform* has been instituted to give the peasants more land.

_____ 4. The Indian government has attempted to speed up industrialization through *five-year plans.*

_____ 5. Because of a lack of necessary *capital* to finance industrial growth, India has had to borrow money.

_____ 6. India lacks the necessary *mineral resources* needed for industrial growth.

_____ 7. India's major *agricultural products* include rice, wheat, jute, tea, sugar cane, and cotton.

_____ 8. The average annual *per capita income* in India is about $70 000.

_____ 9. Cotton and textile industries produce the largest number of *manufactured products* in India.

_____ 10. India generally has an *unfavourable balance of trade.*

_____ 11. India's *major exports* include burlap and tea; its *major imports* include rice and various foodstuffs.

II. *Directions:* Take each of the italicized words and phrases from part I and place each under the heading to which it most closely relates. Place a check next to any word or phrase listed under more than one heading.

Agriculture	Industry	Trade	Standard of Living

III. *Directions:* Based on the information organized in part II and your own knowledge, check any of the following statements for which you can give an example.

_____ 1. Economic growth is determined largely by private enterprise.

_____ 2. Government has a strong influence over the economy.

_____ 3. Industrial production is a major source of a nation's wealth.

_____ 4. To maintain a favourable balance of trade, a country must export more than it imports.

FIGURE 10.9   **Concept Guide on India's Economy**

"PICTURE COMPOSITION"

I. *Directions:* As you read Chapter 12 in the textbook assigned pages, check the following statements that are specifically supported by the reading.

_____ 1. Composition may be defined as a pleasing arrangement of subject matter in the picture area.

_____ 2. Light is to the photographer as paint is to the artist.

_____ 3. There are no fixed rules that will ensure good composition in every picture.

_____ 4. There are only principles that may be applied to help achieve pleasing composition.

_____ 5. Pictures should never tell a story.

_____ 6. Simplicity is the secret of many good pictures.

_____ 7. Choose a subject that will lend itself to a simple, pleasing arrangement.

_____ 8. Check your camera angle carefully.

_____ 9. Camera angle is unimportant.

_____ 10. Poor background and foreground are errors of amateur photographers.

_____ 11. The "Golden Section" is a subject placement guide.

_____ 12. In photo composition, one should pay heed to balance.

_____ 13. Two subjects of different sizes should be farther apart than two subjects of equal size.

_____ 14. There are four basic line forms in photography.

_____ 15. Use horizontal lines to show peace and tranquillity.

_____ 16. Vertical lines show strength and power.

_____ 17. The diagonal line is said to represent action, speed, and movement.

_____ 18. The Hogarth Curve is said to be the most beautiful line in the world.

II. Categorize the statements you have checked under one of these column headings:

Rules of Composition   Techniques

FIGURE 10.10 Concept Guide for "Picture Composition"

THE INCAS OF PERU: "ENLARGING THE EMPIRE"

I. *Directions:* Read the chapter "Enlarging the Empire" in your textbook. As you read, check the following statements that say what the author said.

_____ 1. Unlike the nation as a whole, the capital housed no commoners.

_____ 2. The general, finding himself near an area with many villagers, ordered his men to rob the villagers of their gold and jewellery and burn the fields.

_____ 3. These assignments did provide the necessary labour for public works, and they also took troublemakers away from their own people for a while.

_____ 4. By means of this pyramid of authority, orders were transmitted to all parts of the empire.

_____ 5. Such methods and policies were a new experience for commoners, but their lives did not change much.

_____ 6. Crimes against the state were the most serious and were punishable by death.

_____ 7. Noblemen received special food, fine clothing, and many wives.

_____ 8. Panchacutec would quickly promote men who were able and trustworthy to important positions.

_____ 9. The people wanted to barter for extra food and goods with their neighbours, instead of travelling all the way to the marketplace in Cuzco.

II. *Directions:* Place the number of each statement you checked in the box next to the concept that it supports. A statement may be used more than once.

Concepts	Supporting ideas
1. Great empires are highly organized.	_____
2. Some people are more privileged than others.	_____
3. Unnecessary destruction during war should be avoided.	_____
4. Societies run smoothly when people are busy.	_____
5. Rewards and punishments keep people in control.	_____

FIGURE 10.11 Concept Guide for "Enlarging the Empire"

Page 128. Read the title. Write a definition of a permissible lie. Give an example of this type of lie.

Page 128, par. 1. Do you agree with this quotation? Why or why not?

Pages 128-129. Read paragraphs 2-6 slowly and carefully. What aspects of TV were borrowed from radio? Write them down. From personal experience, do you think TV reflects reality? Jot an answer down, and then continue reading.

Pages 129-130. Read paragraphs 7-15 quickly. What specific types of commercials are being discussed?

Pages 130-131. Read paragraphs 16-26 to find out the author's opinion of this type of commercial.

Page 131. Read paragraph 7. The author gives an opinion here. Do you agree?

Pages 131-133. Read to page 133, paragraph 45. You can skim this section, slowing down to read parts that are especially interesting to you. What are some current popular phrases or ideas in advertising? Think of some commercials you've seen on TV. List another word or idea or fad that's used in a lot of advertising.

Pages 133-134. Read paragraphs 45-50 quickly. Give your own example of a sex-based advertisement.

Page 134, par. 51. According to the author, what is a good test for an advertisement? Do you agree? Would most advertisements pass or fail the test? Try out a few.

Page 134, par. 52. Restate Comant's quote in your own words.

After reading the assignment, summarize what you read in 100 words or less.

FIGURE 10.12   **Selective Reading Guide for "Advertising: The Permissible Lie"**

The teacher begins ... by determining the overall purpose for a particular reading assignment. Second, he selects those sections of the reading are necessary to achieve this purpose.

Most important ... he eliminates from the assignment any and all sections that are irrelevant to the purpose. Third, for those relevant sections that remain, the teacher determines, *based on his own model reading behaviours*, what a student must operationally do to achieve the purpose—step by step, section by section. (p. 381; emphasis added)

The premise behind the selective reading guide is that teachers understand how to process information from their own subject matter areas. Figure 10.12 illustrates how an English teacher developed a selective reading guide that mixes written questions with appropriate signals for processing the material.

In elementary and middle school situations, selective reading guides have been called reading road maps (Wood 1988). For maturing readers, teachers add a visual dimension to the guide. Study the reading road map in Figure 10.13 developed by a middle school science teacher. Notice how he guides students through the life functions of bacteria by using various kinds of cues, signals, and statements. The guide provides location cues to focus students' attention on relevant segments of text, speed signals to model flexibility in reading, and mission statements that initiate tasks that help students think and learn with texts.

The examples presented in this chapter should give you some idea of how guides may be used and developed for different instructional purposes across a wide range of texts. We encourage you to develop and experiment with several study guides for potentially difficult text assignments in your content area.

LOOKING BACK, LOOKING FORWARD

When learners are not able to handle difficult texts on their own, a teacher supports their efforts to make meaning by *scaffolding* their interactions with texts. With the use of study

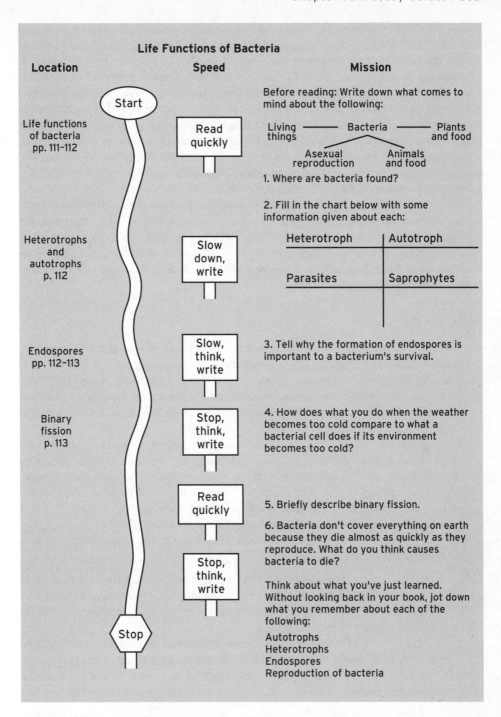

Life Functions of Bacteria

Location	Speed	Mission

Start

Before reading: Write down what comes to mind about the following:

Living things ——— Bacteria ——— Plants and food

Asexual reproduction   Animals and food

Life functions of bacteria pp. 111–112

Read quickly

1. Where are bacteria found?

2. Fill in the chart below with some information given about each:

Heterotroph	Autotroph
Parasites	Saprophytes

Heterotrophs and autotrophs p. 112

Slow down, write

Endospores pp. 112–113

Slow, think, write

3. Tell why the formation of endospores is important to a bacterium's survival.

Binary fission p. 113

Stop, think, write

4. How does what you do when the weather becomes too cold compare to what a bacterial cell does if its environment becomes too cold?

Read quickly

5. Briefly describe binary fission.

6. Bacteria don't cover everything on earth because they die almost as quickly as they reproduce. What do you think causes bacteria to die?

Stop, think, write

Think about what you've just learned. Without looking back in your book, jot down what you remember about each of the following:

Autotrophs
Heterotrophs
Endospores
Reproduction of bacteria

Stop

FIGURE 10.13   **A Reading Road Map**

guides, teachers provide instructional support to allow students to interact with and respond to difficult texts in meaningful ways. We explored and illustrated four types of guides: three-level guides, pattern guides, concept guides, and selective reading guides.

Three-level guides allow readers to interact with text, constructing meaning at different levels of abstraction and conceptual complexity: literal, interpretive, and applied levels. Pattern guides help students become aware of the importance of text organization and learn how to search for relationships in text. Teachers may adapt pattern guide formats to match major organizational structures in their content materials. Concept guides are a variation of three-level guides and help readers distinguish important information from less important information. Selective reading guides show students how to think with text by modelling the reading behaviours necessary to read texts effectively.

Despite efforts to scaffold instruction in ways that facilitate text learning, some students will continually struggle with reading. Even though the best of readers may struggle with text in certain situations, the struggling reader often has given up on reading as a way of learning. Chapter 11 takes a closer look at the literacy needs of the struggling reader. As you read about struggling readers, focus your attention on the role of explicit instruction in the development and use of reading strategies.

MINDS-ON

1. Select a popular book, film, or song that most members of your small group know. Discuss each of the following levels of comprehension communicated in that work: (a) literal (in the lines), (b) interpretive (between the lines), (c) applied (beyond the lines).
2. Some teachers believe that because literal comprehension is necessary to answer "higher-level" questions, it is unnecessary to ask literal-level questions. Do you agree? Do you think we would agree?
3. The basic premise of a study guide is to provide instructional support for students for whom the text is too difficult to handle independently. How might study guides be especially well suited to below-level students who have low self-esteem and little confidence in their ability to meet success with content material? In what ways will the purpose of meeting the individual needs of academically at-risk students be better served through their use? Provide specific examples when possible.
4. Reflect on the use of study guides in your content area. Do you agree or disagree with the following statements:

    a. Study guides provide students with direction and organization for their reading.
    b. Study guides give students the chance to respond to texts in meaningful ways.
    c. Study guides are not meant to be used every day or with every reading assignment; that would reduce their effectiveness.
    d. Levels of comprehension are not as discrete as they may seem, but their division and treatment as separate entities are necessary to address each aspect of comprehension.
    e. If students become used to the support study guides offer, they will always be teacher-dependent.

5. If a study guide is offered as an independent activity, students will get little out of it; failure will be just as frequent as with the traditional question-laden worksheet. Students need to be led through the use of study guides, sometimes working independently, sometimes working together. Reflect on the role of the content teacher in designing and using study guides for learning.

HANDS-ON

1. Choose a brief content area reading selection. Working as two groups, one group should prepare a selective reading guide, and the other a concept guide on the material. Meet together to share the completed products and to discuss the ways in which they are similar and dissimilar and the advantages and disadvantages of each.
2. Working in small groups or with a partner, prepare pattern guides for each of the major types of expository text organization (cause and effect, comparison and contrast, description, sequence, and problem and solution). Follow the guidelines for construction given in this chapter. The organizational pattern should guide your design and usage of the guide, so each will vary in appearance. Compare and contrast the resulting guides and frames of mind, and try to determine if one is better than the others for a particular content or organizational pattern.
3. Work together to create a three-level guide for an article from an electronic media source, a newspaper, or an educational journal. Follow the guidelines for construction presented in this chapter.

SUGGESTED READINGS

Armstrong, D. P., Patberg, J., & Dewitz, P. (1988). Reading guides: Helping students understand. *Journal of Reading, 31,* 532–541.

Bean, T. W., & Ericson, B. O. (1989). Text previews and three-level study guides for content area critical reading. *Journal of Reading, 32,* 337–341.

Bowd, A., McDougall, D., & Yewchuk, C. (1998). Learning: cognitive processes. In *Educational psychology for Canadian teachers* (Toronto: Harcourt Brace), pp. 106–133.

Brown, A. L., & Campione, J. C. (1994). Guided discovery in a community of learners. In K. McGilly (Ed.), *Classroom lessons: Integrating cognitive theory and classroom practice.* Cambridge, MA: MIT Press.

Brownlie, F., & Close, S. (1992). *Beyond chalk and talk: Collaborative strategies for the middle and high school years.* Markham, ON: Pembroke Publishers.

Davey, B. (1986). Using textbook activity guides to help students learn from textbooks. *Journal of Reading, 29,* 489–494.

Guthrie, J. T., McGough, K., Bennett, L., & Rice, M. E. (1996). Concept-oriented reading instruction: An integrated curriculum to develop motivations and strategies for reading. In L. Baker, P. Afflerbach, & D. Reinking (Eds.), *Developing engaged readers in school and home communities.* Hillsdale, NJ: Erlbaum.

Herber, H. L. (1978). Levels of comprehension. In *Teaching reading in content areas* (2nd ed.). Upper Saddle River, NJ: Prentice Hall.

Herber, H. L. (1985). Levels of comprehension: An instructional strategy for guiding students' reading. In T. Harris, & E. Cooper (Eds.), *Reading, thinking, and concept development: Strategies for the classroom.* New York: College Entrance Examination Board.

Mooney, M. (1995). Guided reading: The reader in control. *Teaching PreK–8, 25,* 54–58.

Olson, M., & Longnion, B. (1982). Pattern guides: A workable alternative for content teachers. *Journal of Reading, 25,* 736–741.

Rosenshine, B., & Meister, C. (1992). The use of scaffolds for teaching higher-level cognitive strategies. *Educational Leadership, 49*(7), 26–33.

Wood, K. D., Lapp, D., & Flood, J. (1992). *Guiding readers through text: A review of study guides.* Newark, DE: International Reading Association.

chapter eleven

Struggling Readers

Gzowski gave me the opportunity to continue. He showed me that perseverance works and that there was hope in learning. Peter Gzowski gave learners hope through literacy and in turn literacy allowed him to be humble.

–Murd Nicholson (Yukon Learner Representative to the Movement for Canadian Literacy)

ORGANIZING PRINCIPLE

Sometimes learning to read isn't easy. Neither is learning with academic texts. Students often struggle with reading in the content areas. When Peter Gzowski, famous Canadian broadcaster, turned his interests to the development of literacy, he had little idea of how many lives he would touch. When he died on January 24, 2002, the outpouring of gratitude and affection, especially from struggling readers, may well have made Gzowski blush. On websites such as that of the Movement for Canadian Literacy (http://www.literacy.ca), newly skilled readers and writers were able to express themselves, as Murd Nicholson does above, and share their abilities in an electronic medium.

Struggling learners often lack strategies—the kinds of reading strategies necessary to learn effectively with text. One of the realities facing teachers across all content areas today is that many students make little use of reading as a tool for learning. Either they read academic texts superficially or find ways to circumvent the process altogether. Those people who listened to Peter Gzowski on the radio were learning about Canada through engagement with an oral text, and our society values this way of gaining knowledge; however, the ability to read well enough to learn with print texts is another one of the keys to independent and lifelong learning. Gzowski became involved with campaigns to raise money to support reading and writing, despite his already established role in radio communication.

When students struggle with reading, teachers need to become coaches. Through our instructional support and guidance, we can build students' confidence and competence as readers by showing them how to think strategically about reading and how to use reading strategies to learn with text. By using *explanation*, *modelling*, *practice*, and *application* (the cornerstones of explicit instruction), we can help struggling students develop alternatives to feeling helpless during reading. When teachers assume the role of coach, they make explicit what good readers do to cope with the kinds of comprehension problems they encounter in academic texts.

When asked, "What do you teach?" do you respond, "I teach social studies (or mathematics or science or physical education or any one of the subject areas in the school curriculum)?" Or do you say, "I teach students?" The distinction is a subtle but important one. Today's teacher is a teacher of all kinds of students, with different language and cultural backgrounds and academic needs. Struggling readers need teachers who know as much and care as much about their students as their subject matter.

How can teachers be responsive to the literacy needs of struggling readers while maintaining high standards for content learning? The organizing principle of this chapter builds on teachers' ability to provide explicit instruction in the development and use of reading strategies: **one of the important ways that teachers respond to the literacy needs of struggling readers is to scaffold instruction so that students become aware of and competent with strategies that support learning with text.**

CHAPTER OVERVIEW

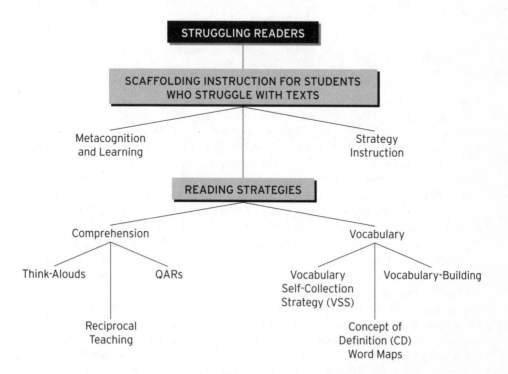

FRAME OF MIND

1. Why are struggling readers at risk in text learning situations?

2. How can a teacher scaffold instruction in ways that make students aware of and competent in the use of strategies for text learning?

3. What is *metacognition*, and why is it important for struggling readers to develop metacognitive knowledge and skills?

4. How do think-alouds, QARs, and reciprocal teaching provide instructional support for students who have difficulty answering questions and comprehending text?

5. How do concept of definition (CD), vocabulary self-selection (VSS), and vocabulary-building strategies help students develop strategies for understanding unfamiliar concepts encountered during reading?

Take a moment to study and reflect on the important ideas and relationships depicted in the chapter overview. Use the Frame of Mind questions, along with the chapter overview, to anticipate the content and structure of the chapter. Before reading, ask yourself, "How knowledgeable am I about the ideas targeted in the overview? What do I expect to learn from my study of this chapter?"

Even the best of readers will struggle with reading at some time, in some place, with some text. A good reader on occasion will get lost in the author's line of reasoning, become confused by the way the text is organized, or run into unknown words that are difficult to pronounce let alone define. Perhaps main ideas are too difficult to grasp or the reader simply lacks prior knowledge to make connections to the important ideas in the text. Regardless of the comprehension problem, often it's only temporary. The difference between good readers and poor readers is that when good readers struggle with text, they know what to do to get out of trouble. When a text becomes confusing or doesn't make sense, good readers recognize that they have a repertoire of reading strategies at their command that they can use to work themselves out of the difficulty.

Throughout this book, we have argued that the real value of reading lies in its uses. Whether we use reading to enter into the imaginative world of fiction; learn with academic texts; meet workplace demands; acquire insight and knowledge about people, places, and things; or understand a graphic on a website, readers, to be successful, must adapt their skills and strategies to meet the comprehension demands of a particular task at hand. Reading isn't as much a struggle as it is a challenge for those readers who know what to do.

We developed the text passage in Box 11.1 to demonstrate how easy it is for good readers to experience what it means to struggle with reading. More often than not, a good reader will approach the passage as a challenge and use a repertoire of reading strategies to construct meaning from the text. The passage, in the form of a short parable, poses a particular problem for readers as it tells the story of a king with kind but misguided intentions.

As you read the story, did the substitution of consonants *x*, *z*, *q*, and *v* for the vowels *e*, *a*, *o*, and *i* cause you to struggle as a reader? Probably so. The progressive substitution of the consonants for vowels undoubtedly slowed down your *reading fluency*—the ability to read in a smooth, conversational manner—and may even have affected your accuracy in recognizing some words. Just think about some of the students in classrooms today who struggle with reading. They may experience difficulty because they read in a slow and halt-

BOX 11.1	**The Kingdom of Kay Oss**

Once in the land of Serenity, there ruled a king called Kay Oss. The king wanted to be liked by all of his people. Onx day thx bxnxvolxnt dxspot dxcidxd that no onx in thx country would bx rxsponsiblx for anything. So hx dxcrxxd zn xnd to work in his kingdom.

Zll of thx workxrs rxstxd from thxvr dzvly lzbours. "Blxss Kvng Kzy Oss," thxy xxclzvmxd! Thx fzrmxrs dvdn't hzrvxst thx crops. Thx Kvng's zrmy dvsbzndxd. Zll of thx mxrchznts vn thx kvngdom wxnt on zn xxtxndxd vzcztvon to thx Fzr Xzst. Thx shop ownxrs hung svgns on thxvr doors thzt szvd, "Gonx Fvshvng Vndxfvnvtxly."

Nqw thx lzw mzkxrs vn thx lznd of Sxrxnvty wxrx vxry wvsx. But zs wvsx zs thxy wxrx, thxy dvd nqt wznt tq zct zgzvnst thx kvng's wvshxs. Xvxn thxy stqppxd wqrkvng! So thx kvng dxcvdxd thzt thx bxst fqrm qf gqvxrnmxnt wzs nqnx zt zll. Zs tvmx wxnt qn, thx lznd of Sxrxnvty bxgzn tq splvt zt thx sxzms znd vt lqqkxd lvkx thvs: bcx dqufghj klzm nqxp qqt rqst vqxwxxz bqxc dqf ghzj kqlxmmnxp.

ing manner, word-by-word, and have trouble recognizing words quickly and accurately. They spend so much time and attention on trying to "say the words" that comprehension suffers and, as a result, the reading process breaks down for them.

Did you find this the case with the King Kay Oss passage? Probably not. Even though the substitution of consonants for vowels slowed down your rate of reading, chances are you were still able to comprehend the passage and construct meaning from it. This is because skilled readers do not use a single strategy to make sense of text. They know how to search for and make use of different types of information to construct meaning. Skilled readers have at their command *multiple strategies* for reading.

For example, as you read about King Kay Oss, you probably made some use of information clues among the letter/sound associations in the passage. Part of your ability to read "Onx day thx bxnxvolxnt dxspot dxcidxd ... " depended on the recognition of some of the consonants' and vowels' letter/sound associations that were not altered in the passage. However, these letter/sound associations provided no clues to meaning. In order to construct meaning, you had to make use of other types of information in the passage. Your prior knowledge, including knowledge of syntax and grammatical relationships, helped you anticipate some of the words in the passage that "had to come next" in order to sound like language. For instance, as you read, "Zs tvmx, _____ _____" you probably predicted that "went" and "on" would follow.

Moreover, skilled readers use prior knowledge to anticipate the meaning of known words or construct meaning for unknown words. Take another look at the third paragraph in the passage. As you read, "As time went on, the land of Serenity began to split at the seams and it looked like this:" you may have made the inference that "it" referred to Serenity and "this" referred to the string of unknown words that followed. These words convey no letter/sound or grammatical clues. They represent total confusion and disorder!

By analogy, then, you may have inferred that the land of Serenity looked like it was in a state of total confusion and disorder much like the string of unknown words. Some skilled readers may even have concluded that there is a word to describe what happened in Serenity a long time ago. The word is *chaos*.

The expression *struggling reader* often refers to low-achieving students who have major difficulties with reading. They lack fluency, have trouble decoding polysyllabic words, and make little sense of what they read. As we suggested in Chapter 1, low-achieving students who struggle with reading are genuine in their resistance to any type of learning that involves text. Teachers who have worked with low-achieving students are no strangers to resistant learners. All too often low-achievers are overage, underprepared, and weighed down with emotional problems. They score low on proficiency tests and are tracked in basic classes for most of their academic lives.

How students achieve as readers reflects such factors as motivation, self-concept, prior knowledge, and the ability to use language to learn. For some struggling students, reading is a painful reminder of a system of schooling that has failed them. They wage a continual battle with reading as an academic activity. The failure to learn to read effectively has contributed to these students' disenchantment with and alienation from school. Although struggling readers may have developed some reading skills and strategies, these are often inappropriate for the comprehension demands inherent in potentially difficult texts. As a result, their participation in reading-related activities, such as writing or discussion, is marginal. Getting through reading assignments to answer homework questions is often the only reason to read, if they read at all.

Learned helplessness is an expression often associated with the struggling reader. It refers to students' perceptions of themselves as being unable to overcome failure. Unsuccessful readers usually sabotage their efforts to read by believing that they can't succeed at tasks that require reading. They struggle because they command a limited repertoire of strategies, lacking knowledge of and control over the procedural routines needed to engage in meaningful transactions with texts. Rarely do struggling readers consider what their role should be as readers. Rather than take an active role in constructing meaning, they often remain passive and disengaged.

Not only do struggling readers lack competence with reading skills and strategies, but they also lack confidence in themselves to make meaning with texts. They believe that they can't learn from reading. As a result, they are often ambivalent about the act of reading and fail to value what reading can do for them. For one reason or another, struggling readers have alienated themselves from the world of print.

Because reading is situational and depends on the task at hand, low-achieving students may not be the only ones who struggle with reading. Average and above-average students, who are on a fast track to go to university or college, might also struggle with reading. Often these students go through the motions but are likely to conceal some of their difficulties with reading. Although they may have developed reading fluency, the ability to read print smoothly and accurately, average and above-average students who struggle as readers usually don't know what to do with texts beyond just saying the words. They appear *skillful* in the mechanics of reading but aren't *strategic* enough in their ability to handle the comprehension demands inherent in the texts that they are reading.

Students who struggle with texts, regardless of ability level, often get lost in a maze of words as they sit down with a text assignment or scroll through an electronic page on a computer screen. The text doesn't make sense to them in ways that permit them to think deeply about ideas encountered during reading. Reading is a strategic act, which is another way of saying that successful readers use *cognitive and metacognitive strategies* so that they can understand, respond to, and even question and challenge the author's ideas. Throughout the chapters in Part 2 of this book, we have examined instructional strategies that help all readers think and learn with text. Nevertheless, students who struggle continually with text often need explicit instruction in the development and use of strategies. They struggle with reading, writing, and talking to learn content in classrooms. One of the dilemmas students face is that few effectively learn how and when to use strategies to construct meaning during tasks that require meaning.

SCAFFOLDING INSTRUCTION FOR STUDENTS WHO STRUGGLE WITH TEXTS

In Chapter 1, we introduced the concept of instructional scaffolding as a way of guiding students in their development as independent learners. Scaffolding, as you may recall, serves to support students as they engage in various tasks that require reading, writing, and discussion. It gives them a better chance to be successful in handling the linguistic and conceptual demands inherent in content area texts than if they are left to their own devices. Providing literacy supports for students, however, doesn't necessarily mean telling them, "You should do it this way in my class." Scaffolding instruction goes beyond imperatives. A struggling reader needs not only exhortation but also a good model or two. A key feature of instructional scaffolding is the demonstration and modelling of strategies that students need to be successful with content area texts. To scaffold instruction effectively, teachers need to understand the role that metacognition plays in comprehension and learning.

Metacognition and Learning

Metacognition involves awareness of, knowledge about, regulation of, and ability to control one's own cognitive processes (Brown, Bransford, Ferrara, & Campione 1983; Flavell 1976, 1981). Simply, it is our ability to think about and control our own learning.

Metacognition, as it applies to reading, has two components. The first is metacognitive *knowledge*; the second is *regulation*. Metacognitive knowledge includes self-knowledge and task knowledge. Self-knowledge is the knowledge students have about themselves as learners. Task knowledge is the knowledge they have about the skills, strategies, and resources necessary for the performance of cognitive tasks. The second component, self-regulation, involves the ability to monitor and regulate comprehension through strategies and attitudes that capitalize on metacognitive knowledge (Baker & Brown 1984). Self- and task knowledge and self-regulation are tandem concepts. The former are prerequisites for the latter. Together, self-knowledge, task knowledge, and self-regulation help explain how maturing readers can begin to assume the lion's share of the responsibility for their own learning.

As teachers, we have metacognition in our particular subject areas. Translating our metacognition into lessons that students understand is the crux of content area teaching. Science teachers, for example, have a metacognition of science. They have knowledge about themselves as scientists; they have knowledge of the tasks of science; and they have the ability to monitor and regulate themselves when conducting experiments, writing results, or reading technical material. Science teachers can monitor and regulate themselves because they know how to perform a set of core process strategies. They know how to observe, classify, compare, measure, describe, organize information, predict, infer, formulate hypotheses, interpret data, communicate, experiment, and draw conclusions. These are the same strategies a student taking a science course is expected to learn. A science teacher's job is to get students to think like scientists. The best way for students to learn to think like scientists is to learn to read, experiment, and write like scientists (L. Baker 1991).

Showing students how to think like scientists, historians, literary critics, mathematicians, health care professionals, artists, or auto mechanics puts them on the road to independent learning. To be independent learners, students need to know the whats, whys, hows, and whens of strategic reading and thinking. They should know enough to be able to recognize the importance of (1) using a variety of strategies to facilitate comprehension and learning, (2) analyzing the reading task before them, (3) reflecting on what they know or don't know about the material to be read, and (4) devising plans for successfully completing the reading and for evaluating and checking their progress in accomplishing the task (Brown 1978).

Teachers need to know if students know enough about their own reading and learning strategies to approach content area text assignments flexibly and adaptively. Different text assignments may pose different problems for the reader to solve. For this reason, when assigned text material, students must be aware of the nature of the reading task and the way to handle it. Is the student sophisticated enough to ask questions about the reading task? To make plans for reading? To use and adapt strategies to meet the demands of the text assignment? Or does a student who struggles with text approach every text assignment in the same manner—plowing through with little notion of why, when, or how to read the material? Plowing through cumbersome text material only once is more than students who struggle with reading can cope. The prospect of rereading or reviewing isn't a realistic option for them. However, teachers are in a position to show students that working with the material doesn't necessarily entail the agony of slow, tedious reading.

To be in command of their own reading, students must know what to do when they run into trouble. This is what comprehension monitoring and self-regulation are all about. Do students have a repertoire of strategies within reach to get out of trouble if they become confused or misunderstand what they are reading?

The experienced reader responds to situations in text in much the same way that the experienced driver responds to situations on the road. Reading and driving become fairly automatic processes until something happens. As Milton (1982) notes, "Everything is fine for experienced drivers as long as they are in familiar territory, the car operates smoothly, they encounter no threat from other drivers, weather, road conditions, or traffic.... But, let even one factor become problematic, and drivers shift more attention to the process of driving" (p. 23).

And so it goes for the reader who suddenly gets into trouble with a text assignment. Attention shifts from automatic processing to strategies that will help learners work their way out of a jam. The problem encountered may parallel the driver's: unfamiliar territory or getting temporarily lost. However, in the learner's case, it is the text, procedure, or problem that is unfamiliar and difficult. It doesn't take much to get lost in the author's line of reasoning, the text organization, the scientific process, or a mathematical formula.

Other problems that may disrupt smooth reading are a concept too difficult to grasp, word identification, or the inability to identify the important ideas in the text. These problems represent major roadblocks that, if left unattended, may hamper the reader's attempts to get the gist of the text passage or to construct meaning. It is in problem situations such as these that metacognitive processes play an important role in learning with text.

Linda Baker (1991) recommends six questions for students to ask themselves when they read to help monitor their comprehension:

1. Are there any words I don't understand?
2. Is there any information that doesn't agree with what I already know?
3. Are there any ideas that don't fit together because I can't tell who or what is being talked about?
4. Are there any ideas that don't fit together because I can't tell how the ideas are related?
5. Are there any ideas that don't fit together because I think the ideas are contradictory?
6. Is there any information missing or not clearly explained? (p. 10)

One way to help struggling readers think about what they do when they read is to have them take the inventory in Box 11.2 on pages 314 and 315. Vincent Miholic (1994) developed the inventory from the body of research on metacognitive strategies. "Correct" responses to each item on the inventory are marked with a +, whereas "incorrect" responses are marked with a –. Teachers who use the inventory with a class should be sure to cover both the + and – rows.

Not only does the inventory pique students' curiosity about strategic learning, but it also gives them a concrete idea of important strategies. Miholic (1994) suggests that the inventory invites students to become aware of the knowledge they need in order to apply strategies to various text-learning situations. In addition, it serves as a vehicle for modelling and demonstration. He warns against emphasizing scores on the inventory. It should be used more as a springboard to create strategy awareness through discussion.

Strategy Instruction

Strategy instruction helps students who struggle with text become aware of, use, and develop control over learning strategies (Brown & Palincsar 1984). Explicit teaching provides an alternative to blind instruction. In blind instructional situations, students are taught what to do, but this is where instruction usually ends. Although directed to make use of a set of procedures that will improve reading and studying, students seldom grasp the rationale or payoff underlying a particular strategy. As a result, they attempt to use the strategy with little basis for evaluating its success or monitoring its effectiveness. Explicit instruction, however, attempts not only to show students *what* to do, but also *why*, *how*, and *when*. Pearson (1982) concludes that such instruction helps "students develop independent strategies for coping with the kinds of comprehension problems they are asked to solve in their lives in schools" (p. 22).

Strategy instruction has four components: *assessment, awareness, modelling and demonstration*, and *application*. By way of analogy, teaching students to be strategic readers provides experiences similar to those needed by athletes who are in training. To perform well with texts, students must understand the rules, rehearse, work on technique, and practise. A coach (the teacher) is needed to provide feedback, guide, inspire, and share the knowledge and experiences that she or he possesses.

BOX 11.2	**Metacognitive Reading Awareness Inventory**

There's more than one way to cope when you run into difficulties in your reading. Which ways are best? Under each question here, put a checkmark beside *all* the responses you think are effective.

1. What do you do if you encounter a word and you don't know what it means?
   + a.   Use the words around it to figure it out.
   + b.   Use an outside source, such as a dictionary or expert.
   + c.   Temporarily ignore it and wait for clarification.
   − d.   Sound it out.

2. What do you do if you don't know what an entire sentence means?
   + a.   Read it again.
   − b.   Sound out all the difficult words.
   + c.   Think about the other sentences in the paragraph.
   − d.   Disregard it completely.

3. If you are reading science or social studies material, what would you do to remember the important information you've read?
   − a.   Skip parts you don't understand.
   + b.   Ask yourself questions about the important ideas.
   + c.   Realize you need to remember one point rather than another.
   + d.   Relate it to something you already know.

4. Before you start to read, what kind of plans do you make to help you read better?
   − a.   No specific plan is needed; just start reading toward completion of the assignment.
   + b.   Think about what you know about the subject.
   + c.   Think about why you are reading.
   − d.   Make sure the entire reading can be finished in as short a period of time as possible.

5. Why would you go back and read an entire passage over again?
   + a.   You didn't understand it.
   − b.   To clarify a specific or supporting idea.
   + c.   It seemed important to remember.
   + d.   To underline or summarize for study.

Assess What Students Know How to Do The assessment component of strategy instruction is tryout time. It gives the teacher an opportunity to determine the degree of knowledge the students have about a strategy under discussion. Moreover, assessment yields insight into how well the students use a strategy to handle a reading task. For these reasons, assessing the use of a strategy should occur in as natural a context as possible. Assessment can usually be accomplished within a single class period if these steps are followed:

6. Knowing that you don't understand a particular sentence while reading involves understanding that

+   a.   the reader may not have developed adequate links or associations for new words or concepts introduced in the sentence.
+   b.   the writer may not have conveyed the ideas clearly.
+   c.   two sentences may purposely contradict each other.
−   d.   finding meaning for the sentence needlessly slows down the reader.

7. As you read a textbook, which of these do you do?

+   a.   Adjust your pace depending on the difficulty of the material.
−   b.   Generally, read at a constant, steady pace.
−   c.   Skip the parts you don't understand.
+   d.   Continually make predictions about what you are reading.

8. While you read, which of these are important?

+   a.   Know when you know and when you don't know key ideas.
+   b.   Know what it is that you know in relation to what is being read.
+   c.   Know that confusing text is common and usually can be ignored.
−   d.   Know that different strategies can be used to aid understanding.

9. When you come across a part of the text that is confusing, what do you do?

+   a.   Keep on reading until the text is clarified.
+   b.   Read ahead and then look back if the text is still unclear.
+   c.   Skip those sections completely; they are usually not important.
−   d.   Check to see if the ideas expressed are consistent with one another.

10. When you come across a part of the text that is confusing, what do you do?

+   a.   Almost all of the sentences are important; otherwise, they wouldn't be there.
+   b.   The sentences that contain the important details or facts.
+   c.   The sentences that are directly related to the main idea.
−   d.   The ones that contain the most details.

Source: From Vincent Miholic, "An Inventory to Pique Students' Metacognitive Awareness" (1994). *Journal of Reading, 38*(2), 84–86. Reprinted with permission of the author and the International Reading Association.

1. *Assign students a text passage of approximately 1000–1500 words.* The selection should take most students 10 to 15 minutes to read.

2. *Direct students to use a particular strategy.* For example, suppose the strategy involves writing a summary of a text selection. Simply ask students to do the things they normally do to read a passage and then write a summary of it. Allow adequate time to complete the task.

3. *Observe the use of the strategy.* Note what students do. Do they underline or mark important ideas as they read? Do they appear to skim the material first to get a general idea of what to expect? What do they do when actually constructing the summary?

4. *Ask students to respond in writing to several key questions about the use of the strategy.* For example, "What did you do to summarize the passage? What did you do to find the main ideas? Did you find summarizing easy or difficult? Why?"

Create Strategy Awareness Assessment is a springboard to making students aware of the *why* and *how* of a study strategy. During the awareness step, a give-and-take exchange of ideas takes place between teacher and students. As a result, students should recognize the *rationale* and *process* behind the use of a strategy. To make students more aware of a learning strategy, consider the following activities:

1. *Discuss the assessment.* Use your observations and students' reflective responses to the written questions.

2. *Set the stage by leading a discussion of* why *the strategy is useful.* What is the payoff for students? How does it improve learning?

3. *Engage in activities that define the rules, guidelines, or procedures for being successful with the strategy.*

4. *Have students experience using the strategy.* They can practise the rules or procedures on a short selection from the textbook.

Awareness provides students with a clear picture of the learning strategy. The *why* and *how* are solidly introduced, and the road has been paved for more intensive modelling and demonstration of the strategy.

Model and Demonstrate Strategies Once the *why* and a beginning sense of the *how* are established, the students should receive careful follow-up in the use of the strategy. Follow-up sessions are characterized by demonstration through teacher modelling, explanations, practice, reinforcement of the rules or procedures, and more practice. The students progress from easy to harder practice situations, and from shorter to longer text selections. The following activities are recommended:

1. *Use an overhead transparency to review the steps students should follow.*

2. *Demonstrate the strategy.* Walk students through the steps. Provide explanations. Raise questions about the procedures.

3. *As part of a demonstration, initiate a think-aloud procedure to model how to use the strategy.* By thinking aloud, the teacher shares with the students the thinking processes he or she uses in applying the strategy. Thinking aloud is often accomplished by reading a passage out loud and stopping at key points in the text to ask questions or provide prompts. The questions and prompts mirror the critical thinking required to apply the strategy. Once students are familiar with the think-aloud procedure, encourage them to demonstrate and use it during practice sessions. Later in the chapter we explain in more detail the role that think-alouds play in modelling strategies.

4. *Reinforce and practice the strategy.* Use trial runs with short selections from the textbook. Debrief the students with questions after each trial run: Did they follow the steps? How successful were they? What caused them difficulty? Have them make

learning-log entries. Often, a short quiz following a trial run shows students how much they learned and remembered as a result of using the study strategy.

The demonstration sessions are designed to provide experience with the strategy. Students should reach a point where they have internalized the steps and feel in control of the strategy.

Apply Strategies The preceding components of strategy instruction should provide enough practice for students to know *why*, *how*, and *when* to use the study strategies that have been targeted by the teacher for emphasis. Once students have made generalizations about strategy use, regular class assignments should encourage its application. Rather than assign a text selection accompanied by questions to be answered for homework, frame the assignment so that students will have to apply certain study strategies.

COMPREHENSION STRATEGIES

Readers who struggle with texts are usually unaware of strategies that will help them construct meaning. Teachers can use *think-alouds*, *reciprocal teaching*, and *question–answer relationships (QARs)* to scaffold students' use of comprehension strategies.

Using Think-Alouds to Model Comprehension Strategies

In think-alouds, teachers make their thinking explicit by verbalizing their thoughts while reading orally. Davey (1983) explains that this process helps readers clarify their understanding of reading and their understanding of how to use strategies. Students will more clearly understand the strategies after a teacher uses think-alouds because they can see how a mind actively responds to thinking through trouble spots and constructing meaning from the text.

Davey (1983) suggests five basic steps when using think-alouds. First, select passages to read aloud that contain points of difficulty, ambiguities, contradictions, or unknown words. Second, while orally reading and modelling thinking aloud, have students follow silently and listen to how trouble spots are thought through. Third, have students work with partners to practise think-alouds by taking turns reading short, carefully prepared passages and sharing thoughts. Fourth, have students practise independently, using a checklist as shown in Figure 11.1 to involve all students while verifying use of the procedures. Finally,

While I was reading, how did I do? (Put an X in the appropriate column.)				
	Not very much	A little bit	Much of the time	All of the time
Made predictions	_____	_____	_____	_____
Formed pictures	_____	_____	_____	_____
Used "like-a"	_____	_____	_____	_____
Found problems	_____	_____	_____	_____
Used fix-ups	_____	_____	_____	_____

FIGURE 11.1   **Checklist for Self-Evaluation of Think-Alouds**

Source: From Beth Davey, "Think Aloud–Modeling the Cognitive Processes of Reading Comprehension" (1983, October). *Journal of Reading, 27*(1), 44–47. Copyright © 1983 by the International Reading Association. All rights reserved. Used by permission of the International Reading Association.

to provide for transfer, integrate practice with other lessons, and provide occasional demonstrations of how, why, and when to use think-alouds. Five points can be made during think-alouds:

1. *Students should develop hypotheses by making predictions.*
2. *Students should develop images by describing pictures forming in their heads from the information being read.*
3. *Students should link new information with prior knowledge by sharing analogies.*
4. *Students should monitor comprehension by verbalizing a confusing point.*
5. *Students should regulate comprehension by demonstrating strategies.*

Let's look at how each of these points can be modelled in a middle school earth science class.

Develop Hypotheses by Making Predictions Teachers might model how to develop hypotheses by making predictions from the title of a chapter or from subheadings within the chapter. Suppose you were teaching with an earth science text. You might say, "From the heading 'How Minerals Are Used,' I predict that this section will tell about things that are made out of different minerals." The text continues:

> Some of the most valuable minerals are found in ores. An *ore* is a mineral resource mined for profit. For example, bauxite (BAWK-sight) is an ore from which aluminum is taken. Iron is obtained from the ore called hematite (HEE-muh-tight). Bauxite and hematite are metallic minerals.
>
> Metallic minerals are metals or ores of metals. Gold, iron, and aluminum are examples of metals. Metals are important because of their many useful properties.
>
> One useful property of many metals is malleability (mal-ee-uh-BIL-uh-tee). *Malleability* is the ability to be hammered without breaking. Malleability allows a metal to be hammered into thin sheets.

Develop Images To model how to develop imaging, at this point you might stop and say, "I have a picture in my head from a scene I saw in a movie about the Old West. I see a blacksmith pumping bellows in a forge to heat up an iron horseshoe. When the iron turns a reddish orange, he picks it up with his tongs, and he hammers. The sparks fly, but slowly the horseshoe changes shape to fit the horse's hoof." The text continues:

> Another property of many metals is ductility (duk-TIL-uh-tee). *Ductility* is the ability to be pulled and stretched without breaking. This property allows a metal to be pulled into thin wires.

Share Analogies To model how to link new information with prior knowledge, you might share the following analogies. "This is like a time when I tried to eat a piece of pizza with extra cheese. Every time I took a bite, the cheese kept stretching and stretching into these long strings. It is also like a time when I went to a fair and watched people make taffy. They got this glob of candy and put it on a machine that just kept pulling and stretching the taffy, but it never broke." The text continues:

> Metals share other properties as well. All metals conduct heat and electricity. Electrical appliances and machines need metals to conduct electricity. In addition, all metals have a shiny, metallic lustre.

Monitor Comprehension To model how to monitor comprehension, you can verbalize a confusing point: "This is telling me that metals have a metallic lustre. I don't know what that is. I'm also confused because I thought this section was going to be about things that are made out of different minerals. This is different from what I expected."

Regulate Comprehension To model how to correct lagging comprehension, you can demonstrate a strategy: "I'm confused about what *metallic lustre* means, and I don't know why the authors are talking about this when I expected them to talk about stuff made out of minerals. Maybe if I ignore the term *metallic lustre* and keep on reading, I'll be able to make some connections to what I expected and figure it all out." The text continues:

> Very shiny metals, like chromium, are often used for decorative purposes. Many metals are also strong. Titanium (tigh-TAY-nee-um), magnesium (mag-NEE-zee-um), and aluminum are metals that are both strong and lightweight. These properties make them ideal building materials for jet planes and spacecraft.

"Oh, they're talking about properties of metals that make them especially good for making certain things, like aluminum for jets because it is strong and lightweight. Now I understand why they're talking about properties. I'll bet chrome and chromium are just about the same, because I know chrome is the shiny stuff on cars. I think *metallic lustre* must mean something like shiny because chromium reminds me of chrome."

Think-alouds are best used at the beginning of lessons to help students learn the whats and hows of constructing meaning with text. The next teaching strategy, *reciprocal teaching*, is an excellent follow-up to think-alouds. Reciprocal teaching helps students learn how to apply the strategy learned during a think-aloud so that they can understand the author's message.

Using Reciprocal Teaching to Model Comprehension Strategies

When using reciprocal teaching, you model how to use four comprehension activities (generating questions, summarizing, predicting, and clarifying) while leading a dialogue (Palinscar & Brown 1984). Then students take turns assuming the teacher's role. A key to the effectiveness of this strategy is adjusting the task demand to support the students when difficulty occurs. That is, when students experience difficulty, you provide assistance by lowering the demands of the task. As the process goes on, you slowly withdraw support so that students continue learning. Reciprocal teaching lessons have two phases. The first phase has five steps:

1. *Find text selections that demonstrate the four comprehension activities.*
2. *Generate appropriate questions.*
3. *Generate predictions about each selection.*
4. *Locate summarizing sentences and develop summaries for each selection.*
5. *Note difficult vocabulary and concepts.*

In the second phase, decisions are made about which comprehension activities to teach, based on the students' needs. It also helps determine students' present facility with the activities so that you are prepared to give needed support during the process. Once students are familiar with more than one strategy, reciprocal teaching can be used to model the decision-making process about which strategy to use. Reciprocal teaching can also be used to check whether the comprehension breakdown has been repaired and if not, why not.

A grade 7 social studies teacher recognized that his students were having difficulty understanding important terms in their text that were central to understanding the author's message. He developed a lesson that combined thinking aloud and reciprocal teaching. The first part of his lesson used think-alouds for focusing on vocabulary when lack of understanding of words caused comprehension to break down. He then used reciprocal teaching to scaffold the reasoning process he had modelled during the think-aloud phase of his lesson.

His first steps were to activate prior knowledge, to have students make predictions about the selection, to tell what reasoning process was going to be taught, to tell why the reasoning process was important, and to discuss when it would be used:

Teacher: Today we're going to read about the Halifax Explosion of 1917. How many of you have heard of the explosion? [Students respond.] Look at the pictures at the bottom of page 195. What do you see in the photographs?

Student: There are a whole bunch of children's pictures on top of a picture of a wrecked train and a lot of other rubble in the background.

Teacher: Right. Look at page 194. What is the title of this article?

Student: "The day war came to Halifax."

Teacher: Good. Now there's something I want you to know about this selection. There are some new terms that are important for you to figure out so that you can understand the author's message. Before we read the selection, I'm going to teach you how to figure them out so that when you come to them, you'll be able to figure them out and understand the author's message on your own.

His second step was to think out loud to model *when* the reasoning process should be used:

Teacher: I'm going to pretend that I don't know a term in the first sentence of this article. Watch what happens. "Halifax—the doomed ships steamed unwaveringly toward collision." Hmmm. [Teacher pretends he doesn't understand the term *unwaveringly*.] I'll skip it for now because the rest of the sentence should help me understand what it means. "Like two trains on the same narrow track." Hmmm. Now, I know trains headed toward each other will collide unless they switch tracks. "Or so it seemed to Barbara Orr, gazing out her front window at the morning traffic in the harbour below." Okay, so now I think the author is going to tell me a story to illustrate what *unwaveringly* means when you are talking about ships instead of trains, but I still don't really know what *unwaveringly* means.

His third step was to think out loud *how* to use the reasoning process to repair the comprehension breakdown:

Teacher: I'll sound it out. I can see the word *waver*, and the other parts are easy to say, so un-waver-ing-ly. That still doesn't tell me what it means. Let's see, *waver* must have something to do with wave—like waves on a beach or radio waves that are curved. [Teacher reads sentences over again.] And I know from language arts class that *un* at the beginning of a word means *not*. So maybe the ships are not curving away from each other, but going straight for each other, so they hit. That makes sense now.

His fourth step was to check how the students interpreted the information by asking them to tell or show when and how to use the reasoning process:

Teacher: Now, how would you figure out the hard word in this sentence?

Student: At first I'd keep on reading because it might tell you later.

Teacher: That's good. Sometimes when you read a little further, you are given a definition. What else did I think about when that didn't work?

Student: Sounding out the word.

Teacher: Sometimes that helps, too, but there is something else to try. Watch and listen again. [Repeat procedure with another term to demonstrate use of root words and prefixes.]

His fifth step was to review the title and the pictures and ask for predictions before reading:

Teacher: Now we're going to read the selection about the Halifax explosion. Look at the pictures on pages 197, 199, and 200; then read the title again. In your own words, predict what you think this selection is about. What do you expect to learn? [Students make predictions; teacher gives positive reinforcement for making predictions, jots them on the board, and then summarizes predictions.]

Teacher: Now remember, there are difficult terms in this selection, so when you come to one, try to figure it out the way I showed you.

His sixth step was to read aloud a small portion of the text.

His seventh step was to ask a question about the content, invite students to answer, and then ask individuals to share questions they had generated:

Teacher: My question is, "Why did the ships fail to change course when they were on a collision course?"

Student: Because they were stubborn.

Teacher: Who was stubborn?

Student: The captains of the ships.

Teacher: Correct. Does anyone else have a question?

His eighth step was to summarize what had been read by identifying the gist of that section and how he had arrived at that summary:

Teacher: My summary is that the captains could have prevented the disaster if they had responded more quickly. I thought of that summary because the author tells us everything that happened and the captains were always delaying. At the end of the section, the author tells us that the court says they should have reversed course, but I know that ships take a lot of time to stop and then go in a different direction. Do you have anything that should be added to my summary?

His ninth step was to check on the reasoning process to see if it was working, helping him figure out difficult terms:

Teacher:	Is there an unclear meaning in this paragraph?
Student:	Yes. It says the carillion was on the crown of Fort Needham.
Teacher:	Can a fort have a crown?
Student:	No.
Teacher:	That's right if you are thinking about a crown that the Queen might wear. What is the author doing here?
Student:	He's using the word crown to mean top.
Teacher:	Yes, so what does he mean?
Student:	He's saying that carillion bells were on the top of the Fort in a new tower.
Teacher:	Good reasoning. Are there any other parts of this paragraph that are unclear? [No student response.]

His tenth step was to ask the students to make predictions about the next segment by using the first paragraph of the next section and what they had already learned. He then selected a student to be the next "teacher."

After students took turns playing the role of teacher, his final step was to close the lesson by inviting students to summarize the content of the entire selection as well as when, why, and how to use the reasoning process.

Using Question–Answer Relationships (QARs) to Model Comprehension Strategies

The type of question asked to guide comprehension should be based on the *information readers need to answer the question*. Therefore, teachers must help students *become aware of* likely sources of information as they respond to questions (Pearson & Johnson 1978).

A reader draws on two broad information sources to answer questions: information in the text and information inside the reader's head. For example, some questions have answers that can be found directly in the text. These questions are *textually explicit* and lead to answers that are "right there" in the text.

Other questions have answers that require students to think about the information they have read in the text. Students must be able to search for ideas that are related to one another and then put these ideas together in order to answer the questions. These questions are *textually implicit* and lead to "think and search" answers.

Still other questions require students to rely mainly on prior knowledge and experience. In other words, responses to these questions are more inside the reader's head than in the text itself. These questions are *schema-based* and lead to "author and you" and "on your own" answers.

"Right there," "think and search," "author and you," and "on your own" are mnemonics for question–answer relationships (Raphael 1982, 1984, 1986). Many kinds of responses can be prompted by textually explicit questions, by textually implicit questions, and by schema-based questions. However, the success that students experience when responding to a certain type of question depends on their ability to recognize the relationship between the question and its answer. Let's explore in more detail how students can be taught to be more strategic in their awareness and use of question–answer relationships.

QARs make explicit to students the relationships that exist among the type of question asked, the text, and the reader's prior knowledge. In the process of teaching QARs, you help students become aware of and skilled in using learning strategies to find the information they need to comprehend at different levels of response to the text.

The procedures for learning QARs can be taught directly to students by reading teachers and can be reinforced by content area specialists. Keep in mind, however, that students may come to your class totally unaware of what information sources are available for seeking an answer, or they may not know when to use different sources. In this case, it is worth several days' effort to teach students the relationship between questions and answers. It may take up to three days to show students how to identify the information sources necessary to answer questions. The following steps, which we have adapted for content area situations, are suggested for teaching QARs:

1. *Introduce the concept of QARs.* Show students a chart or an overhead transparency containing a description of the four basic question–answer relationships. (We recommend a chart that can be positioned in a prominent place in the classroom. Students may then refer to it throughout the content area lessons.) Point out the two broad categories of information sources: "in the text" and "in your head." Figure 11.2 on page 324 is adapted from a chart recommended by Raphael (1986).

2. *Begin by assigning students several short passages from the textbook.* (These should be no more than two to five sentences in length.) Follow each reading with one question from each of the QAR categories on the chart. Then discuss the differences between a "right there" question and answer, a "think and search" question and answer, an "on your own" question and answer, and an "author and you" question and answer. Your explanations should be clear and complete. Reinforce the discussion by assigning several more short text passages and asking a question for each. Students will soon begin to catch on to the differences among the four QAR categories. The example in Box 11.3 on pages 326 and 327 illustrates how a science teacher in the middle grades introduced the QAR categories to her students.

3. *Continue the second day by practising with short passages.* Use one question for each QAR category per passage. First, give students a passage to read along with questions *and* answers *and* identified QARs. Why do the questions and answers represent one QAR and not another? Second, give students a passage along with questions and answers; this time they have to identify the QAR for each. Finally, give students passages, decide together which strategy to use, and have them write their responses.

4. *Review briefly on the third day.* Then assign a longer passage (75–200 words) with up to six questions (at least one each from the four QAR categories). First, have students work in groups to decide the QAR category for each question and the answers for each. Next, assign a second passage, comparable in length, with five questions for students to work on individually. Discuss their responses either in small groups or with the whole class. You may wish to work with several class members or colleagues to complete the QAR exercise in Box 11.4 on page 328. It was developed by a secondary school English teacher as part of a short story unit.

Where Are Answers to Questions Found?

In the Text:

Right There

The answer is in the text. The words used in the question and the words used for the answer can usually be found in the same sentences.

Think and Search

The answer is in the text, but the words used in the question and those used for the answer are not in the same sentence. You need to think about different parts of the text and how ideas can be put together before you can answer the question.

Or

In Your Head:

On Your Own

The text got you thinking, but the answer is inside your head. The author can't help you much. So think about it, and use what you know already about the question.

Author and You

The answer is not in the text. You need to think about what you know, what the author says, and how they fit together.

FIGURE 11.2 Introducing QARs

5. *Apply the QAR strategy to actual content area assignments.* For each question asked, students decide on the appropriate QAR strategy and write out their answers.

Once students are sensitive to the different information sources for different types of questions and know how to use these sources to respond to questions, variations can be made in the QAR strategy. For example, you might have students generate their own questions to text assignments—perhaps two for each QAR strategy. They then write down the answers to the questions as they understand them, except that they leave one question unanswered from the "think and search" category and one from the "on your own" or "author and you" category. These are questions about which the student would like to hear the views of others. During the discussion, students volunteer to ask their unanswered questions. The class is invited first to identify the question by QAR category and then to contribute answers, comments, or related questions about the material.

A second variation involves discussions of text. During question-and-answer exchanges, preface a question by saying, "This question is *right there* in the text," or "You'll have to *think and search* the text to answer," or "You're *on your own* with this one," or "The answer is a combination of the *author and you*. Think about what the author tells us and what we already know to try and come up with a reasonable response." Make sure that you pause several seconds or more for "think time." Think time, or "wait time," is critical to responding to textually implicit and schema-based questions. Gambrell (1980) found that increasing think time to five seconds or longer increases the length of student responses as well as the quality of their speculative thinking.

Once students are familiar with QARs, they can be used in combination with a variety of interactive strategies that encourage readers to explore ideas through text discussions.

Modelling comprehension strategies through think-alouds, reciprocal teaching, and QARs provides the instructional support that will help students do more than simply read the words on a page. These procedures scaffold students' use of strategies that will help them read texts in a more thoughtful and thought-provoking manner. Another dimension of strategy instruction is to show diverse learners how to generate meaning for unfamiliar words and concepts that they encounter during reading.

VOCABULARY STRATEGIES

Diverse learners will often encounter an enormous number of unfamiliar words during reading that may pose comprehension problems for them. Strategy instruction, therefore, should take into account tactics and procedures that will help students build meaning for important concept terms. *Vocabulary self-collection strategy (VSS)*, *concept of definition (CD) word maps*, and *vocabulary-building strategies* scaffold students' ability to define concepts in the context of their use.

Vocabulary Self-Collection Strategy

Vocabulary self-collection strategy (VSS) promotes the long-term acquisition of language in an academic discipline (Haggard 1986). As a result of the repeated use of the strategy, students learn how to make decisions related to the importance of concepts and how to use context to determine what words mean. VSS begins once students read and discuss a text assignment. The teacher asks students, who are divided into teams, to nominate one word

BOX 11.3	**An Introduction to QARs in a Science Class**

1. Everyone has some idea of what growth means. People, plants, and animals grow, but what changes occur when a person or a plant grows? Two changes usually occur during the growth process. There is an increase in height and a gain in weight.

   Question: How many changes usually occur in the growth process?

   Answer: Two

   QAR: RIGHT THERE   __X__

            THINK AND SEARCH   _____

            ON YOUR OWN   _____

            AUTHOR AND YOU   _____

   Rationale (developed during class discussion): This is an example of a "right there" question because the answer is easy to find and the words used to make the question are also in the answer.

2. New cells must be added as an organism grows. Cells that die or are worn away must be replaced. New cells are produced by a process called *mitosis*. During mitosis, one cell divides to become two cells.

   Question: What would happen if our cells stopped dividing?

   Answer: Our bodies would stop growing and we would eventually die because cells that died or were worn away would not be replaced.

   QAR: RIGHT THERE   _____

            THINK AND SEARCH __X__

            ON YOUR OWN   _____

            AUTHOR AND YOU   _____

   Rationale (developed during class discussion): The answer is in the text but harder to find. The words to the question and the answer are not in the same sentence.

3. Growth in height is not steady during the life of a human. There are times when you grow very fast. At other times, you grow slowly. Adults do not grow in height at all. Your most rapid growth took place before you were born. Rapid growth continues through the first two years of life.

Question: What were the times in your life when you or someone you know grew rapidly?

Answers: My nine-year-old brother (pants needed hemming); young babies; myself at puberty; secondary school students

QAR: RIGHT THERE   _____

THINK AND SEARCH _____

ON YOUR OWN   __X__

AUTHOR AND YOU   _____

Rationale (developed during class discussion): To answer a question like this, you have to use what you know already. The answer is in your head, not the text. You're "on your own."

4. Two provisions are necessary for a tree to grow more than one kind of fruit. First, the branches of different fruit trees must be properly spliced onto the original tree. Second, the different fruit of all of the branches must belong to the same genus. Many orange trees, for example, have produced grapefruits, lemons, and limes.

Question: If you were a fruit grower, would you be able to grow bananas on an apple tree?

Answer: It's impossible. Bananas are a tropical fruit. I know that bananas and apples are not related to one another like oranges, grapefruits, and lemons, which are citrus fruits.

QAR: RIGHT THERE   _____

THINK AND SEARCH _____

ON YOUR OWN   _____

AUTHOR AND YOU   __X__

Rationale (developed during class discussion): To answer this question, you need to take what the author tells you and connect it to what you know. The answer is not in the text but in your head. However, you need to use information in the text and link it to what you know to respond to the question.

BOX 11.4	**QAR Awareness in an English Class**

"I never throw nothing away; I kept the alder branch your father cut to find my water. I don't understand, it hasn't dried out."

Moved as I touched the branch, kept out of I don't know what sense of piety—and which really wasn't dry—I had the feeling that my father was watching me over my shoulder; I closed my eyes and, standing above the spring my father had discovered, I waited for the branch to writhe, I hoped the sound of gushing water would rise to my ears.

The alder stayed motionless in my hands.... (*From "A Secret Lost in the Water" by Roch Carrier*)

1. *Question:* What is the narrator doing?

   Answer: _____

   QAR: _____

2. *Question:* Why did the narrator touch the branch?

   Answer: _____

   QAR: _____

3. *Question:* What was the narrator listening for?

   Answer: _____

   QAR: _____

4. *Question:* How would you describe the narrator?

   Answer: _____

   QAR: _____

5. *Question:* How does the narrator feel at the end of the passage?

   Answer: _____

   QAR: _____

6. *Question:* Why do children sometimes ignore the lessons of their parents?

   Answer: _____

   QAR: _____

that they would like to learn more about. The word must be important enough for the team to share it with the class. The teacher also nominates a word. Here are several suggested steps in VSS:

1. *Divide the class into nominating teams of two to five students.* Together the students on a nominating team decide which word to select for emphasis in the text selection.
2. *Present the word that each team has selected to the entire class.* A spokesperson for each team identifies the nominated word and responds to the following questions:

a. *Where is the word found in the text?* The spokesperson reads the passage in which the word is located or describes the context in which the word is used.
b. *What do the team members think the word means?* The team decides on what the word means in the context in which it is used. They must use information from the surrounding context and may also consult reference resources.
c. *Why did the team think the class should learn the word?* The team must tell the class why the word is important enough to single out for emphasis.

To introduce VSS to the students, the teacher first presents his or her nominated word to the class, modelling how to respond to the three questions. During the team presentations, the teacher facilitates the discussion, writes the nominated words on the board with their meanings, and invites class members to contribute additional clarifications of the words.

To conclude the class session, students record all the nominated words and their meanings in a section of their learning logs or in a separate vocabulary notebook. These lists may be used for review and study. As a consequence of VSS, the teacher has a set of student-generated words that can be incorporated into a variety of follow-up extension activities, as suggested in Chapter 5.

Concept of Definition Word Maps

Although VSS provides opportunities to define and explore the meanings of words used in text readings, many students are not aware of the types of information that contribute to the meaning of a concept. Nor have they internalized a strategy for defining a concept based on the information available to them. In addition, words in a text passage often provide only partial contextual information for defining the meaning of a concept.

Concept of definition (CD) word maps provide a framework for organizing conceptual information in the process of defining a word (Schwartz 1988; Schwartz & Raphael 1985). Conceptual information can be organized in terms of three types of relationships: the general class or category in which the concept belongs, the attributes or properties of the concept and those that distinguish it from other members of the category, and examples or illustrations of the concept. Students from elementary school through secondary school can use CD to learn how to construct meaning for unknown words encountered in texts.

CD instruction supports vocabulary and concept learning by helping students internalize a strategy for defining and clarifying the meaning of unknown words. The hierarchical structure of a concept has an organizational pattern that is reflected by the general structure of a CD word map (see Figure 11.3 on page 330).

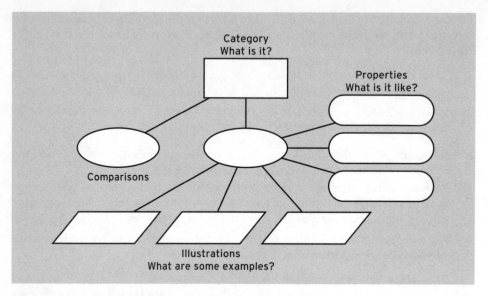

FIGURE 11.3 **General Structure for a CD Word Map**

Source: From Robert Schwartz, "Learning to Learn: Vocabulary in Content Area Textbooks" (1988, November). *Journal of Reading, 32*(2), 108–118. Copyright © 1988 by the International Reading Association. All rights reserved. Used by permission of the author and the International Reading Association.

In the centre of the CD word map, students write the concept being studied. Working outward, they then write the word that best describes the general class or superordinate concept that includes the target concept. The answer to "What is it?" is the general class or category. Students then provide at least three examples of the concept as well as three properties by responding, respectively, to the questions, "What are some examples?" and "What is it like?" Comparison of the target concept is also possible when students think of an additional concept that belongs to the general class but is different from the concept being studied. Figure 11.4 provides an example of a CD word map for the word *tiger*.

Because students use the general CD word map as a framework for defining unknown concepts that they encounter during reading, a teacher can easily combine CD instruction with VSS. Schwartz (1988) recommends a detailed plan for modelling CD with students. The plan includes demonstrating the value of CD by connecting its purpose to how people use organizational patterns to aid memory and interpretation; introducing the general structure of a CD word map, explaining how the three probes define a concept, and walking students through the completion of a word map; and applying CD to an actual text selection.

Two caveats are relevant to CD instruction: CD works best with concept words that function as nouns, but the procedure may be used, with some adaptation, with action words as well. Also, a potential misuse of CD occurs when teachers reproduce the general CD word map on the copier and expect students to define lists of words at the end of a text chapter. This is not the intent of CD instruction. Instead, students should internalize the process through demonstration and actual use, applying it as they need it in actual text learning. Ultimately, the goal of CD instruction is to have students own the strategy of defining unknown words in terms of category, property, and example relationships.

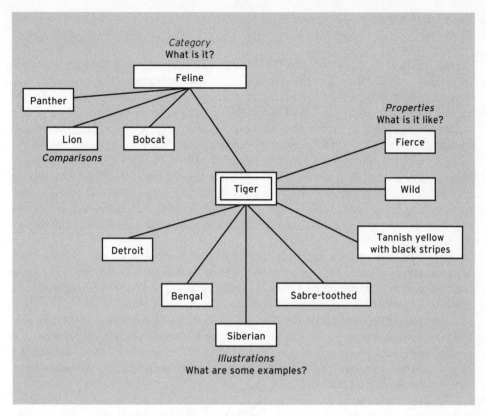

FIGURE 11.4 CD Map for the Word *Tiger*

Vocabulary-Building Strategies

Showing diverse learners how to construct meaning for unfamiliar words encountered during reading helps them develop strategies needed to monitor comprehension and build on their own vocabularies. Demonstrating how to use *context*, *word structure*, and the *dictionary* provides students with several basic strategies for vocabulary learning that will last a lifetime. With these strategies, students can search for information clues while reading so that they can approximate the meanings of unknown words. These clues often reveal enough meaning to allow readers who struggle with text to continue reading without "short-circuiting" the process and giving up because the text does not make sense.

You can scaffold the use of vocabulary-building strategies before assigning material to be read. If one or more words represent key concepts—and the words lend themselves to demonstration—you can model the inquiry process necessary to construct meaning. The demonstration is brief, often lasting no more than five minutes.

There are three types of demonstrations that will make students aware of vocabulary-building strategies. The first is to model how to make sense of a word in the context of its use, the second involves an analysis of a word's structure, and the third combines context and word structure. Usually these demonstrations require the use of visuals, such as an overhead transparency or a chalkboard. After the brief demonstration, guide students to practise and apply the strategy that you just modelled so that they can become proficient in its use.

Using Context to Approximate Meaning Constructing meaning from context is one of the most useful strategies at the command of proficient readers. Showing readers who struggle how to make use of context builds confidence and competence and teaches the inquiry process necessary to unlock the meaning of troublesome technical and general vocabulary encountered during reading. Using context involves using information surrounding a difficult word to help reveal its meaning. Every reader makes some use of context automatically. Strategy instruction, however, is needed when the text provides a *deliberate context* to help the reader with concept terms that are especially difficult. Often the text author will anticipate that certain words will be troublesome and will provide information clues and contextual aids to help readers with meaning. In these instances, students will benefit from a strategy that allows them to use the deliberate context to construct meaning.

Even though textbook authors may consciously or unconsciously use deliberate contexts for unknown words, constraints in the material itself or the reader's own background limit the degree to which context reveals word meaning. The teacher and students must know how context operates to limit meaning as well as to reveal it.

Deighton (1970) identified several factors that limit the use of context: (1) What a context may reveal to a particular reader depends on the reader's experience, (2) the portion of context that reveals an unfamiliar word must be located reasonably close to the word if it is to act effectively, and (3) there must be some clear-cut connection between the unfamiliar term and the context that clarifies it.

The use of context, as you have probably concluded, is mostly a matter of inference. Inference requires readers to see an explicit or implicit relationship between the unfamiliar word and its context or to connect what they know already with the unknown term. It can't be assumed that students will perceive these relationships or make the connections on their own. Most students who struggle with text simply don't know how to use a deliberate context provided by an author. Three kinds of information in particular are useful to struggling readers: *typographic*, *syntactic*, and *semantic* clues.

TYPOGRAPHIC CLUES. Typographic or format clues make use of footnotes, italics, boldface print, parenthetical definitions, pictures, graphs, charts, and the like. A typographic clue provides a clear-cut connection and a direct reference to an unknown word. Many students tend to gloss over a typographic aid instead of using it to spotlight the meaning of a difficult term. The teacher can rivet attention to these aids with minimal expenditure of class time.

For example, consider the way a science teacher modelled a strategy for revealing the meaning of the word *enzymes*, which was presented in boldface type in the text. Before assigning a text section titled "Osmosis in Living Cells," the teacher asked students to turn to the relevant page. Then he asked, "Which word in the section on osmosis stands out among the others?" The students quickly spotted the word *enzymes*. "Why do you think this word is highlighted in boldface type?" he asked. A student replied, "I guess it must be important." Another student said, "Maybe because it has something to do with osmosis—whatever that is." The teacher nodded approvingly and then asked the class to see if they could figure out what *enzymes* meant by reading this sentence: "Chemical substances called **enzymes** are produced by cells to break down large starch molecules into small sugar molecules."

The science teacher continued the demonstration by asking two questions: "What are enzymes?" and "What do they do?" The students responded easily. The teacher concluded the walk-through with these words: "Words that are put in large letters or boldfaced print are important. If you pay attention to them as we just did, you will have little trouble figuring out what they mean. There are four other words in boldfaced type in your reading assignment. Look for them as you read and try to figure out what they mean."

SYNTACTIC AND SEMANTIC CLUES. Syntactic and semantic clues in content materials should not be treated separately. The grammatical relationships among words in a sentence or the structural arrangement among sentences in a passage often helps clarify the meaning of a particular word.

Syntactic and semantic clues are much more subtle than typographic clues. Table 11.1 on pages 334 and 335 presents a summary of the most frequently encountered syntactic and semantic clues.

The chalkboard or an overhead transparency is valuable for helping students visualize the inquiry process necessary to reveal meaning. For example, if a *definition clue* is used, as in this example from Table 11.1—"Entomology is the study of insects, and biologists who specialize in this field are called entomologists"—it may be appropriate first to write the sentence on the board. During the modelling discussion, you can then show how *is* and *are called* provide information clues that reveal meaning for *entomology* and *entomologists*.

A simple strategy would be to cross out *is* and *are called* in the sentence and replace them with equal signs (=):

Entomology ~~is~~ = the study of insects, and biologists who specialize in this field ~~are called~~ = entomologists.

A brief discussion will reinforce the function of the verb forms *is* and *are called* in the sentence.

The definition clue is the least subtle of the syntactic and semantic clues. However, all the clues in Table 11.1 require students to make inferential leaps. Consider one of the examples from the mood and tone clue: "The tormented animal screeched with horror and writhed in pain as it tried desperately to escape from the hunter's trap." Suppose this sentence came from a short story about to be assigned in an English class. Assume also that many of the students would have trouble with the word *tormented* as it is used in the sentence. If students are to make the connection between *tormented* and the mood created by the information clues, the teacher will have to ask several effective clarifying questions.

The demonstration begins with the teacher writing the word *tormented* on the board. She asks, "You may have heard or read this word before, but how many of you think that you know what it means?" Student definitions are put on the board. The teacher then writes the sentence on the board. "Which of the definitions on the board do you think best fits the word *tormented* when it's used in this sentence?" She encourages students to support their choices. If none fits, she will ask for more definitions now that students have seen the sentence. She continues questioning, "Are there any other words or phrases in the sentence that help us get a feel for the meaning of *tormented*? Which ones?"

The inquiry into the meaning of *tormented* continues in this fashion. The information clues (*screeched with horror*, *writhed in pain*, *desperately*) that establish the mood are

TABLE 11.1	Syntactic and Semantic Contextual Clues	
Type of Clue	Explanation	Examples[a]
1. Definition	The author equates the unknown word to the known or more familiar, usually using a form of the verb *be*.	*Entomology* **is** the study of insects, and biologists who specialize in this field **are called** *entomologists*. A *critical review* **is** an attempt to evaluate the worth of a piece of writing.
2. Linked synonyms	The author pairs the unknown word with familiar synonyms or closely related words in a series.	Kunte Kinte was the victim of **cruel**, **evil**, *malevolent*, and **brutal** slave traders. The member of parliament from Ontario possessed the traits of an honest and just leader: **wisdom**, **judgment**, *sagacity*.
3. Direct description: examples, modifiers, restatements	The author reveals the meaning of an unknown word by providing additional information in the form of appositives, phrases, clauses, or sentences.	*Example clue:* Undigested material **such as fruit skins, outer parts of grain, and the stringlike parts of some vegetables** forms *roughage*. *Modifier clues: Pictographic writing,* **which was the actual drawing of animals, people, and events**, is the forerunner of written language. *Algae,* **nonvascular plants that are as abundant in water as grasses are on land**, have often been called "grasses of many waters." *Restatement clue:* A billion dollars a year is spent on *health quackery.* **In other words, each year in North America, millions of dollars are spent on worthless treatments and useless gadgets to "cure" various illnesses.**

underlined and discussed. The teacher concludes the modelling activity by writing five new words on the board and explaining, "These words are also in the story that you are about to read. As you come across them, stop and think. How do the words or phrases or sentences surrounding each word create a certain feeling or mood that will allow you to understand what each one means?"

When modelling the use of context in Table 11.1, it's important for students to discover the information clues. It's also important for the teacher to relate the demonstration to several additional words to be encountered in the assignment. Instruction of this type will

Type of Clue	Explanation	Examples[2]
4. Contrast	The author reveals the meaning of an unknown word by contrasting it with an antonym or a phrase that is opposite in meaning.	You have probably seen animals perform tricks at the zoo, on television, or in a circus. Maybe you taught a dog to fetch a newspaper. **But learning tricks--usually for a reward--is very different from** *cognitive problem solving.*
		It wasn't a *Conestoga* like Pa's folks came in. **Instead, it was just an old farm wagon drawn by one tired horse.**
5. Cause and effect	The author establishes a cause-and-effect relationship in which the meaning of an unknown word can be hypothesized.	The *domestication* of animals probably began when young animals were caught or strayed into camps. **As a result, people enjoyed staying with them and made pets of them.**
		A family is *egalitarian* **when both husband and wife make decisions together and share responsibilities equally.**
6. Mood and tone	The author sets a mood (ironic, satirical, serious, funny, etc.) in which the meaning of an unknown word can be hypothesized.	A sense of *resignation* engulfed my thoughts as **the feeling of cold greyness was everywhere around me.**
		The *tormented* animal **screeched with horror and writhed in pain as it tried desperately to escape** from the hunter's trap.

[2] Italics denote the unknown word. Boldface type represents information clues that trigger context revelation.

have a significant cumulative effect. If students are shown how to use contextual clues for two or three words each week, over the course of an academic year they will have 80 to 120 applications in the process.

Word Structure A word itself provides information clues about its meaning. The smallest unit of meaning in a word is called a *morpheme*. Analysis of a word's structure, *morphemic analysis*, is a second vocabulary-building strategy that students can use to predict meaning. When readers encounter an unknown word, they can reduce the number of feasible guesses about its meaning considerably by approaching the whole word and identifying its parts. When students use morphemic analysis in combination with context, they have a powerful strategy at their command.

Student readers often find long words daunting. Olsen and Ames (1972) put long or polysyllabic words into four categories:

1. *Compound words made up of two known words joined together.* Examples: *commonwealth, matchmaker*.

2. *Words containing a recognizable stem to which an affix (a prefix, combining form, or suffix) has been added.* Examples: *surmountable, deoxygenize, unsystematic, microscope.*

3. *Words that can be analyzed into familiar and regular pronounceable units.* Examples: *undulate, calcify, subterfuge, strangulate.*

4. *Words that contain irregular pronounceable units so that there is no sure pronunciation unless one consults a dictionary.* Examples: *louver, indictment.*

Content vocabulary terms from categories 1 and 2 (compound words and recognizable stems and affixes) are the best candidates for instruction. You can readily demonstrate techniques for predicting the meanings of these words, since each of their isolated parts will always represent a meaning unit.

In some instances, a word from category 3 may also be selected for emphasis. However, there is no guarantee that students will bring prior knowledge and experience to words that comprise the third category. Long phonemically regular words lend themselves to syllabication. Syllabication involves breaking words into pronounceable sound units or syllables. The word *undulate*, for example, can be syllabicated (un-du-late). However, the syllable *un* is not a meaning-bearing prefix.

Many words from category 3 are derived from Latin or Greek. Students who struggle with texts will find these words especially difficult to analyze for meaning because of their lack of familiarity with Latin or Greek roots. Occasionally, a word such as *strangulate* (derived from the Latin *strangulatus*) can be taught because students may recognize the familiar word *strangle*. They might then be shown how to link *strangle* to the verb suffix *-ate* (which means "to cause to become") to hypothesize a meaning for *strangulate*. Unfortunately, the verb suffix *-ate* has multiple meanings, and the teacher should be quick to point this out to students. This procedure is shaky, but it has some payoff.

Words from category 2 warrant instruction because English root words are more recognizable, obviously, than Latin or Greek ones. Whenever feasible, teach the principles of structural word analysis using terms that have English roots. Certain affixes are more helpful than others, and knowing which affixes to emphasize during instruction will minimize students' confusion.

The most helpful affixes are the combining forms, prefixes, or suffixes that have single, invariant meanings. Deighton's (1970) monumental study of word structure has helped identify affixes that have single meanings. (See Appendix C for a summary of Deighton's findings.)

Many other commonly used prefixes have more than one meaning or have several shades of meaning. Because of their widespread use in content terminology, you should also consider these variant-meaning prefixes for functional teaching. (See Appendix D for a list of prefixes with varying meanings.)

The tables of affixes are resources for you. Don't be misled into thinking that students should learn long lists of affixes in isolation to help them analyze word structure. This approach is neither practical nor functional. We recommend instead that students be taught affixes as they are needed to analyze the structure of terms that will appear in a reading assignment.

For example, an English teacher modelled how to analyze the meaning of *diviner* before students were to encounter the term in an assignment from Margaret Laurence's *The Diviners*. She wrote the word on the board, underlining the base word *divine*, and asked students for several synonyms for the base word. Student responses included *religious*, *holy*, and *good*. Then she explained that *-er* was a noun suffix meaning "one who." She said, "Now let's take a look at *divine*. Have you ever heard of other words with the same root word *divine*, such as *divination* or *divinity*? The suffix *-ation* means "a process of" and *-ity* means "a state of." What meaning do these words all have in common? Students responded and also remembered that they had already read a short story titled *A Secret Lost in the Water* that concerned a diviner who found underground water by using a branch as a divining rod. Through this process, relating the known to the unknown, students predicted that a diviner in Laurence's novel would be a person who receives messages about spiritual matters. They recorded their ideas in their reading journal for future reference.

Using the Dictionary as a Strategic Resource The use of context and word structure are strategies that give struggling readers insight into the meanings of unknown words. Rarely does context or word structure help learners derive precise definitions for keywords. Instead, these vocabulary-building strategies keep readers on the right track so that they are able to follow a text without getting bogged down or giving up.

There are times, however, when context and word structure reveal little about a word's meaning. In these instances, or when a precise definition is needed, a dictionary is a logical alternative and a valuable resource for students.

Knowing when to use a dictionary is as important as knowing how to use it. A content teacher should incorporate dictionary usage into ongoing plans but should avoid a very common pitfall in the process of doing so. When asked, "What does this word mean?" the teacher shouldn't automatically reply, "Look it up in the dictionary."

To some students, "Look it up in the dictionary" is another way of saying "Don't bug me" or "I really don't have the time or the inclination to help you." Of course, this may not be the case at all. However, from an instructional perspective, that hard-to-come-by teachable moment is lost whenever we routinely suggest to students to look up a word in the dictionary.

One way to make the dictionary a functional resource is to use it to verify educated guesses about word meaning revealed through context or word structure. For example, if a student asks you for the meaning of a vocabulary term, an effective tactic is to bounce the question right back: "What do you think it means? Let's look at the way it's used. Are there any clues to its meaning?" If students are satisfied with an educated guess because it makes sense, the word need not be looked up. But if students are still unsure of the word's meaning, the dictionary is there.

When students go into a dictionary to verify or to determine a precise definition, more often than not they need supervision to make good decisions. Keep these tips in mind as you work on dictionary usage.

1. *Help students determine the "best fit" between a word and its definition.* Students must often choose the most appropriate definition from several. This poses a real dilemma for young learners. Your interactions will help them make the best choice of a definition and will provide a behaviour model for making such a choice.

2. *If you do assign a list of words to look up in a dictionary, choose them selectively.* A few words are better than many. The chances are greater that students will learn several key terms thoroughly than that they will develop vague notions about a large number.

3. *Help students with the pronunciation key in a glossary or dictionary as the need arises.* This does not mean, however, that you will teach skills associated with the use of a pronunciation key in isolated lessons. Instead, it means guiding and reinforcing students' ability to use a pronunciation key as they study the content of your course.

Vocabulary development is a gradual process, "the result of many encounters with a word towards a more precise grasp of the concept the word represents" (Parry 1993, p. 127). If this is the case, students who struggle with demanding text material will benefit from vocabulary-building strategies that make use of context clues, word structure, and appropriate uses of reference tools such as the dictionary. Johnson and Steele (1996) found that with ESL learners, the use of *personal word lists* provided excellent strategy practice and application in the use of vocabulary-building strategies.

The use of personal word lists would be of value not only to ESL students but also to all students who need explicit support in the use of vocabulary-building strategies. The personal word list technique emphasizes the need for students to self-select important concept words and incorporates key principles learned from the VSS strategy discussed earlier in the chapter. Students then complete a personal word list, which may be part of a vocabulary notebook or learning log. The personal word list is divided into four columns as illustrated in Figure 11.5. For each word entry, students list (1) the word, (2) what the word means, (3) the clues used to construct meaning for the word (context, word structure, or a combination of the two), and (4) a dictionary definition, when it is appropriate to consult the dictionary for a definition. Figure 11.5 illustrates an ESL student's personal word list entries (Johnson & Steele 1996).

Word	What I Think It Means	Clues (context or structure)	Dictionary Definition (if needed)
sacred	religious	they were entering a sacred building that loomed out of the night to give them what haven and what <u>blessing</u> they yearned for.	
vexation	displeasure	<u>but something would come up,</u> some vexation that was like a fly <u>buzzing</u> around their heads.	
lurch	movement	she took a step toward the porch lurching	a sudden movement forward or sideways

FIGURE 11.5 An ESL Student's Personal Word List

Source: From Denise Johnson, "So Many Words, So Little Time: Helping College ESL Learners Acquire Vocabulary-Building Strategies" (1996, February). *Journal of Adolescent and Adult Literacy, 39*(5), 351. Copyright © 1996 by the International Reading Association. All rights reserved. Used by permission of the author and the International Reading Association.

LOOKING BACK, LOOKING FORWARD

Struggling readers exhibit a learned helplessness characterized by a lack of control over reading strategies, a poor self-image, and an ambivalent attitude toward reading. As a result, they tend to avoid reading or being held accountable for reading in school. Students who struggle with text challenge teachers to look for and experiment with instructional strategies that will actively involve them in the life of the classroom.

Teachers reach struggling readers by scaffolding instruction in ways that support content literacy and learning. Throughout this book, we explore scaffolded instruction designed to help all students learn with texts. In this chapter, we concentrated on the role of explicit instruction in the development and use of reading strategies.

Strategic classrooms are places where students learn how to learn. We explored how to teach for metacognition so that students will be more aware of, confident in, and competent in their use of learning strategies. Explicit instruction includes modelling comprehension and vocabulary strategies and demonstrating their use in text learning. Think-alouds, reciprocal teaching, and question–answer relationships (QARs), vocabulary self-collection strategy (VSS), concept of definition (CD) word maps, and vocabulary-building strategies are several learner-oriented strategies that we emphasized in this chapter.

Continuing opportunities for teachers to grow professionally are essential if the literacy practices in this book are to become part of the instructional repertoire of content area teachers. Chapter 12 offers supportive strategies for teachers who want to plan and initiate reflective, inquiry-based professional development programs in literacy and learning across the curriculum.

MINDS-ON

1. Picture a science class of 25 students from very diverse backgrounds—different social classes, different ethnicity, and varying achievement levels. Many of the students struggle with text materials. Describe some classroom strategies you might use to respond to struggling readers while maintaining high standards of content literacy and learning.
2. Review the opening section of this chapter, "Organizing Principle." Take turns with members of a small discussion group sharing examples of passages that demonstrated the QAR principles of (a) "right there," (b) "think and search," (c) "on your own," and (d) "author and you." How might these same principles be used with a piece of literature, a scientific explanation, or a work of art?
3. Use your knowledge of root words, suffixes, and prefixes to create five original words. Then write mock "dictionary" entries for each. Next, write a short paragraph incorporating each of the five words in their proper context. Exchange your paragraph with a partner, and see if you can determine the meanings of the original words. Discuss the semantic and structural techniques you have both used. What strategies might be used to teach the meanings of these words to someone else?

HANDS-ON

1. Bring several copies of a favourite poem or short text to class. Following the "think-aloud" guidelines in the chapter, model the checklist for self-evaluation by (a) developing hypotheses by making predictions, (b) developing images, (c) sharing analogies, (d) monitoring comprehension, and (e) regulating comprehension.
2. Using a passage from a content area text, develop one example of each of the four QAR categories: (a) "right there," (b) "think and search," (c) "on your own," and (d) "author and you."

SUGGESTED READINGS

Allen, J. (1995). *It's never too late: Leading adolescents to lifelong literacy.* Portsmouth, NH: Heinemann.

Allen, J. (2000). *Yellow brick roads: Shared and guided paths to independent reading, 4–12.* Portland, ME: Stenhouse.

Allington, R. L., Boxer, N. J., & Broikou, K. H. (1987). Jeremy, remedial reading and subject matter classes. *Journal of Reading, 30,* 643–645.

Blachowicz, C. (1991). Vocabulary instruction in content areas for special needs learners: Why and how? *Reading, Writing, and Learning Disabilities, 7,* 297–308.

Booth, D. (2002). *Even hockey players read: Boys, literacy and learning.* Markham, ON: Pembroke Publishers.

Buikema, J., & Graves, M. (1993). Teaching students to use content clues to infer word meanings. *Journal of Reading, 36,* 450–457.

Ehlinger, J., & Pritchard, R. (1994). Using think alongs in secondary content areas. *Reading Research and Instruction, 33,* 187–206.

Ezell, H., Hunsicker, S., Quinque, M., & Randolph, E. (1996). Maintenance and generalization of QAR reading comprehension strategies. *Reading Research and Instruction, 36,* 64–81.

Jobe, R., & Dayton-Sakari, M. (1999). *Reluctant readers: Connecting students and books for successful reading experiences.* Markham, ON: Pembroke Publishers.

Jobe, R., & Dayton-Sakari, M. (2002). *Info-Kids: How to use nonfiction to turn reluctant readers into enthusiastic learners.* Markham, ON: Pembroke Publishers.

Johnston, P., & Winograd, P. (1990). Passive failure in reading. *Journal of Reading Behavior, 17,* 279–301.

Kang, H-W, & Golden, A. (1994). Vocabulary learning and instruction in a second or foreign language. *International Journal of Applied Linguistics, 4*(1), 57–77.

Robb, L. (2000). *Teaching reading in middle school: A strategic approach to teaching that improves comprehension and thinking.* New York: Scholastic.

Roller, C. M. (1996). *Variability not disability: Struggling readers in a workshop classroom.* Newark, DE: International Reading Association.

Tovani, C. (2000). *I read it, but I don't get it: Comprehension strategies for adolescent readers.* Portland, ME: Stenhouse.

Walker, B. J. (1992). *Supporting struggling readers.* Markham, ON: Pippen Publishing.

part three

Professional Development

chapter twelve

Growth and Reflection in the Teaching Profession

Be not afraid of growing slowly,
Be afraid only of standing still.

-Chinese proverb

ORGANIZING PRINCIPLE

Teachers are professionals. Their preparation does not end with their initial certification but is an ongoing process, much like that of a developing reader and writer. In fact, national professional education organizations recognize the essential role that professional development plays in successful education reform. Teacher preparation and professional development is a process that moves along a continuum, from preservice preparation to certification (NCATE 2000).

To be sure, a certain amount of growth will occur naturally, as colleagues observe each other teach, share exciting and worthwhile innovations and strategies, and make decisions about instruction. Yet teachers also need purposeful, planned support similar to that given students through instructional scaffolding. Providing necessary support to enable teachers to experience growth and reflection would mean understanding that diversity exists *among teachers* and planning for active and meaningful learning in professional communities.

Teachers at different stages in their careers are also at different levels of expertise in their craft. Simply becoming aware of what is happening in the classroom and learning to tap into the immense body of practical knowledge acquired through experience can result in more reflective teaching and effective professional growth. Engaging in collaboration with colleagues and participating in strategies such as writing and representing, dialoguing, problem solving, using technology, and action research provide support for teachers who seek to improve their own teaching. Professional development plans, to be most useful, would be individually designed for teachers at different points in their careers.

This chapter begins with the importance of direction and purpose, collaboration, decision making, and problem solving in professional development. It also explores challenges, themes, and trends that will help teachers in their professional development and growth. Above all, it communicates a belief that powerful adult learning situations can be created: **participating in planned, reflective, and inquiry-based professional development in content area reading leads to professional growth and improved instruction.**

Study the chapter overview. What do you already know about professional development? About what do you need to learn more?

Then use the key questions in the Frame of Mind section as a guide to help you interact with and respond to the chapter's ideas about professional growth and reflection.

CHAPTER OVERVIEW

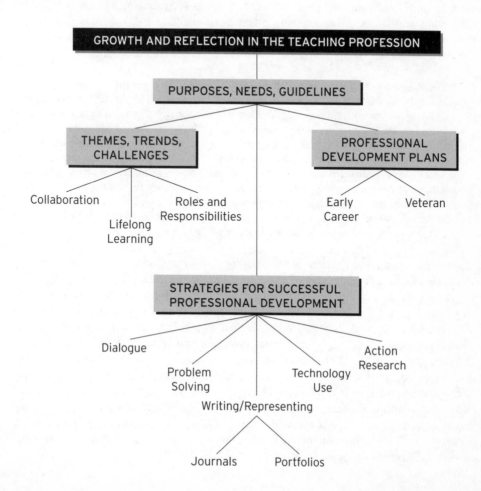

FRAME OF MIND

1. Why are teachers expected to participate in continuing professional development?

2. What are some of the different purposes for engaging in professional development?

3. How are teachers' roles and responsibilities changing?

4. Select a strategy for successful professional development. How would you use it for growth and reflection?

5. In what ways are individual professional development plans different for an early-career teacher (Darby) and a veteran teacher (Farouk)? In what ways are they similar?

Professional development has become synonymous with change and growth—and fortunately so. Expectations and requirements of teachers are changing as rapidly as today's classrooms and learners. For example, when Newfoundland and Labrador reviewed its thinking on professional development, it became clear that overly simplistic approaches, such as one-shot workshops delivered by visiting experts were not working:

> If educators are to accept the lessons related to professional development ..., they must be committed to both individual and organizational learning. While it is clear that individuals can learn without any contribution from the organization, it is also apparent that learning can be helped or hindered by the organization. Additionally, because schools are human endeavours, it makes intuitive sense that organizational learning will not occur unless individuals are learning. This interactive model of learning in which individuals and the organization are interdependent requires a new constructivist approach to professional development that has its foundation in research and theory. Also, it requires systems thinking and a focus on student outcomes. Our current mental images of professional development must be challenged, and new images must be constructed in order for our schools to become centres of continuous learning that will serve our students in the new millennium. (Brown & Sheppard 1997, n.p.)

Change takes time. Teachers who experiment with and adopt content area reading strategies are changing the nature of instruction; they are adults engaging in lifelong learning. As such, they participate in professional development for a variety of reasons and in a variety of ways. First, they may want to obtain better information and to be able to use it more rationally. Second, they may question their own beliefs, coming to a better understanding of themselves, and finding better ways of communicating with their colleagues and with parents and students. And third, they may change practices when they discover that as they engage in new experiences and pilot and reflect on new strategies, they begin to re-examine problems in teaching and learning. They inquire, thinking intuitively about alternative solutions. Professional development in content area reading involves beginning and experienced teachers in purposeful, planned change in interaction with others in the organization. What is the result of engaging in this worthwhile process over the long haul? Growth for teachers and students.

PURPOSES, NEEDS, AND GUIDELINES

Whose purpose should professional development programs serve? Whose needs should be met? For novice teachers, learning to teach and learning to interact with one's colleagues are important needs. More experienced teachers may want to learn what strengths each of their colleagues can contribute to a professional development plan. The district central office must take into account the implementation of new policies such as inclusion. Consider, if you will, a continuum of the various authentic purposes that drive professional development.

On one end, as illustrated in Figure 12.1, are the needs of the institution, the school district, the administrators, the schools, and the program being initiated in an individual school. On this end of the continuum reside pressing demands on administration and staff in this assessment-driven, examination-oriented age of educational reform.

Proficiency test scores and their rankings displayed district by district in the local newspaper preoccupy superintendents who must deal daily with economic and political realities, in addition to having bottom-line responsibility for meeting instructional goals. They are, without a doubt, more aware of and more accountable to multiple stakeholder groups (parents, school board members, business leaders, community advocates, and legislators) than ever before.

On the other end of the continuum are teachers who are at different stages in their careers. As Fessler and Christensen (1994) state, all teachers are at some point in their career cycle. They are at different stages of expertise in their craft and may need different types of growth and development activities. High-quality professional development plays an essential role in educational reform. Rigorous and relevant content, strategies, and organizational supports all contribute to the preparation and career-long development of teachers. Professional development, which is part of a system-wide effort to prepare, support, and advance teachers at all levels of their careers, is recommended.

The incentives appropriate for beginning teachers and for veteran, experienced teachers may be different. For teachers who are beginning their careers, praise from students, written praise, and gaining control over their instructional decisions are appropriate incentives. Professional development must meet all of the following criteria:

■ It focuses on teachers as central to school reform yet includes all members of the school community.

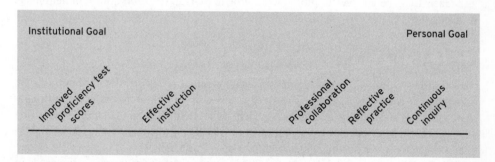

FIGURE 12.1 **Purposes of Professional Development**

- It respects and nurtures the intellectual capacity of teachers and others in the school community.
- It reflects the best research and practice in teaching, learning, and leadership.
- It is planned principally by those who will participate in that development.
- It enables teachers to develop expertise in content, pedagogy, and other essential elements in teaching to high standards.
- It enhances leadership capacity among teachers, principals, and others.
- It requires ample time and other resources that enable educators to develop their individual capacity and to learn and work together.
- It promotes commitment to continuous inquiry and improvement embedded in the daily life of schools.
- It is driven by a coherent long-term plan that incorporates professional development among a broad set of strategies to improve teaching and learning.
- It is evaluated on the basis of its impact on teacher effectiveness, student learning, leadership, and the school community, and this evaluation guides subsequent professional development efforts.

PROFESSIONAL THEMES, TRENDS, AND CHALLENGES

"The complexity of teaching is well recognized: A teacher makes over 3000 non-trivial decisions daily" (Danielson 1996, p. 2). As professional development moves away from the training model, a focus on helping teachers make sense of this complexity within the context of their own experiences is emerging. Teachers have an immense body of practical knowledge acquired through experience, yet many are explicitly unaware of this and hence fail to tap it to further their professional growth.

Examination of this practical knowledge should be continuous and can be demanding, as the process of change and growth is not easy. Another trend is a lessening of reliance on outside experts and an increased call for teachers to engage in reflective inquiry, resulting in better teaching.

Better teaching can "mean that the teacher *knows* more about what teaching is and how it best works for him or her, is more *aware* of what is happening in the classroom as he or she teaches, and is more purposeful in the pedagogical *decisions* that he or she makes" (Baird 1992, p. 33). Simply becoming aware of the myriad aspects of one's daily practice as a teacher can be a powerful professional growth tool, and collaboration can help make it successful.

COLLABORATION

"Relationships with colleagues are an important element of teachers' contribution to the school and district. Professional educators are generous with their expertise and willingly share materials and insights, particularly with those less experienced than they" (Danielson 1996, p. 113). The essence of collaboration is conversation-colleagues sitting down together and engaging in serious dialogue about the "stuff" of teaching.

Whether the topic is school-wide activities, common curricular themes, new trends in technology, an article from a professional publication, or their own personal journal entries, the activity of teachers sharing ideas and insights with one another is a powerful one. The rapport and trust that grow between individuals break down the walls of isolation that can exist when teachers work alone in their individual classrooms. Teachers exchange roles and become learners from each other, gaining from each other's perspectives and expertise. Just as we try to realize the potential of our students by maximizing their strengths, so can we, as teachers, grow as professionals by learning from each other. This can and should be an ongoing process—across experience levels and subjects taught.

Creating partnerships is not simply a matter of goodwill. True collaboration creates a sense of connectedness that brings with it responsibility. Nevertheless, collaboration is a powerful trend in professional development today. When teachers make connections, they form a community, thereby counteracting the isolation that pervades the teaching profession. For "when teachers are engaged together in thinking aloud about their work and its consequences," the results are a greater sense of professionalism and a stronger and more cohesive instructional program (Griffin 1991, p. 250). There is also some risk, as veteran teachers know.

In the school district of Vista in Newfoundland, a group of teachers who were classmates in a university course decided to take their professor's introduction to ThinkWave software and try to apply it to their school's needs. The software was used to increase communication between parents and the school by making information about their children available on the web. While the teachers enjoyed working together to learn the technology, convince the school to adopt its use, and introduce it to students and parents, they were also discouraged by the very modest success of the project. Many parents did not use the technology because they did not have easy access to the internet, nor did they take opportunities to learn to use it, although they were invited to workshops (Barbour 2002, n.p.). Professional development needs to take into account the interaction among various stakeholders in the school organization.

Lifelong Learning

"Continuing development is the mark of a true professional, an ongoing effort that is never completed. Educators committed to attaining and remaining at the top of their profession invest much energy in staying informed and increasing their skills. They are then in a position to exercise leadership among colleagues" (Danielson 1996, p. 115).

One of the skills we try to foster in our students is that of becoming lifelong learners. Often we fail to include ourselves in that community of learners. By modelling those habits of learning, though, we not only guide our students but also enrich the personal and professional knowledge base from which we teach. Whatever career stage a teacher is in, there are new insights and perspectives to be gained to enliven, reinspire, and deepen one's commitment to the profession. For, as Griffin (1991) says, "development indicates forward motion, links activities and events in coherent ways, considers people as individuals at varying stages of expertise, and focuses attention on working toward an end in view, a vision of the possible" (p. 247).

At the very least, professional developers who want to improve professional development in content area reading according to these concepts would involve teachers at different career stages in program planning. The perceived usefulness of the planned activity is important and will depend on the group's mix of experiences and career stages. Both the second-year teacher still sorting out the curriculum in social studies and the veteran down the hall going through the motions need and deserve to have relevant activities for professional growth.

Recasting Roles and Responsibilities

As school reform efforts become part of the daily way of life for educators, so does the notion of change as it applies to the daily activities of teachers in schools. No longer can teachers go into their rooms, close the doors, and interact with only their own students throughout the day. Schools are opening up, not only for students but also for teachers, administrators, parents, and university personnel. "In almost all schools, many opportunities exist for educators to assume additional responsibilities, thereby enhancing the culture of the entire school" (Danielson 1996, p. 113).

Teachers can extend their duties and responsibilities beyond their classroom doors. "Professional educators [can] make many contributions to the life of a school" (Danielson 1996, p. 113). Schools and districts undertaking major projects increasingly include teachers in the design, planning, and implementation of these new ideas. Such activities often require a considerable investment of time and mental energy. When viewed as authentic professional growth opportunities, however, professional educators find the time to become involved. In addition to the personal knowledge and experience gained through participation, teachers are able to interact with one another on a level different from the classroom, thereby making an additional contribution to education.

As school-based and university-based personnel attempt collaboration and engage in lifelong learning, their roles begin to change. Initiatives of school and university collaboration in systemic reform through strategic intervention require teachers, administrators, and faculty who are willing to explore new roles and responsibilities. These explorations link educators from prekindergarten through adult education in the reform of education. In recently recast roles, educators may be doing any or all of the following:

- Defining performance indicators and authentic performance tasks
- Developing portfolios of assessment techniques
- Networking with colleagues in other schools, districts, and universities around the world through technology
- Modelling teaching strategies and demonstrating their usefulness in performance-based assessments
- Redesigning curriculum around constructivism, interdisciplinary teams, inclusion, and reflective practice

Constructivism, in which learning is viewed as the learner's process of constructing knowledge and personal meaning from new experiences, has very direct implications for teaching and learning in the classroom and in professional development. Taking responsibility for one's own learning, building shared understandings, and using reader response techniques in classrooms, in which meaning is constructed socially, affect how teachers conceptualize their own roles and design their own professional development. Teachers' engaging in the process of reflection, self-examination, and problem solving in efforts to inquire into their own practice represents a fundamental change. Collectively, these themes, trends, and challenges occurring in the midst of school reform dictate the importance of *doing what works* in professional development.

STRATEGIES FOR SUCCESSFUL PROFESSIONAL DEVELOPMENT

There is no blueprint for staff development. Instead, a number of successful professional growth and development opportunities and approaches embrace the principles of current reform efforts. They are "serious and systematic, ... engaging a group of professional educators who work together, a staff, in activities designed specifically to increase the power and authority of their shared work" (Griffin 1991, p. 244).

Teachers who want a successful content area reading program in their schools need more than knowledge and enthusiasm if this important aspect of instruction is to become a reality. Certain support strategies can be used to increase success as colleagues engage in what can best be described as a process of change. When teachers work together to grow professionally, support is essential for change to occur in the school. During professional development, relevant experiences, such as those listed in Table 12.1, need to be provided by teachers and for teachers who want to grow in their ability to deliver content area reading strategies.

"Show me what to do on Monday morning" is a legitimate demand. Often, however, this concern is misinterpreted to mean that classroom teachers are anti-theoretical and anti-research. What teachers are actually saying is, "Show me how to improve my craft. Let me experience the process first, and if it makes sense, let's discuss why it works." Let us explore some of the most effective strategies for professional growth and reflection.

TABLE 12.1	Strategies to Support Change

- Small-group seminars for reflective dialogue
- Journal writing and sketching with response/feedback
- Regularly scheduled meetings with a predictable pattern
- Discussion of research theory and literature with other teachers
- Modelling a strategy with peers
- Microteaching lessons in follow-up session (lesson demonstrations)
- Peer coaching (coworkers give feedback to one another as they use strategies with their classes)
- Guided practice (facilitator leads participants in trying out strategies)
- Structured feedback session (facilitator elicits participant response after strategy is tried)
- Peer support teams (coworkers share the ups and downs that accompany change)
- Mentor and lead teacher models
- On-site and off-site consultants
- Telephone and email hotlines
- Visiting functional sites either in one's own or another building

Source: From "Professional Development," by Jo Anne L. Vacca and Maryann Mraz. Reprinted by permission of the publisher from Wepner, Feeley, and Strickland, *The Administration and Supervision of Reading Programs* (3rd ed.) (New York: Teachers College Press, © 2001 by Teachers College, Columbia University. All rights reserved.).

Using writing and representing, dialogue, problem solving, technology, and action research is congruent with a reflective stance that *teachers* rather than experts hold the knowledge necessary to improve teaching. Teachers can and do become aware of their intuitive knowledge through the process of reflection. "Reflection promotes knowledge on practice, which is the heart of professional growth" (Vacca, Vacca, & Bruneau 1997, p. 445).

Writing and Representing

Writing is a major strategy that teachers can use to grow professionally; writing engages teachers in a process of reflection and self-examination. Writing can be a powerful tool for expressing individual reflection and response. According to Arhar, Holly, and Kasten (2001), "Writing is a powerful process for learning; for describing, synthesizing, analyzing, and interpreting experience; for coming to terms with what we know, how we know it, and why it is important—if it is—to know (p. 229)." In writing, you explore connections between teaching and professional development; you identify and think about your own circumstances and how your experiences influence and shape your teaching and professional development. Some teachers may also find visual representations helpful. Drawing sketches and creating diagrams of how you "see" your teaching is another powerful way to explore your ideas and emotions.

Journals Journals can be both verbal (words) and visual (pictures and diagrams). Waldron (1994) studied five art teachers (teaching kindergarten through grade 12) who kept *journals* for three months. The art teachers, who ranged in experience from three to 20 years, were given journal notebooks, but the format for their entries was intentionally left unstructured so that they could articulate their insights in their own voices. Waldron analyzed the entries for the kinds of thoughts and concerns that novice and veteran art teachers had about their experience; samples of these entries are displayed in Box 12.1. She also wanted to find out what stages the art teachers had passed through in their engagement with reflection on practice. Had teachers been able to articulate previously unexpressed concerns about their individual practice? The researcher contacted the teachers individually once a week to answer their questions about the process, to address any personal concerns, and to offer them consistent encouragement to continue making entries systematically and thoughtfully.

These teachers reported that getting used to keeping journals was a slow process. Some initial entries had been conversational; others were more self-critical, asking lots of questions. One teacher who had already been thinking about her teaching "questioned, analyzed, and began resolving issues for herself." The journal writing seemed "to bring things to consciousness" for the writers. One wrote, "Revelations come and go and sometimes you are lucky enough to be holding a pen in your hand when one strikes you" (Waldron 1994, p. 105).

Journals can serve teachers well as a personal and professional growth tool. This technique, however, requires both time and patience to cultivate. For example, even a 12-week period seemed to be an insufficient amount of time. But the journal entries remained consistent in length and depth. They seemed to accomplish the purpose of "explicating thoughts for the participants" (Waldron 1994, p. 105).

BOX 12.1	**Thoughts About Teaching Expressed in Journals**

Diane, 16 years' experience:

2/18—The drawing unit is making me feel good. The students love what we've been working on—I keep stressing our goals and what we are focusing on so they *know why* they are doing *what* they are doing. I've always been told what a successful teacher I am, but it has only been lately that I've felt clear about what I'm really doing.

Yet there are days that I want to get out so bad I can't stand it. Not so much the kids, but all the other "stuff"—especially the lack of respect for teachers, the constant "blaming" for kids and their lack of education, the moronic treatment of teachers by administrators. We really are not treated as professional adults. It makes me *MAD!!* We are not allowed to leave the building, we are talked down to, we have to "report in" for everything like children. Sometimes I feel the students have more rights than teachers.

Claire, 3 years' experience:

3/22—You know—how does a person do it?—Teach I mean? It seems like you get very little feedback when you're doing good—but they don't hesitate to tell you when you are bad.

4/8—When I make art I spend a lot of time on one project and do fewer projects with more time invested. When I teach, I am still trying out a variety of different approaches because I'm so new—I don't think what I am doing is good enough yet. (Hmmm—I think the same about my art!) I feel like I can always improve—I expect good craft from my students and I do good craft myself.

Source: From *Reflective Practice in Art Education: An Inquiry Model for Staff Development*, by Deborah Z. Waldron. Copyright © 1994 by Deborah Z. Waldron. Reprinted by permission.

Student teachers too can benefit from the use of "field journals" to inquire into their growing understanding of what it means to be a teacher (Rousseau 2000). These journals could also be kept electronically and include pictures of class events and exemplary student work. Connecting teachers on listservs can help to make sharing easier.

Portfolios For both beginning and veteran teachers, another powerful technique that focuses on writing is the development of *portfolios*. A natural bridge from preservice education to the first years of teaching, portfolios are also practical for teachers in mid-career. As purposeful collections of information involving collaboratively chosen artifacts, portfolios can serve teachers in much the same way they do students. For example, portfolios are valuable in evaluating the progress of learners in the classroom. Teachers can use portfolios to assess their own progress in implementing a program, incorporating portfolios into their planning process.

Content area teachers are encouraged to view their diverse students as active readers and writers while meeting their special learning needs. What better way to understand the developmental nature of students than for teachers to be involved themselves in the development of their own portfolios? As Graves (1992) states, "We need more policy makers, administrators, and teachers who know portfolios *from the inside*. Their decisions about portfolio use must include the reality of living and growing with the process of keeping one" (p. 5).

The person responsible for professional development might meet with teachers to discuss their expectations of personal portfolio development. Dates can be set for periodic sharing and for the "final" portfolios to be presented (although, ideally, a portfolio would be continued throughout a teacher's career). What are appropriate pieces to include in a portfolio? Some items that could be part of this portfolio are "journal entries, letters to colleagues, anecdotal writing, formal writing, written plans for classroom lessons, levels-of-use checklists, and script tapes" (George, Moley, & Ogle 1992, p. 54). Visual components are also very useful. Teachers can be encouraged to videotape and audiotape lessons and take photographs of student work.

The group would meet periodically to share the material from their portfolios and the experiences they have had in selecting this material. This approach gives "educators first-hand experience with a strategy they may be using with their students and also encourages teachers to look at their own continuing development" (Vacca & Genzen 1995, p. 150). There are, nevertheless, cautions about the reliance on portfolios without a complete professional development program. "If clear connections are not made between teaching, reflect on and assessment, it seems that portfolios will achieve ends that are more superficial than substantive" (Castle 1999). Portfolios are only one part of a teacher's continuing education.

Dialogue

Another major strategy for teachers seeking professional growth is engaging in collegial dialogue. Sharing in meaningful conversation with professional colleagues works well with writing techniques such as keeping journals and logs and developing a portfolio.

In her study, Waldron (1994) combined journal writing with dialogue sessions to engage the five visual arts teachers in systematic reflection over 12 weeks. Her intent was to describe the processes of reflective teaching and collegial dialogue of inservice art teachers. To find out how teachers think about their episodes of practice—how they make sense of them and how they learn from them—she invited them to five seminar sessions, each lasting 90 minutes. Sometimes their written entries addressed personal concerns about individual practice and reactions to aspects of the collegial dialogue in seminar sharing sessions. According to one experienced teacher, "I've found I'm reflecting more carefully and slowing down my high-speed chase through the days." Another reported that she enjoyed the gatherings, but "I still find it hard to find the time to write it all down." The first two seminar sessions were spent establishing rapport and group identity, telling stories, and discussing many topics. As the teachers grew comfortable with one another, they focused more on common situations, ideas, and solutions. The dialogue sessions were useful in exploring concerns, frustrations, and personal and professional issues identified by both early-career and veteran art teachers, often in their journals. Frustrations expressed by early-career art teachers dealt more often with "constraints they felt to be directed at them personally which infringed upon their time, while veteran art teachers were more often frustrated by outward directed concerns, those that interacted with the school, community, and field" (p. 129). Waldron concludes that changes were evident in the teachers' growth in the *process* of engaging in collegial dialogue.

As teachers interact in group meetings over time and try to make sense of their experiences, they grow in several ways. According to Clemente (1992), who observed teachers in a two-year school/university urban-change project, they talked about expanding their own roles and taking curricular risks. The teachers clearly supported one another in this urban school system as they gained new perspectives on their roles. Furthermore, as the teachers interacted in meetings over time, their people-to-people skills seemed to improve. Several of the teachers showed movement toward the level of introspective questioning. As one teacher said, "Am I doing what I am supposed to be doing? Now I question everything I do" (p. 183). During the informal meetings, where participants gathered to talk about their classroom practice, frustrations were vented. These were sessions where teachers chose to work with others who had similar philosophies as a means of improving their teaching practices. These "situational aspects" were "supportive oases of confidence, trust, rapport, and friendship" (p. 185).

Where teachers were philosophically similar to each other, there was less confrontation and better communication. "In these situations ... communication ... went smoothly because there was a basis of trust and confidence in one another" (p. 191). Clemente's work corroborates Holly's (1989) findings that the increased opportunity to interact with other teachers, regardless of the setting, is perceived as beneficial by teachers, who viewed their colleagues as valuable resources. By engaging in a common conversation, teachers can begin to see themselves as professionals working toward a single goal—the improvement of teaching and learning.

Problem Solving

By engaging in mutual inquiry or problem solving, teachers reflect on their own practice, which strengthens teaching ability. In fact, classroom decision-making from a reflective viewpoint *requires* concrete problem solving. Reflection enables content area reading teachers to consider what works in their classrooms as they attempt to solve day-to-day problems.

One time-tested inquiry model is action planning. Before implementing the basic steps in action planning, it's important to identify needs, concerns, and interests of the larger teaching staff; an informal survey could accomplish this.

Once the survey results are analyzed, the faculty team follows some rather explicit procedures to develop an action plan that looks like this:

I. Define the Problem

    A. The problem as we understand it:

        Large vocabulary and concept load in secondary school textbooks

    B. The following people are involved in the problem:

        Teachers in selecting and teaching vocabulary terms and students who act uninterested

    C. Other factors relevant to the problem:

        Pressures to get through the content and produce acceptable test scores

D. One aspect of the problem we need to change:

Finding more effective ways of teaching vocabulary to students

II. Plan for Change

A. Exactly what are we trying to accomplish?

Find better ways to use social studies and history subject matter as a natural context for the development of students' vocabularies.

B. What behaviour is implied?

History and social studies teachers will identify keywords, show students interrelationships, preteach, and guide students. Students will understand and use strategies they are shown.

C. Who is going to do it?

Each team member will meet with several other teachers to get their input, then come back to the team. Eventually, most of the history and social studies staff and their students will be involved.

D. Can it be done?

Yes. There is every reason to expect support from the staff because the problem is a real one and we all expect improvement.

E. What tangible evidence will indicate change?

Teachers will be meeting to share vocabulary strategies, and students will be observed improving their vocabularies in class and using this knowledge and skill in tests.

III. Take Action Steps

A. Actions that need to be taken:
   1. Discussions with and memo to faculty
   2. Selecting consultant
   3. Arranging workshops for faculty with and without consultant
   4. Formative evaluations of progress
   5. Concerted effort in classroom vocabulary instruction
   6. Post-assessment of teachers, consultant, students; summative evaluation compiled

B. For each action, Persons responsible/Timing/Necessary resources:
   1. Team and principal/January/School office budget
   2. Team and faculty/January/Team requesting money from district staff-development committee
   3. Principal/February/Principal
   4. Team and principal/February, March/Released time for workshops budgeted; consultant
   5. Team and faculty/April/Materials reproduced
   6. Team, principal, and planning committee/May/Principal; report disseminated

Technology Use

Learning to use technology has revolutionized the way educators access information and communicate with each other. With technology, teachers can choose to address specific individual interests or classroom needs and receive almost instant feedback. They can

- Infuse technology into teaching practices in different subjects
- Investigate skills students need to function in the twenty-first century
- Design a classroom or school webpage
- Meet people in various occupations
- Connect with students and teachers in other communities

There is, quite literally, a whole world of professional development opportunities available to today's teacher on the internet. The path to professional growth can be as simple as an email correspondence with a colleague or two to share ideas and lesson plans. More extensive connections can also be established by exploring the educational offerings of numerous websites and their accompanying links. Nearly every professional organization, journal, and magazine also has a site on the internet that can provide teachers with valuable resources and references. In addition, the internet is a good place to look for grant and funding information for kindergarten through grade 12 programs in many subject areas.

Most of the major online service providers have entire sections dedicated to teachers and education. Listservs and conversation exchange areas are set up for educators to interact.

Curricular references can also be found by searching using other relevant terms, such as "social studies teaching," "physical education," and "health education." Box 12.2 on pages 358 and 359 provides a sampling of the websites, mailing lists, and newsgroups available on the internet for professional growth, lesson planning, and conversations with colleagues.

The internet is, indeed, an appropriate starting point for building cross-disciplinary connections also, as the information can be collected so easily and quickly. Teachers can work independently, learning in areas of specific interest to themselves, or they can interact with colleagues across disciplines, grade levels, and geographic areas. The possibilities are endless.

Action Research

Action research is enjoying a resurgence in popularity through the teacher-as-researcher movement. When classroom teachers pursue action research, they investigate questions that they themselves have generated about teaching and learning. Beginning with the questions, "What do I think?" and "How will I know?" teacher-researchers gather evidence in their classrooms to test their hypotheses and then evaluate their results (Gove & Kennedy-Calloway 1992). Although it's probably true that "all good teachers participate in teacher research because they reflect about students' learning (and their own)" (Patterson & Shannon 1993, p. 8), it's not often that they do so as part of planned professional development.

One systematic, common-sense procedure that we've found effective is to begin by designing an inquiry plan such as the one in Figure 12.2 on page 360. In this particular plan, developed by Gary, an experienced grade 6 teacher in a suburban school district, the focus of concern is the newly mandated process of inclusion: teaching diverse learners with diverse needs in the same classroom. A critical issue throughout education, inclusion is a good example of a topic that cuts across all subject areas and that relates to both the classroom learning level and the school organizational level.

BOX 12.2	**Nothing but Net**

Resources, Mailing Lists, and Newsgroups for Professional Growth

INFORMATION AND PLANNING RESOURCES

CM: Canadian Review of Materials
www.umanitoba.ca/outreach/cm

This electronic review of Canadian books and videos allows teachers to make more informed choices for their classroom library and their own professional reading.

Textual Studies in Canada
www.caribou.bc.ca/ae/engml/tsc

Covers cultural text in Canada, including literature, visual arts, and interdisciplinary studies.

The Global Schoolhouse
www.globalschoolhouse.org

Connects with students around the world for project-oriented learning.

Canada's School Net
www.schoolnet.ca

A database of educational resources in Canada.

Canadian Education on the Web
www.oise.utoronto.ca/~mpress/eduweb/eduweb.html

Contains lesson plans and links to other resources.

PBS TeacherSource
www.pbs.org/teachersource/

Provides information, lesson plans, and links to resources related to television programs appearing on the Public Broadcasting Service stations.

Statistics Canada
www.statscan.ca

Includes statistics on the nature and growth of education.

Educating.net
www.educating.net

"A portal to the world of knowledge."

LISTSERVS/MAILING LISTS

Discussion Group for Curricular Issues

Community Learning Network
www.cln.org/lists/home.html

Issues related to education, grades K-12.

Discussion Groups for Language Arts

KIDLIT-L
listserv@bingvmb.bitnet

Children's literature.

The main benefit to working through several drafts of the plan, first individually and then with colleagues, is that it helps build confidence in the teacher-researcher. Before much time had elapsed, for example, Gary found himself immersed in conducting the action research. By the time he revised his inquiry plan, he was moving from step 3 to step 4 in the action research process:

1. *Identify a problem or situation.*
2. *Formulate specific research questions.*

Teachers Applying Whole Language (TAWL)

www.stfx.ca/people/rjmackin/ed467/
listservs.htm

Whole language.

Mailing Lists Related to Children's Literature

www.ucalgary.ca/~dkbrown/
listserv.html

Several mailing lists relating to children's literature.

University of British Columbia's School of Library, Archival and Information Studies

www.slais.ubc.ca/courses/libr522a/03-04-wt2/
www-links.htm

A collection of web links for children's literature.

Discussion Groups for Mathematics

MATHSED-L

listserv@deakin.edu.au

Discussion for mathematics educators.

NCTM-L

listproc@sci-ed.fit.edu

National Council of Teachers of Mathematics discussions.

Discussion Groups for Science

Science Education

www.mste.uiuc.edu/listservs/
subjectsearch.html#Science

A very large clearinghouse of education mailing lists.

CYBERMARCH-NET

majordomo@igc.apc.org

Environmental education.

IMSE-L

listserv@uwf.cc.uwf.edu

Sponsored by the Institute for Math and Science Education.

T321-L

listserv@mizzou1.missouri.edu

Science in elementary schools.

TIMS-L

listserv@uicvm.uic.edu

Sponsored by the Teaching Integrated Mathematics and Science (TIMS) Project.

Discussion Group for Social Studies

SchoolNet

www.schoolnet.ca

A large, well-maintained site for a variety of educational issues.

3. *Determine the method and procedure for investigating the question.*
4. *Carry out research; collect data.*
5. *Look at the data; analyze them; draw conclusions.*
6. *Make decisions based on the results of the research.*

Action research, as a strategy for professional development, incorporates the first three strategies of empowerment: writing and representing, dialogue, and problem solving. It

Action Research: Teachers identifying and
answering their most pressing questions,
finding solutions, and engaging in
practice-centred inquiry

Name: <u>Gary Hargrove</u>

Planning Your Study:

1. What is being studied in your field? <u>Inclusion, graded vs. nongraded, assessment, portfolios</u>

2. What are you interested in studying? <u>Inclusion</u>

3. How do you choose to go about it? <u>(see below)</u>

Inquiry Plan

Purpose	Research Questions	Procedures
1. To determine the positive effects of inclusive schooling 2. To determine how an inclusive classroom in grade 6 and 7 can be organized to benefit the teachers and the students	1. How do teachers provide a supportive environment in which students with "regular" and special needs can grow together? 2. What types of teaching strategies and approaches should be used to ensure success? 3. In what ways do the students intereact in the classroom? 4. How are teachers of grades 6 and 7 currently adjusting to the new program?	Interview teachers involved in the process of inclusion. Interview students in inclusive classrooms Observe classrooms in the morning and afternoon over a three-week period Interview teachers who have never dealt with inclusion.

FIGURE 12.2 **An Inquiry Plan for Action Research**

can be especially helpful to content area teachers who try many of the instructional strategies suggested in this book. They gain experience with innovations while receiving support from colleagues, changing their own teaching, and growing professionally.

PROFESSIONAL DEVELOPMENT PLANS

Professional development activities will naturally vary over the course of a teacher's career, as one's professional focus and interests move from internal to external with years of experience. An early-career teacher, for example, might spend more time and energy trying out various techniques in the classroom and dealing with classroom management issues. A 15-year veteran teacher, by contrast, might be looking for alternative ways to contribute to the profession or otherwise dealing with burnout issues. There are a number of successful strategies for growth and reflection in the teaching profession. With some planning, they can be used to benefit teachers at all points throughout their career. Let's see how two teachers, a novice and a veteran, put together individual plans for professional development.

Entry-Year Grade 7 Teacher

Darby is a first-year teacher in a grade 7 classroom. Her *primary* concern is gaining a sense of mastery and comfort with being "in charge"—not only of all the daily operations of her classroom but also of the educational life of her students! The journal could be her most indispensable tool to make sense of it all. By keeping a notebook on her desk, Darby can write down random thoughts, concerns, questions, and reflections whenever she has the chance. Reading the entries every so often can provide Darby with insight into her own thinking as a teacher. If she can find a like-minded colleague (maybe even a veteran teacher) with whom to share the discoveries revealed in her journal, it can initiate conversations, furnish each teacher with fresh perspectives, and generate new ideas to use in the classroom.

Darby's special curricular interest is mathematics. By joining a professional organization, such as the National Council of Teachers of Mathematics, she can stay abreast of current thinking in the field, as well as learn practical, often hands-on, ideas for her teaching. Subscribing to a teacher's journal or magazine can also keep Darby connected with the larger field of education without being overwhelming.

Many organizations sponsor workshops and conferences throughout the year. By attending even one a year, Darby would renew and recharge her energy and enthusiasm. She would interact with fellow teachers, view the latest in curriculum materials, and pick up lots of ideas for her classroom.

Darby will soon begin making application to university for admission into the new middle school education program. As part of her course requirements, she may well be engaged in doing learning logs, using technology to access information, and planning to begin action research.

Veteran Art Teacher

Farouk, an art teacher, has taught at every level, from kindergarten to grade 12, but is currently at a middle school. Throughout his 19-year career, Farouk, who has a master's degree in curriculum and instruction, has kept a journal. Though his entries were sometimes far between, he always remembered to record his thoughts, plans, and reflections on the first workday of the school year as a way to centre himself and reconnect to the work at hand. Rereading these entries gives Farouk an idea of how his perspective has evolved over the years. He often discusses his thinking with several colleagues with whom he has worked for many years. They've grown together.

Farouk has also maintained an active membership in a number of professional organizations during his career, including both province- and national-level art education associations. These connections have given him a broader perspective on his field and allowed him to both learn from and share with colleagues, by attending and presenting at conferences and subscribing to publications. The provincial association provides Farouk with a close network of supportive colleagues and lots of practical teaching ideas. The national association enriches Farouk's interest in the more academic scholarly theory and research side of art education and keeps him in tune with the national issues and scope of the field.

Farouk began by simply attending one provincial conference a year, early in his career. Then, after earning his master's degree over a four-year period, he tried presenting a session at a provincial conference and then attended a national conference in Toronto. The next step was to write a proposal and become a presenter at the national level. All these activities became avenues for Farouk to grow as a teacher and a professional.

Farouk has found four other avenues that keep him "charged" and excited about teaching. One is taking part in a small group of middle school teachers who set out to collaborate on developing a project that would break down disciplinary boundaries. They initiated an entirely new curriculum opportunity for their school—a school garden. They have researched interdisciplinary connections, organized school and community people to plan and build the garden, and worked together to gather resources and support for the project. His art students even covered an entire outside wall of the school with a garden mural.

A second avenue for Farouk is serving as a mentor for fieldwork and student teaching interns from a nearby university's teacher education program. He tries to take one student a semester, spending extra time during and after the regular school day talking with and listening to his mentee. Farouk attends one or two meetings a year at the university in connection with his responsibilities and has become friendly with several of his counterparts from other local school districts.

Third, Farouk has explored the possibilities of grant writing. Funds are available from numerous sources for creative and innovative curriculum programs for students. Farouk has discovered that writing grants have provided him with an unanticipated benefit: he has had to articulate his beliefs about education, his goals for the art education of his students, and his own perspective on teaching, thereby clarifying why he does what he does. He has written many grants and received some, but he has learned a lot about himself and teaching in the process, regardless of the outcome.

Fourth, Farouk recently discovered for himself the benefit of "primary source" professional development. He participated in a workshop on Mayan archaeology, for educators, on-site in Belize. Being *in* the environment while studying it, and learning how to transmit that knowledge to students, truly made a difference. First hand experiences of this kind are both personally and professionally enriching. Farouk prepared for this experience by reading and studying about the Maya and the rain forest. One source he used was the online program Mayaquest. This interactive curriculum, used in many classrooms, involved the contributions of Mayan experts in a number of fields and provided Farouk with extensive background information, both for himself as a professional and for use with his students in the classroom.

The next step for Farouk, as he nears the last phase of his teaching career, is to share what he has learned with others. This he can do by continuing to mentor novice teachers or by starting a study group in which the members simply discuss concerns they have—perhaps using their own journals. He can write articles for the publications he has read for years. And he can continue to attend and present at conferences—to inspire his newer colleagues to continue their own learning as they foster the learning of their students.

Accreditation of Teacher Education

While not every province in Canada has an accreditation process for faculties of education (and thus of their students and future teachers), Ontario is a notable exception. The Ontario College of Teachers, created in 1996, has a mandate to license, govern, and regulate the practice of teaching in Ontario (Elliot & Faubert-McCabe 2002). Faculties must apply to be accredited to produce teachers who could meet the Standards of Practice for the Teaching Profession (1998).

British Columbia is another example. Its College of Teachers (BCCT) exerted a great deal of influence over preservice faculties of education until 2003 when the government and the deans of education in British Columbia decided to evaluate their teacher education programs without undue influence from the BCCT. Are teachers who have graduated from government-accredited institutions more effective than those from nonaccredited institutions? More research needs to be conducted on this important issue, especially in Canada, where teacher education programs vary from province to province.

LOOKING BACK, LOOKING FORWARD

We have focused in this chapter on growth and reflection in the teaching profession as a developmental, continuing process for content area teachers. To attract and retain good teachers who will incorporate content area reading into their instructional repertoires, professional growth opportunities are designed on the principles of lifelong learning and planned change. They are the result of collaborative inquiry—among teachers, administrators, specialists, and consultants—who reflect on their own practice.

Professional development programs with clear purposes are more likely to be perceived as relevant by the participants. Hence planners of professional development may deal with a range of purposes, from improved proficiency test scores to teachers' becoming reflective practitioners.

We can learn from what works. Many effective programs are described in reports and brochures. Recurring characteristics of these programs are incorporated into the guidelines and principles of professional development. In planning for professional development where opportunities for reflection and inquiry are highly valued, there are a number of strategies. Building on teachers' orientation to learning as adults, their experiences, and their career stage, we proposed five strategies: *writing and representing* for a personal sense of purpose, *dialoguing* and *problem solving* with colleagues, *using technology* for information and communication, and inquiring through *action research*.

Finally, we illustrated through two teachers, Darby and Farouk, ways in which strategies that promote growth and reflection can be integrated into individual plans for professional development, whether early or later in one's career.

MINDS-ON

1. Imagine that you are part of a committee in charge of planning a professional development program for teachers in your school. Considering the wide range of experience levels among the teachers, what different types of growth and development activities might you devise to meet individual needs?

2. Reflect on a time when you teamed with one or more people on a project. What were some of the benefits derived from the collaboration? What were some of the drawbacks? If you are a preservice teacher, speculate on how your experience might be similar or different in a school context; if you are an inservice teacher, reflect on an actual in-school collaboration.

3. How do professionals in various fields improve their craft through reflection? In what way can reflection enhance a teacher's professional growth? How might portfolios, journals, and diaries aid in this process?

4. Examine the following professional development needs: (a) to obtain better information and to be able to use it more rationally, (b) to reconsider one's own beliefs in order to come to a better understanding of oneself, and (c) to explore alternative strategies for improving one's teaching and learning. Where would you place your own professional needs, and how do they compare with those of others in your group?

HANDS-ON

1. As part of a program for professional development, the administration at your school has decided to encourage teachers to develop professional portfolios. You have been asked to participate on a committee to develop guidelines for the items that might be included. Some colleagues have suggested journal entries, letters to colleagues and students, anecdotal writing, formal writing, lesson plans, checklists, and videotapes of lessons. After searching the web for existing provincial guidelines, what would you add to and delete from this list? Why?

2. Team with several people in the class who teach or will be teaching in your content area and develop a survey to identify needs and concerns of your teaching colleagues. Then complete the survey and analyze the results.

3. Think of yourself as a teacher-researcher. Come up with a question that you believe could be answered by a classroom experiment. Conduct the experiment and share the results with the class.

4. Define teachers' career cycles in relation to a category. You might choose levels of expertise, levels of personal needs, levels of experience, or any other category you find appropriate. Using this category, create a chart of teacher career cycles and suggest appropriate professional development activities for each stage.

SUGGESTED READINGS

Begoray, D. (2000). Positive effect from negative affect: Language arts teacher candidates reconstructing professional images. *Journal of Professional Studies*, 8(1), 22–31.

Brown, J., & Sheppard. B. (1997). Professional development: What do we know and where are we going? http://www.mun.ca/educ/faculty/mwatch/win97/pdfinal.htm.

Castle, J. (1999). Preservice teachers' perceptions of their portfolio experience. *Journal of Professional Studies, 6*(2), 34–43.

Danielson, C. (1996). *Enhancing professional practice: A framework for teaching.* Alexandria, VA: Association for Supervision and Curriculum Development.

Elliot, A., & Faubert-McCabe, P. (2002). Catalyst for institutional renewal: An accreditation story told through two lenses. *Journal of Professional Studies, 9*(2), 32–42.

Morin, F. (1994). A professional development model for planned change in arts education. *Canadian Journal of Research in Music Education, 35*(7), 5–12.

Murphy, E., & Laferriere, T. (2003). Virtual communities for professional development: Helping teachers map the territory in landscapes without bearings. *Alberta Journal of Educational Research, 49*(2), 70–82.

National Board for Professional Teaching Standards. (2000). Washington, DC. http://www.nbpts.org.

Patterson, L., Santa, C., Short, K., & Smith, K. (Eds.). (1993). *Teachers are researchers: Reflection and action*. Newark, DE: International Reading Association.

Rousseau, N. (2000). Student teachers' reflective inquiry as reported in their field journals. *Journal of Professional Studies, 8*(1), 53–59.

Appendix A

Internet Addresses for Content Areas

The websites that we have selected illustrate additional possibilities for locating information resources on the internet in various content areas. Because the web is a fluid and continually changing medium, some of the locations listed here may no longer be in operation.

THE ARTS

The Royal British Columbia Museum
http://www.rbcm.gov.bc.ca

The Louvre Museum
http://www.louvre.fr/louvrea.htm

ArtNet
http://www.artnet.com

A Fine Arts Search Engine
http://www.artcyclopedia.com/museums.html

Art and Architecture History
http://rubens.anu.edu.au

Bayly African Mask Exhibit
http://cti.itc.virginia.edu/~bcr/African_Mask.html

The First Impressionist Exhibition, 1874
http://www.artchive.com/74nadar.htm

Downloadable Folk Songs with Lyrics
http://www.mudcat.org/threads.cfm

The Experience Music Project
http://www.emplive.com

The Fine Art Forum
http://www.msstate.edu/Fineart_Online/home.html

The Essentials of Music, an Overview of Classical Music
http://www.essentialsofmusic.com

A Passion for Jazz
http://www.apassion4jazz.net

Canadian Music Centre
http://www.musiccentre.ca

Children's Music Web
http://www.childrensmusic.org

Music Education
http://datadragon.com/education

ENGLISH LANGUAGE ARTS

The National Library and Archives Canada
http://www.nlc-bnc.ca

Culture Canada
http://culturecanada.gc.ca/

The Internet Public Library
http://ipl.org

H-Net, Humanities and Social Sciences Resources
http://www2.h-net.msu.edu

Quotations
http://www.quotationspage.com

Children's Literature
http://www.armory.com/~web/notes.html

Jolly Rogers Repository of Resources for Teen Readers
http://jollyroger.com/treasureisland.html

Children's Writings
http://www.ucalgary.ca/~dkbrown/writings.html

Research Paper Resources
http://owl.english.purdue.edu/workshops/hypertext/ResearchW/

The Purdue Writing Lab Online
http://owl.english.purdue.edu

Shakespeare Resources
http://www.shakespeare-online.com

Canadian Poets
http://www.library.utoronto.ca/canpoetry/index_poet.htm

Virtual Green Gables
http://www.gov.pe.ca/greengables/index.php3

The Dickens Page
http://lang.nagoya-u.ac.jp/~matsuoka/Dickens.html

The C. S. Lewis Web Site
http://cslewis.drzeus.net

The Lewis Carroll Home Page
http://www.lewiscarroll.org/carroll.html

The Little Prince by Antoine de Saint Exupéry
http://www.angelfire.com/hi/littleprince/

Classics and Antiquity Links
http://classics.mit.edu/

The Encyclopedia Mythica
http://www.pantheon.org

Mayan Folktales
http://www.folkart.com/~latitude/folktale/folktale.htm

Mythweb
http://www.mythweb.com

The Labyrinth: Medieval Studies Resources
http://labyrinth.georgetown.edu

FOREIGN LANGUAGE

Canadian Language Associations
http://www.caslt.org/research/association_lang_can.htm

The French Immersion Teacher's Guide to the Internet
http://www.stemnet.nf.ca/~elmurphy/emurphy/travel.html

Webspañol
http://www.geocities.com/Athens/Thebes/6177/

Linguistic Funland
http://www.linguistic-funland.com

Columbia Index of Language Lessons
http://www.col-ed.org/cur/

Foreign Language Teaching Technologies
http://www.cortland.edu/flteach

Foreign Language Resource Center
http://www.educ.iastate.edu/nflrc/

Ethnologue
http://www.ethnologue.com

Say Hello in More Than 800 Different Languages
http://www.elite.net/~runner/jennifers/

Newspapers of the World
http://www.onlinenewspapers.com

HEALTH LESSONS AND LINKS

Sexuality and U
http://www.sexualityandu.ca/eng/

Sexuality, Health, and Relationship Education
http://www.share-program.com

Canadian Health Network
http://www.canadian-health-network.ca

The Canadian Red Cross
http://www.redcross.ca

Health World Online
http://healthy.net

The Calorie Control Council
http://www.caloriecontrol.org

BrainPOP: Health
http://www.brainpop.com/health/seeall.weml

MATHEMATICS

Coolmath.com
http://www.coolmath.com

Columbia Index of Mathematics Lesson Plans
http://www.col-ed.org/cur/

Geometry Online
http://math.rice.edu/~lanius/Geom/

Online Math Lessons
http://score.kings.k12.ca.us/lessons.html

Math.com
http://www.math.com

Webmath
http://school.discovery.com/homeworkhelp/webmath/

Education Place Brain Teasers
http://www.eduplace.com/math/brain/

Brain Teasers and Math Puzzles
http://www.syvum.com/teasers/

FunBrain.com
http://www.funbrain.com/index.html

MathStories.com
http://www.mathstories.com

Aunty Math: Math Challenges for K-5 Learners
http://www.dupagechildrensmuseum.org/aunty/index.html

Connect 4
http://www2.allmixedup.com/connect/connect.cgi?render=1

Math History
http://www-gap.dcs.st-and.ac.uk/~history

The National Council of Teachers of Mathematics (United States)
http://nctm.org

The Birthday Problem
http://www.mste.uiuc.edu/reese/birthday/intro.html

The Monty Hall Problem Probability Page
http://www.cut-the-knot.com/probability.html

Mathematics Miscellany
http://www.cut-the-knot.com/content.shtml

SCIENCE

Environment Canada: The Green Lane
http://www.ec.gc.ca

Canadian Weather
http://www.weatheroffice.ec.gc.ca/canada_e.html

BrainPOP: Science
http://www.brainpop.com/science/seeall.weml

Columbia Index of Science Lessons
http://www.col-ed.org/cur/science.html

Canadian Geographic
http://canadiangeographic.ca

The National Geographic Society Online
http://www.nationalgeographic.com

Canadian Geography Resources
http://www.canadainfolink.ca/geog.htm

Test Your Geography Knowledge
http://www.lizardpoint.com/fun/geoquiz/

Species at Risk
http://www.speciesatrisk.gc.ca

The Global Warming Information Page
http://www.globalwarming.org

Eco Net
http://www.igc.org/home/econet/index.html

Royal Astronomical Societies of Canada
http://starfinders.cvnet.net/links.htm

Down-to-Earth Astronomy
http://oposite.stsci.edu

NASA Science in the Classroom
http://quest.arc.nasa.gov/index.html

Herzburg Institute of Astrophysics
http://hia.nrc.ca

Exploratorium
http://www.exploratorium.edu

StarGazer
http://www.outerbody.com/stargazer/

Astronomy
http://www.astronomy.com/home.asp

Space.com, Daily News on Space Exploration
http://www.space.com/missionlaunches/

The Search for Extraterrestrial Intelligence
http://www.seti.org

The National Science Foundation (United States)
http://www.nsf.gov

The National Museum of Natural History
http://www.mnh.si.edu

Discovery Channel Canada
http://www.exn.ca

Volcano World
http://volcano.und.nodak.edu

Artificial Intelligence
http://www-aig.jpl.nasa.gov

Dinosauria
http://www.dinosauria.com

When Dinosaurs Were Gone
http://www.dinosgone.org http://www.dinosgone.org

WhaleNet
http://whale.wheelock.edu

Teacher Resources on Whales
http://ww.stemnet.nf.ca/CITE/whaleteacher.htm

Horticulture for Kids
http://aggie-horticulture.tamu.edu/kindergarden/ delete

The SeaWiFS Project, Earth Imagery
http://seawifs.gsfc.nasa.gov/SEAWIFS.html

Ask An Expert
http://askanexpert.com

Hydrology
http://www.ghcc.msfc.nasa.gov

The Bug Club
http://www.ex.ac.uk/bugclub/

Quirks and Quarks
http://radio.cbc.ca/programs/quirks/

SOCIAL STUDIES

Historica
http://www.histori.ca

Canada: Heirloom Series
http://collections.ic.gc.ca/heirloom_series/

Canada in the Making
http://www.canadiana.org/citm/

National Library of Canada: Canadian History
http://www.nlc-bnc.ca/history/index-e.html

Canadiana: The Canadian Resource Page
http://www-2.cs.cmu.edu/afs/cs.cmu.edu/user/clamen/misc/Canadiana

Images Canada
http://www.imagescanada.ca

Hudson's Bay Company's Digital Collections
http://collections.ic.gc.ca/hbc/

First Nations Histories
http://www.tolatsga.org/Compacts.html

Aboriginal Studies Virtual Library
http://www.ciolek.com/WWWVL-Aboriginal.html

Native American Resources
http://www.hanksville.org/NAresources/

First Nations Voices
http://www.gallery.ca/english/default_1149.htm

Mi'kmaq Portraits Collection
http://museum.gov.ns.ca/mikmaq/index.htm

Native American Portraits and History
http://www.npg.si.edu/col/native/index.htm

The National Museum of the American Indian
http://www.nmai.si.edu

Vikings
http://www.pc.gc.ca/lhn-nhs/nl/meadows/index_e.asp

Virtual Museum of New France
http://www.civilisations.ca/vmnf/vmnfe.asp

Henry Hudson
http://www.ianchadwick.com/hudson/

Inuit and Englishmen: The Nunavut Voyages of Martin Frobisher
http://www.civilization.ca/hist/frobisher/frint01e.html

Canadian Railway History
http://imagescn.technomuses.ca/photoessays/railways/railways01.cfm

Indepth: Chinese Immigration
http://www.cbc.ca/news/indepth/chinese/

Famous Canadians
http://www.cln.org/themes/famous.html

Women from Canada's Past
http://www.niagara.com/~merrwill/

Canadian Women's Rights
http://www.womennet.ca

Canadian Composer Harry Somers
http://www.harrysomers.com/aboutHS.htm

The Underground Railroad
http://education.ucdavis.edu/NEW/STC/lesson/socstud/railroad/contents.htm

1920s Canada
http://www.micromedia.ca/Timeline/1920-1929.htm

Farming and Rural Life in Canada
http://www.tv.cbc.ca/newsinreview/feb99/farm/farm.htm

The Mad Trapper of Rat River
http://www.usask.ca/education/ideas/tplan/sslp/yukon/ratriver.htm

Canadian War Museum
http://www.civilization.ca/cwm/cwme.asp

Canadian Military History
http://www.nlc-bnc.ca/2/38/index-e.html

War of 1812
http://www.warof1812.ca

Canada in World War I
http://www.archives.ca/05/0518_e.html

A Multimedia History of World War I
http://www.firstworldwar.com

Trenches on the Web: WW I History
http://www.worldwar1.com/tlindex.htm

Pierre Trudeau
http://cbc.ca/news/indepth/trudeau/archives.html

Canadian Constitutional Acts, 1867 to 1982
http://laws.justice.gc.ca/en/const/index.html

Canadian Constitutional Documents
http://www.solon.org/Constitutions/Canada/English/index.html

Prime Minister of Canada
http://www.pm.gc.ca

Canadian Genealogy and History
http://www.islandnet.com/~jveinot/cghl/cghl.html

Genealogy Today
http://www.genealogytoday.com/ca/

RCMP Organized Crime
http://www.rcmp-grc.gc.ca/organizedcrime/index_e.htm

Canadian Softwood Dispute
http://www.Canada.com/national/features/softwooddispute/

Internet Modern History Sourcebook
http://www.fordham.edu/halsall/mod/modsbook.html

The Dead Sea Scrolls
http://www.ibiblio.org/expo/deadsea.scrolls.exhibit/intro.html

Links to Greek History
http://www.showgate.com/medea/grklink.html

The Roman Empire
http://www.geocities.com/Athens/Forum/6946/rome.html

Roman History and Artifacts
http://www.forumromanum.org

Mayan History
http://www.crystalinks.com/mayanhistory.html

K-12 African Studies Resources
http://www.sas.upenn.edu/African_Studies/K-12/AFR_GIDE.html

African Timelines
http://www.cocc.edu/cagatucci/classes/hum211/timelines/htimelinetoc.htm

100+ Links to Indigenous Asian and Middle Eastern Resources
http://www.cwis.org/wwwvl/indig-vl.html#asia

The Middle East Institute
http://www.mideasti.org

Middle Eastern Cultural Information by Country
http://www.mideasttravelnet.com/mideastsite/

The Aaron Copeland Collection
http://memory.loc.gov/ammem/achtml/achome.html

The Reformation
http://www.mun.ca/rels/reform/

China the Beautiful
http://www.chinapage.com/china.html

Modern Japanese History
http://www.jiyuu-shikan.org/e/index.html

Holocaust and Anti-Racism Organization Links
http:www.vhec.org/links/links.html

History Television
http://www.historytelevision.ca

Jewish History
http://www.nmajh.org/images/007.htm

Russian History
http://www.departments.bucknell.edu/russian/

Anglo-Boer War
http://www.anglo-boer.co.za

The History of India
http://www.historyofindia.com

An American Timeline
http://www.americasstory.com/cgi-bin/page.cgi/jb/

The Salem Witch Trials
http://www.salemwitchmuseum.com

Boston Tea Party
http://pages.infinit.net/aaricia/tea/bosto2.htm

American Civil War History
http://www.civilwar.com

WPA Slave Narratives
http://newdeal.feri.org/asn/

The American Civil Rights Movement
http://www.cr.nps.gov/nr/travel/civilrights/intro.htm

Battlefield Vietnam
http://www.pbs.org/battlefieldvietnam/

Propaganda Research
http://www.propagandacritic.com

The International Monetary Fund
http://www.imf.org

Anthropology Net
http://www.anthro.net

Atomic Archive
http://www.atomicarchive.com

VOCATIONAL EDUCATION

Canadian University and College Information Site
http://www.uc411.com/careermap.asp

Canada's National Centre for Occupational Health and Safety Information
http://www.ccohs.ca

Career: The Journal of Industrial Teacher Education
http://scholar.lib.vt.edu/ejournals/JITE/

Financial Aid in Canada
http://www.campusaccess.com/campus_web/educ/e2fin.htm

Useful Web Sites in Technical and Vocational Education
http://www.umanitoba.ca/unevoc/link.shtml

Appendix B

Graphic Representations with Text Frames

Graphic representations are visual illustrations of verbal statements. Frames are sets of questions or categories that are fundamental to understanding a given topic. Here are shown nine "generic" graphic forms with their corresponding frames. Also given are examples of topics that could be represented by each graphic form. These graphics show at a glance the key parts of the whole and their relations, helping the learner to comprehend text and solve problems.

Spider Map

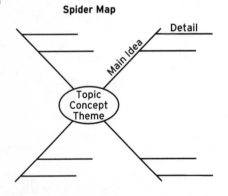

Used to describe a central idea: a thing (a geographic region), process (meiosis), concept (altruism), or proposition with support (experimental drugs should be available to AIDS victims). Key frame questions: What is the central idea? What are its attributes? What are its functions?

Used to describe the stages of something (the life cycle of a primate); the steps in a linear procedure (how to neutralize an acid); a sequence of events (how feudalism led to the formation of nation-states); or the goals, actions, and outcomes of a historical figure or character in a novel (the rise and fall of Napoleon). Key frame questions: What is the object, procedure, or initiating event? What are the stages or steps? How do they lead to one another? What is the final outcome?

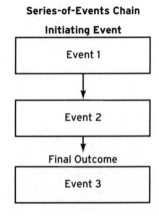

Used for time lines showing histor-ical events or ages (grade levels in school), degrees of something (weight), shades of meaning (Likert scales), or ratings scales (achieve-ment in school). Key frame ques-tions: What is being scaled? What are the end points?

Continuum/Scale

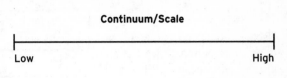

Low

High

Compare/Contrast Matrix

	Name 1	Name 2
Attribute 1		
Attribute 2		
Attribute 3		

Used to show similarities and dif-ferences between two things (peo-ple, places, events, ideas, etc.). Key frame questions: What things are being compared? How are they similar? How are they different?

Used to represent a problem, attempted solutions, and results (the national debt). Key frame ques-tions: What was the problem? Who had the problem? Why was it a problem? What attempts were made to solve the problem? Did those attempts succeed?

Problem/Solution Outline

Problem

| Who |
| What |
| Why |

Solution

Attempted Solutions	Results
1. 2.	1. 2.

| End Result |

Network Tree

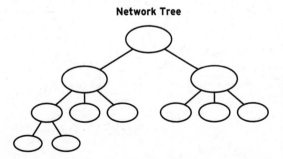

Used to show causal information (causes of poverty), a hierarchy (types of insects), or branching pro-cedures (the circulatory system). Key frame questions: What is the superordinate category? What are the subordinate categories? How are they related? How many levels are there?

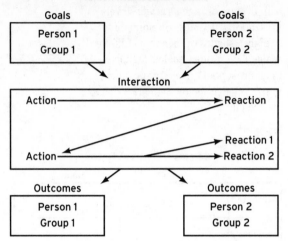

Used to show the nature of an interaction between persons or groups (European settlers and aboriginal peoples). Key frame questions: Who are the persons or groups? Did they conflict or cooperate? What was the outcome for each person or group?

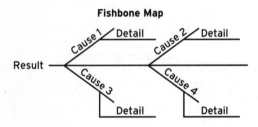

Used to show the causal interaction of a complex event (an election, a nuclear explosion) or complex phenomenon (juvenile delinquency, learning disabilities). Key frame questions: What are the factors that cause X? How do they relate? Are the factors that cause X the same as those that cause X to persist?

Used to show how a series of events interact to produce a set of results again and again (weather phenomena, cycles of achievement and failure, the life cycle). Key frame questions: What are the critical events in the cycle? How are they related? In what ways are they self-reinforcing?

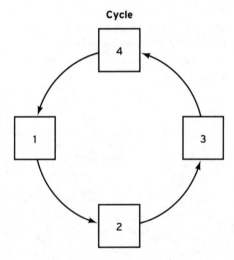

Source: © 1988 North Central Regional Educational Laboratory. Reprinted with permission.

Appendix C

Affixes with Invariant Meanings

Affix	Meaning	Example
Combining Forms		
anthropo-	man	anthropoid
auto-	self	autonomous
biblio-	book	bibliography
bio-	life	biology
centro-, centri-	centre	centrifugal
cosmo-	universe	cosmonaut
heter-, hetero-	different	heterogeneous
homo-	same	homogeneous
hydro-	water	hydroplane
iso-	equal	isometric
lith-, litho-	stone	lithography
micro-	small	microscope
mono-	one	monocyte
neuro-	nerve	neurologist
omni-	all	omnibus
pan-	all	panchromatic
penta-	five	pentamerous
phil-, philo-	love	philanthropist
phono-	sound	phonology
photo-	light	photosynthesis
pneumo-	air, respiration	pneumonia
poly-	many	polygon
proto-	before, first in time	prototype
pseudo-	false	pseudonym

tele-	far	television
uni-	one	unicellular

Prefixes

apo-	separate or detached from	apocarpous
circum-	around	circumvent
co-, col-, com-, con-, cor-	together or with	combine
equi-	equal	equivalent
extra-	in addition	extraordinary
intra-	within	intratext
mal-	bad	malpractice
mis-	wrong	mistreatment
non-	not	nonsense
syn-	together or with	synthesis

Noun Suffixes

-ana	collection	Canadiana
-archy	rule or government	oligarchy
-ard, -art	person who does something to excess	drunkard, braggart
-aster	inferiority or fraudulence	poetaster
-bility	quality or state of being	capability
-chrome	pigment, colour	autochrome
-cide	murder or killing of	insecticide
-fication, -ation	action or process of	classification, dramatization
-gram	something written or drawn	diagram
-graph	writing, recording, drawing	telegraph, lithograph
-graphy	descriptive science of a specific subject or field	planography, oceanography
-ics	science or art of	graphics, athletics
-itis	inflammation or inflammatory disease	bronchitis
-latry	worship of	bibliolatry
-meter	measuring device	barometer
-metry	science or process of measuring	photometry
-ology, -logy	science, theory, or study of	phraseology, paleontology
-phobia	fear	hypnophobia
-phore	bearer or producer	semaphore

-scope	instrument for observing or detecting	telescope
-scopy	viewing, seeing, or observing	microscopy
-ance, -ation, -ion, -ism, -dom, -ery, -mony, -ment, -tion	quality, state, or condition; action or result of an action	tolerance, adoration, truism, matrimony, government, sanction
-er, -eer, -ess, -ier, -ster, -ist, -trix	agent, doer	helper, engineer, countess, youngster, shootist, executrix

Adjective Suffixes

-able, -ible	worthy of or inclined to	debatable, knowledgeable
-aceous, -ative, -ish, -ive, -itious	pertaining to	impish, foolish, additive, fictitious
-acious	tendency toward or abundance of	fallacious
-est	most	greatest
-ferous	bearing, producing	crystalliferous
-fic	making, causing, or creating	horrific
-fold	multiplied by	fivefold
-form	having the form of	cuneiform
-ful	full of or having the quality of	masterful, useful, armful
-genous	generating or producing	androgenous, endogenous
-ic	characteristic of	seismic, microscopic
-less	lacking	toothless
-like	similar to	lifelike
-most	most	innermost
-ous, -ose	possessing, full of	joyous, grandiose
-wise	manner, direction, or positions	clockwise

Appendix D

Commonly Used Prefixes
with Varying Meanings

Prefix	Meaning	Example
ab-	from, away, off	abhor, abnormal, abdicate
ad-	to, toward	adhere, adjoin
ante-	before, in front of, earlier than	antecedent, antediluvian
anti-	opposite of, hostile to	antitoxin, antisocial
be-	make, against, to a great degree	bemoan, belittle, befuddle
bi-	two, twice	biped, bivalve
de-	away, opposite of, reduce	deactivate, devalue, devitalize
dia-	through, across	diameter, diagonal
dis-	opposite of, apart, away	dissatisfy, disarm, disjointed
en-	cause to be, put in or on	enable, engulf
epi-	upon, after	epitaph, epilogue, epidermis
ex-	out of, former, apart, away	excrete, exposition
hyper-	above, beyond, excessive	hyperphysical, hypersensitive
hypo-	under, less than normal	hypodermic, hypotension
in-, il-, im-, ir-	not, in, into, within	inept, indoors
inter-	between, among	interscholastic, interstellar
neo-	new, young	neophyte, neo-Nazi
ortho-	straight, corrective	orthotropic, orthopedic
per-	through, very	permanent, perjury
peri-	around, near, enclosing	perimeter, perihelion
post-	after, behind	postwar, postorbital
pre-	before, in place, time, rank, order	preview, prevail

pro-	before, forward, for, in favour of	production, prothorax, pro-conscription
re-	again, back	react, recoil
sub-, sur-, sug-, sup-	under, beneath	subordinate, subsoil, substation
super-	above, over, in addition	superhuman, superlative, superordinate
syn-	with, together	synthesis, synchronize
trans-	across, beyond, through	transatlantic, transconfiguration, transa
✢ction		
ultra-	beyond in space, excessive	ultraviolet, ultramodern
un-	not, the opposite of	unable, unbind

Selected Bibliography

Allen, J. (1995). *It's never too late: Leading adolescents to lifelong literacy.* Portsmouth, NH: Heinemann.

Allen, J. (2000). *Yellow brick roads: Shared and guided paths to independent reading, 4–12.* Portland, ME: Stenhouse.

Alvarez, M. C. (1996). Explorers of the universe: Students using the World Wide Web to improve their reading and writing. In B. Neate (Ed.), *Literacy saves lives* (pp. 140–145). Herts, England: United Kingdom Reading Association.

Alvermann, D. E. (1991). The discussion web: A graphic aid for learning across the curriculum. *Reading Teacher, 45*(2), 92–99.

Alvermann, D. E. (1996). Peer-led discussions: Whose interests are served? *Journal of Adolescent and Adult Literacy, 39,* 282–289.

Alvermann, D. E., & Moore, D. W. (1991). Secondary school reading. In P. D. Pearson, R. Barr, M. L. Kamil, & P. Mosenthal (Eds.), *Handbook of reading research* (2nd ed., pp. 951–983). New York: Longman.

Anderson, J. O. (1999). Modeling the development of student assessment. *Alberta Journal of Educational Research, 45*(3), 278–287.

Anderson, R. C. (1994). Role of the reader's schema in comprehension, learning, and memory. In R. Ruddell, M. Ruddell, & H. Singer (Eds.), *Theoretical models and processes of reading* (4th ed., pp. 469–482). Newark, DE: International Reading Association.

Anthony, R. J., Johnson, T. D., Mickelson, N. I., & Preece, A. (1991). *Evaluating literacy: A perspective for change.* Toronto: Irwin Publishing.

Applebee, A. N. (1991). Environments for language teaching and learning: Contemporary issues and future directions. In J. Flood, J. M. Jensen, D. Lapp, & J. R. Squire (Eds.), *Handbook of research on teaching the English language arts* (pp. 549–558). New York: Macmillan.

Arhar, J., Holly, M., & Kasten, W. (2000). *Action research for teachers.* Columbus, OH: Merrill.

Armbruster, B. B., Anderson, T. H., & Ostertag, J. (1987). Does text structure/summarization instruction facilitate learning from expository text? *Reading Research Quarterly, 22,* 331–346.

Ash, B. H. (1992). Student-made questions: One way into a literary text. *English Journal, 81*(5), 61–64.

Asselin, M. (2001). Grade 6 research process instruction: An observation study. *Alberta Journal of Educational Research, 47*(2), 123–140.

Atwell, N. (1989). *Coming to know: Writing to learn in the intermediate grades.* Portsmouth, NH: Heinemann.

Au, K. H. (1993). *Literacy instruction in multicultural settings.* Orlando, FL: Harcourt Brace.

Azzolino, A. (1990). Writing as a tool for teaching mathematics: The silent revolution. In T. Cooney & E. Hirsh (Eds.), *Teaching and learning mathematics in the 1990's.* Reston, VA: National Council of Teachers of Mathematics.

Bainbridge, J., & Malicky, G. (2000). *Constructing meaning: Balancing elementary language arts.* Toronto: Harcourt.

Baird, J. R. (1992). Collaborative reflection, systematic enquiry, better teaching. In T. Russell & H. Munby (Eds.), *Teachers and teaching from classroom to reflection* (pp. 33–48). Bristol, PA: Falmer Press.

Baker, L. (1991). Metacognition, reading, and science education. In C. M. Santa & D. E. Alvermann (Eds.), *Science learning: Processes and applications* (pp. 12–13). Newark, DE: International Reading Association.

Bamford, R. A., & Kristo, J. V. (Eds.). (1998). *Making facts come alive: Choosing quality nonfiction literature, K–8.* Norwood, MA: Christopher-Gordon.

Bamford, R. A., & Kristo, J. V. (2000). *Checking out nonfiction K–8: Good choices for best learning.* Norwood, MA: Christopher-Gordon.

Banks, J. A. (1994). *An introduction to multicultural education.* Boston, MA: Allyn & Bacon.

Barbour, M. (2002). Bridging the home and school: A case study of one web-enabled technology. *International Electronic Journal for Leadership in Learning, 6*(11). Retrieved March 2, 2004, from http://www.ucalgary.ca/~iejl/volume6/barbour.html.

Barnes, D. (1995). Talking and learning in the classroom: An introduction. *Primary Voices K–6, 3*(1), 2–7.

Barnes, D., Britton, J., & Rosen, H. (1969). *Language, the learner, and school.* New York: Penguin.

Barrentine, S. J. (1999). *Reading assessment: Principles and practices for elementary teachers.* Newark, DE: International Reading Association.

Barton, J. (1995). Conducting effective classroom discussions. *Journal of Reading, 38,* 346–350.

Bayer, C. S. (1990). *Collaborative-apprenticeship learning: Language and thinking across the curriculum, K–12.* Mountain View, CA: Mayfield.

Begoray, D. (1996). The borrowers: Issues in using previously composed text. *English Quarterly, 28*(2&3), 60–69.

Begoray, D. (2000). Positive effect from negative affect: Language arts teacher candidates reconstructing professional images. *Journal of Professional Studies, 8*(1), 22–31.

Begoray, D. (2001). Through a class darkly: Visual literacy in the classroom. *Canadian Journal of Education, 26*(2), 201–217.

Begoray, D. (2002). Not just reading any more: Literacy, community and the pre-service teacher. *English Quarterly, 34*(3&4), 34–45.

Begoray, D. (2003). Sign, sign, everywhere a sign: Multiplying literacies in the preservice language arts curriculum. In J. Worthy, D. Schallert, C. M. Fairbanks, B. Maloch, & J. V. Hoffman (Eds.), *Fifty-second National Reading Conference Yearbook* (pp. 128–138). Oak Creek, WI: National Reading Conference.

Beuhl, D. (1991, Spring). Frames of mind. *The Exchange: Newsletter of the IRA Secondary Reading Interest Group,* pp. 4–5.

Blachowicz, C. L. Z., & Fisher, P. J. L. (1994). Vocabulary instruction. In A. C. Purves, *Encyclopedia of English studies and language arts.* New York: Scholastic.

Blachowicz, C. L. Z., & Fisher, P. J. L. (1996). *Teaching vocabulary in all classrooms.* Columbus, OH: Merrill.

Bleich, D. (1978). *Subjective criticism.* Baltimore: Johns Hopkins University Press.

Booth, D. (2002). *Even hockey players read: Boys, literacy and learning.* Markham, ON: Pembroke Publishers.

Borasi, R., Sheedy, J. R., & Siegel, M. (1990). The power of stories in learning mathematics. *Language Arts, 67,* 174–189.

Boudreau, R., Wood, E., Willoughby, T., & Specht, J. (1999). Evaluating the efficacy of elaborative strategies for remembering expository text. *Alberta Journal of Educational Research, 45*(2), 170–183.

Bowd, A., McDougall, D., & Yewchuk, C. (1998). Learning: Cognitive processes. In *Educational psychology for Canadian teachers* (pp. 106–133). Toronto: Harcourt Brace.

Bright, R. (1995). *Writing instruction in the intermediate grades: What is said, what is done, what is understood.* Newark, DE: International Reading Association.

Britton, J. (1975). *Language and learning.* London: Allen Lane.

Bromley, K. (1993). *Journaling: Engagements in reading, writing, and thinking.* New York: Scholastic.

Brooks, J., & Brooks, M. (1993). *The case for constructivist classrooms.* Alexandria, VA: Association for Curriculum and Supervision Development.

Brown, A. L., & Campione, J. C. (1994). Guided discovery in a community of learners. In K. McGilly (Ed.), *Classroom lessons: Integrating cognitive theory and classroom practice.* Cambridge, MA: MIT Press.

Brown, A. L., & Palinscar, A. S. (1984). Reciprocal teaching of comprehension-fostering and comprehension-monitoring activities. *Cognition and Instruction, 1,* 117–175.

Brown, J., & Sheppard. B. (1997). Professional development: What do we know and where are we going? http://www.mun.ca/educ/faculty/mwatch/win97/pdfinal.htm.

Brownlie, F., & Close, S. (1992). *Beyond chalk and talk: Collaborative strategies for the middle and high school years.* Markham, ON: Pembroke Publishers.

Brozo, W. G. (1989). Applying a reader response heuristic to expository text. *Journal of Reading, 32,* 140–145.

Brozo, W. G. (1990). Learning how at-risk readers learn best: A case for interactive assessment. *Journal of Reading, 33,* 522–527.

Bruner, J. (1986). *Actual minds, possible worlds.* Cambridge, MA: Harvard University Press.

Bruner, J. (1990). *Acts of meaning.* Cambridge, MA: Harvard University Press.

Calfee, R. C., Dunlap, K. L., & Wat, A. Y. (1994). Authentic discussion of texts in middle grade schooling: An analytic-narrative approach. *Journal of Reading, 37,* 546–556.

Carlsen, W. S. (1991). Questioning in classrooms: A sociolinguistic perspective. *Review of Educational Research, 61,* 157–178.

Carr, E. G., & Ogle, D. M. (1987). K-W-L plus: A strategy for comprehension and summarization. *Journal of Reading, 30,* 626–631.

Castle, J. (1999). Preservice teachers' perceptions of their portfolio experience. *Journal of Professional Studies, 6*(2), 34–43.

Cooney, T., Bell, K., Fisher-Cauble, D., & Sanchez, W. (1996). The demands of alternative assessment: What teachers say. *Mathematics Teacher, 89,* 484–487.

Countryman, J. (1992). *Writing to learn mathematics: Strategies that work, K–12.* Portsmouth, NH: Heinemann

Crapse, L. (1995). Helping students construct meaning through their own questions. *Journal of Reading, 38,* 389–390.

Crue, W. (1932, February). Ordeal by Cheque. *Vanity Fair.*

Cullinan, B. E. (1993). *Fact and fiction: Literature across the curriculum.* Newark, DE: International Reading Association.

Cummins, J. (1994). The acquisition of English as a second language. In K. Spangenberg-Urbschat & R. Pritchard (Eds.), *Kids come in all languages: Reading instruction for ESL students* (pp. 36–62). Newark, DE: International Reading Association.

Curry, J. (1989). The role of reading instruction in mathematics. In D. Lapp, J. Flood, & N. Farnan (Eds.), *Content area reading and learning: Instructional strategies* (pp. 187–197). Upper Saddle River, NJ: Prentice Hall.

Daisey, P. (1994). The value of trade books in secondary science and mathematics instruction: A rationale. *School Science and Mathematics, 94,* 130–137.

Daisey, P. (1997). Promoting literacy in secondary content area classrooms with biography projects. *Journal of Adolescent and Adult Literacy, 40,* 270–278.

Danielson, C. (1996). *Enhancing professional practice: A framework for teaching.* Alexandria, VA: Association for Supervision and Curriculum Development.

Davey, B. (1983). Think aloud: Modeling the cognitive processes of reading comprehension. *Journal of Reading, 27,* 44–47.

Davies, A., Politano, C., & Cameron, C. (1993). *Making themes work: building connections.* Winnipeg: Peguis Publishing.

Delpit, L. (1995). *Other people's children: Conflict in the classroom.* New York: The New Press.

Delpit, L. D. (1988). The silenced dialogue: Power and pedagogy in educating other people's children. *Harvard Educational Review, 58,* 280–298.

Dillon, D. R. (1983). Showing them that I want them to learn and that I care about who they are: A micro-ethnography of the social organization of a secondary low-track English-reading classroom. *American Education Research Journal, 26,* 227–259.

Doige, L. A. C. (1999). Beyond cultural differences and similarities: Student teachers encounter Aboriginal children's literature. *Canadian Journal of Education, 24*(4), 383–397.

Donelson, K. L., & Nilsen, A. P. (1997). *Literature for today's young adults* (5th ed.). New York: Longman.

Dufflemeyer, F. (1994). Effective anticipation guide statements for learning from expository prose. *Journal of Reading, 37,* 452–457.

Early, M. (1989). Using key visuals to aid ESL students' comprehension of content classroom texts. *Reading-Canada-Lecture, 7,* 202–212.

Edwards, P. (1967). *Equiano's travels: The interesting narrative of the life of Olaudah Equiano or Gustavus Vassa, the African.* New York: Praeger.

Egoff, S., & Saltman, J. (1990). *The new republic of childhood: A critical guide to Canadian children's literature in English.* Toronto: Oxford University Press.

Ehlinger, J., & Pritchard, R. (1994). Using think alongs in secondary content areas. *Reading Research and Instruction, 33,* 187–206.

Eisner, E. W. (1985). *The educational imagination: On the design and evaluation of school programs* (2nd ed.). New York: Macmillan.

Elliot, A., & Faubert-McCabe, P. (2002). Catalyst for institutional renewal: An accreditation story told through two lenses. *Journal of Professional Studies, 9*(2), 32–42.

Esses, V. M., & Gardner, R. C. (1996). Multiculturalism in Canada: Context and current status. Retrieved November 16, 2003, from http://www.cpa.ca/cbjsnew/1996/ful_edito.html.

Ezell, H., Hunsicker, S., Quinque, M., & Randolph, E. (1996). Maintenance and generalization of QAR reading comprehension strategies. *Reading Research and Instruction, 36,* 64–81.

Farr, R., & Tone, B. (1998). *Assessment portfolio and performance* (2nd ed.). Orlando, FL: Harcourt Brace.

Fazio, B. (1992). Students as historians—writing their school's history. *The Social Studies, 83,* 64–67.

Fessler, R., & Christensen, J. (1994, February). *The teacher career cycle: A model for career-long teacher education.* Paper presented at the meeting of the American Association of Colleges of Teacher Education, Chicago.

Fetterman, D. M. (1989). *Ethnography step by step.* Thousand Oaks, CA: Sage.

Finkel, A., & Conrad, M. (1998). *History of the Canadian peoples,* vol. 2. Toronto: Addison Wesley Longman.

Flavell, J. H. (1981). Cognitive monitoring. In P. Dickson (Ed.), *Communication skills.* Orlando, FL: Academic Press.

Fogarty, R. (1994, March). Thinking about themes: Hundreds of themes. *Middle School Journal, 25,* 30–31.

Fry, E. (1977). Fry's readability graph: Clarifications, validity, and extension to level 17. *Journal of Reading, 21,* 242–252.

Fulwiler, T. (1987). *Teaching with writing.* Portsmouth, NH: Boynton/Cook.

Gambrell, L. B., & Almasi, J. F. (Eds.). (1996). *Lively discussions! Fostering engaged reading.* Newark, DE: International Reading Association.

Garner, R., & Gillingham, M. (1987). Students' knowledge of text structure. *Journal of Reading Behavior, 29,* 247–259.

Garrett-Petts, W. F., & Lawrence, D. (1996). *Integrating visual and verbal literacies.* Winnipeg: Inkshed Publications.

Gaskins, I. W., Satlow, E., Hyson, D., Ostertag, J., & Six, L. (1994). Classroom talk about text: Learning in science class. *Journal of Reading, 37,* 558–565.

Gere, A. R. (Ed.). (1985). *Roots in the sawdust: Writing to learn across the disciplines.* Urbana, IL: National Council of Teachers of English.

Ghosh, R. (1996). *Redefining multicultural education.* Toronto: Harcourt Brace Canada.

Goodlad, J. (1984). *A place called school.* New York: McGraw-Hill.

Gordon, C., Sheridan, M., & Paul, W. (1998). *Content literacy for secondary teachers.* Toronto: Harcourt Brace.

Gove, M., & Kennedy-Calloway, C. (1992). Action research: Empowering teachers to work with at-risk students. In J. Vacca (Ed.), *Bringing about change in schools* (pp. 14–22). Newark, DE: International Reading Association.

Graves, D. (1992). Portfolios: Keep a good idea growing. In D. Graves & B. Sunstein (Eds.), *Portfolio portraits* (pp. 1–12). Portsmouth, NH: Heinemann.

Graves, M., & Graves, B. (1994). *Scaffolding reading experiences: Designs for student success.* Norwood, MA: Christopher-Gordon.

Graves, M. F., & Slater, W. (1996). Vocabulary instruction in content areas. In D. Lapp, J. Flood, & N. Farnan (Eds.), *Content area reading and learning: Instructional strategies.* Boston, MA: Allyn & Bacon.

Greabell, L. C., & Anderson, N. (1992). Applying strategies from the directed reading-thinking activity to a directed mathematics activity. *School Science and Mathematics, 92,* 42–44.

Greenlee-Moore, M. E., & Smith, L. L. (1996). Interactive computer software: The effects on young children's reading achievement. *Reading Psychology, 17,* 43–64.

Gunnery, S. (1998). *Just write! Ten practical workshops for successful student writing.* Markham, ON: Pembroke Publishers.

Guthrie, J. T., McGough, K., Bennett, L., & Rice, M. E. (1996). Concept-oriented reading instruction: An integrated curriculum to develop motivations and strategies for reading. In L. Baker, P. Afflerbach, & D. Reinking (Eds.), *Developing engaged readers in school and home communities.* Hillsdale, NJ: Erlbaum.

Guthrie, J. T., & Wigfield, A. (2000). Engagement and motivation in reading. In M. Kamil, P. Mosenthal, P. D. Pearson, & R. Barr (Eds.), *Handbook of reading research,* volume 3 (pp. 403–424). Mahwah, NJ: Erlbaum.

Haggard, M. R. (1986). The vocabulary self-collection strategy: Using student interest and world knowledge to enhance vocabulary growth. *Journal of Reading, 29,* 634–642.

Hamilton, S. (2003). What's history got to do with it? Department of Canadian Heritage. http://www.pch.gc.ca/special/dcforum/info-bg/07_e.cfm1.

Hancock, J. (Ed.). (1999). *Teaching literacy using information technology.* Newark, DE: International Reading Association.

Hancock, M. R. (1993). Exploring and extending personal response through literature journals. *Reading Teacher, 46,* 466–474.

Herber, H. L. (1985). Levels of comprehension: An instructional strategy for guiding students' reading. In T. Harris & E. Cooper (Eds.), *Reading, thinking, and concept development: Strategies for the classroom.* New York: College Entrance Examination Board.

Hiebert, E. H. (Ed.). (1991). *Literacy for a diverse society: Perspectives, practices, policies.* New York: Teachers College Press.

Hill, M. (1991). Writing summaries promotes thinking and learning across the curriculum—but why are they so difficult to write? *Journal of Reading, 34,* 536–539.

Hoffman, J. (1992). Critical reading/thinking across the curriculum: Using I-charts to support learning. *Language Arts, 69,* 121–127.

Hoffman, J. V. (1979). The intra-act procedure for critical reading. *Journal of Reading, 22,* 605–608.

Holly, M. L. (1989). *Writing to grow: Keeping a personal-professional journal.* Portsmouth, NH: Heinemann.

Holston, V., & Santa, C. (1985). RAFT: A method of writing across the curriculum that works. *Journal of Reading, 28,* 456–457.

Hynd, C. R., McNish, M. E., Guzzetti, B., Lay, K., & Fowler, P. (1994). *What high school students say about their science texts.* Paper presented at the annual meeting of the College Reading Association, New Orleans.

International Reading Association. (1999). *High-stakes assessments in reading: A position paper of the International Reading Association.* Newark, DE: Author.

International Reading Association and National Council of Teachers of English. (1994). *Standards for the assessment of reading and writing.* Newark, DE: International Reading Association.

Irwin, J. W., & Doyle, M. A. (1992). *Reading/writing connections: Learning from research.* Newark, DE: International Reading Association.

Jackson, F. R., & Cunningham, J. W. (1994). Investigating secondary content teachers' and preservice teachers' conceptions of study strategy instruction. *Reading Research and Instruction, 34,* 111–135.

Jacobs, H. H. (Ed.). (1989). *Interdisciplinary curriculum: Design and implementation.* Alexandria, VA: Association for Supervision and Curriculum Development.

Jacobsen, M., Clifford, P., & Friesen, S. (2002). Preparing teachers for technology integration: Creating a culture of inquiry in the context of use and teacher educators. *Contemporary Issues in Technology and Teacher Education, 2*(3). Retrieved March 1, 2004, from http://www.cite-journal.org/vol2/iss3/currentpractice/article2.cfm.

Jasper, K. C. (1995). The limits of technology. *English Journal, 84*(6), 16–17.

Jobe, R., & Dayton-Sakari, M. (1999). *Reluctant readers: Connecting students and books for successful reading experiences.* Markham, ON: Pembroke Publishers.

Johnson, D. W., Johnson, R. T., & Holubec, E. J. (1994). *The new circles of literacy: Cooperation in the classroom and school.* Alexandria, VA: Association for Supervision and Curriculum Development.

Johnson, D. W., & Steele, V. (1996). So many words, so little time: Helping college ESL learners acquire vocabulary-building strategies. *Journal of Adolescent and Adult Literacy, 39,* 348–357.

Johnston, P., & Winograd, P. (1990). Passive failure in reading. *Journal of Reading Behavior, 17,* 279–301.

Jones, B. F., Pierce, J., & Hunter, B. (1988–1989). Teaching students to construct graphic representations. *Educational Leadership, 46*(4), 20–25.

Jones, R., & Stott, J. (2000). *Canadian children's books: A critical guide to authors and illustrators.* Don Mills, ON: Oxford University Press.

Jongsma, E., & Farr, R. (1993). A themed issue on literacy assessment. *Journal of Reading, 36,* 516–600.

Kang, H. (1994). Helping second language readers learn from content area text through collaboration and support. *Journal of Reading, 37,* 646–652.

Kang, H-W., & Golden, A. (1994). Vocabulary learning and instruction in a second or foreign language. *International Journal of Applied Linguistics, 4*(1), 57–77.

Kibbey, M. (1995). The organization and teaching of things and the words that signify them. *Journal of Adolescent and Adult Literacy, 39,* 208–223.

Kintsch, W., & van Dijk, T. (1978). Toward a model of text comprehension and production. *Psychological Review, 85,* 363–394.

Kletzien, S. B., & Baloche, L. (1994). The shifting muffled sound of the pick: Facilitating student-to-student discussion. *Journal of Reading, 37,* 540–545.

Knoeller, C. P. (1994). Negotiating interpretations of text: The role of student-led discussions in understanding literature. *Journal of Reading, 37,* 572–580.

Kovacs, E. (1994). *Writing across cultures: A handbook on writing poetry & lyrical prose.* Portland, OR: Blue Heron Publishing.

Krogness, M. (1995). *Just teach me, Mrs. K: Talking, reading, and writing with resistant adolescent learners.* Portsmouth, NH: Heinemann.

Langer, J. A., & Applebee, A. N. (1987). *How writing shapes thinking.* Urbana, IL: National Council of Teachers of English.

Lapkin, S. (1998). *French second language education in Canada: Empirical studies.* Toronto: University of Toronto Press.

Lapp, D., & Flood, J. (1995). Strategies for gaining access to the information superhighway: Off the side street and on to the main road. *Reading Teacher, 48,* 432–436.

Leu, D. J., Jr. (1996). Sarah's secret: Social aspects of literacy and learning in a digital information age. *Reading Teacher, 50,* 162–165.

Leu, D. J., Jr., & Leu, D. D. (2000). *Teaching with the Internet: Lessons from the classroom* (3rd ed.). Norwood, MA: Christopher-Gordon.

Levstik, L. S. (1990). Research directions: Mediating content through literary texts. *Language Arts, 67,* 848–853.

Lindemann, E. (1982). *A rhetoric for writing teachers.* New York: Oxford University Press.

Lounsbury, J. H. (Ed.). (1992). *Connecting the curriculum through interdisciplinary instruction.* Columbus, OH: National Middle School Association.

Luongo-Orlando, K. (2001). *A project approach to language learning: Linking literary genres and themes in elementary classrooms.* Markham, ON: Pembroke Publishing.

MacGinitie, W. H. (1993). Some limits of assessment. *Journal of Reading, 36,* 556–560.

Macrorie, K. (1980). *Searching writing.* Rochelle Park, NJ: Hayden.

Manning, M., Manning, G., & Long, R. (1994). *Theme immersion: Inquiry-based curriculum in elementary and middle schools.* Portsmouth, NH: Heinemann.

Manzo, A. V. (1969). The ReQuest procedure. *Journal of Reading, 11,* 123–126.

Manzo, A. V. (1975). Guided reading procedure. *Journal of Reading, 18,* 287–291.

Marshall, N. (1996). The students: Who are they and how do I reach them? In D. Lapp, J. Flood, & N. Farnan (Eds.), *Content area reading and learning: Instructional strategies* (pp. 27–38). Boston, MA: Allyn and Bacon.

Maxwell, R. (1996). *Writing across the curriculum in middle and high schools.* Boston: Allyn and Bacon.

McAloon, N. M. (1994). Content area reading: It's not my Job! *Journal of Reading, 37,* 332–334.

McCullen, C. (1998). The electronic thread: Research and assessment on the Internet. *Middle Ground, 1*(3), 7–9.

McGowan, T., & Guzzetti, B. (1991, January–February). Promoting social studies understanding through literature-based instruction. *Social Studies,* pp. 16–21.

McIntosh, M. (1991, September). No time for writing in your class? *Mathematics Teacher,* 423–433.

Meinbach, A. M., Rothlein, L., & Fredericks, A. D. (1995). *The complete guide to thematic units: Creating the integrated curriculum.* Norwood, MA: Christopher-Gordon.

Meltzer, M. (1994). *Nonfiction for the classroom.* New York: Teachers College Press.

Met, M. (1994). Teaching content through a second language. In F. Genesee (Ed.), *Educating second language children* (pp. 159–182). Cambridge, England: Cambridge University Press.

Metropolitan Toronto School Board. (1995). *Getting it all together: Curriculum integration in the transition years.* Markham, ON: Pembroke Publishers.

Miholic, V. (1994). An inventory to pique students' metacognitive awareness. *Journal of Reading, 38*(2), 84–86.

Mike, D. G. (1996). Internet in the schools: A literacy perspective. *Journal of Adolescent and Adult Literacy, 40,* 4–13.

Mikulecky, L. (1990). Literacy for what purpose? In R. L. Venezky, D. A. Wagner, & B. S. Ciliberti (Eds.), *Toward defining literacy* (pp. 24–34). Newark, DE: International Reading Association.

Moje, E. B. (1996). "I teach students, not subjects": Teacher-student relationships as contexts for secondary literacy. *Reading Research Quarterly, 31,* 172–195.

Moje, E., Brozo, W., & Haas, J. (1994). Portfolios in a high school classroom: Challenges to change. *Reading Research and Instruction, 33,* 275–292.

Mooney, M. (1995). Guided reading: The reader in control. *Teaching PreK–8, 25,* 54–58.

Moore, D. W. (1996). Contexts for literacy in secondary schools. In D. J. Leu, C. K. Kinzer, & K. A. Hinchman (Eds.), *Literacies for the twenty-first century: Research and practice* (pp. 15–46). Chicago: National Reading Conference.

Moore, D. W., Readence, J. E., & Rickelman, R. (2000). *Prereading activities for content area reading* (3rd ed.). Newark, DE: International Reading Association.

Morin, F. (1994). A professional development model for planned change in arts education. *Canadian Journal of Research in Music Education, 35*(7), 5–12.

Moss, J. F. (1994). *Using literature in the middle grades: A thematic approach.* Norwood, MA: Christopher-Gordon.

Murphy, E., & Laferriere, T. (2003). Virtual communities for professional development: Helping teachers map the territory in landscapes without bearings. *Alberta Journal of Educational Research, 49*(2), 70–82.

Murray, D. M. (1980). Writing as process: How writing finds its own meaning. In T. R. Donovan & B. W. McClelland (Eds.), *Eight approaches to teaching composition* (pp. 80–97). Urbana, IL: National Council of Teachers of English.

Nagy, P. (2000). The three roles of assessment: Gatekeeping, accountability, and instructional diagnosis. *Canadian Journal of Education, 25*(4), 262–279.

Neal, J. C., & Moore, K. (1991). *The very hungry caterpillar* meets *Beowulf* in secondary classrooms. *Journal of Reading, 35,* 290–296.

Neilsen, L. (1998). Playing for real: Performative texts and adolescent identities. In D. Alvermann, K. Hinchman, S. Phelps, & S. Waff (Eds.), *Reconceptualizing the Literacies in Adolescents' Lives* (pp. 3–26). Mahwah, NJ: Erlbaum.

Noden, H. R. (1995). A journey through cyberspace: Reading and writing in a virtual school. *English Journal, 84*(6), 19–26.

Noden, H. R., & Vacca, R. T. (1994). *Whole language in middle and secondary classrooms.* New York: HarperCollins.

Ogle, D. M. (1992). KWL in action: Secondary teachers find applications that work. In E. K. Dishner, T. W. Bean, J. E. Readence, & D. W. Moore (Eds.), *Reading in the content areas: Improving classroom instruction* (3rd ed., pp. 270–281). Dubuque, IA: Kendall-Hunt.

Palmer, R. G., & Stewart, R. A. (1997). Nonfiction trade books in content area instruction: Realities and potential. *Journal of Adolescent and Adult Literacy, 40,* 630–641.

Pantaleo, S. (2002). A canon of literature in Canadian elementary schools? *English Quarterly, 34*(1&2), 19–26.

Parry, K. (1993). Too many words: Learning the vocabulary of an academic subject. In T. Huckin, M. Haynes, & J. Coady (Eds.), *Second language reading and vocabulary learning* (pp. 109–129). Norwood, NJ: Ablex.

Parsons, L. (1994). *Expanding response journals in all subject areas.* Markham, ON: Pembroke Publishers.

Patterson, L., Santa, C., Short, K., & Smith, K. (Eds.). (1993). *Teachers are researchers: Reflection and action.* Newark, DE: International Reading Association.

Patterson, L., & Shannon, P. (1993). Reflection, inquiry, action. In L. Patterson, C. M. Santa, K. Short, & K. Smith (Eds.), *Teachers are researchers: Reflections and action* (pp. 7–11). Newark, DE: International Reading Association.

Pearson, J. W., & Santa, C. M. (1995). Students as researchers of their own learning. *Journal of Reading, 38,* 462–469.

Peregoy, S. F., & Boyle, O. F. W. (1997). *Reading, writing, & learning in ESL: A resource book for K–12 teachers* (2nd ed.). New York: Longman.

Peresich, M. L., Meadows, J. D., & Sinatra, R. (1990). Content area cognitive mapping for reading and writing proficiency. *Journal of Reading, 34,* 424–432.

Piper, T. (2001). *And then there were two: Children and second-language learning.* Portsmouth, NH: Heinemann.

Preece, A. (1995). Talking about learning: Making reflection meaningful in elementary classroom. *English Quarterly, 23*(4), 18–21.

Pressley, M. (2000). What should comprehension instruction be the instruction of? In M. Kamil, P. Mosenthal, P. D. Pearson, & R. Barr (Eds.), *Handbook of reading research,* volume 3 (pp. 545–562). Mahwah, NJ: Erlbaum.

Raphael, T. E. (1986). Teaching question-answer relationships. *Reading Teacher, 39,* 516–520.

Reinking, D. (1995). Reading and writing with computers: Literacy research in a post-typographic world. In K. A. Hinchman, D. J. Leu, Jr., & C. K. Kinzer (Eds.), *Perspectives on literacy research and practice* (pp. 17–33). Chicago: National Reading Conference.

Reinking, D. (1997). Me and my hypertext: A multiple digression analysis of technology and literacy. *Reading Teacher, 50,* 626–643.

Resnick, L. B., & Resnick, D. P. (1991). Assessing the thinking curriculum: New tools for educational reform. In J. Gifford & D. O'Connor (Eds.), *Changing assessments.* Boston: Kluwer.

Rhodes, L. (Ed.). (1993). *Literacy assessment: A handbook of instruments.* Portsmouth, NH: Heinemann.

Robb, L. (2000). *Teaching reading in middle school: A strategic approach to teaching that improves comprehension and thinking.* New York: Scholastic.

Roller, C. M. (1996). *Variability not disability: Struggling readers in a workshop classroom.* Newark, DE: International Reading Association.

Rose, B. (1989). Writing and mathematics: Theory and practice. In P. Connolly & T. Vilardi (Eds.), *Writing to learn mathematics and science* (pp. 19–30). New York: Teachers College Press.

Rose, S. A., & Fernlund, P. M. (1997). Using technology for powerful social studies learning. *Social Education, 13*(6), 160–166.

Rosenblatt, L. M. (1982). The literary transaction: Evocation and response. *Theory into Practice, 21,* 268–277.

Rosenshine, B., & Meister, C. (1992). The use of scaffolds for teaching higher-level cognitive strategies. *Educational Leadership, 49*(7), 26–33.

Rousseau, N. (2000). Student teachers' reflective inquiry as reported in their field journals. *Journal of Professional Studies, 8*(1), 53–59.

Rubin, D. L. (1990). Introduction: Ways of thinking about talking and learning. In S. Hynds & D. L. Rubin (Eds.), *Perspectives on talk and learning* (pp. 1–17). Urbana, IL: National Council of Teachers of English.

Ruddell, M. R. (1994). Vocabulary knowledge and comprehension: A comprehension-process view of complex literacy relationships. In R. B. Ruddell, M. R. Ruddell, & H. Singer (Eds.), *Theoretical models and processes of reading* (4th ed.). Newark, DE: International Reading Association.

Ruddell, M. R. (1996). Engaging students' interest and willing participation in subject area and learning. In D. Lapp, J. Flood, & N. Farnan (Eds.), *Content area reading and learning: Instructional strategies* (2nd ed.). Boston, MA: Allyn and Bacon.

Rumelhart, D. E. (1982). Schemata: The building blocks of cognition. In J. Guthrie (Ed.), *Comprehension and teaching: Research reviews* (pp. 3–26). Newark, DE: International Reading Association.

Sadoski, M., & Paivio, A. (2001). *Imagery and text: A dual coding theory of reading and writing.* Mahwah, NJ: Erlbaum.

Salisbury, R. (1934). A study of the transfer effects of training in logical organization. *Journal of Educational Research, 28,* 241–254.

Santa, C., Havens, L., & Harrison, S. (1996). Teaching secondary science through reading, writing, studying, and problem-solving. In D. Lapp, J. Flood, & N. Farnan (Eds.), *Content area reading and learning: Instructional practices* (2nd ed., pp. 165–180). Boston: Allyn and Bacon.

Santa, C. M., & Havens, L. T. (1991). Learning through writing. In C. M. Santa & D. E. Alvermann (Eds.), *Science learning: Processes and applications* (pp. 122–133). Newark, DE: International Reading Association.

Schumm, J. S., Vaughn, S., & Saumell, L. (1992). What do teachers do when the textbook is tough: Students speak out. *Journal of Reading Behavior, 24,* 481–503.

Scott, J. A., & Nagy, W. E. (1994). Vocabulary development. In A. C. Purves, *Encyclopedia of English studies and language arts.* New York: Scholastic.

Shanahan, T. (Ed.). (1990). *Reading and writing together: New perspectives for the classroom.* Norwood, MA: Christopher-Gordon.

Short, K. G., & Armstrong, J. (1993). Moving toward inquiry: Integrating literature into science curriculum. *The New Advocate, 6,* 183–199.

Slavin, R. E. (1995). *Cooperative learning: Theory, research, and practice* (2nd ed.). Boston, MA: Allyn and Bacon.

Smith, F. (1988). *Understanding reading* (4th ed.). Hillsdale, NJ: Erlbaum.

Stahl, S. (1986). Three principles of effective vocabulary instruction. *Journal of Reading, 29,* 662–668.

Stenmark, J. K. (1991). Math portfolios: A new form of assessment. *Teaching Pre-K–8, 21,* 62–66.

Stevenson, C., & Carr, J. F. (Eds). (1993). *Integrated studies in the middle grades: "Dancing through walls."* New York: Teachers College Press.

Taba, H. (1967). *Teacher's handbook for elementary social studies.* Reading, MA: Addison-Wesley.

Taylor, W. (1953). Close procedure: A new tool for measuring readability. *Journalism Quarterly, 30,* 415–433.

Tchudi, S., & Huerta, M. (1983). *Teaching writing in the content areas: Middle school/junior high.* Washington, DC: National Education Association.

Tchudi, S., & Yates, J. (1983). *Teaching writing in the content areas: Senior high school.* Washington, DC: National Education Association.

Thorndike, E. (1917). Reading and reasoning: A study of mistakes in paragraph reading. *Journal of Educational Psychology, 8,* 323–332.

Tiedt, I. M. (2000). *Teaching with picture books in the middle school.* Newark, DE: International Reading Association.

Tierney, R. J. (1998). Literacy assessment reform: Shifting beliefs, principled possibilities, and emerging practices. *Reading Teacher, 51,* 374–390.

Tierney, R. J., Carter, M. A., & Desai, L. E. (1991). *Portfolio assessment in the reading– writing classroom.* Norwood, MA: Christopher-Gordon.

Tierney, R. J., & Shanahan, T. (1991). Research on reading-writing relationships: Interactions, transactions, and outcomes. In P. D. Pearson, R. Barr, M. Kamil, & P. Mosenthal (Eds.), *Handbook of reading research* (2nd ed., pp. 246–280). New York: Longman.

Tobias, S. (1989). Writing to learn science and mathematics. In P. Connolly & T. Vilardi (Eds.), *Writing to learn mathematics and science* (pp. 47–61). New York: Teachers College Press.

Tompkins, G. E. (1990). *Teaching writing: Balancing process and product.* Columbus, OH: Merrill.

Tovani, C. (2000). *I read it, but I don't get it: Comprehension strategies for adolescent readers.* Portland, ME: Stenhouse.

Vacca, J. L., & Mraz, M. (2000). Professional development. In S. Wepner, J. Feeley, & D. Strickland (Eds.), *The administration and supervision of reading programs* (3rd ed.). New York: Teachers College Press.

Vacca, J. L., Vacca, R. T., & Gove, M. K. (2000). *Reading and learning to read* (4th ed.). New York: Addison Wesley Longman.

Vacca, R. T. (2001). Making a difference in adolescents' school lives: The visible and invisible aspects of content area literacy. In S. J. Samuels & A. E. Farstrup (Eds.), *What research has to say about reading instruction* (3rd ed.). Newark, DE: International Reading Association.

Vacca, R. T., & Padak, N. D. (1990). Who's at risk in reading? *Journal of Reading, 33,* 486–489.

Vacca, R. T., Vacca, J. L., & Bruneau, B. (1997). Teachers reflecting on practice. In J. Flood, S. B. Heath, & D. Lapp (Eds.), *Handbook for literacy educators: Research on teaching the communicative and visual arts* (pp. 445–450). Newark, DE: International Reading Association.

Valencia, S. (1990). A portfolio approach to classroom reading assessment: The whys, whats, and hows. *Reading Teacher, 43,* 338–340.

Valencia, S., McGinley, W. J., & Pearson, P. D. (1990). *Assessing reading and writing: Building a more complete picture for middle school assessment.* Champaign: University of Illinois, Center for the Study of Reading.

Vars, G. F. (1993). *Interdisciplinary teaching in the middle grades: Why and how.* Columbus, OH: National Middle School Association.

Vogt, M. E. (1996). Creating a response-centered curriculum with discussion groups. In L. B. Gambrell & J. F. Almasi (Eds.), *Lively discussions! Fostering engaged reading.* Newark, DE: International Reading Association.

Wade, S. E., Trathen, W., & Schraw, G. (1990). An analysis of spontaneous study strategies. *Reading Research Quarterly, 25,* 147–166.

Walker, B. J. (1992). *Supporting struggling readers.* Markham, ON: Pippen Publishing.

Wang, M. C., Reynolds, M. C., & Walberg, H. J. (1994–1995). Serving students at the margins. *Educational Leadership, 52*(4), 12–17.

Ward, A., & Bouvier, R. (2001). *Resting lightly on Mother Earth: The Aboriginal experience in urban educational settings.* Calgary: Detselig Enterprises.

Weaver, C., Chaston, J., & Peterson, S. (1995). *Theme exploration: A voyage of discovery.* Portsmouth, NH: Heinemann.

Wepner, S. B., Valmont, W. J., & Thurlow, R. (Eds.). (2000). *Linking literacy and technology: A guide for K–8 classrooms.* Newark, DE: International Reading Association.

Wiggins, G. (1993). Assessment to improve performance, not just monitor: Assessment reform in the social sciences. *Social Science Record, 30,* 5–12.

Wilcox, S. (1997). Using the assessment of students' learning to reshape thinking. *Mathematics Teacher, 90,* 223–229.

Wilkinson, L. E., & Silliman, E. R. (2000). Classroom language and literacy learning. In M. Kamil, P. Mosenthal, P. D. Pearson, & R. Barr (Eds.), *Handbook of reading research,* volume 3 (pp. 337–360). Mahwah, NJ: Erlbaum.

Williams, B. (1995). *The internet for teachers.* Foster City, CA: IDG Books Worldwide.

Willinsky, J. (1990). *The new literacy: Redefining reading and writing in the schools.* New York: Routledge.

Wills, H. (1993). *Writing is learning: Strategies for math, science, social studies and language arts.* Bloomington, IN: Edinfo Press.

Wilson, R. J. (1996). *Assessing students in classrooms and schools*. Scarborough, ON: Allyn and Bacon.

Wineburg, S., & Grossman, P. (1998). Creating a community of learners among high school teachers. *Phi Delta Kappan, 79,* 350–353.

Wolf, K., & Siu-Runyan, Y. (1996). Portfolio purposes and possibilities. *Journal of Adolescent and Adult Literacy, 40,* 30–37.

Wollman-Bonilla, J. (1991). *Response journals.* New York: Scholastic.

Wood, K. D., Lapp, D., & Flood, J. (1992). *Guiding readers through text: A review of study guides.* Newark, DE: International Reading Association.

Name Index

Subject Index